2023
青岛统计年鉴

QINGDAO STATISTICAL YEARBOOK

（总第 44 期　　VOL.44）

青 岛 市 统 计 局
国家统计局青岛调查队 编

QINGDAO MUNICIPAL BUREAU OF STATISTICS
NBS SURVEY OFFICE IN QINGDAO

中国统计出版社
China Statistics Press

图书在版编目（CIP）数据

青岛统计年鉴．2023 = Qingdao Statistical Yearbook 2023：汉英对照 / 青岛市统计局，国家统计局青岛调查队编．-- 北京：中国统计出版社，2023.9
ISBN 978-7-5230-0263-6

Ⅰ．①青… Ⅱ．①青… ②国… Ⅲ．①统计资料－青岛－2023－年鉴－汉、英Ⅳ．① C832.523-54

中国国家版本馆 CIP 数据核字（2023）第 185218 号

青岛统计年鉴 2023

作　　者 / 青岛市统计局　国家统计局青岛调查队
责任编辑 / 周小睿
执行编辑 / 周小睿　刘琛
装帧设计 / 中闻集团青岛印务有限公司
出版发行 / 中国统计出版社有限公司
地　　址 / 北京市丰台区西三环南路甲 6 号
邮政编码 /100073
电　　话 / 邮购（010）63376909　书店（010）68783171
网　　址 / http://www.zgtjcbs.com
印　　刷 / 中闻集团青岛印务有限公司
经　　销 / 新华书店
开　　本 / 890mm × 1240mm　1/16
字　　数 / 880 千字
印　　张 / 27.5　彩页 1.25
版　　别 / 2023 年 9 月第 1 版
版　　次 / 2023 年 9 第 1 次印刷
定　　价 / 280.00 元

如有印装差错，由本社发行部调换。

编辑委员会

编者说明

一、《青岛统计年鉴 2023》是一部全面反映青岛市国民经济和社会发展情况、信息高度密集的资料工具书。

二、本年鉴共包括发展成果图、统计公报、统计表、附录四大部分。

统计表部分收录了 2022 年青岛市经济和社会等各方面的统计数据，以及中华人民共和国成立以来重要年份和改革开放以来的主要统计数据，包括：综合，人口，就业与工资，固定资产投资，对外经济贸易，城市建设、环境保护，能源消耗，财政、金融和保险业，价格指数，人民生活，农业，工业，服务业，建筑业，运输、邮电，批发和零售业，住宿、餐饮业和旅游，教育、科技和文化，体育、卫生和民政、司法。

为方便读者正确使用年鉴资料，各篇章前设有《简要说明》，概括介绍各篇主要内容和资料来源；篇末附有《主要统计指标解释》。

三、本年鉴部分历史数据已根据经济普查、农业普查、人口普查数据进行了修订调整，在此之前公布的数据凡与本年鉴数字不符的一律以本年鉴为准。

四、部门分区市数据按照所属职能部门提供的区市名称范围划分。

五、本年鉴中的符号说明：年鉴各表中的“空格”表示该项统计指标数据不足本表最小单位数、数据不详或无该项数据；“#”表示其中的主要项。

六、《青岛统计年鉴》自公开出版以来，受到社会各界的关心和支持，对于年鉴的内容和编辑工作提出了许多宝贵的意见，对此我们深表谢意。限于我们的水平，欢迎读者继续对年鉴的不足之处给予批评和指正，帮助我们进一步改进年鉴编辑工作，以期更好地为广大读者服务。

《青岛统计年鉴》编委会

2023 年 7 月

Editor's Note

Ⅰ. *Qingdao Statistical Yearbook 2023* is a very important reference book, which reflects various aspects of Qingdao's social and economic development and contains High-density information.

Ⅱ.The yearbook contains the following four parts: achievement graphs, statistic gazette, statistics and appendixes.

Statistics contains all kinds of data on Qingdao's social and economic development in 2022, and data in significant year or data since the beginning of reform and opening up, including: General Survey; Population; Employment and Wages; Investment in Fixed Assets; International Trade and Economic Cooperation; City Construction and Environmental Protection; Consumption of Energy; Government Finance, Financial and Insurance; Price Indices; People's Livelihoods; Agriculture; Industry; service Enterprises; Construction; Transport, Postal and Telecommunication Services; Wholesale and Retail Trades; Hotels, Catering Services and Tourism; Education, Science & Technology and Culture; Sports, Public Health and Civil Affairs, Judicial Affairs.

In brief introduction at the beginning of each chapter, main coverage, data sources and statistical coverage are concerned. Meanwhile explanatory notes on major statistical indicators have been attached for readers to use the data correctly.

Ⅲ. All of the data in the book are in accordance with new administrative division.

Some of the data have been adjusted on the basis of statistics of economic census. In any case the data of this book shall be deemed as the authentic ones.

Ⅳ. Departmental district city data is divided according to the range of district and city names provided by the functional department to which it belongs.

Ⅴ.Explanation of symbols in this yearbook: "blanks" in the tables in the yearbook indicate that the statistical indicator data is insufficient to the minimum unit number in this table, the data is unknown or there is no such data; "#" indicates the main item.

Ⅵ. Since the publication of the "*Qingdao Statistical Yearbook*", it has received care and support from all walks of life, and has put forward many valuable opinions on the content and editing of the yearbook, for which we are deeply grateful. Limited to our level, readers are welcome to continue to criticize and correct the deficiencies of the yearbook, and to help us further improve the editing of the yearbook in order to better serve the readers.

Editorial Board

July, 2023

全市生产总值构成（%）

Composition Of Gross Domestic Product（%）

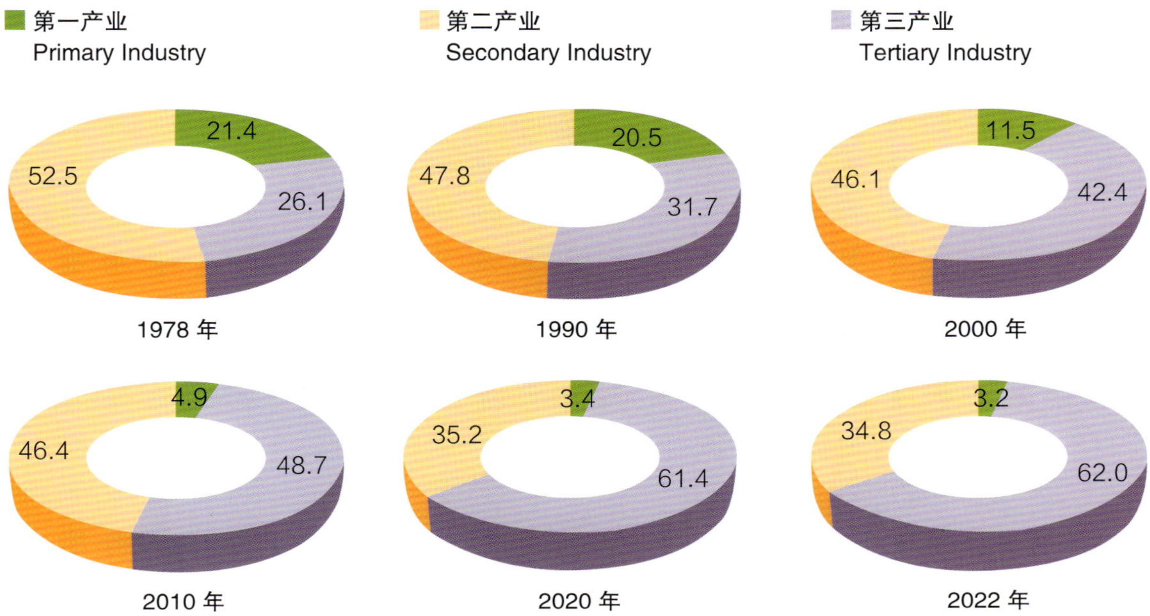

全市生产总值（亿元）

Gross Domestic Product（100 million yuan）

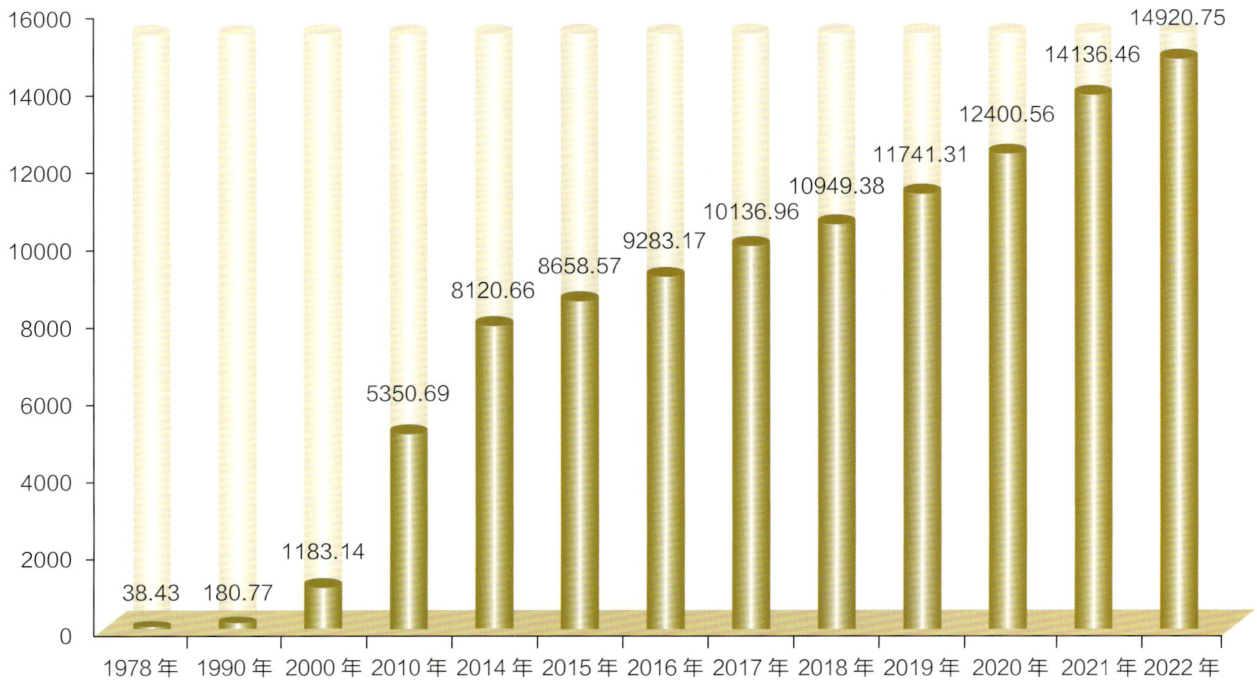

农林牧渔业总产值（亿元）

Gross Output Value Of Agriculture, Forestry, Animal Husbandry and Fishery (100 million yuan)

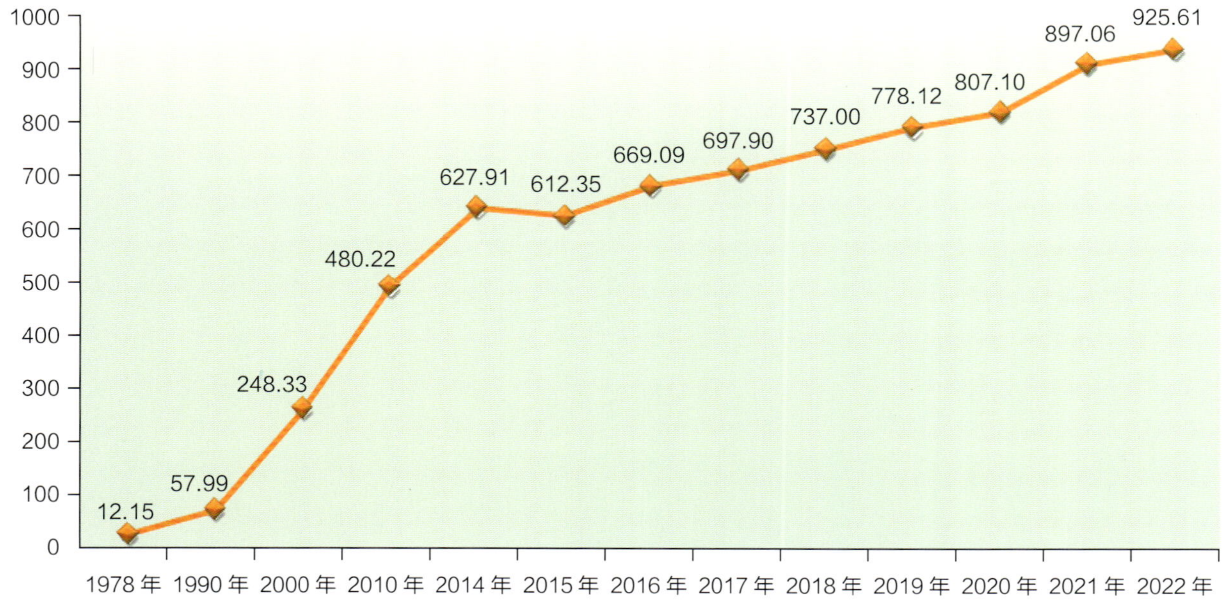

主要农产品产量（万吨）

Output Of Farm Products (10 000 tons)

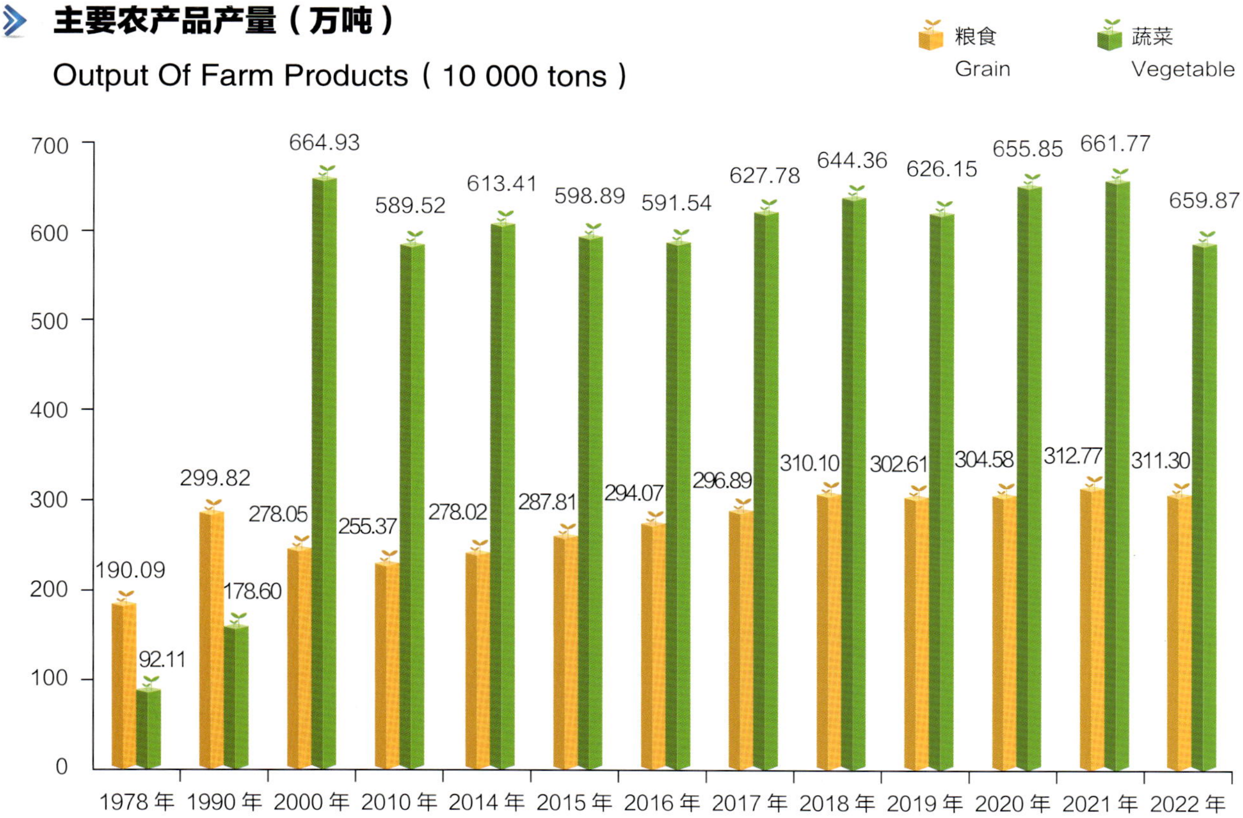

规模以上工业企业单位数（个）

Number Of Industrial Enterprises Above Designateo Size（unit）

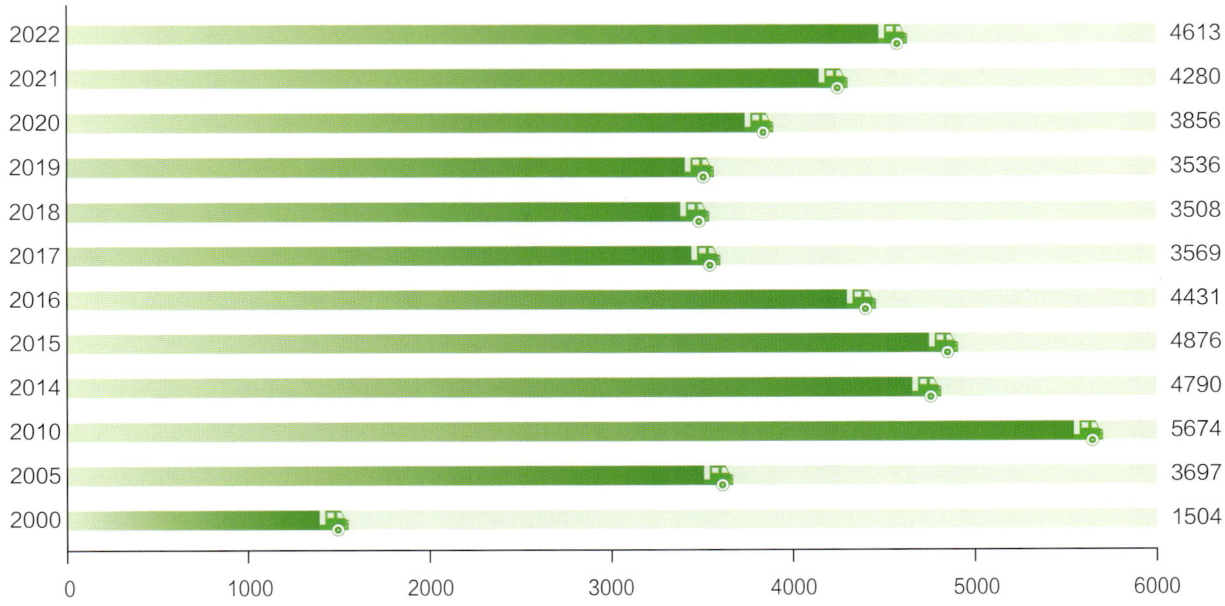

规模以上工业实现利润总额（亿元）

The Total Profits Made By The Industries Above The Designated Size（100 million yuan）

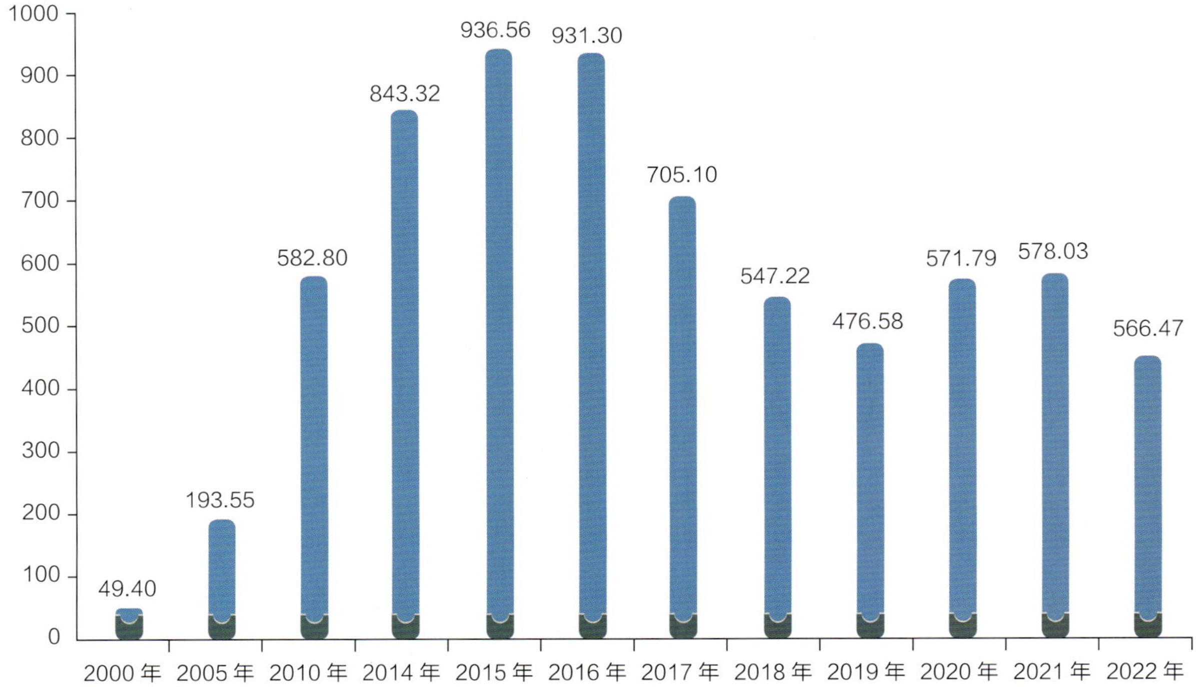

房地产开发投资额（亿元）

Investment In Real Estate Development (100 million yuan)

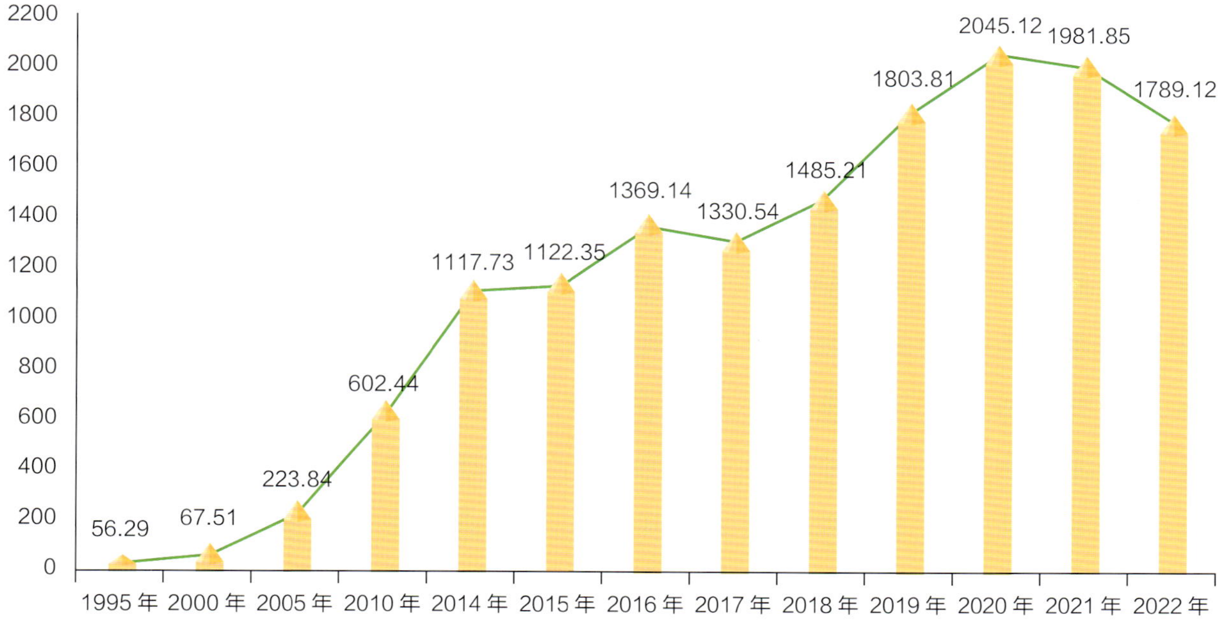

房屋销售面积（万平方米）

Floor Space Of Commercial Buildings Sold (10 000 sq.m)

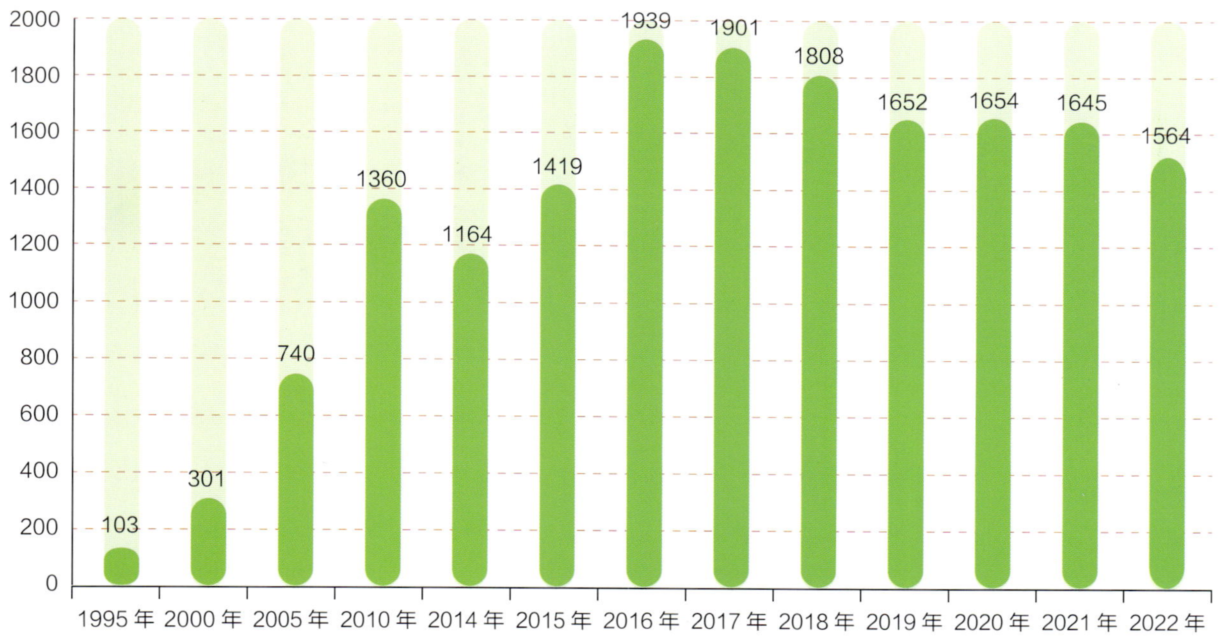

消费构成（%）（2022 年）

2022 Composition Of Consumption（%）

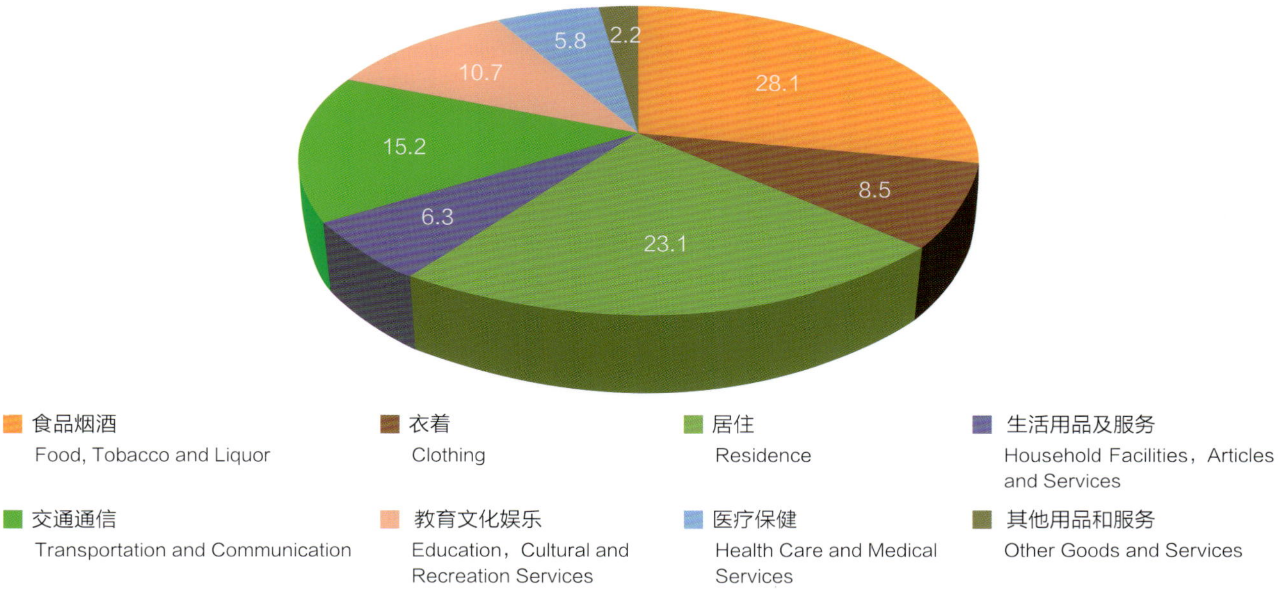

社会消费品零售总额（亿元）

Total Retail Sales Of Consumer Goods（100 million yuan）

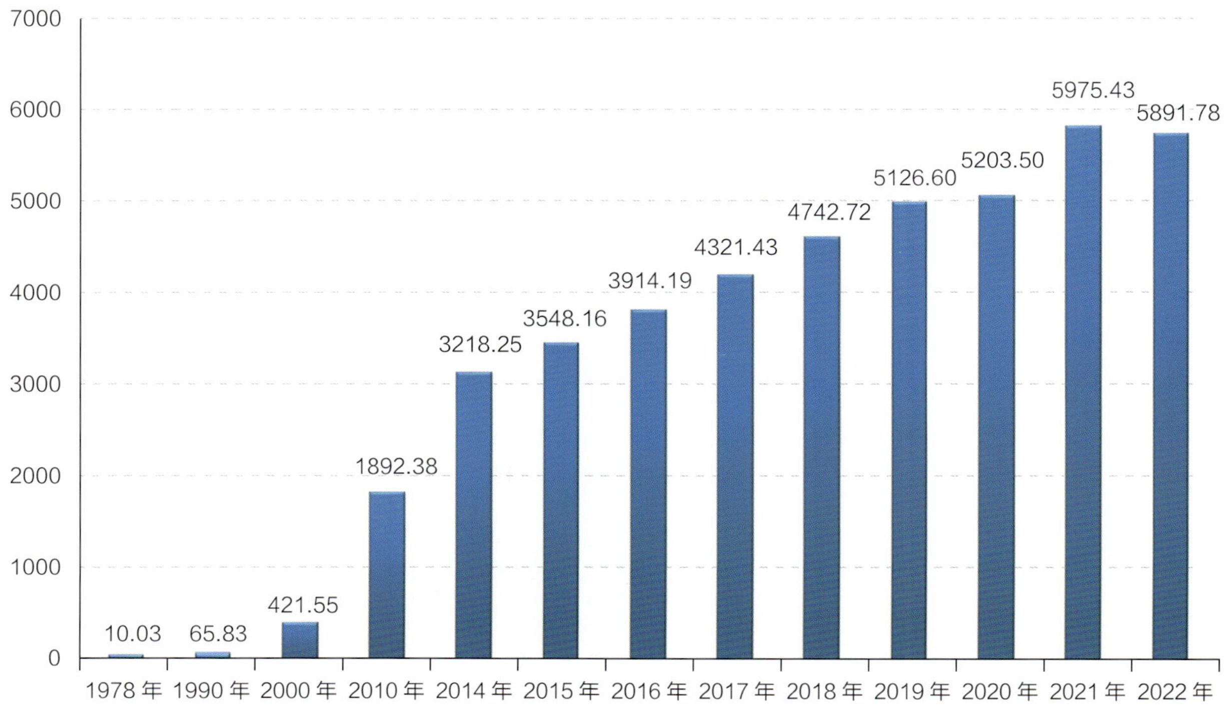

旅游总人数（万人次）

Number Of Tourists（10 000 person-times）

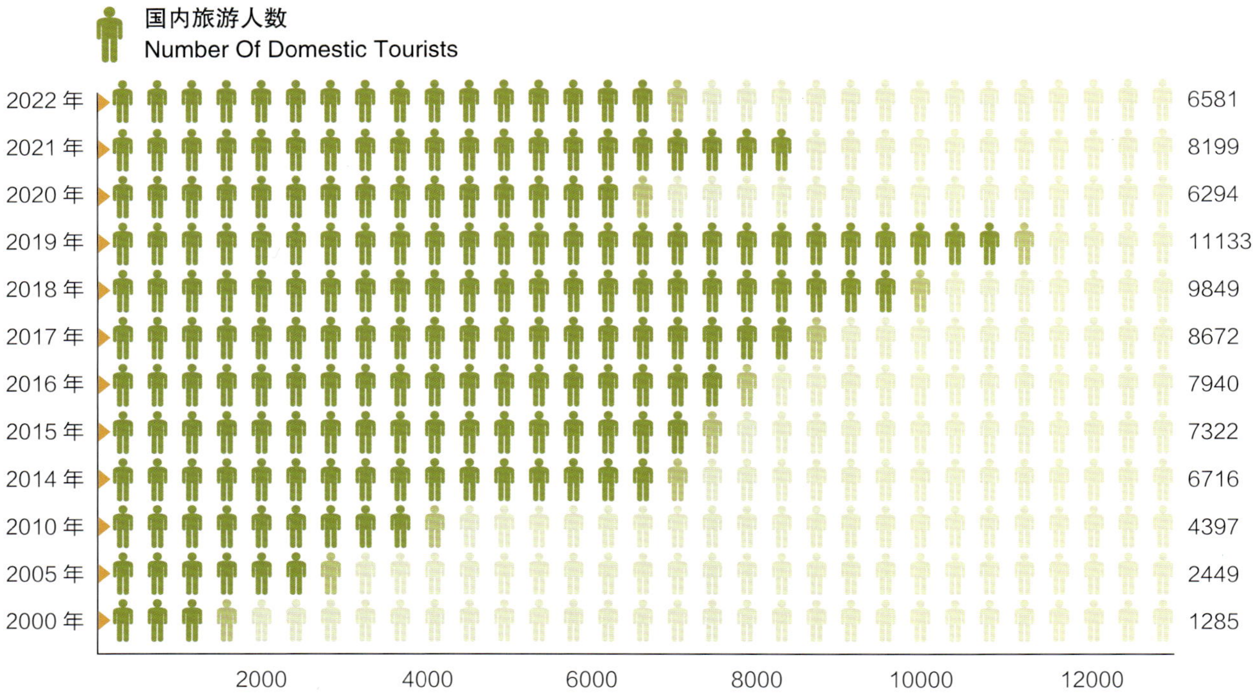

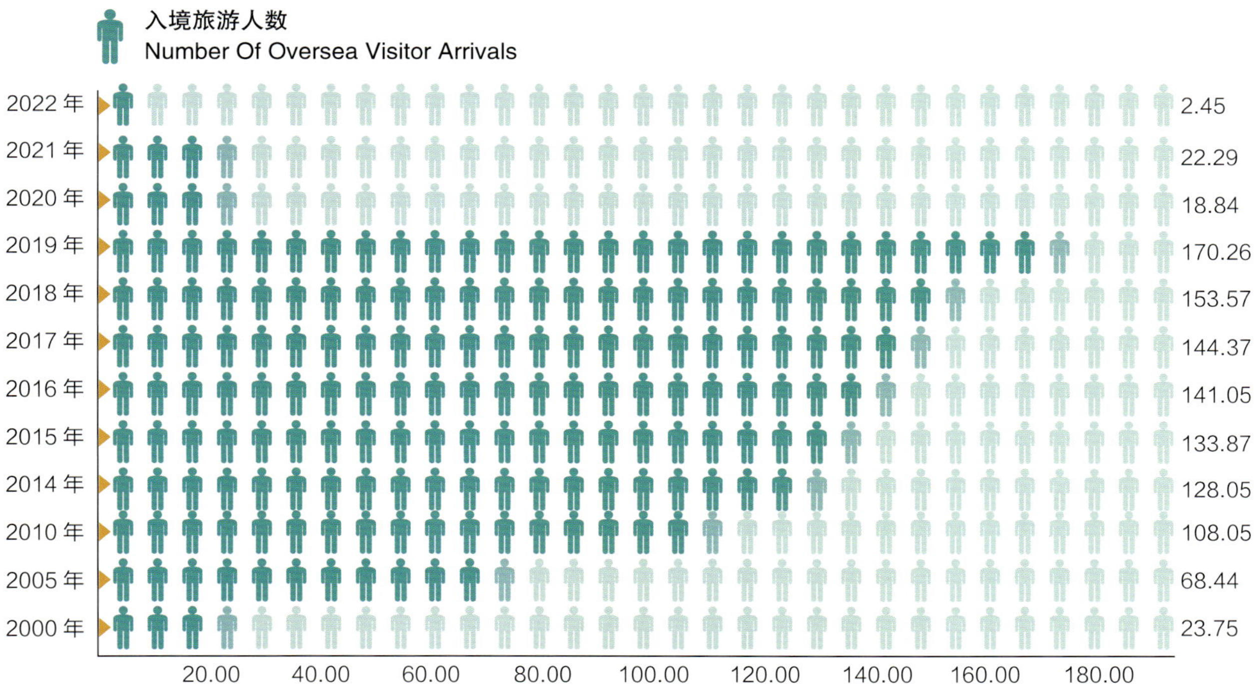

注：2022 年统计口径不含海员数。

Note：The statistical caliber of 2022 does not include the number of seafarers.

地方财政收入（亿元）

Revenue Of Local Government Finance（100 million yuan）

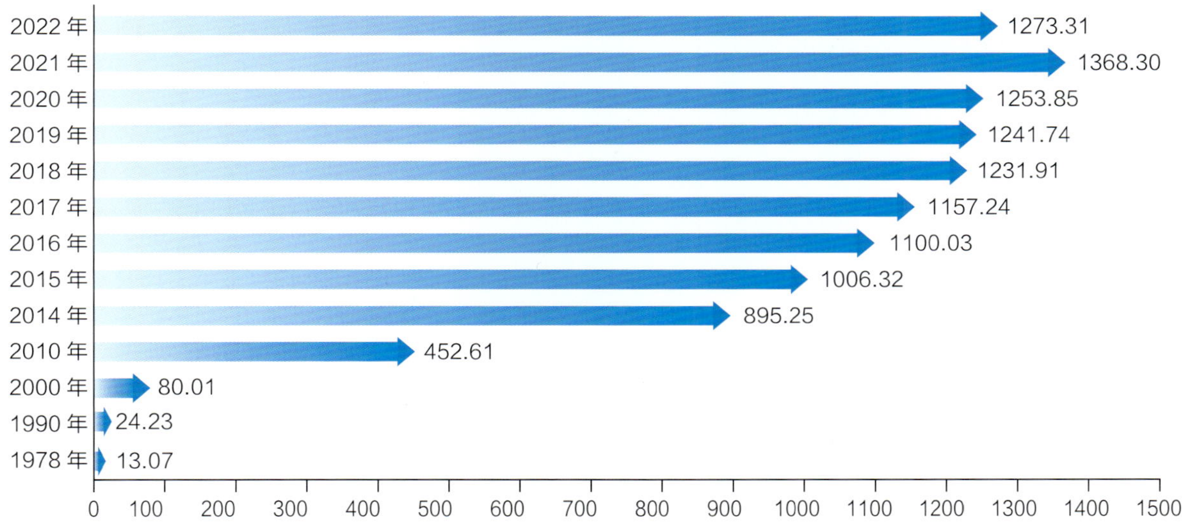

注：2002 年以后财政收入为一般预算收入数。

Note：Since 2002，revenue of government finance refers to general budgetary revenue.

金融机构年末人民币存贷款余额（亿元）

Year-end Savings Deposits And Loans Of Financial Institution（100 million yuan）

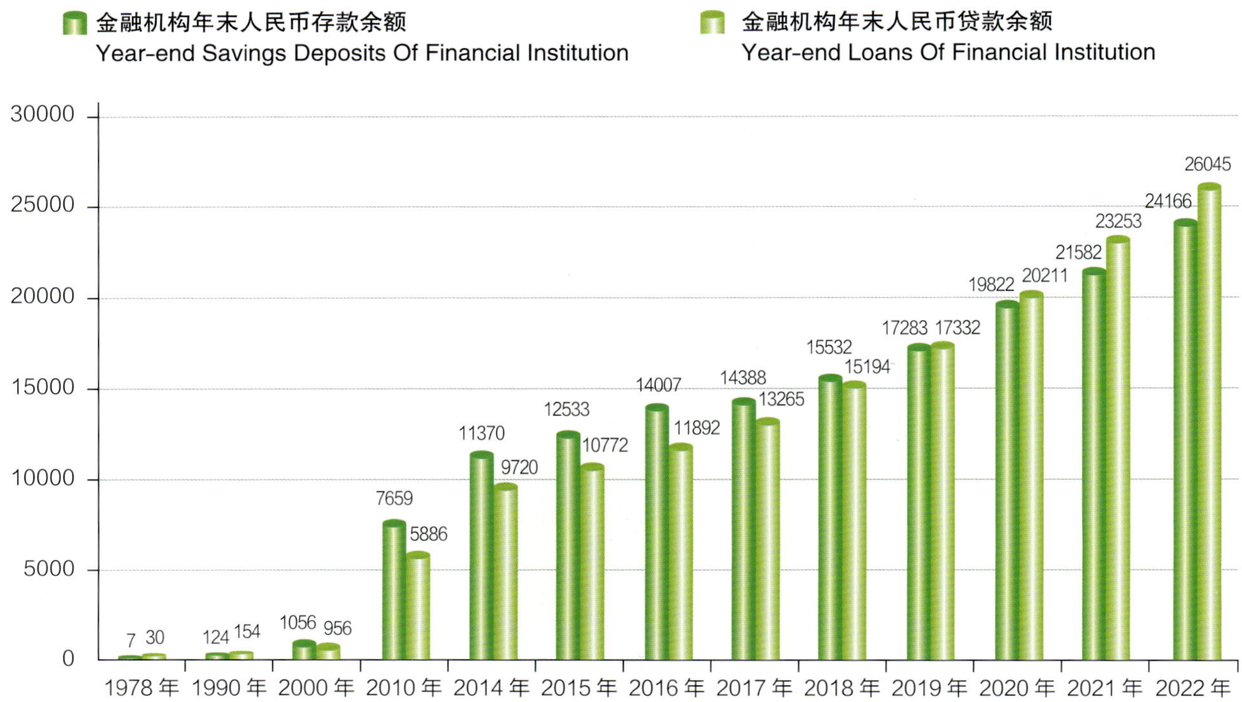

社会就业人数（万人）

Social Employment（10 000 persons）

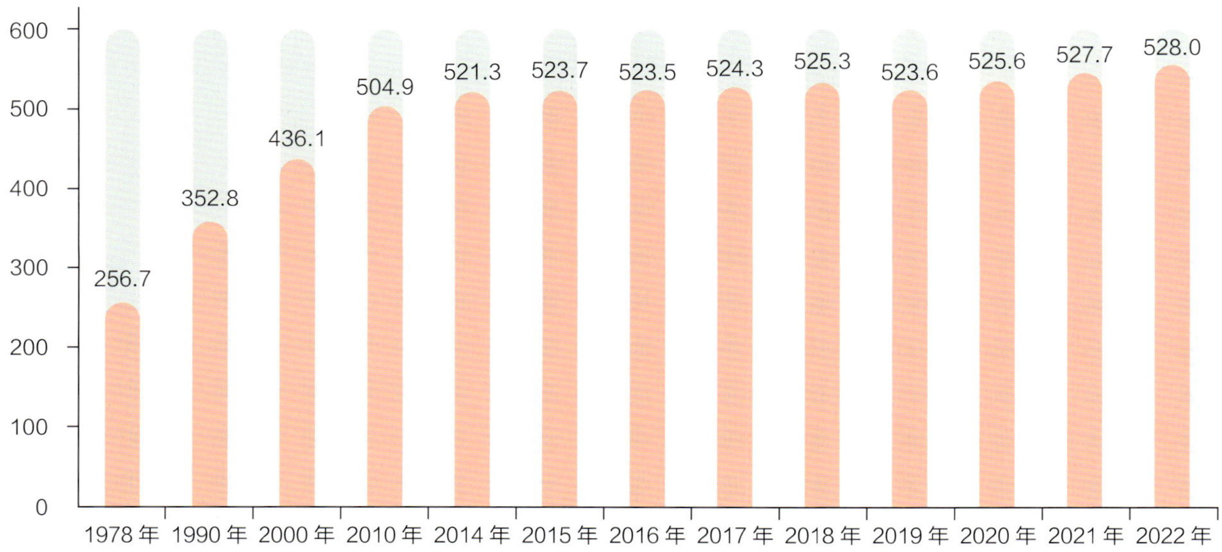

城镇非私营单位平均工资（元）

Average Salary of Urban Non-Private Units（yuan）

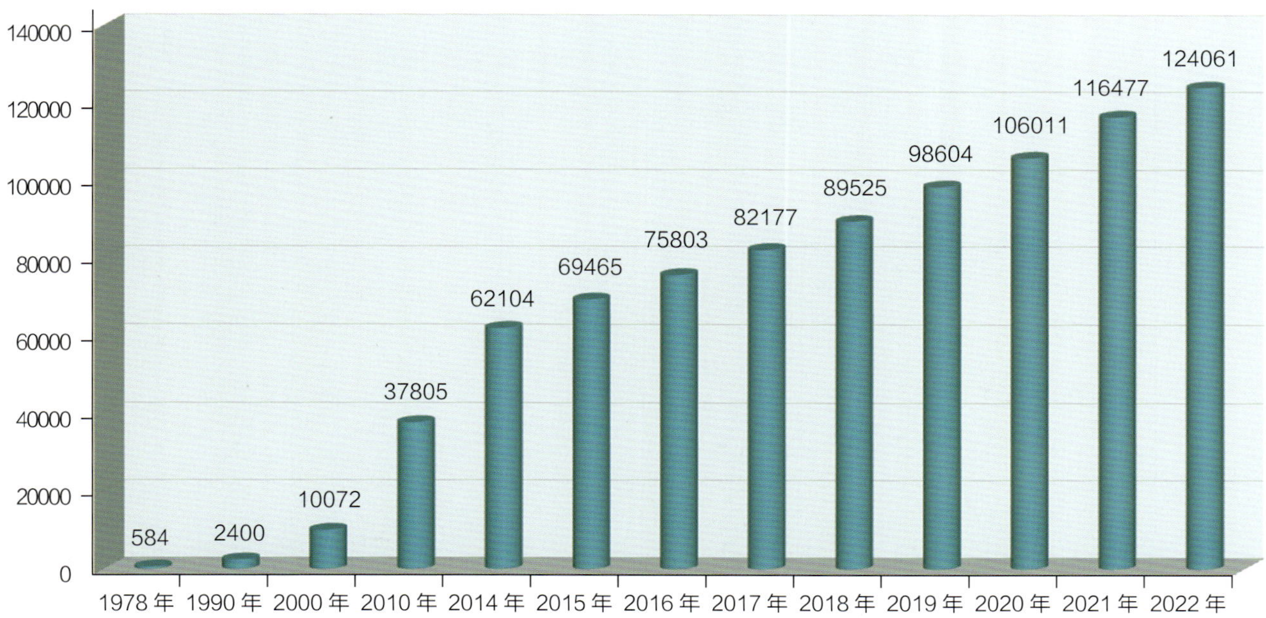

居民消费价格指数（上年= 100）

Consumer Price Indices（preceding year = 100）

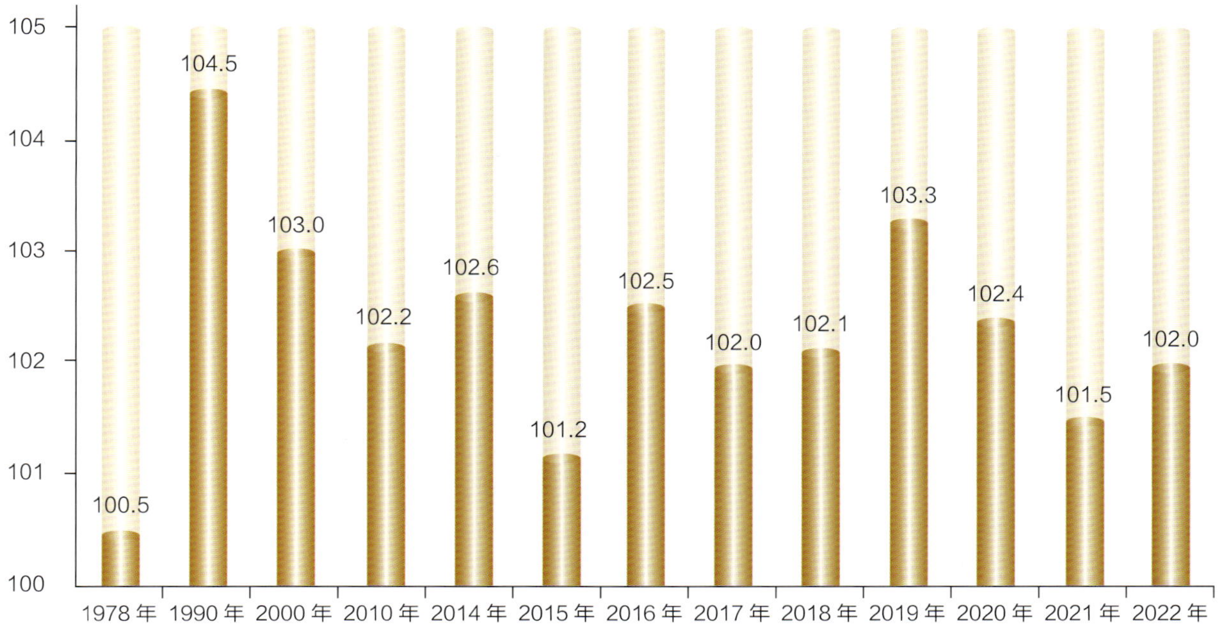

商品零售价格指数（上年= 100）

Retail Price Indices（preceding year = 100）

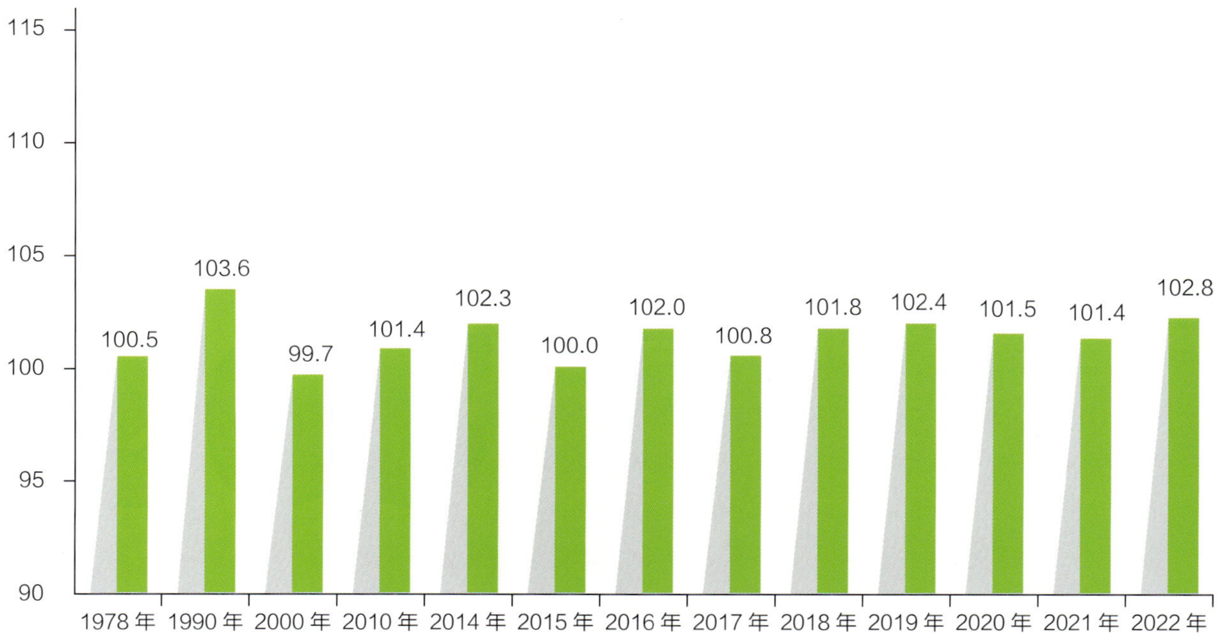

城市建成区面积（平方公里）

Developed Area Of the City（sq.km）

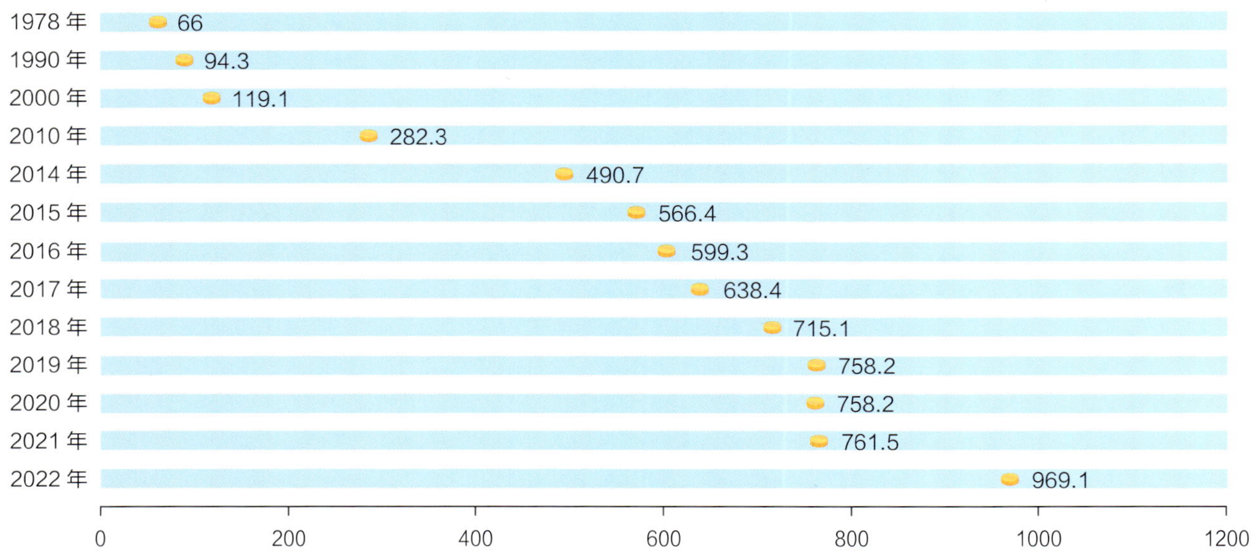

道路面积（万平方米）

Roads Area（10 000 sq.m）

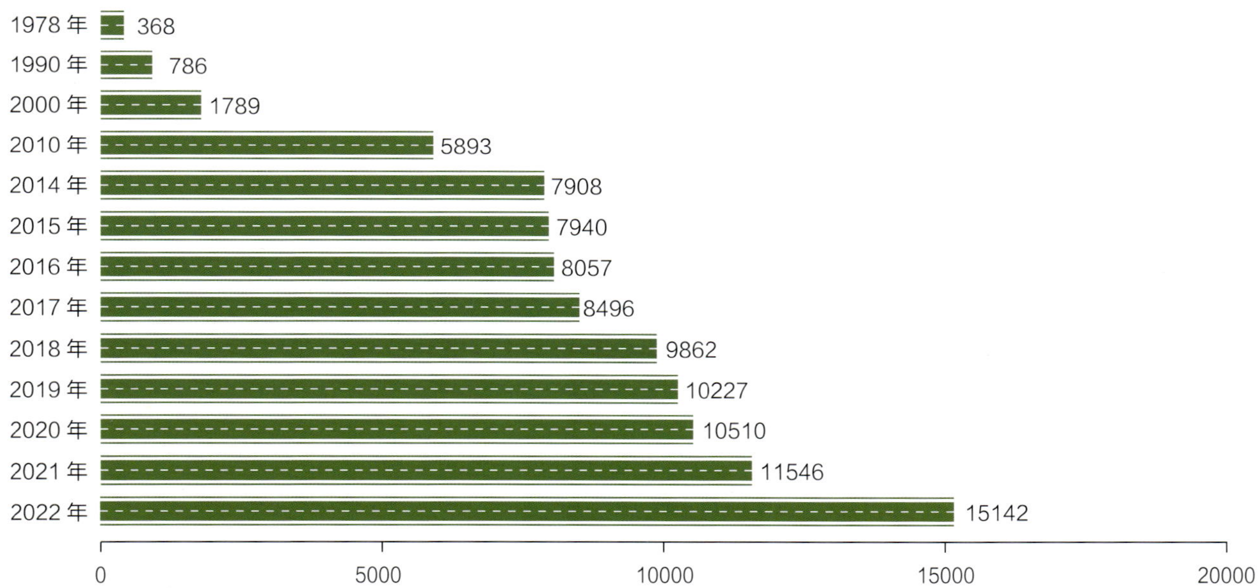

注：由于城市的发展变化，2022 年起，城市建设数据涵盖胶州市、平度市、莱西市数据。

Note：Due to the growth and changes of the city, from 2022, the data of urban development covers that of Jiaozhou, Pingdu and Laixi.

医疗卫生机构（个）

Health Care Institutions (unit)

普通高校在校人数（万人）

Students Enrollment Of Regular Institutions Of Higher Education (10 000 persons)

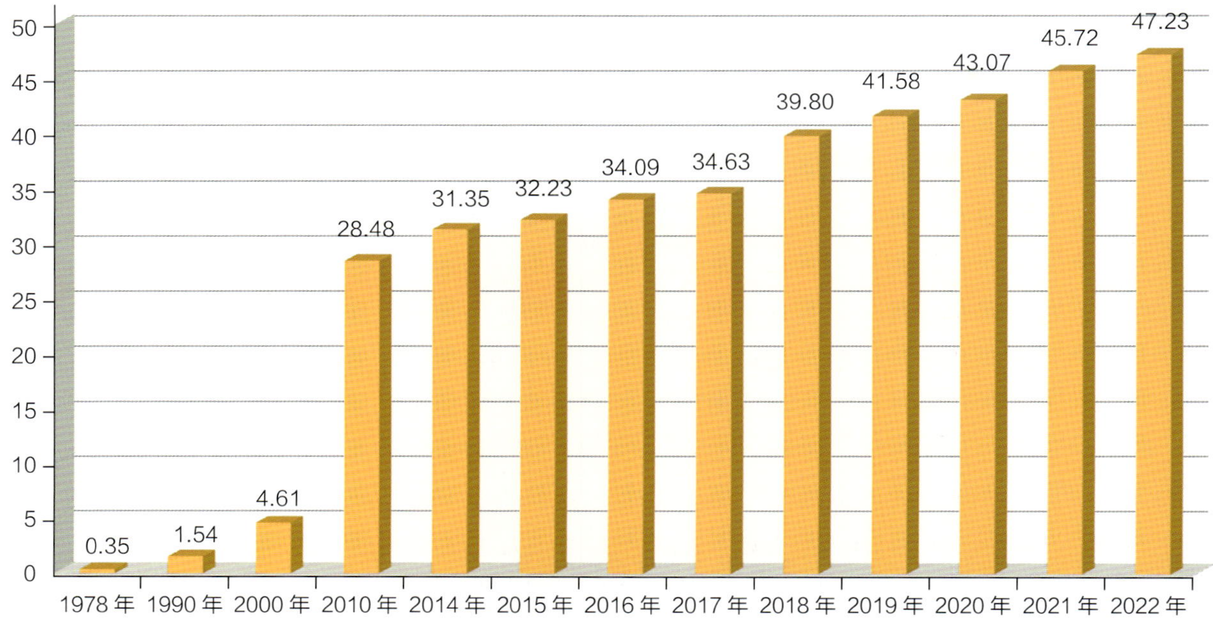

目　　录
CONTENTS

一、综　　合
Chapter 1.　GENERAL SURVEY

三、就业与工资
Chapter 3.　EMPLOYMENT AND WAGES

四、固定资产投资
Chapter 4.　INVESTMENT IN FIXED ASSETS

五、对外经济贸易
Chapter 5.　INTERNATIONAL TRADE AND ECONOMIC COOPERATION

六、城市建设、环境保护
Chapter 6.　CITY CONSTRUCTION AND ENVIRONMENTAL PROTECTION

七、能源消耗
Chapter 7. CONSUMPTION OF ENERGY

八、财政、金融和保险业
Chapter 8. GOVERNMENT FINANCE, FINANCIAL AND INSURANCE

九、价格指数
Chapter 9.　PRICE INDICES

十、人民生活
Chapter 10.　PEOPLE'S LIVELIHOODS

十一、农　业
Chapter 11.　AGRICULTURE

十二、工　业
Chapter 12.　INDUSTRY

十三、服务业
Chapter 13. SERVICE ENTERPRISES

十四、建筑业
Chapter 14.　CONSTRUCTION

十五、运输、邮电
Chapter 15.　TRANSPORT，POSTAL AND TELECOMMUNICATION SERVICES

十六、批发和零售业
Chapter 16.　WHOLESALE AND RETAIL TRADES

十七、住宿、餐饮业和旅游
Chapter 17.　HOTELS，CATERING SERVICES AND TOURISM

十八、教育、科技和文化
Chapter 18.　EDUCATION, SCIENCE & TECHNOLOGY AND CULTURE

十九、体育、卫生和民政、司法

Chapter 19.　SPORTS，PUBLIC HEALTH AND CIVIL AFFAIRS，JUDICIAL AFFAIRS

附　录
APPENDIX

2022 年
青岛市国民经济和社会发展
统　计　公　报 [1]

青岛市统计局

国家统计局青岛调查队

（2023 年 3 月 31 日）

2022 年，全市上下坚持以习近平新时代中国特色社会主义思想为指导，紧紧围绕迎接党的二十大、学习宣传贯彻党的二十大精神，深入落实习近平总书记对山东、对青岛工作的重要指示要求，完整、准确、全面贯彻新发展理念，主动服务和融入新发展格局，高效统筹疫情防控和经济社会发展，全市经济社会顶住压力持续发展，呈现持续恢复、进中提质良好态势，新时代社会主义现代化国际大都市建设迈出坚实步伐。

一、综　合

综合实力持续增强。初步核算，全市实现生产总值 [2] 14920.75 亿元，按可比价格计算，比上年增长 3.9%。其中，第一产业增加值 478.05 亿元，增长 2.2%；第二产业增加值 5197.34 亿元，增长 2.8%；第三产业增加值 9245.36 亿元，增长 4.5%。三次产业结构为 3.2∶34.8∶62.0。

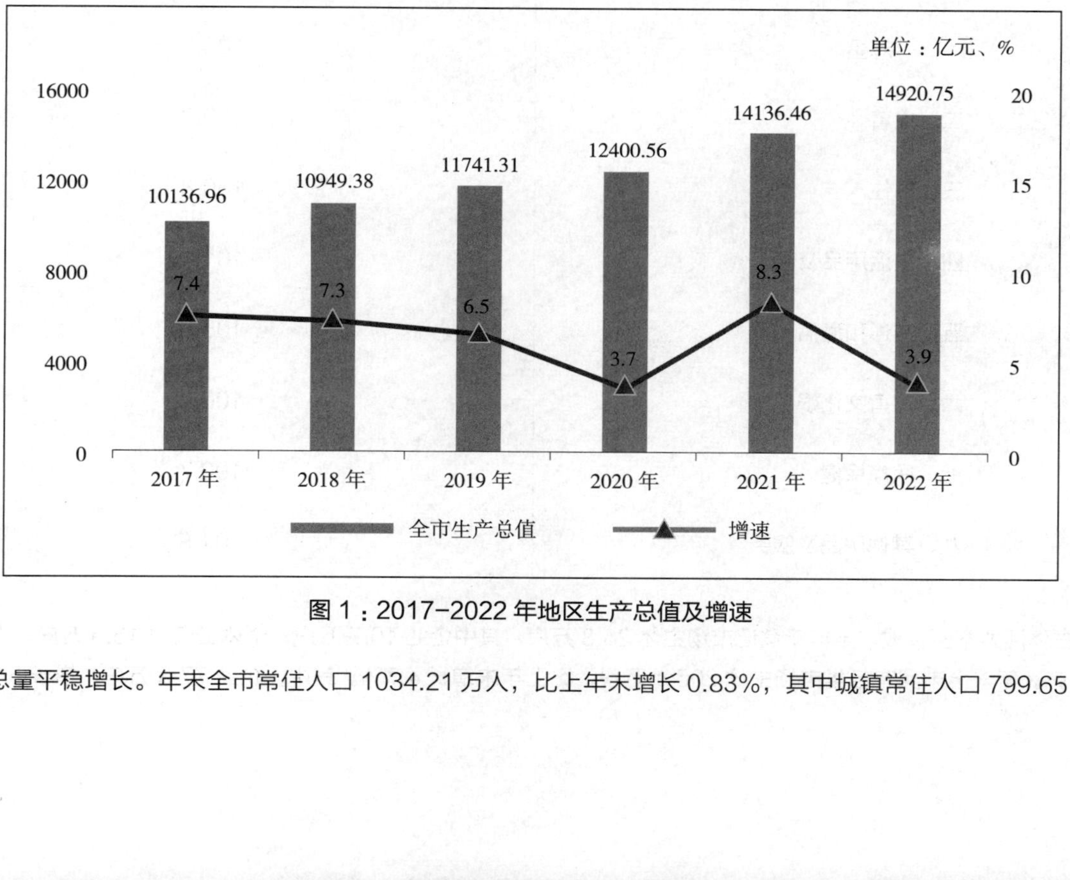

图 1：2017-2022 年地区生产总值及增速

人口总量平稳增长。年末全市常住人口 1034.21 万人，比上年末增长 0.83%，其中城镇常住人口 799.65 万人，常住人口城镇化率为 77.32%，比上年末提高 0.15 个百分点。

就业形势总体稳定。城镇新增就业 36.5 万人，其中失业人员再就业 6.3 万人，困难群体再就业 3.8 万人。

居民消费价格温和上涨。全年居民消费价格指数（CPI）为 102.0。分类别看，食品烟酒类价格指数为 103.0，衣着类价格指数为 100.8，居住类价格指数为 100.8，生活用品及服务类价格指数为 101.4，交通通信类价格指数为 105.8，教育文化娱乐类价格指数为 100.3，医疗保健类价格指数为 100.7，其他用品及服务类价格指数为 101.5。

表 1：2022 年居民消费价格指数

指　标	全年（上年同期 =100）
居民消费价格总指数	102.0
非食品价格指数	101.8
服务价格指数	100.8
消费品价格指数	102.9
一、食品烟酒	103.0
食品	103.4
#粮食	106.2
鲜菜	105.5
猪肉	91.7
鸡蛋	105.7
二、衣着	100.8
三、居住	100.8
四、生活用品及服务	101.4
五、交通和通信	105.8
六、教育文化娱乐	100.3
七、医疗保健	100.7
八、其他用品及服务	101.5

市场主体活力不断释放。全年新登记市场主体 26.3 万户，其中企业 10.7 万户，个体工商户 15.5 万户，农民专业合作社 612 户。年末全市实有各类市场主体 205.1 万户，比上年末增长 4.7%。其中，企业 77.3 万户，增长 5.6%；个体

工商户 126.1 万户，增长 4.3%；农民专业合作社 1.7 万户。实有民营经济市场主体 201.6 万户，增长 4.8%，占全部市场主体的比重为 98.3%。

动能转换加速突破。全年“四新”经济[3]增加值占 GDP 的比重达到 34.2%，比上年提高 1.3 个百分点；“四新”经济投资增长 20.8%，占全部投资的比重为 58.2%。规模以上工业[4]中，高技术制造业增加值比上年增长 17.3%，占规模以上工业的比重为 11.6%，比上年提高 1.4 个百分点；工业战略性新兴产业增加值增长 10.6%，占规模以上工业的比重为 29.5%，比上年提高 5.0 个百分点。生产性服务业增加值比上年增长 6.5%，占全市生产总值的比重为 36.7%；现代服务业增加值增长 3.7%，占全市生产总值的比重为 28.8%。

二、农　业

农业生产稳步提升。全年农林牧渔业总产值 925.6 亿元，比上年增长 3.0%。其中，农业产值 443.1 亿元，增长 3.2%；林业产值 4.2 亿元，增长 8.6%；牧业产值 176.9 亿元，下降 0.6%；渔业产值 234.0 亿元，增长 4.2%；农林牧渔专业及辅助性活动产值 67.4 亿元，增长 9.1%。全年农林牧渔业增加值 512.64 亿元，比上年增长 2.6%。

种植业平稳发展。全年粮食播种面积 48.2 万公顷，蔬菜播种面积 10.8 万公顷，花生播种面积 6.9 万公顷。全年粮食产量 311.3 万吨，比上年下降 0.5%；蔬菜及食用菌产量 659.9 万吨，下降 0.3%；花生产量 31.2 万吨，下降 8.2%；水果（含果用瓜）产量 121.9 万吨，增长 1.8%。

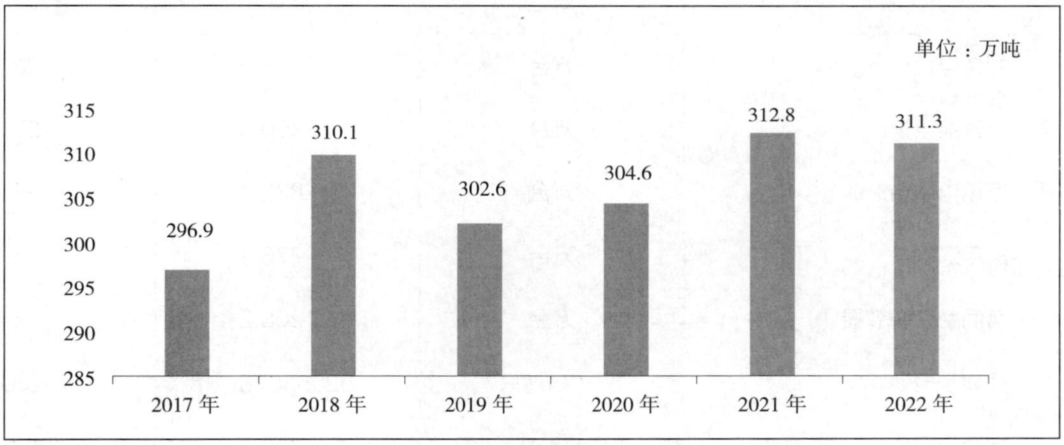

图 2：2017-2022 年粮食产量

表 2：2022 年主要种植业产品产量及增速

指　标	产量（万吨）	增长（%）
粮食	311.3	-0.5
夏粮	141.5	-1.0
秋粮	169.8	-0.03
油料	31.2	-8.2
蔬菜及食用菌	659.9	-0.3
水果	121.9	1.8
园林水果	83.1	3.2

林牧渔业稳步增长。全年完成荒山造林面积 0.067 万公顷。全年肉类产量 52.0 万吨，禽蛋产量 26.9 万吨，牛奶产量 29.6 万吨。全年水产品产量（不包括远洋捕捞）99.3 万吨，比上年下降 1.9%；海、淡水养殖面积 3.78 万公顷，增长 1.6%。

现代农业加快建设。市级以上现代农业产业园达到 11 个，产业强镇达到 43 个，绿色园艺标准园达到 202 个，畜禽养殖标准化示范场达到 185 个。国家地理标志保护产品达到 54 个。农机总动力 760 万千瓦，比上年增加 2.9 万千瓦。农作物生产综合机械化水平达到 91.02%。

三、工业与建筑业

工业生产平稳增长。全年工业增加值 3966.45 亿元，比上年增长 2.7%。规模以上工业增加值增长 3.8%。在规模以上工业中，分门类看，采矿业增长 3.2%，制造业增长 3.8%，电力、热力、燃气及水生产和供应业增长 1.2%；分大类行业看，35 个工业大类行业中 22 个行业增加值较上年增长，增长面为 62.9%，其中电气机械和器材制造业、化学原料和化学制品制造业、通用设备制造业、计算机通信和其他电子设备制造业、专用设备制造业等重点行业分别增长 8.0%、24.7%、6.1%、18.9% 和 13.6%。新产品快速增长，太阳能工业用超白玻璃、锂离子电池、多晶硅产量分别增长 4.9 倍、65.6% 和 30.6%。全年规模以上工业企业产销率为 97.2%。

表 3：2022 年规模以上工业主要产品产量及增速

产品名称	单位	产量	增长（%）
彩色电视机	万台	2545.6	28.1
智能电视	万台	2390.6	27.1
家用电冰箱	万台	832.1	−7.1
家用洗衣机	万台	776.1	6.2
房间空气调节器	万台	1208.2	5.0
锂离子电池	只（自然只）	52053076	65.6
啤酒	万千升	203.0	2.0
橡胶轮胎外胎	万条	4637.6	−8.0
平板玻璃	万重量箱	853.0	−14.5
太阳能工业用超白玻璃	平方米	676773.1	490.7
多晶硅	千克	52811.9	30.6
粗钢	万吨	435.0	33.9
动车组	辆	464	−7.8
城市轨道车辆	辆	964	−39.3
金属集装箱	万立方米	1522.6	−33.7

部分行业利润稳步增长。全年规模以上工业企业营业收入比上年增长 2.1%，利润总额下降 10.5%。规模以上装备制造业实现利润 304.4 亿元，比上年增长 1.7%，占规模以上工业的比重为 59.3%，比上年提高 6.4 个百分点。消费品制造业实现利润 104.1 亿元，比上年增长 6.9%，其中农副食品加工业、酒饮料和精制茶制造业、医药制造业利润分别增长 55.3%、20.4% 和 11.1%。

建筑业稳健发展。全年建筑业增加值 1250.56 亿元，比上年增长 3.0%。全市具有资质等级的总承包、专业承包建筑业企业 961 家，完成建筑业总产值 3580.2 亿元，比上年增长 8.6%；签订合同额 8606 亿元，增长 16.2%。

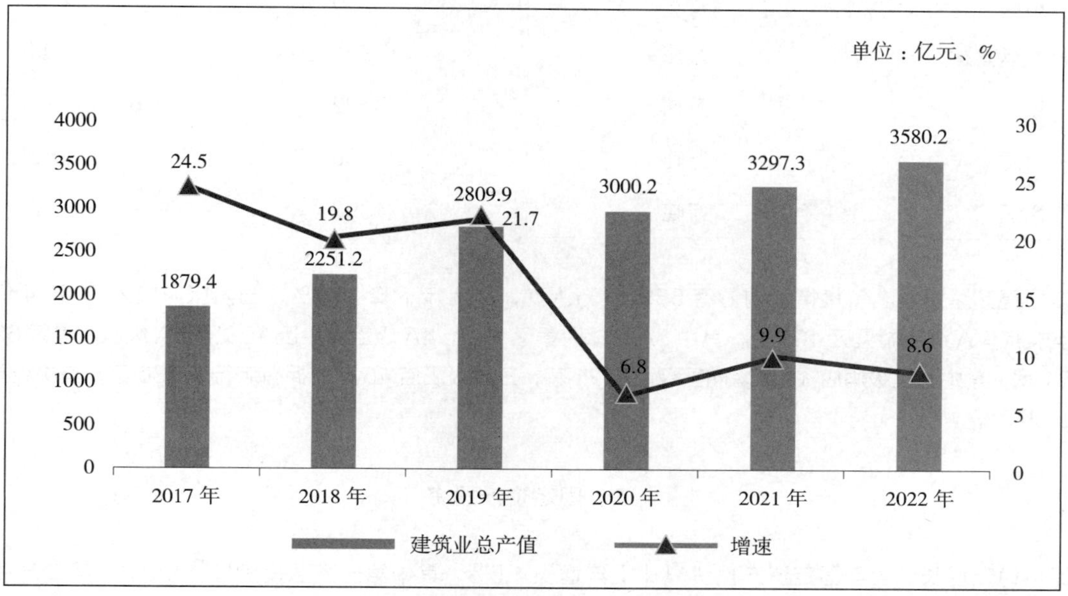

图 3：2017-2022 年建筑业总产值及增速

四、服务业

服务业支撑有力。全年服务业增加值 9245.36 亿元，比上年增长 4.5%，占全市生产总值的比重为 62.0%，对经济增长的贡献率为 73.8%，其中批发和零售业增加值增长 4.0%，交通运输、仓储和邮政业增加值增长 9.8%，住宿和餐饮业增加值增长 1.5%，金融业增加值增长 6.9%，信息传输、软件和信息技术服务业增加值增长 12.1%，租赁和商务服务业增加值增长 1.4%。规模以上服务业[5]实现营业收入 3884.4 亿元，比上年增长 6.6%。服务业新动能表现活跃，互联网和相关服务、软件和信息技术服务业、研究和试验发展营业收入分别增长 42.2%、17.8% 和 54.0%。

交通运输承压运行。全年铁路、公路、水路共完成货运量 4.0 亿吨，比上年下降 0.6%；完成客运量 2991 万人次，下降 41.9%。全年港口吞吐量 6.6 亿吨，比上年增长 4.3%；外贸吞吐量 4.7 亿吨，增长 3.2%；集装箱吞吐量 2567 万标准箱，增长 8.3%。年末拥有空中国内航线 220 条，国际航线 22 条，港澳台地区航线 2 条；全年航空旅客吞吐量 972 万人次，比上年下降 39.4%；航空货邮吞吐量 22 万吨，下降 7.4%。年末全市机动车保有量 355 万辆，比上年增长 5.4%，其中私人汽车 308 万辆，增长 5.3%。

邮政电信持续向好。全年完成邮电业务总量 245.5 亿元，比上年增长 19.7%。其中，邮政业务总量 92.1 亿元，增长 4.6%；电信业务总量 153.4 亿元，增长 31.1%。快递业务量 8.1 亿件，增长 4.8%。固定宽带互联网用户 499 万户，增长 0.1%。全市移动电话用户 1345.3 万户，增长 3.9%。国家级互联网骨干直联点建成开通，新建 5G 基站 10204 个，累计建成并开通 5G 基站 30154 个。

表 4：2022 年主要运输方式完成的运输量及增速

指　标	单 位	运输量	增长 (%)
旅客发送量	万人	2991	-41.9
铁路	万人	1210	-36.7
公路	万人	1694	-45.6
水运	万人	86	-27.7
货运运输量	万吨	39711	-0.6
铁路	万吨	8622	1.5
公路	万吨	26696	-6.0
水运	万吨	4393	43.2

旅游市场复苏趋缓。全年接待国内游客 6581.3 万人次，比上年下降 19.7%，国内旅游收入 1006.4 亿元，下降 28.7%。年末拥有 A 级旅游景区 101 处，其中 5A 级旅游景区 1 处，4A 级旅游景区 25 处，3A 级旅游景区 62 处。拥有星级酒店 81 家，其中五星级酒店 11 家，四星级酒店 21 家，三星级酒店 46 家。拥有旅行社 630 家，其中经营出境旅游业务旅行社 56 家。

五、固定资产投资

投资保持稳定增长。全年固定资产投资 [6] 比上年增长 4.5%，其中第一产业投资增长 1.0%，第二产业投资增长 15.6%，第三产业投资增长 0.8%。

投资结构不断优化。全年制造业投资比上年增长 13.2%，其中高技术制造业投资增长 75.0%。战略性新兴产业投资增长 18.3%，占固定资产投资的比重为 38.5%。基础设施投资、社会民生投资增长 23.2% 和 17.1%，比上年分别提高 27.0 个和 30.1 个百分点。

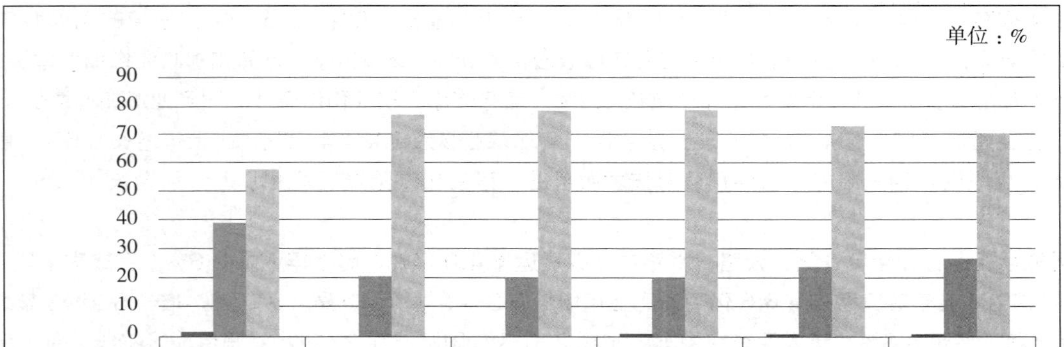

	2017 年	2018 年	2019 年	2020 年	2021 年	2022 年
第一产业	1.7	0.9	0.6	1.3	1.5	1.5
第二产业	39.9	21.5	20.9	20.6	24.9	27.4
第三产业	58.4	77.6	78.5	78.1	73.6	71.1

图 4：2022 年三次产业投资占固定资产投资比重

房地产市场低位运行。全年房地产开发投资 1789.1 亿元，比上年下降 9.7%，其中住宅投资 1316.2 亿元，下降 11.1%。商品房销售面积 1563.7 万平方米，比上年下降 4.9%，其中住宅销售面积 1264.1 万平方米，下降 11.0%。

表 5：2022 年房地产开发投资、商品房销售面积及增速

分 类	房地产开发投资（亿元）	增长（%）	商品房销售面积（万平方米）	增长（%）
总计	1789.1	−9.7	1563.7	−4.9
住宅	1316.2	−11.1	1264.1	−11.0
办公楼	95.7	−22.6	143.4	90.0
商业营业用房	114.1	−0.6	110.3	80.7
其他	263.1	0.3	45.9	−48.0

保障性住房供给有效增加。全年开工建设公共租赁住房 1005 套，建设筹集保障性租赁住房 4.58 万套（间）。年末全市正在享受租赁补贴家庭共 1.48 万户，全年发放租赁补贴 11390.42 万元。

六、消费市场

消费市场恢复放缓。全年社会消费品零售总额[7]5891.8 亿元，比上年下降 1.4%。其中，商品零售 5286.1 亿元，下降 1.1%；餐饮收入 605.7 亿元，下降 3.5%。按经营地统计，城镇社会消费品零售额 4862.2 亿元，下降 1.4%；乡村社会消费品零售额 1029.6 亿元，下降 1.2%。限额以上单位实现零售额 2044.0 亿元，增长 2.1%。

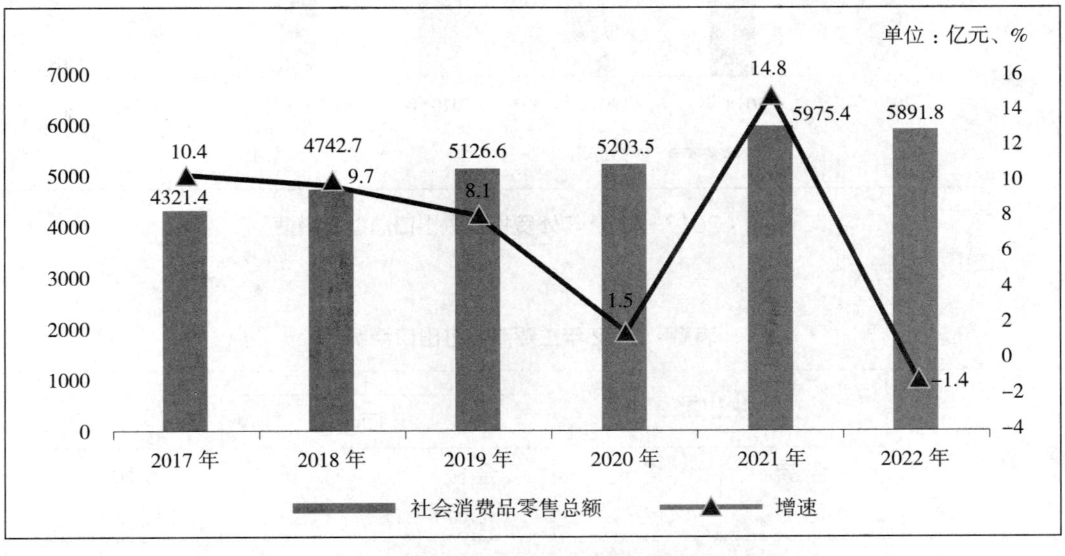

图 5：2017−2022 年社会消费品零售总额及增速

消费升级态势明显。全年限额以上单位商品零售额中，金银珠宝类、化妆品类和可穿戴智能设备商品零售额比上年分别增长 23.3%、18.7% 和 480.8%。绿色升级类消费需求持续释放，新能源汽车、能效等级为 1 级和 2 级的家用电器和音像器材类商品零售额分别增长 123.6% 和 10.3%。

七、对外经济

对外贸易稳步扩大。全年货物进出口总额 9117.2 亿元，比上年增长 7.4%。其中，出口额 5361.1 亿元，增长 9.0%；进口额 3756.1 亿元，增长 5.1%。从企业性质看，民营企业进出口 6366.1 亿元，增长 11.6%，占全市进出口总额的 69.8%；外商投资企业进出口 1559.0 亿元，下降 10.1%；国有企业进出口 1189.6 亿元，增长 14.5%。从出口结构看，机电产品出口 2434.6 亿元，增长 3.6%，占全市出口总额的 45.4%，其中汽车零配件、汽车、船舶出口分别增长 16.6%、102.8% 和 83.9%。从贸易市场看，对排在前三位的东盟、美国、欧盟进出口分别为 1743.3 亿元、1010.8 亿元和 944.7 亿元，增速分别为 28.8%、1.3% 和 -4.5%；对"一带一路"沿线国家进出口 3194.4 亿元，增长 21.0%；对 RCEP 其他成员国进出口 3557.5 亿元，增长 11.4%；对上合组织其他成员国进出口 600.1 亿元，增长 20.1%。

全年青岛口岸对外贸易进出口总额 18446.7 亿元，比上年增长 21.7%。其中，出口额 10587.2 亿元，增长 23.9%；进口额 7859.5 亿元，增长 18.8%。

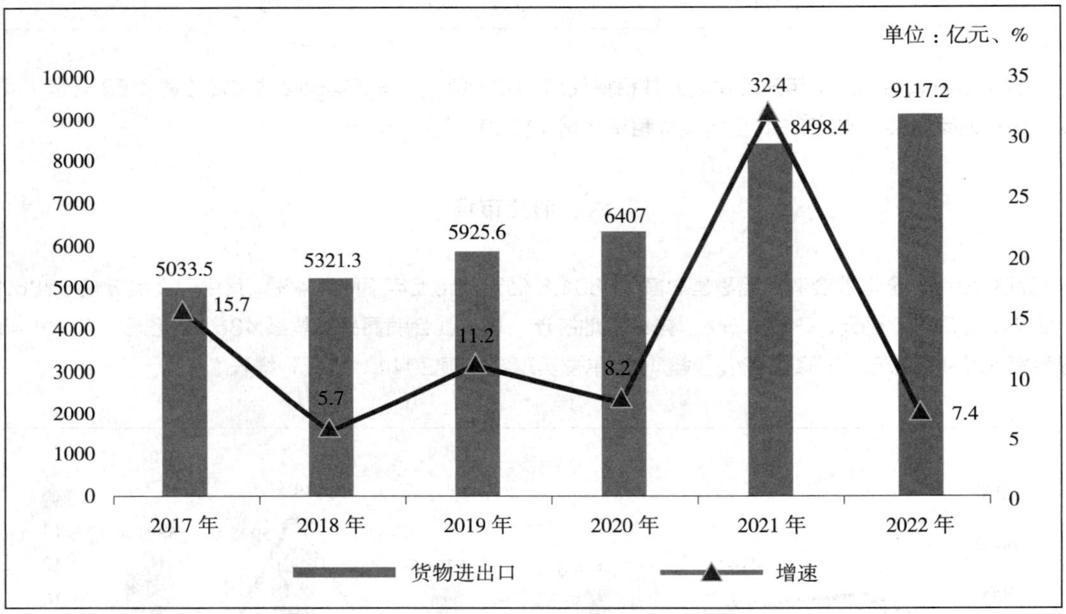

图 6：2017-2022 年外贸货物进出口总额及增速

表 6：2022 年主要商品进出口情况

指　标	进出口		出 口		进 口	
	金 额 （亿元）	增 长 （%）	金 额 （亿元）	增 长 （%）	金 额 （亿元）	增 长 （%）
纺织服装	639.5	7.9	620.3	8.6	19.1	-12.3
农产品	1199.2	13.5	432.7	16.7	766.5	11.8
机电产品	2992.1	1.1	2434.6	3.6	557.5	-9.5
高新技术产品	697.8	-7.6	340.5	-13.1	357.2	-1.7

表 7：2022 年对主要国家和地区货物进出口额及增速

国家和地区	出口额（亿美元）	增长（%）	进口额（亿美元）	增长（%）
亚洲	2524.4	9.3	1899.9	11.7
中国香港	127.5	−45.0	3.6	−1.3
中国台湾	45.8	−2.7	153.2	21.3
日本	501.8	9.3	142.6	−8.3
韩国	466.1	7.3	289.1	0.4
东盟	840.9	33.2	902.4	24.9
南亚	197.2	−5.2	43.1	−36.7
中东	305.3	20.0	333.3	13.8
非洲	278.4	17.8	257.4	36.1
南非	44.9	5.3	26.5	17.1
欧洲	1069.4	6.8	518.4	9.8
欧盟	704.1	3.0	240.5	−21.1
英国	120.8	−10.0	39.9	61.5
俄罗斯	175.8	21.4	180.9	104.9
南美洲	183.9	14.1	504.7	−6.5
巴西	66.2	16.3	366.5	−12.4
北美洲	932.7	6.5	295.6	10.9
美国	758.7	−2.1	252.1	13.0
加拿大	174.0	72.3	39.0	−4.1
大洋洲	154.7	11.2	268.5	−29.3
澳大利亚	128.6	19.4	222.1	−32.9

注：本表非全口径。

利用外资保稳促优。全年新设外商投资企业 693 家，比上年下降 23.7%；合同外资 277.1 亿美元，增长 29.3%。全市实际使用外资 55.1 亿美元，比上年下降 10.6%。其中，制造业实际使用外资 8.5 亿美元，增长 12.6%；现代服务业实际使用外资 24.7 亿美元，占服务业实际使用外资的比重达到 56%。

对外合作稳步推进。全市对外承包工程业务新承揽项目 39 个，新签合同额 21.8 亿美元，比上年下降 30.1%；完成营业额 29.3 亿美元，下降 2.7%。对外劳务合作业务派出各类劳务人员 10688 人。

"一带一路"融合发展。全年全市企业对"一带一路"沿线国家和地区投资项目 24 个，中方协议投资额 7.6 亿美元，比上年下降 37.7%；中方实际投资额 3.9 亿美元，增长 17.4%。

八、财政金融

财政收支扎实稳固。全年一般公共预算收入 1273.2 亿元，扣除留抵退税因素后比上年增长 5.5%，其中税收收入 881.2 亿元，扣除留抵退税因素后增长 3.5%，占一般公共预算收入的比重为 73.7%。全年一般公共预算支出 1696.2 亿元，比上年下降 0.6%。其中，教育支出 332.1 亿元，增长 7.5%；社会保障和就业支出 252.5 亿元，增长 3.9%；卫生健康支出 142.3 亿元，增长 14.5%。全年税务系统组织税收收入（含海关代征）2983.7 亿元，扣除留抵退税因素后比上年增长 9.6%，其中国内税收 2126.3 亿元，增长 2.2%。

金融市场健康发展。全市存贷款余额突破 5 万亿元。年末金融机构本外币存款余额 24992.7 亿元，比上年增长 11.7%，比年初增加 2617.9 亿元；本外币贷款余额 26782.5 亿元，增长 11.2%，比年初增加 2693.5 亿元。全年保险业累计实现保费收入 503 亿元，比上年增长 8.9%。其中，人身险公司保费收入 333 亿元，增长 9.1%；财产险公司保费收入 170 亿元，增长 8.5%。全年证券分支机构证券交易额 75750.5 亿元，比上年增长 6.8%；法人机构证券交易额 75337.6 亿元，增长 14.2%。全年新增境内上市公司 7 家，境内上市公司达到 65 家。在中国证券投资基金业协会登记的私募基金管理人 400 家，基金管理规模 1795.6 亿元，比上年增长 9.5%。

九、人民生活和社会保障

民生质量持续改善。全年全市居民人均可支配收入 53735 元，比上年增长 4.9%。按常住地分，城镇居民人均可支配收入 62584 元，增长 3.9%；农村居民人均可支配收入 27701 元，增长 6.0%。全市居民人均消费支出 32497 元，比上年下降 1.2%，恩格尔系数为 28.1%。按常住地分，城镇居民人均消费支出 37592 元，下降 2.5%；农村居民人均消费支出 17508 元，增长 2.9%。据抽样调查，年末城镇居民人均现住房建筑面积 34.0 平方米，农村居民人均现住房建筑面积 38.7 平方米。

城市品质全面提升。地铁三期规划 7 条线路全部开工建设，4 号线开通运营，运营总里程达到 315 公里。顺利实施 29 个城中村改造，完成 318 个老旧小区更新改造。完成架空线入地 207 公里。打通 42 条未贯通道路，新增 2.2 万个公共停车泊位，16 个位于老城区的停车场建成启用。基本完成 60 个山头公园整治，新建城市绿道 100 公里。年末全市建成区面积 761.5 平方公里。建成区绿化覆盖率为 45.2%，人均公园绿地面积 17.4 平方米。

表 8：2022 年城乡居民人均可支配收入构成情况

指　标	全体居民		城镇居民		农村居民	
	绝对值（元）	增长（%）	绝对值（元）	增长（%）	绝对值（元）	增长（%）
可支配收入	53735	4.9	62584	3.9	27701	6.0
工资性收入	31911	4.7	37635	3.9	15074	3.7
经营净收入	10081	3.9	9793	4.0	10931	4.2
财产净收入	4450	3.0	5805	1.7	463	1.1
转移净收入	7292	8.6	9352	5.1	1233	93.9

表 9：2022 年城乡居民人均消费支出情况

指　标	全体居民		城镇居民		农村居民	
	绝对值（元）	增长（%）	绝对值（元）	增长（%）	绝对值（元）	增长（%）
消费支出	32497	−1.2	37592	−2.5	17508	2.9
食品烟酒	9140	−0.7	10512	−2.0	5103	2.8
衣着	2775	−6.7	3290	−8.5	1258	1.7
居住	7515	−2.5	8812	−3.7	3700	0.4
生活用品及服务	2042	−6.8	2336	−9.1	1178	3.5
交通和通信	4932	1.2	5568	0.2	3059	2.9
教育文化娱乐	3480	3.5	4051	2.0	1801	8.0
医疗保健	1883	5.3	2175	4.6	1025	4.6
其他用品和服务	730	−6.0	847	−8.0	386	2.3

表 10：2022 年每百户居民家庭主要耐用消费品拥有量

指　标	单位	数 量		
		全体居民	城镇居民	农村居民
家用汽车	辆	68	72	59
摩托车	辆	17	9	41
电冰箱（柜）	台	111	112	109
洗衣机	台	106	109	99
热水器	台	100	101	98
空调	台	126	134	104
彩色电视机	台	103	103	105
计算机	台	64	71	45
移动电话	部	239	237	245

社会保障日益完善。年末城镇职工基本养老保险缴费人数 336.27 万人，职工医疗保险参保人数 429.22 万人，失业保险参保人数 281.42 万人，工伤保险参保人数 329.91 万人，生育保险参保人数 322.99 万人。居民养老保险和医疗保险参保人数分别达到 275 万人和 484.92 万人。年末全市城乡居民最低生活保障人数 7.7 万人，城乡居民最低生活保障资金支出 7.6 亿元；城乡特困供养人数 1.3 万人，城乡特困人员救助供养金支出 2.9 亿元。为 9.0 万名困难群众发放救助金 10.5 亿元，为 7.9 万名大病群众报销医疗费 53.9 亿元。全市养老床位 5.3 万张，其中本年新增养老床位 0.2 万张。

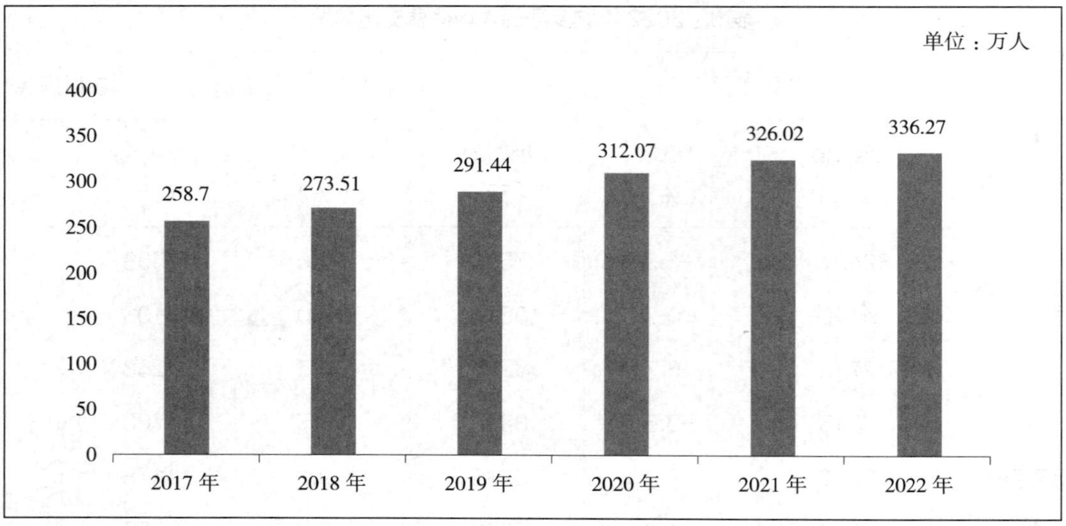

图 7：2017-2022 年城镇职工基本养老保险参保缴费人数

十、科学技术和教育

科创平台加速建设。崂山实验室挂牌运行。国家虚拟现实创新中心（青岛）获批组建。5 家实验室在首批全国重点实验室重组中获得批复，省级以上重点实验室达到 66 家，其中国家级 11 家。新建省级以上技术创新中心 6 家，总数达到 30 家。现有国家知识产权示范企业 23 家，国家知识产权优势企业 196 家。高新技术企业总数达到 6680 家，比上年增加 1126 家。入库国家科技型中小企业达到 7050 家。新培育国家专精特新“小巨人”企业 54 家，总数累计达到 151 家。新引进集聚人才 25.7 万人，人才总量突破 265 万人。

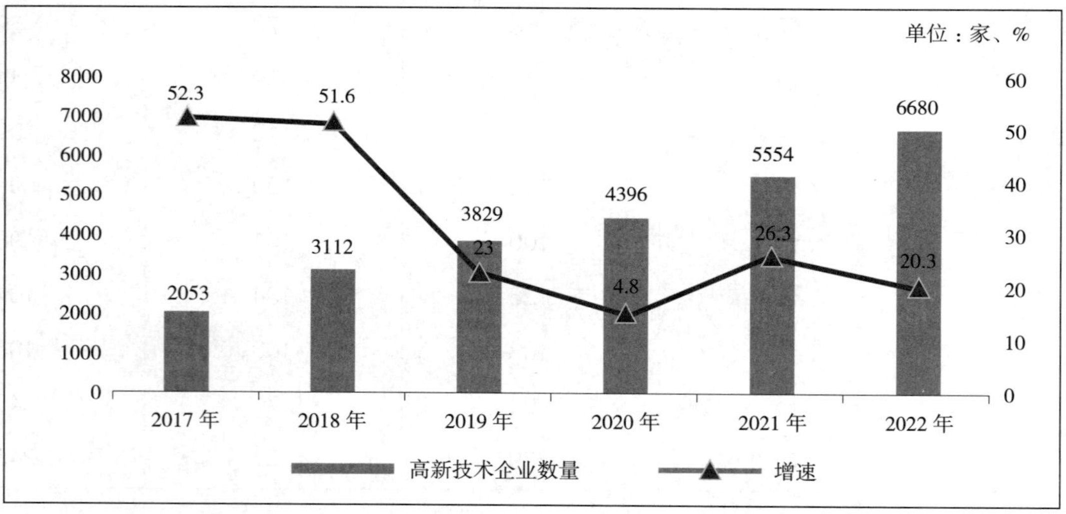

图 8：2017-2022 年高新技术企业数量及增速

科技实力持续增强。初步统计，全市共登记科技成果 405 项，获得省级科技奖励 75 项，其中自然科学奖 13 项，技术发明奖 9 项，科技进步奖 51 项，最高奖项 1 项，青年奖 1 项。技术合同交易额 395 亿元，比上年增长 23.0%。涉海技术合同成交额 40.8 亿元，增长 28.2%。新增有效发明专利 14523 件，比上年增长 42.2%。每万人有效发明专利拥有量 58.99 件，比上年增加 12.17 件。PCT 国际专利申请 2351 件。

教育事业全面发展。全年新建改扩建中小学和幼儿园 112 所，新增公办学位 8.07 万个；改造提升农村薄弱幼儿园 62 所。年末全市共有各类高校（含民办高校）29 所，其中普通高校 26 所。全年研究生招生 2.20 万人，在校研究生 6.73 万人，毕业生 1.46 万人（不含驻青科研院所研究生）。普通本专科招生 12.49 万人，在校生 40.50 万人，毕业生 10.96 万人；中等职业教育招生 2.78 万人，在校生 9.24 万人，毕业生 2.97 万人；普通高中招生 5.79 万人，在校生 15.76 万人，毕业生 4.44 万人；初中招生 9.37 万人，在校生 29.25 万人，毕业生 9.5 万人；普通小学招生 12.54 万人，在校生 66.45 万人，毕业生 9.32 万人；特殊教育招生 0.03 万人，在校生 0.25 万人，毕业生 0.03 万人；幼儿园在园幼儿 35.24 万人。

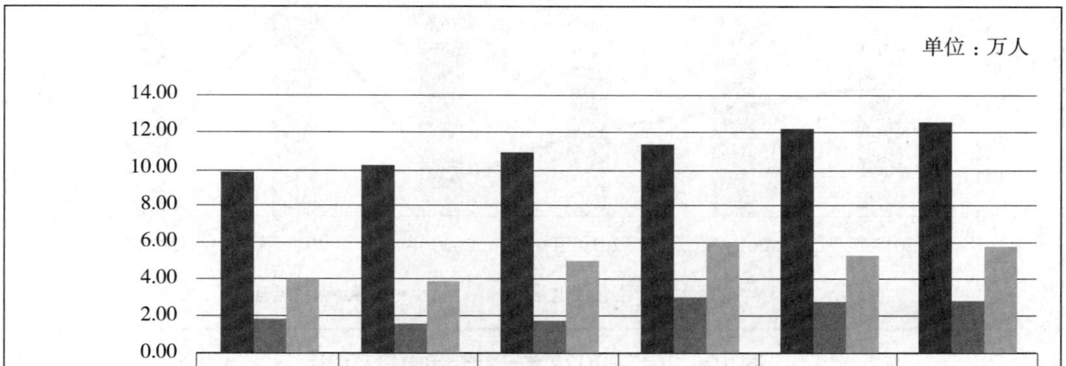

	2017 年	2018 年	2019 年	2020 年	2021 年	2022 年
■普通高校本专科	9.90	10.24	10.91	11.37	12.06	12.49
■中等职业学校	1.80	1.59	1.70	2.97	2.72	2.78
■普通高中	3.96	3.83	4.94	6.03	5.28	5.79

图 9：2017-2022 年各类学校招生人数

十一、卫生、文化和体育

医疗卫生水平不断提升。年末全市共有医疗卫生机构 8780 个，其中医院 353 个，基层卫生医疗机构 8290 个。各类卫生技术人员 9.90 万人，其中执业（助理）医师 4.12 万人，注册护士 4.44 万人。全市拥有医疗床位 6.96 万张，其中医院 5.85 万张，卫生院 0.69 万张。

文化供给更加丰富。国家海洋考古博物馆正式签约落地青岛。全年新建全民阅读设施 100 处。年末全市共有影剧院 102 家，文化馆（站）148 个，博物馆 121 个，公共图书馆 11 个，国有文艺院团 9 个，广播电台 6 座、11 套节目，电视台 6 座、17 套节目。全市共有档案馆 12 个。

体育事业蓬勃发展。全年新建体育公园、笼式多功能运动场等体育健身场所 58 处，更新新建健身路径 411 处。我市运动员在第 24 届冬奥会上获得山东冬奥史上首枚奖牌；在第 25 届省运会上获得 277 枚金牌，位居金牌榜第一名。年末全市共有重点体校 1 所，学员 1150 人；业余体校 10 所，学员 2059 人。

十二、能源、环境和安全生产

能源供给更加绿色。全年能源生产量 2836.4 万吨标准煤，比上年下降 1.7%。发电量 196.3 亿千瓦时，比上年增长 4.6%。新能源发电量 36.7 亿千瓦时，增长 10.1%，占全市发电总量的比重为 18.7%，其中风力发电量增长 3.8%，垃圾焚烧发电量增长 6.3%，太阳能发电量增长 315.8%。

能源消费保持平稳。全社会用电量 576.5 亿千瓦时，比上年增长 4.3%。其中，工业用电量 302.1 亿千瓦时，增长 1.4%；服务业用电量 148.8 亿千瓦时，增长 3.5%；城乡居民生活用电量 103.9 亿千瓦时，增长 13.9%。全市规模以上工业综合能源消费量 1754.6 万吨标准煤，比上年增长 9.4%，其中煤炭消费量增长 2.7%，石油消费量增长 1.0%，天然气消费量增长 13.5%。

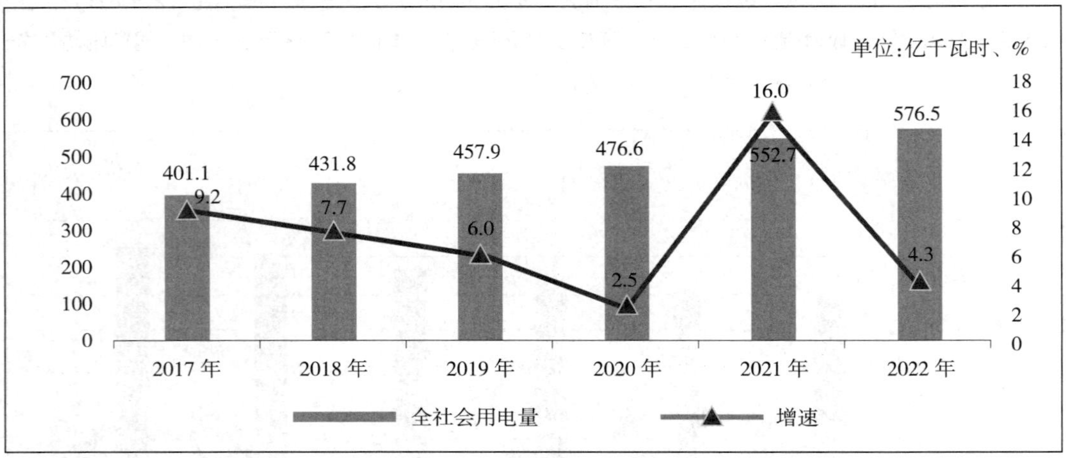

图 10：2017-2022 年全社会用电量及增速

生态环境质量进一步改善。全市年平均气温 13.5℃，平均年降水量 1079.6 毫米。市区空气质量优良天数 323 天，占全年的 88.5%。市区区域环境噪声平均值 54.8 分贝，市区交通干线噪声平均值 69.5 分贝。空气质量连续三年达到国家二级标准。全市主要污染物细颗粒物（PM2.5）、可吸入颗粒物（PM10）年均值分别为 26 和 49 微克 / 立方米，比上年分别改善 7.1% 和 12.5%。20 个国省控地表水考核断面水质全部达标，近岸海域水质优良比例面积达到 99%。

安全生产持续稳定。全市共发生各类生产安全事故 186 起，死亡 98 人，分别比上年下降 13.5% 和 24.0%。亿元 GDP 生产安全事故死亡率 0.0066，十万工矿商贸企业就业人员生产安全事故死亡率 0.58。

注释：

[1] 本公报中数据均为初步统计数，部分数据因四舍五入的原因，存在总计与分项合计不等的情况。

[2] 全市生产总值、三次产业及相关行业增加值按现价计算，增长速度按可比价格计算。

[3]“四新”经济指以国家统计局《新产业新业态新商业模式统计分类（2018）》为基础，由山东省统计局《新技术新产业新业态新模式统计监测制度》界定的具有“新技术、新产业、新业态、新模式”经济特征的生产活动。

[4] 规模以上工业统计范围为年主营业务收入 2000 万元及以上的工业企业。

[5] 规模以上服务业统计范围包括：年营业收入 2000 万元及以上的交通运输、仓储和邮政业，信息传输、软件和信息技术服务业，水利、环境和公共设施管理业，卫生行业法人单位；年营业收入 1000 万元及以上的房地产业（不含房地产开发经营），租赁和商务服务业，科学研究和技术服务业，教育行业法人单位；以及年营业收入 500 万元及以上的居民服务、修理和其他服务业，文化、体育和娱乐业，社会工作行业法人单位。

[6] 固定资产投资统计范围包括：辖区内计划总投资 500 万元及以上建设项目投资，全部房地产开发经营业法人单位开发项目投资，不包括农户投资。

[7] 社会消费品零售总额统计范围包括：从事商品零售活动或提供餐饮服务的法人企业、产业活动单位和个体户。其中，限额以上单位是指年主营业务收入 2000 万元及以上的批发业企业（单位）、500 万元及以上的零售业企业（单位）、200 万元及以上的住宿和餐饮业企业（单位）。

资料来源：本公报中财政数据来自青岛市财政局；税务数据来自青岛市税务局；社会保障、就业、人才等数据来自青岛市人力资源和社会保障局；银行数据来自中国人民银行青岛市中心支行；证券保险数据来自中国证券监督管理委员会青岛监管局、中国银行保险监督管理委员会青岛监管局；水产品数据来自青岛市海洋发展局；林业数据来自青岛市园林和林业局；农业数据来自青岛市农业农村局；交通运输数据来自青岛市交通运输局；邮政数据来自青岛市邮政管理局；宽带、移动电话等数据来自青岛市通信管理局；进出口、外资、对外承包工程、对外劳务合作等数据来自青岛市商务局；旅游数据来自青岛市文化和旅游局；教育数据来自青岛市教育局；科技数据来自青岛市科学技术局；市场主体、专利等数据来自青岛市市场监督管理局；低保数据来自青岛市民政局；体育数据来自青岛市体育局；卫生数据来自青岛市卫生健康委员会；环境数据来自青岛市生态环境局；用电量数据来自青岛供电公司；气象数据来自青岛市气象局；安全生产数据来自青岛市应急管理局；城市建设数据来自青岛市住房和城乡建设局；汽车保有量数据来自青岛市公安局；粮食数据、畜牧数据、居民生活数据、价格数据来自国家统计局青岛调查队；其他数据来自青岛市统计局。

STATISTICS COMMUNIQUE QINGDAO'S ECONOMIC AND SOCIAL DEVELOPMENT IN THE YEAR OF 2022[1]

Qingdao Municipal Statistics Bureau

NBS Survey Office In Qingdao

(March 31, 2023)

In 2022, all people in the city took Xi Jinping Thought on Socialism with Chinese Characteristics for a New Era as the guideline, attentively prepared for the opening of the Party's 20th national congress, studied, publicized and implemented the guiding principles of the 20th CPC National Congress. We fully implemented the important instructions and requirements of Xi Jinping, general secretary of the CPC Central Committee, on the work of Shandong and Qingdao. We applied the new development philosophy in full, in the right way and in all fields of endeavor, actively serving and integrating into the new development paradigm. Great efforts have been made to effectively coordinate COVID-19 pandemic prevention and control measures along with economic and social development. The overall economy reported continuing development despite the pressure, showing a good momentum of continuous recovery and quality improvement and solid strides were taken on a new journey to build a modern socialist international metropolis in the new era.

I. General Survey

The comprehensive economic strength of the city has continued to increase. According to preliminary estimation, the gross domestic product (GDP)[2] in 2022 was 1492.075 billion yuan, up by 3.9 percent over the previous year based on comparable prices. Of this total, the value added of the primary industry was 47.805 billion yuan, up by 2.2 percent over the previous year, that of the secondary industry was 519.734 billion yuan, up by 2.8 percent from 2021, and that of the tertiary industry was 924.536 billion yuan, up by 4.5 percent year on year. The ratio of the three industries was 3.2:34.8:62.0.

The total population grew steadily. The number of permanent residents in Qingdao stood at 10.3421 million at the end of 2022, up by 0.83 percent over the same period last year. Of this total, the number of permanent urban residents was 7.9965 million, accounting for 77.32 percent of the total population in the city, 0.15 percentage points higher over the end of the previous year.

The overall employment situation remained stable. Among the 365,000 new jobs created in urban areas, 63,000 unemployed people found new jobs, and 38,000 people with difficulty finding jobs became employed.

The consumer prices went up moderately. The annual consumer price index (CPI) was 102.0. In terms of categories, the price index of food, tobacco and alcohol was 103.0, that of clothing was 100.8, that of housing was 100.8, that of daily necessities and services was 101.4, that of transportation and communication was 105.8, that of education, culture and entertainment was 100.3, that of health care was 100.7, and that of other goods and services was 101.5 respectively.

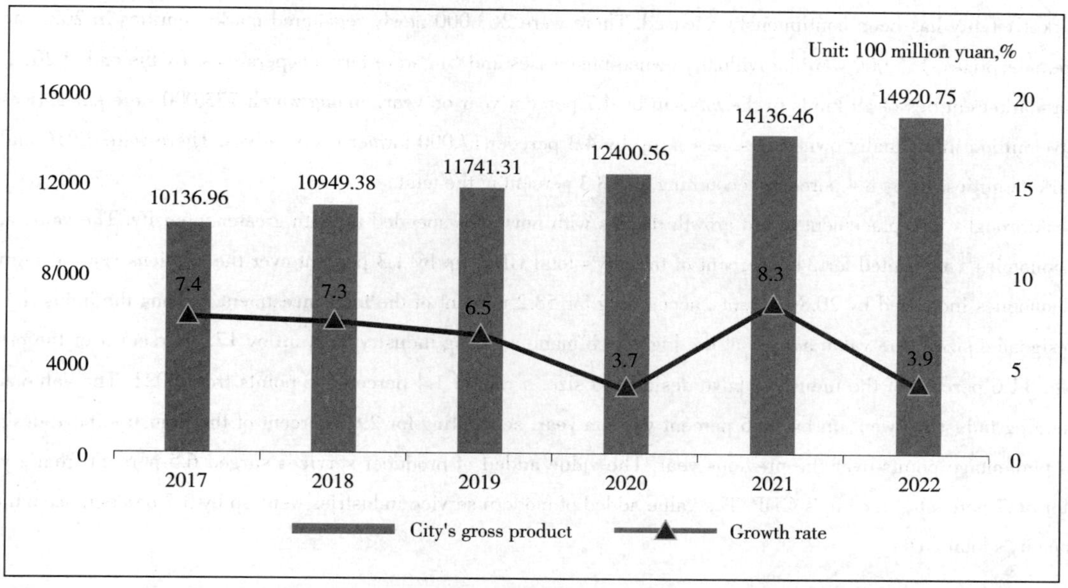

Figure 1: GDP and Growth rate from 2017 to 2022

Table 1: Consumer Price Indices of the City in 2022

Indicators	The whole year（the same period last year=100）
General Consumer Price Indices	102.0
Non–Food Price Indices	101.8
Service Price Indices	100.8
Consumer Goods Price Indices	102.9
1. Food, Tobacco and Liquor	103.0
Food	103.4
#Grain	106.2
Vegetables	105.5
Pork	91.7
Egg	105.7
2. Clothing	100.8
3. Residence	100.8
4. Supplies and Services	101.4
5. Transportation and Communication	105.8
6. Education, Culture and Recreation	100.3
7. Medical Care	100.7
8. Other supplies and services	101.5

The market vitality has been continuously released. There were 263,000 newly registered market entities in 2022, among which 107,000 were enterprises, 155,000 were individually owned businesses and 612 were farm cooperatives. By the end of 2022, there were 2.051 million market entities of all kinds in the city, up by 4.7 percent year on year, among which 773,000 were enterprises, up by 5.6 percent; 1.261 million individually owned businesses, up by 4.3 percent;17,000 farmer cooperatives. There were 2.016 million private economic market entities, up by 8.4 percent, accounting for 98.3 percent of the total.

The breakthroughs in replacement of old growth drivers with new ones speeded up with greater intensity. The value added of the Four–new Economies[3] accounted for 34.2 percent of the city's total GDP, up by 1.3 percent over the previous year. The investment in Four–new Economies increased by 20.8 percent , accounting for 58.2 percent of the total investment. Among the industrial enterprises above the designated size[4], the value added of the high–tech manufacturing industry went up by 17.3 percent over the previous year, accounting for 11.6 percent of the industry above designated size, a rise of 1.4 percentage points from 2021. The value added of the strategic emerging industries went up by 10.6 percent year on year, accounting for 29.5 percent of the industry above designated size, a rise of 5.0 percentage points over the previous year. The value added of producer services surged 6.5 percent from a year earlier, accounting for 36.7 percent of the city's GDP. The value added of modern service industries went up by 3.7 percent, accounting for 28.8 percent of the city's total GDP.

Ⅱ . Agriculture

Steady progress was made in agriculture production. The annual total output value of agriculture, forestry, animal husbandry and fishery was 92.56 billion yuan, an increase of 3.0 percent over the previous year. Among the total, the agricultural output value was 44.31 billion yuan, an increase of 3.2 percent; the forestry output value was 420 million yuan, an increase of 8.6 percent; the animal husbandry output value was 17.69 billion yuan, a decrease of 0.6 percent; the fishery output value was 23.4 billion yuan, an increase of 4.2 percent. The output value of agriculture, forestry, animal husbandry and fishery and auxiliary activities was 6.74 billion yuan, up by 9.1 percent. The value added of agriculture, forestry, animal husbandry and fishery was 51.264 billion yuan, up by 2.6 percent over the previous year.

The crop Agriculture developed steadily. The total grain acreage was 482,000 hectares, vegetable acreage 108,000 hectares and peanut acreage 69,000 hectares. The total grain output reached 3.113 million tons, down by 0.5 percent year on year. The output of vegetables and edible fungi was 6.599 million tons, down by 0.3 percent; peanut output was 312,000 tons, down by 8.2 percent from last year; the output of fruits (including melons) was 1.219 million tons, increasing by 1.8 percent year on year.

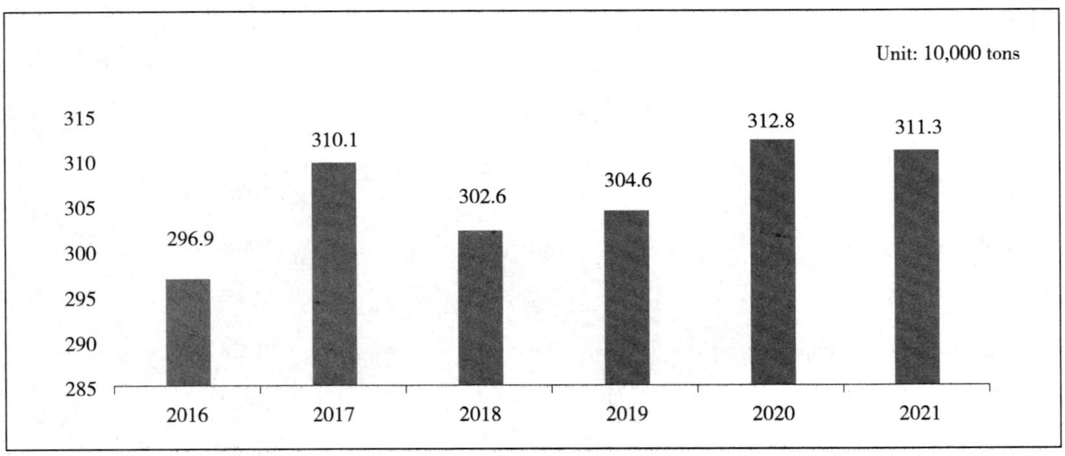

Figure 2 : 2017–2022 Grain Production

Table 2: Output and Growth Rate of Main Planting Products in 2022

Indicators	Yield (10000 tons)	Growth (%)
Grain	311.3	-0.5
Summer grain	141.5	-1.0
Autumn grain	169.8	-0.03
Oilseed	31.2	-8.2
Vegetable and edible fungi	659.9	-0.3
Fruit	121.9	1.8
Garden fruit	83.1	3.2

The forestry, animal husbandry and fishery industries maintained steady growth in the period. Afforested areas on barren hills were 6,70 hectares. The annual output of meat was 520,000 tons, eggs 269,000 tons, and milk 296,000 tons. The annual output of aquatic products (excluding deep-sea fishing) was 993,000 tons, falling 1.9 percent over the previous year. The area of marine and freshwater aquaculture was 37,800 hectares, increasing by 1.6 percent year on year.

Development of modern agriculture was accelerated. At the end of 2022, there were 11 modern agricultural industrial parks at or above the municipal level, 43 strong industrial towns, 202 green horticultural standard parks and 185 livestock and poultry standardization demonstration farms. The number of agricultural products with National geographical indications reached 54. The total power of Agriculture machinery was 7.60 million kW with an increase of 29, 000 over the previous year. The comprehensive mechanization rate for growing crops has reached 91.02 percent.

Ⅲ. Industry and Construction

Industrial production grew steadily. In 2022, the total value added of the industrial sector was 396.645 billion yuan, up by 2.7 percent over the previous year. The value added of industrial enterprises above the designated size increased by 3.8 percent. Of the industrial enterprises above the designated size, in terms of different sectors, mining grew by 3.2 percent, manufacturing by 3.8 percent and electricity, heat, gas and water production and supply by 1.2 percent. In terms of industrial sectors, the value added of 22 of the 35 major industrial industries increased compared with the previous year, with a growth rate of 62.9 percent. Among them, key industries such as electrical machinery and equipment manufacturing, chemical raw materials and chemical products manufacturing, general equipment manufacturing, computer communication and other electronic equipment manufacturing and special equipment manufacturing increased by 8.0 percent, 24.7 percent, 6.1 percent, 18.9 percent and 13.6 percent respectively. New products grew rapidly, and the output of ultra-clear glass for solar industry, lithium-ion batteries, and polysilicon increased by 4.9 times, 65.6 percent and 30.6 percent respectively. The annual sales rate of industrial enterprises above designated size was 97.2 percent.

Profits in some industries grew steadily. The revenue of industrial enterprises above designated size increased by 2.1 percent over the previous year, and the total profit decreased by 10.5 percent. The profits of the equipment manufacturing industry above designated size was 30.44 billion yuan, an increase of 1.7 percent over the previous year, accounting for 59.3 percent of the total, an increase of 6.4 percentage points over the previous year. The profits of the consumer goods manufacturing industry was 10.41 billion yuan, an increase of 6.9 percent over the previous year, of which the profits of the agricultural and sideline food processing industry, the alcoholic beverage and refined tea manufacturing industry, and the pharmaceutical manufacturing industry increased by 55.3 percent, 20.4 percent and 11.1 percent respectively.

Table 3 : Output and Growth Rate of Main Products of Industries Above Designated Size in 2022

Description	Unit	Output	Growth（%）
Color TV sets	10000 sets	2545.6	28.1
Of which: Smart TV	10000 sets	2390.6	27.1
Household refrigerators	10000 sets	832.1	-7.1
Household washing machine	10000 sets	776.1	6.2
Room air conditioners	10000 sets	1208.2	5.0
Lithium-ion batteries	piece (unit)	52053076	65.6
Beer	10000 KL	203.0	2.0
Rubber tire casing	10000 tires	4637.6	-8.0
Plate glass	10000 wt. cases	853.0	-14.5
Ultra-clear glass	sq. m	676773.1	490.7
Polysilicon	kg	52811.9	30.6
Crude steel	10000 tons	435.0	33.9
Motor train units	set	464	-7.8
Urban rail vehicle	set	964	-39.3
Metal shipping containers	10000 cu.m	1522.6	-33.7

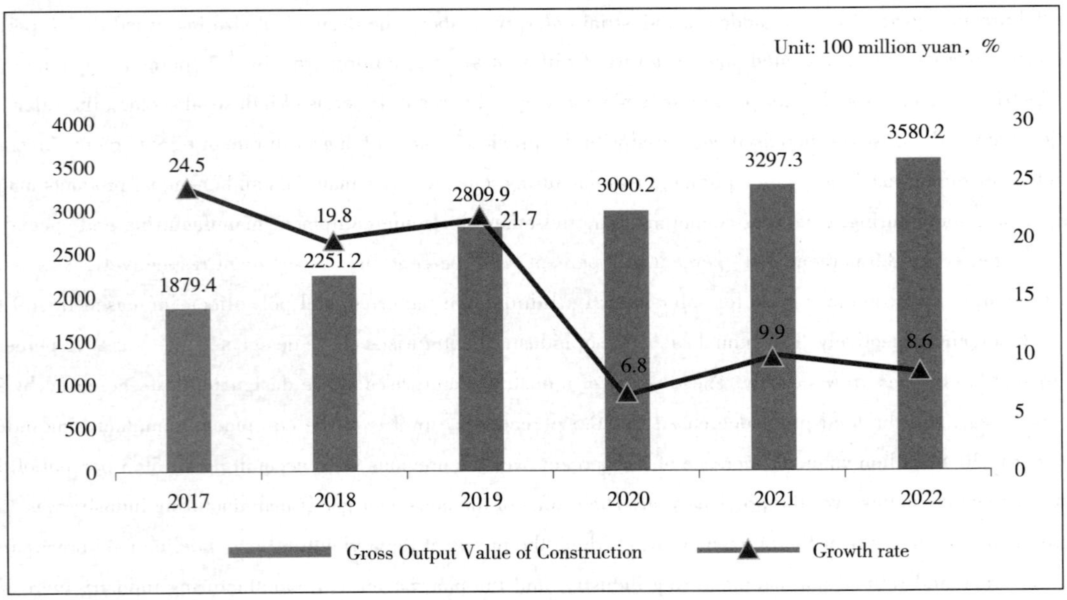

Figure 3 : 2017-2022 Total Output Value and Growth Rate of Construction Industry

The construction industry maintained steady development. The annual value added of the construction industry was 125.056 billion yuan, an increase of 3.0 percent over the previous year. There were 961 general contracting and professional contracting construction enterprises in the city with qualification levels, and the total output value of the construction industry was 358.02 billion yuan, an increase of 8.6 percent over the previous year; the contract value was 860.6 billion yuan, an increase of 16.2 percent.

Ⅳ. Service Sector

The service industry sector provided strong support. The annual value added of the service industry was 924.536 billion yuan, an increase of 4.5 percent over the previous year, accounting for 62.0 percent of the city's GDP and contributing 73.8 percent to the economic growth, of which the value added of the wholesale and retail industry increased by 4.0 percent, that of the transportation, warehousing and postal industry increased by 9.8 percent, that of the accommodation and catering industry increased by 1.5 percent, that of the financial industry increased by 6.9 percent, that of the information transmission, software and information technology service industry increased by 12.1 percent, and that of the leasing and business service industry increased by 1.4 percent. The revenue of service industry above designated size[5] was 388.44 billion yuan, an increase of 6.6 percent over the previous year. The new drivers of the service industry were active, and the revenue of Internet and related services, software and information technology services, research and experimental development increased by 42.2 percent, 17.8 percent and 54.0 percent respectively.

Table 4：Transportation volume and growth rate completed by major transportation modes in 2022

Indicators	Units	Volume	Growth(%)
Passenger Volume	10000 persons	2991	–41.9
Railways	10000 persons	1210	–36.7
Highways	10000 persons	1694	–45.6
Waterways	10000 persons	86	–27.7
Freight volume	10000 tons	39711	–0.6
Railways	10000 tons	8622	1.5
Highways	10000 tons	26696	–6.0
Waterways	10000 tons	4393	43.2

Transportation ran under pressure. An annual total of 400 million tons of freight was transported by railways, highways, and waterways with an decrease of 0.6 percent from last year. Passenger trips totaled 29.91 million, falling 41.9 percent from 2021. The annual port throughput 2022 reached 660 million tons, up by 4.3 percent year on year. Foreign trade throughput was 470 million tons, increasing by 3.2 percent. The container throughput was 25.67 million TEUs, an increase of 8.3 percent. By the end of 2022, there were 220 domestic routes, 22 international routes, 2 routes to Hong Kong, Macao, and Taiwan. The annual air passenger throughput 2022 was 9.72 million, falling by 39.4 percent over the previous year. The air cargo throughput 2022 was 220,000 tons, down by 7.4 percent year on year. By the end of 2022, the number of motor vehicles in the city was 3.55 million, an increase of 5.4 percent over the previous year, including 3.08 million private cars, up by 5.3 percent.

The post and telecommunications industries continued to improve. The total amount of post and telecommunications business completed in 2022 was 24.55 billion yuan, an increase of 19.7 percent over the previous year. Among them, the total amount of postal business was 9.21 billion yuan, an increase of 4.6 percent; that of telecommunications business was 15.34 billion yuan, an increase of 31.1 percent. The express business volume was 810 million pieces, an increase of 4.8 percent. There were 4.99 million fixed broadband Internet users, an increase of 0.1 percent. There were 13.453 million mobile phone users in the city, an increase of 3.9 percent. The national-level Internet backbone direct connection point was completed; 10,204 new 5G base stations were built, and a total of 30,154 5G base stations were built and opened.

The recovery of the tourism market has slowed down. A total of 65.813 million visits were paid for the whole year, with an decrease of 19.7 percent over the previous year, generating revenue of 100.64 billion yuan, falling 28.7 percent year on year. By the end of 2022, there were 101 A-level scenic spot, including one 5A-level scenic spot, twenty-five 4A-level scenic spots, and sixty-two 3A-level scenic spots. There were 81 star-rated hotels, including 11 five-star hotels, 21 four-star hotels and 46 three-star hotels. There were 630 travel agencies, including 56 ones operating outbound tourism business.

V . Fixed-asset Investment

Investment maintained steady growth. The annual investment in fixed assets[6] increased by 4.5 percent over the previous year, of which the investment in the primary industry increased by 1.0 percent, that in the secondary industry increased by 15.6 percent, and that in the tertiary industry increased by 0.8 percent.

The investment structure was continuously optimized. The annual manufacturing investment grew by 13.2 percent over the previous year, of which the high-tech manufacturing investment increased by 75.0 percent. The investment in strategic emerging industries increased by 18.3 percent, accounting for 38.5 percent of fixed asset investment. The investment in infrastructure and in social and people's livelihood increased by 23.2 percent and 17.1 percent, respectively, an increase of 27.0 and 30.1 percentage points over the previous year.

The real estate market was running low. The development investment in real estate was 178.91 billion yuan, down by 9.7 percent over the previous year, of which residential investment was 131.62 billion yuan, a decrease of 11.1 percent. The sales area of commercial housing was 15.637 million square meters, a decrease of 4.9 percent over the previous year, of which the sales area of residential buildings was 12.641 million square meters, down by 11.0 percent.

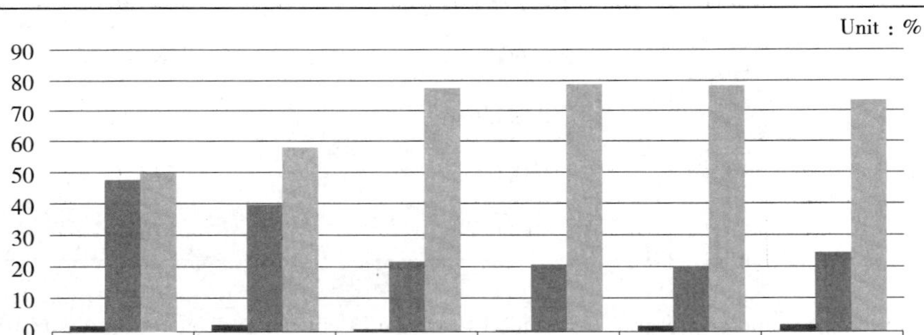

	2017	2018	2019	2020	2021	2022
Primary Industry	1.7	0.9	0.6	1.3	1.5	1.5
Secondary Industry	39.9	21.5	20.9	20.6	24.9	27.4
Tertiary Industry	58.4	77.6	78.5	78.1	73.6	71.1

Primary Industry　Secondary Industry　Tertiary Industry

Figure 4 : The Proportion of Investment in Three Industries in Fixed Asset Investment in 2022

Table 5 : The City's Real Estate Development Investment, Commercial Housing Sales Area and Growth Rate in 2022

Indicators	Real Estate Development Investment (100 million yuan)	Growth (%)	Commercial Housing Sales Area (10000 sq.m)	Increase (%)
Total	1789.1	-9.7	1563.7	-4.9
Residential	1316.2	-11.1	1264.1	-11.0
Office Building	95.7	-22.6	143.4	90.0
Commercial Premises	114.1	-0.6	110.3	80.7
Others	263.1	0.3	45.9	-48.0

The supply of affordable housing has effectively increased. Throughout 2022, 1,005 sets of public rental housing were started to be constructed, and 45,800 sets (rooms) of government-subsidized rental housing were raised for construction. By the end of 2022, there were a total of 14,800 households enjoying rental subsidies in the city, and 113.9042 million yuan of rental subsidies were issued throughout 2022.

Ⅵ. Consumer market

The recovery of the consumer market has slowed down. The total retail sales of consumer goods[7] for the whole year was 589.18 billion yuan, a decrease of 1.4 percent over the previous year. Among them, retail sales of goods were 528.61 billion yuan, down by 1.1 percent; catering revenue was 60.57 billion yuan, down by 3.5 percent. According to the statistics of the place of operation, the retail sales of social consumer goods in urban areas were 486.22 billion yuan, a decrease of 1.4 percent; the retail sales of social consumer goods in rural areas were 102.96 billion yuan, a decrease of 1.2 percent. The retail sales of enterprises above designated size reached 204.40 billion yuan, with an increase of 2.1 percent.

The trend of consumption upgrading was obvious. Among the annual retail sales of units above designated size, the retail sales of gold and silver jewelry, cosmetics and wearable smart devices increased by 23.3 percent, 18.7 percent and 480.8 percent respectively over the previous year. The demand for green upgrades continued to be released, and the retail sales of new energy vehicles, household

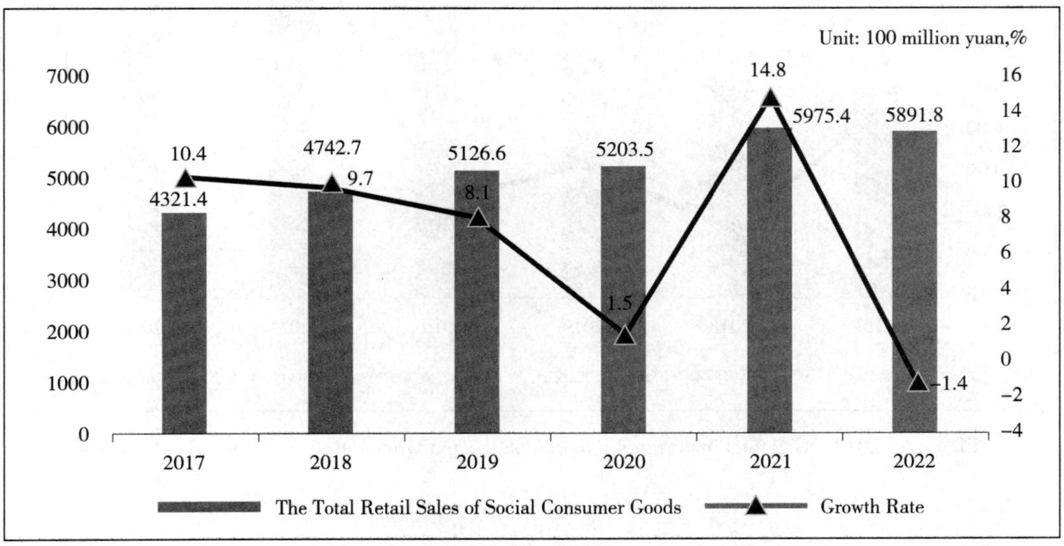

Figure 5 : 2017-2022 Total Retail Sales of Consumer Goods and Growth Rate

appliances with energy efficiency grades 1 and 2, and audio–visual equipment increased by 123.6 percent and 10.3 percent respectively.

Ⅶ. Foreign Economy

Foreign trade expanded steadily. The total value of import and export of goods for 2022 was 911.72 billion yuan, up by 7.4 percent over that of the previous year. Of this total, the value of goods exported was 536.11 billion yuan, up by 9.0 percent; the value of goods imported was 375.61 billion yuan, an increase of 5.1 percent. In terms of the nature of enterprises, the import and export of private enterprises was 636.61 billion yuan, up by 11.6 percent, accounting for 69.8 percent of the city's total value of import and export; the import and export of foreign–invested enterprises was 155.9 billion yuan, a decrease of 10.1 percent; the import and export of state–owned enterprises was 118.96 billion yuan, an increase of 14.5 percent. In terms of export structure, the export of mechanical and electrical products was 243.46 billion yuan, an increase of 3.6 percent, accounting for 45.4 percent of the city's total exports, of which auto parts, automobiles, and ships increased by 16.6 percent, 102.8 percent and 83.9 percent respectively. In terms of the trade market, imports and exports to the top three ASEAN, the United States, and the European Union were 174.33 billion yuan, 101.08 billion yuan, and 94.47 billion yuan respectively, with growth rates of 28.8 percent, 1.3 percent, and –4.5 percent; The imports and exports between China and countries along the Belt and Road was 319.44 billion yuan, an increase of 21.0 percent; the import and export between China and other RCEP member countries was 355.75 billion yuan, up by 11.4 percent; the import and export between China and other SCO member countries was 60.01 billion yuan, an increase of 20.1 percent.

The total value of foreign trade import and export of Qingdao port in the whole year was 1844.67 billion yuan, an increase of 21.7 percent over the previous year. Among them, the export value was 1,058.72 billion yuan, an increase of 23.9 percent; the import value was 785.95 billion yuan, an increase of 18.8 percent.

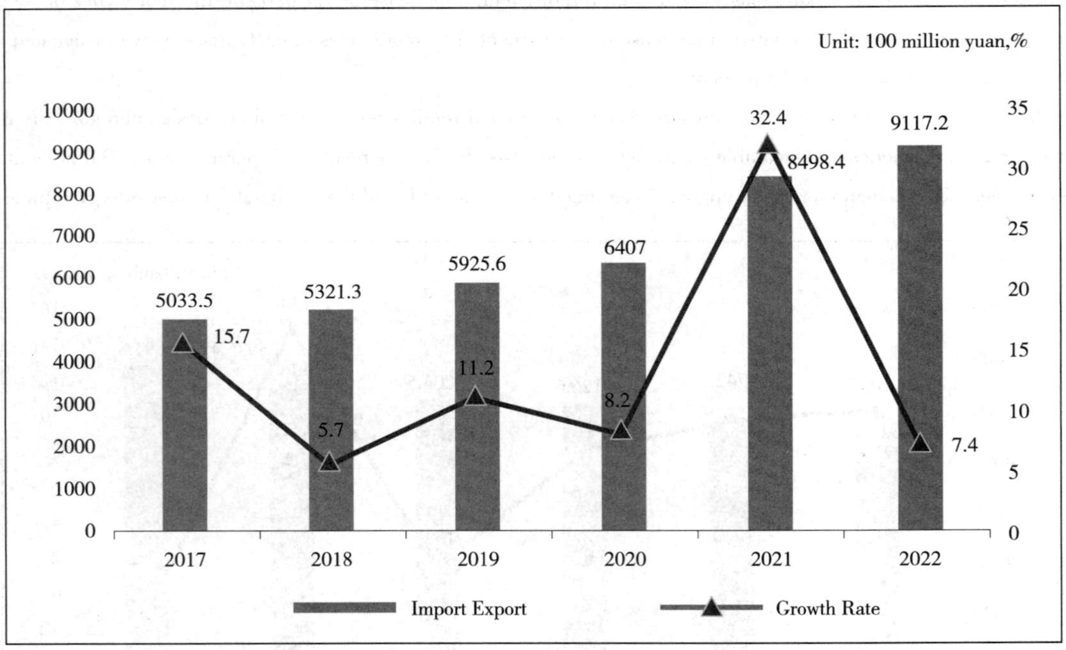

Figure 6 : 2017–2022 total import and Export Volume and Growth Rate of Foreign Trade Goods

Table 6 : Imports and Exports of Major Commodities in 2022

Indicators	Import & Export		Export		Import	
	Amount (100 million yuan)	Growth (%)	Amount (100 million yuan)	Growth (%)	Amount (100 million yuan)	Growth (%)
Textile and Apparel	639.5	7.9	620.3	8.6	19.1	-12.3
Agricultural products	1199.2	13.5	432.7	16.7	766.5	11.8
Electronics	2992.1	1.1	2434.6	3.6	557.5	-9.5
High-tech products	697.8	-7.6	340.5	-13.1	357.2	-1.7

Table 7 : Import and Export Volume and Growth Rate of Goods to Major Countries and Regions in 2022

Country and Region	Export Amount (100 million USD)	Growth (%)	Import Amount (100 million USD)	Growth (%)
Asia	2524.4	9.3	1899.9	11.7
Hong Kong, China	127.5	-45.0	3.6	-1.3
Taiwan, China	45.8	-2.7	153.2	21.3
Japan	501.8	9.3	142.6	-8.3
Korea	466.1	7.3	289.1	0.4
ASEAN	840.9	33.2	902.4	24.9
South Asia	197.2	-5.2	43.1	-36.7
Middle East	305.3	20.0	333.3	13.8
Africa	278.4	17.8	257.4	36.1
South Africa	44.9	5.3	26.5	17.1
Europe	1069.4	6.8	518.4	9.8
EU	704.1	3.0	240.5	-21.1
Britain	120.8	-10.0	39.9	61.5
Russia	175.8	21.4	180.9	104.9
South America	183.9	14.1	504.7	-6.5
Brazil	66.2	16.3	366.5	-12.4
North America	932.7	6.5	295.6	10.9
USA	758.7	-2.1	252.1	13.0
Canada	174.0	72.3	39.0	-4.1
Oceania	154.7	11.2	268.5	-29.3
Australia	128.6	19.4	222.1	-32.9

Note : This table is not full caliber.

The use of foreign capital maintained stability and promoted excellence. The year of 2022 witnessed the establishment of 693 new foreign–invested enterprises, a decrease of 23.7 percent over the previous year; the contracted foreign capital was 27.71 billion US dollars, an increase of 29.3 percent. The city's actual use of foreign capital was 5.51 billion US dollars, a decrease of 10.6 percent over the previous year. Of the total, the actual use of foreign capital in the manufacturing industry was 850 million US dollars, an increase of 12.6 percent; the actual use of foreign capital in the modern service industry was 2.47 billion US dollars, accounting for 56 percent of the total.

Steady progress was made in international cooperation. The city's overseas engineering business newly contracted 39 projects, and the newly signed contract value was 2.18 billion US dollars, a decrease of 30.1 percent over the previous year; the completed turnover was 2.93 billion US dollars, a decrease of 2.7 percent. The number of labor forces sent abroad through overseas labor contracts was 10,688.

The Belt and Road enjoyed integrated development. Throughout 2022, the city's enterprises invested 24 projects in countries and regions along the Belt and Road. The Chinese agreed investment amounted to 760 million US dollars, a decrease of 37.7 percent from the previous year; the actual Chinese investment amounted to 390 million US dollars, an increase of 17.4 percent.

Ⅷ. Finance

Financial revenue and expenditure were solid and stable. The fiscal revenue rose 5.5 percent to hit 127.32 billion yuan in 2022 after deducting the credit refund factors, of which the tax revenue was 88.12 billion yuan, an increase of 3.5 percent after deducting the credit refund factors, accounting for 73.7 percent of the general public budget revenue. The annual general public budget expenditure was 169.62 billion yuan, a decrease of 0.6 percent over the previous year. Among them, the education expenditure was 33.21 billion yuan, an increase of 7.5 percent; the social security and employment expenditure was 25.25 billion yuan, an increase of 3.9 percent; the health care expenditure was 14.23 billion yuan, an increase of 14.5 percent. The annual tax revenue of the tax system (including customs collection) was 298.37 billion yuan, an increase of 9.6 percent over the previous year after deducting the credit refund factor, of which domestic tax revenue was 212.63 billion yuan, an increase of 2.2 percent.

The financial market developed healthily. The city's balance of deposits and loans exceeded 5 trillion yuan. At the end of 2022, the balance of domestic and foreign currency deposits in financial institutions was 2,499.27 billion yuan, up by 11.7 percent over the previous year, and an increase of 261.79 billion yuan from the beginning of 2022; the balance of domestic and foreign currency loans was 2,678.25 billion yuan, up by 11.2 percent, an increase of 269.35 billion yuan from the beginning of 2022. The insurance industry achieved a cumulative premium income of 50.3 billion yuan for the whole year, an increase of 8.9 percent over the previous year. Among them, the premium income of personal insurance companies was 33.3 billion yuan, an increase of 9.1 percent; the premium income of property insurance companies was 17 billion yuan, an increase of 8.5 percent. The annual securities transaction volume of securities branches was 7,575.05 billion yuan, an increase of 6.8 percent over the previous year; the securities transaction volume of legal person institutions was 7,533.76 billion yuan, an increase of 14.2 percent. The year 2022 saw 7 domestic listed companies newly added, bringing the number of domestic listed companies to 65. There were 400 private equity fund managers registered with the Asset Management Association of China, and the fund management scale were 179.56 billion yuan, an increase of 9.5 percent from a year earlier.

Ⅸ. People's Livelihood and Social Security

The quality of people's livelihood continued to improve. The annual per capita disposable income of the city's residents was 53,735 yuan, an increase of 4.9 percent over the previous year. In terms of permanent residence, the per capita disposable income of urban residents was 62,584 yuan, up by 3.9 percent; the per capita disposable income of rural residents was 27,701 yuan, an increase of 6.0 percent. The per capita consumption expenditure of the city's residents was 32,497 yuan, a decrease of 1.2 percent over the previous year, and the Engel's coefficient was 28.1 percent. In terms of permanent residence, the per capita consumption expenditure of urban residents was 37,592 yuan, a decrease of 2.5 percent; the per capita consumption expenditure of rural residents was 17,508 yuan, up by 2.9 percent. According to the sample survey, at the end of 2022, the per capita existing housing construction area of urban residents was 34.0 square meters, and that ofrural residents was 38.7 square meters.

The overall quality of the city has been comprehensively improved. The construction of all 7 lines planned for the third phase of the metro has started, and metroline No.4 has been put into operation, with a total operating mileage of 315 kilometers. The renovation of 29 urban villages and 318 old communities was successfully implementedand completed. 207 kilometers of overhead lines were transferred into the ground. 42 unconnected roads were opened, 22,000 new public parking spaces were added, and 16

Table 8 : The Composition of Per Capita Disposable Income of Urban and Rural Residents in 2022

Description of indicators	Residents		Urban Residents		Rural Residents	
	Absolute Value (yuan)	Growth (%)	Absolute Value (yuan)	Growth (%)	Absolute Value (yuan)	Growth (%)
Disposable income	53735	4.9	62584	3.9	27701	6.0
Salary income	31911	4.7	37635	3.9	15074	3.7
Operating net income	10081	3.9	9793	4.0	10931	4.2
Property net income	4450	3.0	5805	1.7	463	1.1
Transfer net income	7292	8.6	9352	5.1	1233	93.9

Table 9 : Per Capita Consumption Expenditure of Urban and Rural Residents in 2022

Description of indicators	Residents		Urban Residents		Rural Residents	
	Absolute Value (yuan)	Growth (%)	Absolute Value (yuan)	Growth (%)	Absolute Value (yuan)	Growth (%)
Expenditures	32497	−1.2	37592	−2.5	17508	2.9
Food, Tobacco and Liquor	9140	−0.7	10512	−2.0	5103	2.8
Clothing	2775	−6.7	3290	−8.5	1258	1.7
Residence	7515	−2.5	8812	−3.7	3700	0.4
Supplies and Services	2042	−6.8	2336	−9.1	1178	3.5
Transportation and Communication	4932	1.2	5568	0.2	3059	2.9
Education, Culture and Recreation	3480	3.5	4051	2.0	1801	8.0
Medical Care	1883	5.3	2175	4.6	1025	4.6
Other supplies and services	730	−6.0	847	−8.0	386	2.3

Table10 : Ownership of Main Durable Consumer Goods Per 100 Households in 2022

Description of indicators	Unit	Quantity		
		Residents	Urban Residents	Rural Residents
Household automobiles	set	68	72	59
Motorcycles	set	17	9	41
Refrigerators	set	111	112	109
Washing machines	set	106	109	99
Water heaters	set	100	101	98
Air-conditioners	set	126	134	104
Color TV	set	103	103	105
Computers	set	64	71	45
Mobile telephones	set	239	237	245

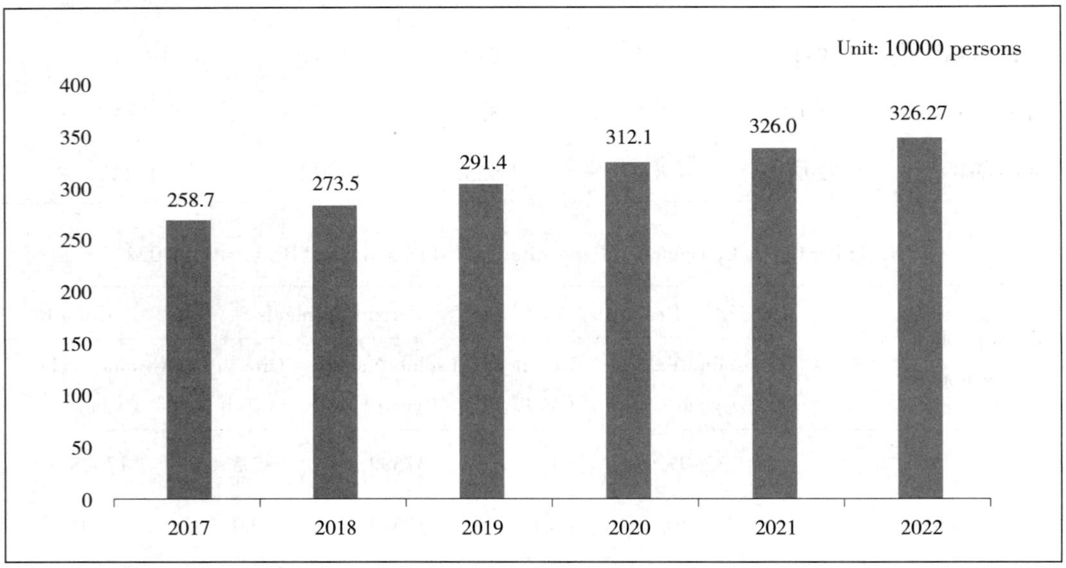

Figure 7 : 2017–2022 Urban Employee Basic Pension Insurance Participation and Payment

parking lots located in the old city were completed and put into use.Basically,the renovation of 60 mountain parks was completed, and 100 kilometers of urban greenways were built. At the end of 2022, the city's built-up area was 761.5 square kilometers. The green coverage rate of the built-up area was 45.2 percent, and the per capita park green area was 17.4 square meters.

Social security has been improved day by day. By the end of 2022, a total of 3.3627 million people participated in basic endowment insurance program for urban workers; 4.2922 million people participated in the program for workers; a total of 2.8142 million people participated in unemployment insurance program; a total of 3.2991 million people participated in work-related injury insurance; a total of 3.2299 million people participated in maternity insurance programs.The number of residents participating in pension insurance and medical insurance reached 2.75 million and 4.8492 million respectively. By the end of

2022, there were 77,000 urban and rural residents living with minimum subsistence allowances in the city, and 760 million yuan was granted as the minimum subsistence allowance fund expenditure to urban and rural residents; there were 13,000 urban and rural extremely poor people to be supported, and the expenditure of assistance and support funds for these people were 290 million yuan.1.05 billion yuan in relief funds was issued to 90,000 needy people, and 5.39 billion yuan was reimbursed in medical expenses for 79,000 seriously ill people. There were 53,000 beds for elderly care in the city, including 2,000 new beds in 2022.

X . Science and Technology and Education

The construction of science and technology innovation platforms was accelerated. Laoshan Laboratory was put into operation. The National Virtual Reality Innovation Center (Qingdao) was approved to be established. Five laboratories were approved in the first batch of national key laboratory reorganization, and the number of key laboratories above the provincial level reached 66, including 11 at the national level. 6 new technological innovation centers above the provincial level were established, bringing the total to 30. There were 23 national demonstration enterprises in IPRs and 196 national enterprises with advantages in IPRs. The total number of high-tech enterprises was 6,680, an increase of 1,126 over the previous year. The number of national science and technology-based SMEs included in the database was 7,050. A total of 54 national enterprises entitled "little giant" using special and sophisticated technologies to produce novel and unique products have been newly cultivated, and the total number has reached 151. 257,000 talents were newly introduced and gathered, and the total number of talents exceeded 2.65 million.

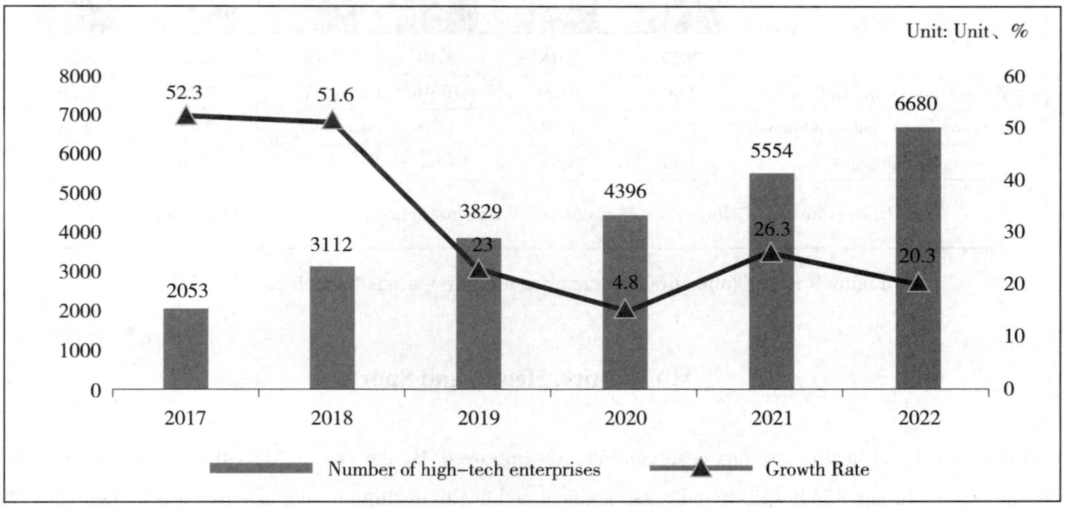

Figure 8 : Number and Growth rate of high-tech enterprises from 2017-2022

The strength of science and technology continued to increase. Preliminary statistics show that 405 scientific and technological achievements have been registered and there were 75 provincial scientific and technological awards, including 13 natural science awards, 9 technological invention awards, 51 scientific and technological progress awards, 1 highest award, and 1 youth award. The transaction volume of technical contracts was 39.5 billion yuan, up by 23.0 percent over the previous year. The turnover of sea-related technology contracts was 4.08 billion yuan, an increase of 28.2 percent. There were 14,523 new effective invention patents, an increase of 42.2 percent over the previous year. The number of valid invention patents per 10,000 people was 58.99, an increase of 12.17 over the previous year and there were 2351 PCT international patent applications.

Education has developed in an all-round way. Throughout in 2022, 112 primary, secondary schools and kindergartens were built, renovated or expanded; and 80,700 new public places were added; 62 kindergartens in rural areas were renovated and upgraded. By the end of 2022, there were 29 colleges and universities (including private colleges) in the city, including 26 regular colleges and universities.In 2022, graduate institutes enrolled 67,300 students with 22,000 new students and 14,600 million graduates. Total enrollment in undergraduate programs in regular higher education institutes was 405,000 with 124,900 new students and 109,600 graduates. The enrollment in secondary vocational education was 92,400, including 27,00 new entrants, and 29,700 graduates. Regular senior secondary schools had 157,600 enrolled students, including 57,900 new entrants, and 44,400 graduates. Students enrolled in junior secondary schools totaled 292,500, including 93,700 new entrants, and 95,000 graduates. The city had a primary education enrollment of 664,500 students, including 125,400 new entrants, and 93,200 graduates. There were 2,500 students enrolled in special education schools, with 300 new entrants and 300 graduates. Kindergartens accommodated 352,400 children.

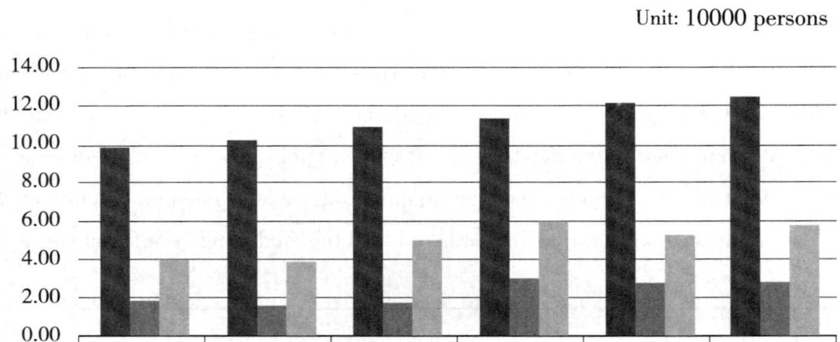

	2017	2018	2019	2020	2021	2022
Universities and Colleges	9.90	10.24	10.91	11.37	12.06	12.49
Secondary Vocational Schools	1.80	1.59	1.70	2.97	2.72	2.78
Normal High School	3.96	3.83	4.94	6.03	5.28	5.79

Universities and Colleges　Secondary Vocational Schools　Normal High School

Figure 9 : The Number of Students Enrolled by Various Schools in 2017–2022

XI . Culture, Health and Sports

The level of medical and health care has been continuously improved. By the end of 2022, there were 8,780 medical and health institutions in the city, including 353 hospitals and 8,290 medical and health institutions at grass–root level. There were 99,000 medical technical personnel, including 41,200 licensed doctors and licensed assistant doctors and 44,400 registered nurses. The city possessed 69,600 beds, of which hospitals possessed 58,500 and health centers had 6,900.

Cultural supply was more abundant. The National Museum of Marine Archeology officially signed a contract with Qingdao. 100 new national reading facilities for all were built throughout 2022. By the end of 2022, the city has had 102 theaters, 148 cultural centers (stations), 121 museums, 11 public libraries, 9 state–owned art troupes, 6 radio stations with 11 programs, and 6 TV stations with 17 programs. There were 12 archives in the city.

Remarkable achievements in sports have been achieved. Throughout 2022, 58 sports and fitness venues such as sports parks and cage multi–functional sports fields were newly built, and 411 fitness paths were updated or newly built. Athletes from our city won the first medal in the history of Shandong Winter Olympics in the 24th Winter Olympics; they won 277 gold medals in the 25th Provincial Games, ranking first in the gold medal list. At the end of 2022, there was one key sports school with 1,150 students in the city; 10 amateur sports schools with 2,059 students.

Ⅻ. Energy, Environment and Safety Production

Energy supply was greener. The annual energy production was 28.364 million tons of standard coal equivalent, a decrease of 1.7 percent over the previous year. The power generation was 19.63 billion kWh, an increase of 4.6 percent over the previous year. New energy power generation was 3.67 billion kWh, an increase of 10.1 percent, accounting for 18.7 percent of the city's total power generation, of which wind power generation increased by 3.8 percent, waste incineration power generation increased by 6.3 percent, and solar power generation increased by 315.8 percent.

Energy consumption remained flat. The electricity consumption of the whole society was 57.65 billion kWh, an increase of 4.3 percent over the previous year. Among them, the electricity consumption of industry was 30.21 billion kWh, an increase of 1.4 percent; the electricity consumption of the service industry was 14.88 billion kWh, an increase of 3.5 percent; the electricity consumption of urban and rural residents was 10.39 billion kWh, an increase of 13.9 percent. The city's industrial comprehensive energy consumption above designated size was 17.546 million tons of standard coal, an increase of 9.4 percent over the previous year, of which coal consumption increased by 2.7 percent, oil consumption increased by 1.0 percent, and natural gas consumption increased by 13.5 percent.

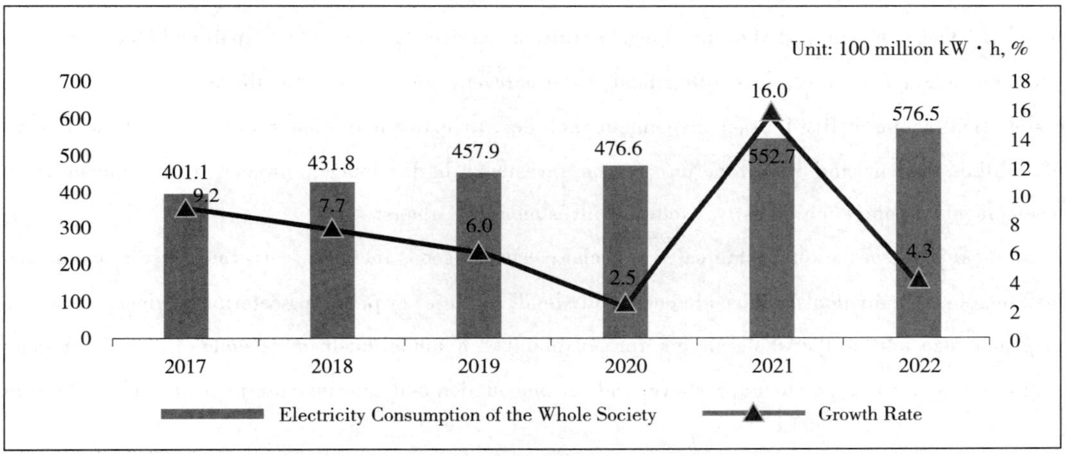

Figure 10 : The Electricity Consumption and Growth Rate of the Whole Society from 2017–2022

The quality of the ecological environment was further improved. The city's annual average temperature was 13.5℃ , and the average annual precipitation is 1079.6 mm. The number of days with good air quality in urban areas was 323, accounting for 88.5 percent of the whole year. The average value of environmental noise in the urban area was 54.8 decibels, and the average value of traffic arterial noise in the urban area was 69.5 decibels. The air quality has reached the national secondary standard for three consecutive years. The annual average values of main pollutants fine particulate matter (PM2.5) and inhalable particulate matter (PM10) were 26 and 49 micrograms per cubic meter, respectively, an improvement of 7.1 percent and 12.5 percent over the previous year. The water quality of the 20 national and provincial control surface water assessment sections all met the standard, and the proportion of coastal waters with good water quality reached 99 percent.

Workplace Safety continued to be stable. A total of 186 workplace accidents of various types occurred in the city, resulting in 98 deaths, a decrease of 13.5 percent and 24.0 percent respectively over the previous year. The death rate of workplace accidents with a GDP of 100 million yuan was 0.0066, and the death rate of workplace accidents for employees of 100,000 industrial, mining and commercial enterprises was 0.58.

Notes :

[1] All figures in this Communiqué are preliminary statistics. Due to the rounding–off reasons, the subentries may not add up to the aggregate totals.

[2] The city's GDP, the value added of the three and related industries are calculated at current prices whereas their growth rates are at comparable price.

[3] The "Four–new" Economies refer to production activities with economic characteristics of "new technology, new industry, new business format and new model",which is defined by the Shandong Provincial Statistics Bureau's Statistical Monitoring System of New Technology, New Industry, New Format and New Model on the basis of the Statistical Classification of New Industry, New Format and New Business model (2018) of the National Bureau of Statistics.

[4] Industrial enterprises above designated size are enterprises with annual business revenue of 20 million yuan and above.

[5] Service enterprises above the designated size refer to legal entities of transport, storage and post, information transmission, software and information technology services, water conservancy, environment and public facilities management, and health industry with annual business revenue of 20 million yuan and above; legal entities of real estate (excluding real estate development and operation), leasing and business services, scientific research and technology services and education with annual business revenue of 10 million yuan and above; and legal entities of services to households, repair and other services and culture, sports and entertainment, and social services with annual business revenue of 5 million and above.

[6] The statistical scope of fixed–asset investment includes: investment in construction projects with a planned total investment of 5 million yuan or more within the jurisdiction, investment in development projects of all impersonal entities in the real estate development and operation industry, excluding investment by farmers.

[7] The statistical scope of the total retail sales of social consumer goods includes: corporate enterprises, industrial activity entities and self–employed individuals engaged in commodity retail activities or providing catering services. Among them, entities above the designated size refer to the wholesale enterprises (units) with annual business revenue of 20 million yuan and above, retail enterprises (units) of 5 million yuan and above, and accommodation and catering enterprises (units) of 2 million yuan and above. unit).

Source: In this Communiqué, the fiscal data are from Qingdao Municipal Finance Bureau; the tax data are from the Qingdao Tax Service, State Taxation Bureau; the data of social security, employment and talents are from the Qingdao Municipal Human Resources and Social Security Bureau; the bank data are from the People´s Bank of China, Qingdao Central sub–branch; the data of securities insurance are from Qingdao Supervision Bureau of China Securities Regulatory Commission and Qingdao Supervision Bureau of China Banking and Insurance Regulatory Commission; the data of aquatic product are from Qingdao Municipal Ocean Development Bureau; forestry data are from Qingdao Municipal Gardening and Forestry Bureau; the data of agricultural machinery are from Qingdao Municipal Bureau of Agriculture and Rural Affairs; transportation data are from Qingdao Municipal Transportation Bureau; postal data are from Qingdao Municipal Postal Administration; the data of broadband, mobile phone and other are from Qingdao Municipal Communications Administration; the data of import and export , foreign investment, foreign contracted projects, and foreign labor service cooperation are from Qingdao Municipal Bureau of Commerce; tourism data are from Qingdao Municipal Culture and Tourism Bureau; educational data come from Qingdao Municipal Education Bureau; the data of scientific and technological are from Qingdao Municipal Science and Technology Bureau; the data of market entities, patents and other data are From Qingdao Municipal Market Regulation Bureau; the data of subsistence allowances are from Qingdao

Civil Affairs Bureau; sports data are from Qingdao Sports Bureau; health data are from Qingdao Municipal Health Commission; environmental data are from Qingdao Municipal Bureau of Ecology and Environment; electricity consumption data are from Qingdao Power Supply Company; meteorological data are from Qingdao Meteorological Bureau; the data of workplace safety are from Qingdao Emergency Management Bureau; the data of urban construction are from Qingdao Housing and Urban–Rural Development Bureau; the data of car ownership are from Qingdao Public Security Bureau; the data of food, animal husbandry, residents′ life and price data are from the National Bureau of Statistics Qingdao Survey Team; all the other data are from the Qingdao Municipal Bureau of Statistics.

综 合 1

GENERAL SURVEY

简要说明

一、本篇资料的主要内容

本篇资料是对我市行政区划、气象情况、分行业法人单位数、各部门机构数和国民经济、社会发展的综合反映，主要包括行政区划、气象情况、分行业法人单位数、各部门机构数、国民经济主要比例关系、国民经济和社会发展主要指标占全国全省比重、国民经济和社会发展主要指标及其增长速度等资料。

二、本篇资料的来源

1. “行政区划”主要包括2022年底各区（市）街道办事处（乡镇）、社区居委会（村民委员会）区划资料，数据来源于市民政局。

2. “气象情况”包括分区市、市区分月气象资料，数据来源于市气象局。

3. “全市生产总值”来源于国民经济核算统计报表，由市统计局国民经济核算处整理提供。

4. 国民经济和社会发展综合部分来源于本年鉴各篇章中的资料，由市统计局国民经济综合统计处加工整理。

Brief Introduction

Ⅰ. Main Content

The information in this article is a comprehensive reflection of Qingdao's administrative divisions, meteorological conditions, the number of legal entities by industry, the number of various departments and institutions, and the national economic and social development, including administrative divisions, meteorological conditions, the number of legal entities by industry, the number of agencies, the main proportions of the national economy, the proportion of the main indicators of national economic and social development in the province, the main indicators of national economic and social development and their increase speed and other information.

Ⅱ. Source of Data

1. "Administrative divisions" mainly include the division data of district (city) sub-district offices (townships) and community neighborhood committees (village committees) at the end of 2022. The data comes from Qingdao Civil Affairs Bureau.

2. "Meteorological conditions" includes monthly meteorological data of district cities and cities, and the data comes from Qingdao Meteorological Bureau.

3. The "Gross Product of the City" comes from the national economic accounting statistical report, which is compiled and provided by the National Economic Accounting Office of Qingdao Statistics Bureau.

4. The comprehensive part of the national economy and social development is derived from the data in each chapter of this yearbook, processed and compiled by the National Economic Comprehensive Statistics Division of Qingdao Bureau of Statistics.

1-1　行政区划(2022 年底)
ADMINISTRATIVE DIVISION (END OF 2022)

单位:个 (unit)

市区名称	Region	街道办事处 Subdistrict Offices	社区居委会 Community Residents' Committees	镇 Town	村民委员会 Villagers' Committees
全　市	**Whole Municipality**	**108**	**1177**	**36**	**908**
市南区	Shinan District	14	50		
市北区	Shibei District	29	137		
李沧区	Licang District	11	123		
崂山区	Laoshan District	5	87		80
黄岛区	Huangdao District	14	231	8	145
城阳区	Chengyang District	8	277		19
即墨区	Jimo District	11	60	4	136
胶州市	Jiaozhou	8	85	4	119
平度市	Pingdu	5	59	12	298
莱西市	Laixi	3	68	8	111

1-2　气象情况 (2022 年)
METEOROLOGY (2022)

市、区名称	Region	平均气温（摄氏度）Average Temperature (℃)	极端气温 Extreme Temperature		降水量（毫米/年）Precipitation (millimeter/year)	日照时数（小时/年）Sunshine Hours (hour/year)	平均气压（百帕）Average Atmospheric Pressure (100 pa)
			最高（摄氏度）Maximum (℃)	最低（摄氏度）Minimum (℃)			
市　区	Urban Area	13.8	34.7	-7.3	1332.0	2324.1	1008.2
崂山区	Laoshan District	13.6	34.7	-6.8	1290.4	2361.8	1010.8
黄岛区	Huangdao District	13.5	36.0	-7.7	1149.0	2197.2	1016.8
即墨区	Jimo District	13.7	36.3	-11.0	959.5	2326.1	1011.7
胶州市	Jiaozhou	13.8	36.8	-8.2	970.7	2442.4	1007.2
平度市	Pingdu	13.4	36.5	-9.7	964.8	2323.5	1009.7
莱西市	Laixi	12.8	36.6	-11.0	891.1	2406.7	1008.1

注：以上为 7 个国家基准站或基本站。
Note: These are 7 national reference or base stations.

1-3　市区分月气象情况 (2022 年)
MONTHLY METEOROLOGY OF URBAN AREA (2022)

月　份	Month	平均气温（摄氏度）Average Temperature (℃)	降水量（毫米）Precipitation (millimeter)	日照时数（小时）Sunshine Hours (hour)
一月	Jan.	1.3	5.0	185.1
二月	Feb.	1.5	0.2	204.9
三月	Mar.	7.6	20.9	190.3
四月	Apr.	12.6	1.8	237.9
五月	May.	17.7	3.5	280.0
六月	Jun.	21.7	349.5	139.2
七月	Jul.	25.5	308.2	151.7
八月	Aug.	26.0	302.7	181.8
九月	Sep.	22.5	222.9	240.7
十月	Oct.	15.7	80.7	185.9
十一月	Nov.	12.3	36.5	132.3
十二月	Dec.	1.2	0.1	194.3
全　年	Annual Total	13.8	1332.0	2324.1

1-4 各部门机构数(2022 年底)

GRASS-ROOTS UNITS IN VARIOUS SECTORS (END OF 2022)

项　目	Item	单位	Unit	机构数 Grass-roots Units
农村基层单位	**Rural Grass-roots Units**			
镇政府	Town Governments	个	unit	36
乡村户数	Number of Rural Households	万户	10000 households	
规模以上工业企业单位	**Industrial Enterprises Above Designated Size**	**个**	**unit**	**4613**
#国有企业	State-owned Enterprises	个	unit	243
集体企业	Collective-owned Enterprises	个	unit	4
外商及港澳台商投资企业	Foreign Funded Enterprises and Enterprises with Funds from Hong Kong, Macao and Taiwan	个	unit	815
交通运输业	**Transportation**			
铁路	Railways	个	unit	4
公路	Highways	个	unit	256
水运	Waterways	个	unit	10
邮电业	**Rostal and Telecommunication Services**			
邮电局(所)	Post Offices	处	unit	266
电信营业网点(自有)	Telecom Business Outlets(self-owned)	个	unit	413
建筑业企业	**Construction Enterprises**	**个**	**unit**	**961**
国有企业	State-owned Enterprises	个	unit	23
集体企业	Collective-owned Enterprises	个	unit	3
其他	Others	个	unit	935
规模以上服务业企业单位	**Service Industry Enterprises Above Designated Size**	**个**	**unit**	**2775**
内资企业	Domestic Funded Enterprises	个	unit	2645
港、澳、台商投资企业	Enterprises with Funds from Hong Kong, Macao and Taiwan	个	unit	46
外商投资企业	Foreign Funded Enterprises	个	unit	84
限额以上批发和零售业、住宿和餐饮业	**Wholesale & Retail Trades, Hotels and Catering Services Above Designated Size**	**个**	**unit**	**5618**
限额以上批发业	Wholesale Trade above Designated Size	个	unit	3713
限额以上零售业	Retail Trade above Designated Size	个	unit	939
限额以上住宿业	Hotel above Designated Size	个	unit	416
限额以上餐饮业	Catering Service above Designated Size	个	unit	550

注：1. 该表邮政局(所)为中国邮政集团公司青岛市分公司提供;电信营业网点(自有)由三大电信运营商提供数据汇总。
　　2. 根据国家统计局 2022 年农林牧渔业统计报表制度取消乡村户数指标。

Note: 1. In the tables, the post offices are provided by Qingdao Branch of China Post Group Corporation; and the Telecom business outlets (self-owned) are from the data summary provided by the three major telecom operators.
　　2. According to the Agricultural, Forestry, Animal husbandry and Fishery Statistical Report System (2022) issued by National Bureau of Statistics, the number of rural households will be canceled.

1-4 续表
Continued

项目	Item	单位	Unit	机构数 Grass-roots Units
教育事业	**Education**			
普通高等学校	Regular Institutions of Higher Education	所	unit	27
普通中等职业学校	Regular Secondary Vocational School	所	unit	53
普通中学	Regular Secondary Schools	所	unit	363
普通小学	Regular Primary Schools	所	unit	672
幼儿园	Kindergartens	所	unit	2274
文化及相关产业	**Culture and Related Industry**			
公共图书馆	Public Libraries	个	unit	11
卫生事业	**Public Health**			
#医院	Hospitals	个	unit	456
民政行政单位	**Civil Affairs Departments**			
#提供住宿的社会服务机构	Social Service Agencies That Provide Accommodation	个	unit	307

1-5 按行业分法人单位数（2022年）

NUMBER OF CORPORATE UNITS BY SECTOR (2022)

单位：个（unit）

行 业	Sector	数量 Number
总 计	**Total**	**598680**
农、林、牧、渔业	Agriculture, Forestry, Animal Husbandry and Fishery	11093
采矿业	Mining	212
制造业	Manufacturing	77045
电力、热力、燃气及水生产和供应业	Electricity, Heat, Gas and Water Production and Supply Industry	909
建筑业	Construction	50338
批发和零售业	Wholesale and Retail Trades	196625
交通运输、仓储和邮政业	Transport, Storage and Post	24502
住宿和餐饮业	Hotels and Catering Services	10232
信息传输、软件和信息技术服务业	Information Transmission, Software and Information Technology Services	29489
金融业	Financial Industry	4636
房地产业	Real Estate	14630
租赁和商务服务业	Leasing and Business Services	87476
科学研究和技术服务业	Scientific Research and Technical Services	42552
水利、环境和公共设施管理业	Management of Water Conservancy, Environment and Public Facilities	4694
居民服务、修理和其他服务业	Resident Services, Repairs and Other Services	11485
教育	Education	8351
卫生和社会工作	Health and Social Work	3290
文化、体育和娱乐业	Culture, Sports and Entertainment Industry	11488
公共管理、社会保障和社会组织	Public Management, Social Security and Social Organization	9633

1-6　国民经济主要平均指标
AVERAGE INDICATORS ON NATIONAL ECONOMY

指　标	Indicator	单位	Unit	2000 年	2005 年
人口密度	Density of Population	人 / 平方公里	person/sq.km	664	695
每户年平均人口	Average Household Size	人	person	3.14	3.12
城镇非私营单位在岗职工年平均工资	The Average Annual Wage of Staff and Workers in the Post in Non–Private Units in Towns and Cities	元	yuan	10072	19086
城镇居民人均可支配收入	Annual Per Capita Disposable Income of Urban Households	元	yuan	7971	12725
农村居民人均可支配收入	Annual Per Capita Net Income of Rural Households	元	yuan	3534	5384
每一播亩平均粮食产量	Output of Grain Per Mu of Sowing Area	千克	kg	411	421
每亩蔬菜平均产量	Average Output of Vegetables Per Mu	千克	kg	2735	2985
每亩茶叶平均产量	Average Output of Tea Per Mu	千克	kg	8.1	16.5
每亩花生平均产量	Average Output of Peanut Per Mu	千克	kg	298	327
每亩棉花平均产量	Average Output of Cotton Per Mu	千克	kg	83	74
每台拖拉机负担耕地面积	Cultivated Area Ploughed by Per Tractor	亩 / 台	mu/unit	56	39
每亩耕地施用化肥量（折纯）	Chemical Fertilizer Consumption Per Mu (convert to pure amount)	千克	kg	45	52
每人平均消费品零售额	Per Capita Retail Sales of Consumer Goods	元	yuan	5965	11445
城市每天平均生活用水量	Daily Residential Consumption of Water	万吨	10000 tons	33.3	34.4
城市每人平均公园绿地面积	Per Capita Public Green Areas	平方米	sq.m	8.5	11.8
每万人拥有医疗床位	Number of Hospital Beds Per 10000 Population	张	bed	34.5	41.3
每万人拥有医生数	Number of Doctors Per 10000 Population	人	person	21.0	20.3
每万人中高等学校学生数	Students Enrollment of Institutions of Higher Education Per 10000 Population	人	person	65	324
每万人中中等学校学生数	Students Enrollment of Secondary Schools Per 10000 Population	人	person	704	768
每万人中小学学生数	Students Enrollment of Primary Schools Per 10000 Population	人	person	757	648

注：1. 自 2015 年开始，全市城乡住户调查统一使用一体化改革后的数据，与原数据相比，城乡居民收支指标的调查范围和口径均存在较大变化。原“城市居民人均可支配收入”调整为“城镇居民人均可支配收入”；原“农民人均纯收入”调整为“农村居民人均可支配收入”。
2. 2008—2017 年农作物数据为根据第三次农业普查结果核定修正后数据。
3. 由于城市的发展变化，2022 年起，城市建设数据涵盖胶州市、平度市、莱西市数据。

Notes：1. Since 2015, the urban and rural households investigation unified the data after the integrated reform, compared with the original data, the investigation scope and the caliber of urban and rural residents' income and expenditure indicators have changed greatly. The original “per capita disposable income of urban residents” is adjusted to be a “per capita disposable income of urban residents” . The original “per capita net income of farmers” is adjusted to “per capita disposable income of rural residents” .
2. Crop data from 2008 to 2017 are revised based on the results of the third agricultural census.
3. Due to the growth and changes of the city, from 2022, the data of urban development covers that of Jiaozhou, Pingdu and Laixi.

2010 年	2012 年	2013 年	2014 年	2015 年	2016 年	2017 年	2018 年	2019 年	2020 年	2021 年	2022 年
677	682										
3.10	3.09										
37501	49052	55363	62104	69465	76616	83539	90840	103108	116115	127228	124601
24380	31349	34356	37346	40370	43598	47176	50817	54484	55905	60239	62584
9326	12366	13905	15434	16730	17969	19364	20820	22573	23656	26125	27701
399	411	407	396	400	404	414	430	425	432	434	431
3689	3887	3957	3963	3889	3760	3931	3796	3883	3992	4046	4071
44	51	49	52	57	74	75	80	75	78	79	79
306	326	314	305	287	294	319	321	305	321	326	320
62	81	81	89	86	82	85	110	105	97	93	81
32			38	38	37	36	36	36	36	31	31
47			37	36	36	36	35	34	34	38	38
24781	32917	37032	41226	45309	49360	53722	57991	61862	62180	70615	68837
34.3	33.2	32.5	40.6	42.1	67.6	50.3	50.6	54.3	58.0	60.0	76.8
14.6	14.6	14.6	14.6	14.6	18.6	17.4	16.3	16.9	19.0	18.0	17.4
47.2	61.4	58.0	60.3	62.0	63.9	69.4	68.2	72.8	77.0	80.1	76.8
23.2	28.1	31.2	32.0	33.5	34.9	38.4	42.3	45.5	47.4	47.2	48.5
373	386	388	402	411.0	430.0	431.0	486.6	500.3	514.6	540.3	554.8
701	635	626	614	596.0	593.0	611.0	612.5	627.8	653.3	675.5	684.2
606	630	642	662	685.0	690.0	685.3	696.9	702.4	721.5	745.1	780.5

1-7　主要年份社会经济主要指标
MAJOR YEAR'S INDICATORS ON SOCIETY AND ECONOMY

指　标	Indicator	单位	Unit	2000 年	2005 年
人口	**Population**				
总人口（年末）	Total Population	万人	10000 persons	706.65	740.91
男性人口	Male	万人	10000 persons	357.74	374.03
女性人口	Female	万人	10000 persons	348.91	366.87
市区人口	Urban Area	万人	10000 persons	234.60	265.43
就业	**Employment**				
社会从业人员	Employment	万人	10000 persons	436.1	467.4
#单位从业人员	Employed Persons in Units	万人	10000 persons	118.3	224.3
经济总量	**Gross Economic Amount**				
全市生产总值（当年价）	GDP（at current price）	亿元	100 million yuan	1183.14	2576.95
第一产业增加值	Primary Industry	亿元	100 million yuan	135.81	168.06
第二产业增加值	Secondary Industry	亿元	100 million yuan	546.12	1292.49
第三产业增加值	Tertiary Industry	亿元	100 million yuan	501.21	1116.4
人均生产总值	Per Capita GDP	元	yuan	15900	31725
农林牧渔业总产值（当年价）	Gross Output Value of Agriculture, Forestry, Animal Husbandry and Fishery（at current price）	亿元	100 million yuan	248.33	320.51
工业总产值（当年价）	Gross Industrial Output Value（at current price）	亿元	100 million yuan	1940.83	5001.78

注：1. 单位从业人员 2004 年以前为职工人数（不含私营企业）。
2. 规模以上固定资产投资数据 2003 年以前为城镇以上统计范围。
3. 2002 年以前地方财政一般预算收支数据为地方财政收支口径。
4. 2008—2017 年农林牧渔业总产值为根据第三次农业普查结果核定修正后数据。
5. 第四次全国经济普查后，对 2000 年至 2018 年历年 GDP 数据进行了修订（以下相关表同）。

Notes：1.Before 2004, the data of employed persons in units refers to the number of staff and workers（excluding private enterprises）.
2.Before 2003, the data of investment in fixed assets above designated size refers to urban investment.
3.Before 2002, the data of general budgetary revenue and expenditure of local government finance refers to revenue and expenditure of local government finance.
4.Gross output value of Agriculture, forestry, animal husbandry and fishery from 2008 to 2017 is revised according to the results of the third agricultural census.
5.After the fourth national economic census, the GDP data from 2000 to 2018 was revised（the following related tables are the same）.

2010 年	2012 年	2013 年	2014 年	2015 年	2016 年	2017 年	2018 年	2019 年	2020 年	2021 年	2022 年
763.64	769.56										
381.92	383.82										
381.72	385.74										
275.50	279.57										
504.9	515.5	517.5	521.3	523.7	523.5	524.3	525.3	523.6	525.6	527.71	528.00
269.4	283.2	293.7	303	309.2	315.6	321.4	330.4	146.6	147.7	147.7	144.4
5350.69	6869.61	7508.7	8120.66	8658.57	9283.17	10136.96	10949.38	11741.31	12400.56	14136.46	14920.75
261.03	305.72	332.1	341.68	356.19	357.4	367.71	386.91	409.98	425.41	470.06	478.05
2482.6	3010.6	3225.9	3389.1	3503.4	3592.80	3849.18	4033.33	4182.76	4381.44	4945.04	5197.34
2607.08	3553.33	3950.68	4389.87	4798.98	5332.96	5920.06	6529.14	7148.57	7593.71	8721.36	9245.36
62148	76636	82463	87677	92157	97430	104905	112129	118978	123828	138849	144870
480.2	567.3	610.6	627.9	612.4	669.1	697.9	737	778.1	807.1	897.1	925.6
11614.83	15306.32	16897.18	17444.21	18019.43	17415.71	13019.73	11389.78				

1-7 续表 1
Continued

指 标	Indicator	单位	Unit	2000 年	2005 年
财政	**Government Finance**				
公共财政预算收入	Public Budget Revenue	亿元	100 million yuan	80.01	176.34
公共财政预算支出	Public Budget Expenditure	亿元	100 million yuan	87.87	203.06
规模以上固定资产投资额	**Investment in Fixed Assets above Designated Size**	**亿元**	**100 million yuan**	**242.68**	**1403.30**
社会消费品零售额	**Total Retail Sales of Consumer Goods**	**亿元**	**100 million yuan**	**421.55**	**847.97**
港口吞吐量	**Volume of Freight Handled in Ports**	**万吨**	**10000 tons**	**8661**	**18727**
集装箱吞吐量	**Volume of Containers Handled**	**万标箱**	**10000 TEUs**	**212.0**	**630.7**
民航货邮吞吐量	**Civil Aviation Cargo and Mail Throughput**	**万吨**	**10000 tons**	**3.44**	**8.91**
对外贸易	**Foreign Trade**				
外贸进出口总额	Imports and Exports	亿美元	100 million USD	108.31	304.55
#出口总额	Exports	亿美元	100 million USD	61.14	175.88
教育、卫生、文化	**Education, Public Health and Culture**				
小学在校学生数	Students Enrollment in Primary Schools	万人	10000 persons	53.49	47.98
普通中学在校学生	Students Enrollment in Regular Secondary Schools	万人	10000 persons	39.85	39.11

2010年	2012年	2013年	2014年	2015年	2016年	2017年	2018年	2019年	2020年	2021年	2022年
452.61	670.18	788.93	895.25	1006.32	1100.03	1157.24	1231.91	1241.74	1253.85	1368.30	1273.31
532.39	765.98	1014.23	1074.71	1222.87	1352.85	1403.03	1561.23	1575.97	1584.65	1706.76	1696.17
3022.48	**4153.91**	**5027.86**	**5766.03**	**6555.70**	**7454.70**	**7777.09**					
1892.38	**2533.16**	**2865.02**	**3218.25**	**3548.16**	**3914.19**	**4321.43**	**4742.72**	**5126.6**	**5203.5**	**5975.4**	**5891.8**
35012	**41465**	**45782**	**47701**	**49749**	**51463**	**51314**	**54250**	**57736**	**60459**	**63029**	**65754**
1201	**1450**	**1552**	**1658**	**1743**	**1805**	**1831**	**1932**	**2101**	**2201**	**2371**	**2567**
16.37	**17.19**	**18.62**	**20.44**	**20.81**	**23.69**	**23.21**	**22.45**	**25.63**	**20.7**	**23.8**	**22.0**
561.49	732.08	779.12	798.88	702.22	4350.67（亿元）	5033.50（亿元）	5321.26（亿元）	5925.58（亿元）	6407.01（亿元）	8498.43（亿元）	9117.2（亿元）
333.51	408.20	419.86	457.77	453.50	2821.91（亿元）	3031.81（亿元）	3172.22（亿元）	3411.90（亿元）	3876.76（亿元）	4921.28（亿元）	5361.1（亿元）
46.27	49.50	49.63	51.65	53.65	54.72	55.05	56.99	58.38	60.4	63.1	66.4
38.00	36.96	36.51	36.26	35.54	35.61	37.22	38.54	40.9	43.0	44.6	45.0

1-7　续表 2
Continued

指　标	Indicator	单位	Unit	2000 年	2005 年
高等学校在校学生	Students Enrollment in Institutions of Higher Education	万人	10000 persons	4.61	23.98
小学专任教师	Full-time Teachers in Primary Schools	万人	10000 persons	3.17	3.17
普通中学专任教师	Full-time Teachers in Regular Secondary Schools	万人	10000 persons	2.63	2.97
医生总数	Doctors	万人	10000 persons	1.49	1.50
医院床位数	Hospital Beds	万张	10000 beds	2.01	2.86
人民生活	**People's Liveli Hoods**				
就业人员工资总额	Total wages of Employed Persons	亿元	100 million yuan	120.4	359.5
城乡人民币储蓄存款余额	Savings Deposit of Urban and Rural Households	亿元	100 million yuan	535	1343
物价指数	**Price Indices**				
商品零售价格指数（以 1950 年价格为 100）	Retail Price Indices（1950=100）	%	%	520.5	495.0
居民消费价格指数（以 1950 年价格为 100）	Consumer Price Indices（1950=100）	%	%	711.9	753.1
#食品价格指数（以 1950 年价格为 100）	Food Price Indices（1950=100）	%	%	800.1	871.8

注：1. 就业人员工资总额 2005 年前统计范围为全部职工不含私营企业，2015 年及以前为在岗职工工资总额。
2. 2015 年“城乡人民币储蓄存款余额”改为“住户存款”。

Notes：1. The total wages of employees before 2005 included all employees excluding private enterprises, and the total wages of employees in 2015 and before were the total wages of employees on the job.
2. In 2015，“balance of RMB deposits in urban and rural areas” changed to “household deposits.”

2010年	2012年	2013年	2014年	2015年	2016年	2017年	2018年	2019年	2020年	2021年	2022年
28.49	29.66	30.02	31.35	32.23	34.09	34.62	39.8	41.58	43.07	45.72	47.23
3.20	3.17	3.28	3.22	3.45	3.42	3.47	3.69	3.53	3.52	3.92	4.05
3.08	3.20	3.18	3.20	3.29	3.39	3.47	3.60	3.98	3.83	3.95	3.97
1.77	2.16	2.41	2.50	2.63	2.76	3.09	3.46	3.78	3.97	4.00	4.13
3.34	4.12	3.97	4.30	4.51	4.73	4.63	5.08	5.85	6.25	6.50	6.54
738.0	1044.3	1251.7	1456.0	1644.4	1852.7	2034.7	2251.7				
2912	3758	4141	4436	5024	5326	5394	5914	6755	8031	9028	10948
526.5	559.6	567.4	580.5	580.5	592.1	596.8	607.6	622.2	631.5	640.3	658.2
854.0	920.9	943.9	968.4	980.0	1004.5	1024.6	1046.1	1080.6	1106.5	1123.1	1145.6
1194.9	1384.6	1458.0	1522.2	1548.1	1625.5	1619.0	1669.2	1862.8	2045.4	2039.3	2108.6

1-8 国民经济主要结构指标
COMPOSITION INDICATORS ON NATIONAL ECONOMY

指　标	Indicator	2000 年	2005 年	2010 年	2012 年
社会从业人员	**Employment**				
产业结构	Industrial Composition				
第一产业	Primary Industry	36.4	22.2	19.5	18.8
第二产业	Secondary Industry	33.9	41.8	41.4	41.0
第三产业	Tertiary Industry	29.7	36.0	39.1	40.2
全市生产总值	**GDP**				
产业结构	Industrial Composition				
第一产业	Primary Industry	11.5	6.5	4.9	4.5
第二产业	Secondary Industry	46.1	50.2	46.4	43.8
第三产业	Tertiary Industry	42.4	43.3	48.7	51.7
农业	**Agriculture**				
农林牧渔业产值结构	Composition of Agriculture, Forestry, Animal Husbandry and Fishery				
# 农业	Agriculture	45.0	39.5	45.8	40.0
林业	Forestry	0.8	0.8	0.4	0.4
畜牧业	Animal Husbandry	27.9	33.4	25.5	26.6
渔业	Fishery	26.4	26.3	24.6	28.8
工业	**Industry**				
轻重工业产值结构	Composition of Output Value of Light and Heavy Industry				
轻工业	Light Industry	64.1	49.4	38.7	39.5
重工业	Heavy Industry	35.9	50.6	61.3	60.5
固定资产投资	**Investment in Fixed Assets**				
投资结构	Composition of Investment				
生产性	Productive	54.0	65.4	53.6	58.4
非生产性	Non-productive	46.0	34.6	46.4	41.6

注：2008—2017 年农业数据为根据第三次农业普查结果核定修正后数据。
Note: Agricultural data from 2008 to 2017 are revised according to the results of the third agricultural census.

单位：%

2013 年	2014 年	2015 年	2016 年	2017 年	2018 年	2019 年	2020 年	2021 年	2022 年
18.8	18.4	18.1	17.8	16.9	16.2	15.7	15.6	15.6	15.0
40.6	39.0	38.6	38.0	37.8	36.4	38.3	31.9	31.9	32.0
40.6	42.6	43.3	44.2	45.3	47.4	46.0	52.5	52.5	53.0
4.4	4.2	4.1	3.9	3.6	3.5	3.5	3.4	3.3	3.2
43.0	41.7	40.5	38.7	38.0	36.9	35.6	35.3	35.0	34.8
52.6	54.1	55.4	57.4	58.4	59.6	60.9	61.3	61.7	62.0
41.7	42.1	40.3	42.5	43.0	44.7	46.3	46.2	47.1	47.9
0.4	0.4	0.4	0.4	0.4	0.5	0.6	0.6	0.5	0.5
25.5	24.8	25.0	24.2	23.8	22.1	21.5	22.3	20.5	19.1
28.0	27.7	29.6	26.6	26.2	26.1	24.9	24	25.1	25.3
39.5	38.8	39.5	39.4	37.6	34.3				
60.5	61.2	60.5	60.6	62.4	65.7				
61.65	57.08	63.16	59.81	53.64					
38.35	42.92	36.84	40.19	46.36					

1-9 平均每天主要社会经济活动

SELECTED INDICATORS ON AVERAGE DAILY SOCIAL AND ECONOMIC ACTIVITIES

指　标	Indicator	单位	Unit	2000 年	2005 年
全市生产总值	GDP	万元	10000 yuan	32415	70601
工业总产值	Gross Industrial Output Value	万元	10000 yuan	53174	137035
农林牧渔业总产值	Gross Output Value of Agriculture，Forestry，Animal Husbandry and Fishery	万元	10000 yuan	6803	8781
主要工业产品产量	Output of Major Industrial Products				
发电量	Electricity	万千瓦时	10000 kW·h	2489	2701
钢材	Rolled-steel	吨	ton	2558	9049
纱	Yarn	吨	ton	191	198
布	Cloth	万米	10000 m	114	141
家用电冰箱	Refrigerator	台	unit	8523	24899
彩色电视机	Color TV Set	台	unit	10395	36282
社会消费品零售总额	Total Retail Sales of Consumer Goods	万元	10000 yuan	11549	23232
固定资产投资	Investment in Fixed Assets above Designated Size	万元	10000 yuan	6649	38446
外贸进出口总额	Imports and Exports	万美元	10000 USB	3707	9047
港口吞吐量	Volume of Freight Handled in Ports	万吨	10000 tons	23.73	51.31

注：1. 固定资产投资包括城镇、农村 500 万元以上投资项目。
2. 一年按照 365 天计算。
3.2008—2017 年农林牧渔业总产值为根据第三次农业普查结果核定修正后数据。

Notes：1. Investment in fixed assets includes construction projects involving an urban or rural investment of 5 million yuan an d over.
2. A year is computed according to 365 days.
3. Gross output value of Agriculture, forestry, animal husbandry and fishery from 2008 to 2017 is revised according to the results of the third agricultural census.

2010 年	2012 年	2013 年	2014 年	2015 年	2016 年	2017 年	2018 年	2019 年	2020 年	2021 年	2022 年
146594	188208	205718	222484	237221	254333	277725	299983	321680	339741	387300	408788
318215	419351	462936	477924	493683	477143	356705	312048				
13157	15541	16728	17203	16777	18331	19120	20192	21318	22112	24576	25359
4984	4787	4935	4885	4754	4805	4981	5271	4947	4725	5148	5377
9136	7525	6312	5830	3853	5243	7996	8764	9211	10663	14927	15464
97	53	92	89	76	92	73	79	111	83	167	112
48	134	141	122	77	68	65	127	31	44	63	67
21951	15754	14366	16714	23893	24170	22429	24290	20050	22521	24351	22798
30444	39452	41426	46984	37704	57855	46658	46443	43299	48626	54431	69743
51846	69402	78494	88171	97210	107238	118395	129938	140455	142562	163700	161419
82808	113806	137751	157973	179608	204238	213071					
15633	20057	21346	21887	19239	119196（万元）	137904（万元）	145787（万元）	162345（万元）	175534（万元）	232834（万元）	249786（万元）
96	114	125	131	136	141	141	149	158	166	173	180

1-10　主要指标占全国全省比重（2022 年）
PERCENTAGE OF MAIN INDICATORS TO CHINA AND SHANDONG（2022）

指　标	Indicator	单位	Unit
一、生产总值	**GDP**	**亿元**	**100 million yuan**
第一产业	Primary Industry	亿元	100 million yuan
第二产业	Secondary Industry	亿元	100 million yuan
第三产业	Tertiary Industry	亿元	100 million yuan
二、年末总人口（常住人口）	**Total Year-end Population（Resident population ）**	**万人**	**10000 persons**
三、主要工业产品产量	**Output of Major Industrial Products**		
发电量	Electricity	亿千瓦时	100 million kW・h
房间空气调节器	Air Conditioner	万台	10000 units
家用电冰箱	Refrigerator	万台	10000 units
彩色电视机	Color TV Set	万台	10000 units
钢材	Rolled-steel	万吨	10000 tons
水泥	Cement	万吨	10000 tons
四、主要农产品产量	**Output of Major Farm Products**		
粮食	Grain	万吨	10000 tons
油料	Oil Plants	万吨	10000 tons
猪牛羊禽肉类产量	Output of Pork, Beef, Mutton And Poultry	万吨	10000 tons
水产品	Aquatic Products	万吨	10000 tons
五、房地产开发投资	**Investment In Real Estate Development**	**亿元**	**100 million yuan**
六、货物进出口总额	**Imports and Exports**	**亿元**	**100 million yuan**
其中：出口	Export	亿元	100 million yuan
进口	Import	亿元	100 million yuan

注：1. 本表全国、全省均为公报数。
2. 青岛市主要工业产品产量数据为本地口径。

Notes：1. The number of the country and province in the table are obtained from the statistical report.
2. The output of main industrial products of qingdao are at local calibre.

全国 China	全省 Shandong	青岛市 Qingdao	青岛市占全国比重 Qingdao/China (%)	青岛市占全省比重 Qingdao/Shandong (%)
1210207	**87435.1**	**14920.75**	**1.2**	**17.1**
88345	6298.6	478.05	0.5	7.6
483164	35014.2	5197.34	1.1	14.8
638698	46122.3	9245.36	1.4	20.0
141175	**10162.79**	**1034.21**	**0.73**	**10.18**
88487.1	5722.6	196.3	0.22	3.43
22247.3	1241.3	1208.2	5.43	97.33
8664.4	832.1	832.1	9.60	100.00
19578.3	2545.6	2545.6	13.00	100.00
134033.5	10529.1	564.4	0.42	5.36
213000	13405.1	456.7	0.21	3.41
68653	5543.80	311.30	0.45	5.62
3654.2	274.0	31.2	0.85	11.39
9227	838.4	52.0	0.56	6.20
6869	843.9	99.3	1.40	11.80
132895	**9225.9**	**1789.1**	**1.35**	**19.39**
420678.2	**33324.9**	**9117.2**	**2.17**	**27.36**
239654.0	20355.8	5361.1	2.24	26.34
181024.2	12969.1	3756.1	2.07	28.96

1-11　主要年份全市生产总值（按当年价格计算）
MAJOR YEAR'S GROSS DOMESTIC PRODUCT（AT CURRENT PRICE）

单位：亿元（100 million yuan）

年　份 Year	全市生产总值 GDP	第一产业 Primary Industry	第二产业 Secondary Industry	#工　业 Industry	第三产业 Tertiary Industry	人均生产总值（元） Per Capita GDP（yuan）
1949	2.87	1.19	1.10		0.58	71
1952	6.74	1.76	3.25	2.95	1.73	163
1957	10.82	2.00	5.76	5.39	3.06	239
1962	9.69	1.11	4.68	4.27	3.90	205
1965	15.50	1.80	8.96	8.48	4.74	325
1970	23.23	3.15	14.46	13.86	5.62	451
1975	29.07	6.93	15.39	14.67	6.75	522
1978	38.43	8.23	20.16	19.15	10.04	663
1980	48.65	9.61	26.15	24.28	12.90	819
1985	82.28	20.06	37.37	34.03	24.84	1311
1988	142.87	30.84	69.99	63.42	42.04	2199
1990	180.77	37.00	86.36	78.94	57.41	2714
1991	205.65	40.56	98.48	89.64	66.61	3053
1992	261.35	41.39	129.67	117.61	90.29	3856
1993	371.90	58.62	182.50	164.35	130.79	5455
1994	510.81	80.21	243.17	218.87	187.43	7436
1995	631.45	106.04	293.07	263.98	232.34	9089
1996	713.60	125.59	320.84	289.87	267.17	10130
1997	802.59	110.71	376.50	342.80	315.39	11235

注：1. 人均生产总值按常住人口计算，2011—2020 年人均生产总值根据第七次人口普查人口修订结果进行了修订（以下相关表同）。
2. 三次产业分类采用《国民经济行业分类》（GB/T 4754—2017）和《三次产业划分规定》（国统字〔2012〕108 号），将农林牧渔业中的农、林、牧、渔专业及辅助性活动以及工业中的开采专业及辅助性活动和金属制品、机械和设备修理业归入第三产业。
3. 全国第四次经济普查后，对 2000 年至 2018 年历年 GDP 数据进行了修订（以下相关表同）。
4. 2022 年 GDP 数据为初步核算数，2021 年 GDP 数据为最终核实数（以下相关表同）。

Notes：1. The per capita GDP is calculated based on the permanent population, and the 2011—2020 per capita GDP has been revised according to the population revision results of the seventh census（the following related tables are the same）.
2. The classification of the three industries adopts the "Classification of National Economic Industries"（GB/T 4754–2017）and the "Regulations on the Classification of the Three Industries"（Guo Tong Zi〔2012〕No. 108）, which classifies the agricultural, forestry, animal husbandry and fishery Professional and ancillary activities, mining professional and ancillary activities in industry, and metal products, machinery and equipment repair businesses are included in the tertiary industry.
3. After the fourth national economic census, the GDP data from 2000 to 2018 was revised（the following related tables are the same）.
4. The GDP data of 2022 is the preliminary accounting data, and that of 2021 is the final verification data（The following related tables are the same.）

1-11 续表 1
Continued

单位：亿元（100 million yuan）

年份 Year	全市生产总值 GDP	第一产业 Primary Industry	第二产业 Secondary Industry	#工业 Industry	第三产业 Tertiary Industry	人均生产总值（元）Per Capita GDP（yuan）
1998	901.19	132.56	407.70	369.89	360.93	12443
1999	1018.97	133.27	466.50	424.15	419.20	13884
2000	1183.14	135.81	546.12	497.34	501.21	15900
2001	1349.98	139.14	625.59	566.71	585.24	17882
2002	1551.42	141.89	728.77	658.00	680.76	20236
2003	1819.03	143.51	877.95	786.49	797.58	23340
2004	2193.60	157.52	1080.95	961.94	955.13	27577
2005	2576.95	168.06	1292.49	1156.53	1116.40	31725
2006	3029.40	173.35	1528.60	1374.12	1327.45	36743
2007	3545.48	191.86	1752.63	1577.15	1600.99	42509
2008	4141.91	210.53	2007.89	1795.88	1923.49	49183
2009	4534.22	216.99	2146.53	1887.38	2170.70	53481
2010	5350.69	261.03	2482.57	2155.73	2607.08	62148
2011	6248.48	288.73	2823.69	2430.66	3136.06	70945
2012	6869.61	305.72	3010.56	2608.44	3553.33	76636
2013	7508.70	332.10	3225.92	2752.90	3950.68	82463
2014	8120.66	341.68	3389.11	2878.71	4389.87	87677
2015	8658.57	356.19	3503.40	2944.80	4798.98	92157
2016	9283.17	357.40	3592.80	2989.24	5332.96	97430
2017	10136.96	367.71	3849.18	3133.78	5920.06	104905
2018	10949.38	386.91	4033.33	3161.34	6529.14	112129
2019	11741.31	409.98	4182.76	3159.86	7148.57	118978
2020	12400.56	425.41	4381.44	3296.87	7593.71	123828
2021	14136.46	470.06	4945.04	3752.88	8721.36	138849
2022	14920.75	478.05	5197.34	3966.45	9245.36	144870

1-12 主要年份全市生产总值构成(以全市生产总值为 100)

COMPOSITION OF MAJOR YRAR'S GROSS DOMESTIC PRODUCT (GROSS DOMESTIC PRODUCT=100)

单位：%

年 份 Year	全市生产总值 GDP	第一产业 Primary Industry	第二产业 Secondary Industry	#工 业 Industry	第三产业 Tertiary Industry
1952	100	26.1	48.2	43.8	25.7
1957	100	18.5	53.3	49.8	28.2
1962	100	11.4	48.3	44.1	40.3
1965	100	11.6	57.8	54.7	30.6
1970	100	13.6	62.2	59.7	24.2
1975	100	23.9	52.9	50.5	23.2
1978	100	21.4	52.5	49.8	26.1
1980	100	19.8	53.7	49.9	26.5
1985	100	24.4	45.4	41.4	30.2
1988	100	21.6	49.0	44.4	29.4
1990	100	20.5	47.8	43.7	31.7
1991	100	19.7	47.9	43.6	32.4
1992	100	15.8	49.6	45.0	34.6
1993	100	15.7	49.1	44.2	35.2
1994	100	15.7	47.6	42.8	36.7
1995	100	16.8	46.4	41.8	36.8
1996	100	17.6	45.0	40.6	37.4
1997	100	13.8	46.9	42.7	39.3
1998	100	14.7	45.2	41.0	40.1
1999	100	13.1	45.8	41.6	41.1
2000	100	11.5	46.1	42.0	42.4
2001	100	10.3	46.3	42.0	43.4

1-12 续表 1
Continued

单位：%

年 份 Year	全市生产总值 GDP	第一产业 Primary Industry	第二产业 Secondary Industry	#工 业 Industry	第三产业 Tertiary Industry
2002	100	9.1	47.0	42.4	43.9
2003	100	7.9	48.3	43.2	43.8
2004	100	7.2	49.3	43.9	43.5
2005	100	6.5	50.2	44.9	43.3
2006	100	5.7	50.5	45.4	43.8
2007	100	5.4	49.4	44.5	45.2
2008	100	5.1	48.5	43.4	46.4
2009	100	4.8	47.3	41.6	47.9
2010	100	4.9	46.4	40.3	48.7
2011	100	4.6	45.2	38.9	50.2
2012	100	4.5	43.8	38.0	51.7
2013	100	4.4	43.0	36.7	52.6
2014	100	4.2	41.7	35.4	54.1
2015	100	4.1	40.5	34.0	55.4
2016	100	3.9	38.7	32.2	57.4
2017	100	3.6	38.0	30.9	58.4
2018	100	3.5	36.9	28.9	59.6
2019	100	3.5	35.6	26.9	60.9
2020	100	3.4	35.3	26.6	61.3
2021	100	3.3	35.0	26.5	61.7
2022	100	3.2	34.8	26.6	62.0

1-13 主要年份全市生产总值增长速度（以上年为 100）

GROWTH RATE OF MAJOR YEAR'S GROSS DOMESTIC PRODUCT（PRECEDING YEAR=100）

单位：%

年 份 Year	全市生产总值 GDP	第一产业 Primary Industry	第二产业 Secondary Industry	第三产业 Tertiary Industry	人均生产总值 Per Capita GDP
1979	12.0	10.6	12.9	11.4	10.4
1980	10.4	4.3	13.1	10.3	9.4
1981	-2.0	-3.6	-1.9	-1.0	-3.2
1982	4.1	5.5	-0.2	11.9	2.6
1983	16.9	42.8	9.3	12.7	15.3
1984	13.0	18.9	11.5	10.3	12.0
1985	9.9	5.4	5.8	21.3	9.3
1986	9.2	2.6	12.1	10.0	8.3
1987	12.0	3.6	16.0	12.0	10.6
1988	13.8	-0.3	21.5	11.2	12.1
1990	9.3	9.8	7.3	12.2	8.0
1991	10.6	16.6	11.6	5.4	9.4
1992	18.2	-1.6	22.9	24.7	17.4
1993	22.4	20.4	21.1	25.5	21.7
1994	14.4	3.7	14.7	19.7	13.5
1995	12.0	10.9	12.1	12.3	10.8
1996	7.2	7.6	7.6	6.5	5.7
1997	11.5	-10.7	16.8	14.1	9.9
1998	12.9	17.6	11.3	13.4	11.3
1999	13.9	4.0	15.5	15.2	12.4
2000	14.3	6.4	14.9	16.0	12.7
2001	13.0	1.8	14.9	13.9	11.3
2002	13.7	3.1	15.5	14.2	11.9
2003	15.4	2.4	18.8	14.5	13.5
2004	15.8	2.7	18.8	14.9	13.5
2005	15.6	0.4	18.1	15.3	13.2

1-13 续表 1
Continued

单位：%

年　份 Year	全市生产总值 GDP	第一产业 Primary Industry	第二产业 Secondary Industry	第三产业 Tertiary Industry	人均生产总值 Per Capita GDP
2006	14.5	0.5	15.3	15.6	12.8
2007	14.6	−2.6	13.8	17.8	13.3
2008	12.5	1.4	10.0	16.6	11.4
2009	11.3	3.0	11.3	12.0	10.5
2010	12.1	1.4	11.2	14.0	10.4
2011	11.0	4.5	11.0	11.8	8.5
2012	9.9	3.2	10.0	10.4	8.0
2013	9.4	2.1	8.5	10.9	7.7
2014	7.8	3.9	7.2	8.6	6.0
2015	7.9	3.6	7.0	9.0	6.3
2016	7.7	2.9	5.7	9.4	6.2
2017	7.4	3.1	5.8	8.7	5.9
2018	7.3	3.4	6.8	7.8	6.1
2019	6.5	1.6	4.7	8.0	5.3
2020	3.7	2.6	3.0	4.1	2.1
2021	8.3	6.7	4.3	10.7	6.5
2022	3.9	2.2	2.8	4.5	2.7
1978—2010 平均每年增长 1978—2010 Average Increase Rate	12.1	5.5	12.6	13.4	10.7
1991—2010 平均每年增长 1991—2010 Average Increase Rate	13.7	4.2	14.8	15.0	12.3
1996—2010 平均每年增长 1996—2010 Average Increase Rate	13.2	2.4	14.2	14.2	11.6
2001—2010 平均每年增长 2001—2010 Average Increase Rate	13.8	1.4	14.7	14.9	12.2
2006—2010 平均每年增长 2006—2010 Average Increase Rate	13.0	0.7	12.3	15.2	11.7
2011—2020 平均每年增长 2011—2020 Average Increase Rate	7.8	3.1	7.0	8.8	6.2
2016—2020 平均每年增长 2016—2020 Average Increase Rate	6.5	2.7	5.2	7.6	5.1

1-14　分市、区生产总值（2022年）
GROSS DOMESTIC PRODUCT BY REGION（2022）

单位：亿元（100 million yuan）

市、区名称	Region	地区生产总值 GDP	第一产业 Primary Industry	第二产业 Secondary Industry	第三产业 Tertiary Industry
市南区	Shinan District	1496.36		155.97	1340.38
市北区	Shibei District	1124.45		233.9	890.55
李沧区	Licang District	612.61		177.52	435.09
崂山区	Laoshan District	1081.17	7.46	347.69	726.03
黄岛区	Huangdao District	4691.85	92.47	1683.7	2915.69
城阳区	Chengyang District	1348.33	20.92	670.29	657.12
即墨区	Jimo District	1513.33	88.72	760.49	664.12
胶州市	Jiaozhou	1541.09	65.98	740.16	734.94
平度市	Pingdu	845.61	127.06	325.95	392.59
莱西市	Laixi	662.37	75.45	250.63	336.29

1-15 全市生产总值构成(2022 年)

COMPOSITION OF GROSS DOMESTIC PRODUCT（2022）

指　标	Indicator	增加值（亿元）Added Value（100 million yuan）	2022 年为 2021 年 % 2022/2021（%）
地区生产总值	**GDP**	**14920.75**	**103.9**
农林牧渔业	Agriculture, Forestry, Animal Husbandry and Fishery	512.64	102.6
#农林牧渔服务业	Agriculture, Forestry, Animal Husbandry and Fishery Service Industry	34.59	109.1
工业	Industry	3966.45	102.7
#开采辅助活动	Mining Auxiliary Activities	0.63	100.0
#金属制品、机械和设备修理业	Metal Products，Machinery and Equipment Repair Industries	19.04	107.5
建筑业	Construction	1250.56	103.0
批发和零售业	Wholesale and Retail Trades	2488.77	104.0
批发业	Wholesale	1623.21	104.9
零售业	Retail Trade	865.56	102.5
交通运输、仓储和邮政业	Transport, Storage and Post	1432.98	109.8
住宿和餐饮业	Hotels and Catering Services	254.27	101.5
住宿业	Hotels	29.10	112.0
餐饮业	Catering Services	225.17	100.3
金融业	Financial Industry	990.88	106.9
房地产业	Real Estate	857.71	98.5
房地产业（K 门类）	Real Estate（K category）	619.32	96.3
自有房地产经营活动	Self-Owned Real Estate Business Activities	238.39	104.5
其他服务业	Other Services	3166.49	104.3
营利性服务业	For-Profit Services	1713.16	103.8
非营利性服务业	Non-Profit Services	1453.33	104.9
第一产业	Primary Industry	478.05	102.2
第二产业	Secondary Industry	5197.34	102.8
第三产业	Tertiary Industry	9245.36	104.5

主要统计指标解释

国内生产总值（GDP）　指按市场价格计算的一个国家（或地区）所有常住单位在一定时期内生产活动的最终成果。国内生产总值有三种表现形态，即价值形态、收入形态和产品形态。从价值形态看，它是所有常住单位在一定时期内生产的全部货物和服务价值超过同期中间投入的全部非固定资产货物和服务价值的差额，即所有常住单位的增加值之和；从收入形态看，它是所有常住单位在一定时期内创造并分配给常住单位和非常住单位的初次收入分配之和；从产品形态看，它是所有常住单位在一定时期内最终使用的货物和服务价值与货物和服务净出口价值之和。在实际核算中，国内生产总值有三种计算方法，即生产法、收入法和支出法。三种方法分别从不同的方面反映国内生产总值及其构成。对于一个地区来说，称为地区生产总值或地区 GDP。

人均 GDP　人均 GDP 是一定时期内 GDP 与同期人口平均数的比值。按照国际标准，人口平均数应该是同期平均常住人口。我国在核算制度中也规定，无论是国家还是地区，人口数都采用常住人口。国家统计局规定从 2004 年开始，过去采用户籍人口计算人均 GDP 的地区，作为过渡性措施，可在两年内同时计算两种口径的人均 GDP（数据后面必须注明是什么口径），两年后取消按户籍人口计算的人均 GDP。我市采用常住人口计算人均 GDP。

三次产业　是根据社会生产活动历史发展的顺序对产业结构的划分，产品直接取自自然界的部门称为第一产业，对初级产品进行再加工的部门称为第二产业，为生产和消费提供各种服务的部门称为第三产业。它是世界上通用的产业结构分类，但各国的划分不尽一致。我国的三次产业划分是：

第一产业是指农、林、牧、渔业（不含农、林、牧、渔服务业）。

第二产业是指采矿业（不含开采辅助活动），制造业（不含金属制品、机械和设备修理业），电力、热力、燃气及水生产和供应业，建筑业。

第三产业即服务业，是指除第一产业、第二产业以外的其他行业。第三产业包括：批发和零售业，交通运输、仓储和邮政业，住宿和餐饮业，信息传输、软件和信息技术服务业，金融业，房地产业，租赁和商务服务业，科学研究和技术服务业，水利、环境和公共设施管理业，居民服务、修理和其他服务业，教育，卫生和社会工作，文化、体育和娱乐业，公共管理、社会保障和社会组织，国际组织，以及农、林、牧、渔业中的农、林、牧、渔服务业，采矿业中的开采辅助活动，制造业中的金属制品、机械和设备修理业。

气候　指地球与大气之间长期能量交换与质量交换所形成的一种自然环境状态，它是多种因素综合作用的结果。气候既是人类生活和生产的环境要素之一，又是供给人类生活和生产的重要资源。气温、降水、湿度等气象要素的多年平均值是用来描述一个地区气候状况的主要参数，而各种气象要素某年、某月的平均值（或总量）则可以反映出该时期天气气候状况的重要特征。

气温　指空气的温度，我国一般以摄氏度（℃）为单位表示。气象观测的温度表是放在离地面约 1.5 米处通风良好的百叶箱里测量的，因此，通常说的气温指的是离地面 1.5 米处百叶箱中的温度。其统计计算方法为：月平均气温是将全月各日的平均气温相加，除以该月的天数而得。

年平均气温　是将 12 个月的月平均气温累加后除以 12 而得。

降水量　指从天空降落到地面的液态或固态（经融化后）水，未经蒸发、渗透、流失而在地面上积聚的深度。其统计计算方法为：月降水量是将全月各日的降水量累加而得。年降水量是将 12 个月的月降水量累加而得。

Explanatory Notes on Main Statistical Indicators

Gross Domestic Product（GDP） refers to the final products at market prices produced by all resident units in a country（or a region）during a certain period of time.Gross domestic product is expressed in three different perspectives, namely value, income, and products respectively. GDP in its value perspective refers to the total value of all goods and services produced by all resident units during a certain period of time, minus the total value of input of goods and services of the nature of non–fixed assets, in other words, it is the sum of the value–added of all resident units. GDP from the perspective of products refers to the value of all goods and services for final consumption by all resident units minus the net exports of goods and services during a given period of time. In the practice of national accounting, gross domestic product is calculated from three approaches,namely production approach, income approach and expenditure approach, which reflect gross domestic product and its composition from different angles. For a certain region, it refers region gross product or region GDP.

Per Capita GDP refers to the ratio of GDP in a certain term and average population in the same term. According to the international standard, average population should be average permanent population in the same term. In the account regulation, population of both the country and the region should be permanent population. In the after two years since 2004, per capita GDP can be calculated at two coverage.i.e. at permanent population and household registered population（the note of coverage should follow the data）. The per capita GDP calculated with household registered population will be abolished after two years. Per capita GDP of Qingdao is calculated at permanent population.

Three Strata of Industries has been classified according to the historical sequence of development. Primary industry refers to extraction of natural resources, secondary industry involves processing of primary products, and tertiary industry provides services of various kinds for production and consumption. The above classification is universal although it varies to some extent from country to country. In China economic activities are categorized into the following three strata of industry：

Primary industry refers to agriculture, forestry, animal husbandry, and fishery（excluding agriculture, forestry, animal husbandry, and fishery service industries）.

The secondary industry refers to mining industry（excluding mining auxiliary activities）, manufacturing industry（excluding metal products, machinery and equipment repair industry）, electricity, heat, gas and water production and supply industry, and construction industry.

The tertiary industry is the service industry, which refers to industries other than the primary industry and the secondary industry. The tertiary industry includes: wholesale and retail industry, transportation, storage and postal industry, accommodation and catering industry, information transmission, software and information technology service industry, financial industry, real estate industry, leasing and business service industry, scientific research and technical service Industry, water conservancy, environment and public facilities management industry, resident service, repair and other service industry, education, health and social work, culture, sports and entertainment industry, public management, social security and social organization, international organization, and agriculture, forestry Agriculture, forestry, animal husbandry, and fishery services in agriculture, animal husbandry and fishery, mining auxiliary activities in mining, and metal products, machinery and equipment repair in manufacturing.

Climate refers to the natural environmental status formed by the long–term exchange of energy and mass between the earth and the air, and is the results of interaction of many factors. Climate is both one of the environment factors and the important resources for the living and production activities of the human being. The average values across several years of meteorological factors such as temperature, rainfall and humidity are used as important parameters to describe the climate of a region, while the average values（or total values）of a given year or month of meteorological factors reflect the key characteristics of climate for that period of time.

Temperature refers to the air temperature. China uses centigrade as the unit. The thermometry used for weather observation is put in a breezy shutter, which is 1.5 meters high from the ground. Therefore, the commonly used temperature refers to the temperature in the breezy shutter 1.5 meters away from the ground. The calculation method is as follows: Monthly average temperature is the summation of average daily temperature of one month divided by the actual days of that particular month.

Annual average temperature is the summation of monthly average of a year divided by 12 months.

Volume of Precipitation refers to the deepness of liquid state or solid state (thawed) water falling from the sky to the ground that has not been evaporated, infiltrated or run off. The calculation method is as follows: Monthly precipitation is the summation of daily precipitation of a month. Annual precipitation is the summation of 12 months precipitation of a year.

人 口 2

POPULATION

简要说明

一、本篇资料的主要内容

本篇资料主要反映全市人口方面的基本情况，包括全市主要年份和区（市）的户数、人口数、人口密度、土地面积数据、常住人口、城镇化率、计划生育等数据。另外还对中华人民共和国成立以来开展的七次人口普查主要数据进行了比较。

二、本篇资料的来源

本篇资料分别来源于国家开展的人口普查、人口抽样调查和市公安局的户籍登记资料，由市统计局人口就业和社会科技文化统计处整理提供。

Brief Introduction

Ⅰ. Main Content

The information in this part mainly reflects the basic situation of the city's population, including the number of households, population, population density, land area data, permanent resident population, urbanization rate, family planning and other data in the major years and districts (cities) of the city. In addition, the major data of the seven censuses conducted since the founding of the People's Republic of China were compared.

Ⅱ. Source of Data

The data in this article are derived from the national population census, population sample survey and household registration data of Qingdao Public Security Bureau, compiled and provided by the Population Employment and Social Science, Technology and Culture Statistics Department of Qingdao Statistics Bureau.

2-1 主要年份全市户籍人口数
MAJOR YEAR'S TOTAL REGISTERED POPULATION

单位：人（person）

年份 Year	总人口 Total Population	按性别分 Grouped by Gender 男 Male	 女 Female	平均人口 Average Population
1949	4056550	1997293	2059257	4054431
1952	4233586	2125392	2108194	4203428
1957	4822756	2424729	2398027	4773862
1962	4627432	2319658	2307774	4578313
1965	4901670	2461629	2440041	4859712
1970	5391852	2720633	2671219	5337282
1975	5742206	2904347	2837859	5717456
1978	5853321	2959800	2893521	5841638
1980	5961129	3015357	2945772	5937187
1985	6267223	3185409	3081814	6253157
1988	6516920	3319534	3197386	6474541
1989	6571597	3348454	3223143	6544259
1990	6666482	3392253	3274229	6619040
1991	6709277	3411776	3297501	6687880
1992	6731072	3420886	3310186	6720175
1993	6753497	3431149	3322348	6742285
1994	6785291	3446019	3339272	6769394
1995	6846346	3476300	3370046	6815819
1996	6902677	3502600	3400077	6874512
1997	6954391	3527588	3426803	6928534
1998	6995666	3545403	3450263	6975029
1999	7029707	3561061	3468646	7012687
2000	7066481	3577367	3489114	7048094
2001	7104875	3595652	3509223	7085678
2002	7156537	3619778	3536759	7130706
2003	7206806	3644032	3562774	7181672
2004	7311228	3692991	3618237	7259017
2005	7409052	3740309	3668743	7360140
2006	7493812	3779891	3713921	7451432
2007	7579910	3816620	3763290	7536861
2008	7615647	3824665	3790982	7597779
2009	7629161	3823534	3805627	7622404
2010	7636392	3819240	3817152	7632777
2011	7663612	3826931	3836681	7650002
2012	7695585	3838205	3857380	7679599

注：截至出书前，未从公安部门获得青岛市 2013—2022 年户籍人口信息。
Note：Data come from the Qingdao Municipal Public Security Bureau，and the Data of 2013—2022 are absent.

2-2 主要年份全市户数、人口数、人口密度（户籍）

MAJOR YEAR'S HOUSEHOLDS, POPULATION AND DENSITY OF POPULATION（WITH PERMANENT RESIDENCE）

年　份 Year	总户数（万户）Total Households（10000 households）		总人口（万人）Total Population（10000 persons）		平均每户人口（人）Average Persons Per Household（person）		人口密度（人/平方公里）Density of Population（person/sq.km）	
	全市 Whole Municipality	市区 Urban Area	全市 Whole Municepality	市区 Urban Area	全市 Whole Municepality	市区 Urban Area	全市 Whole Municepality	市区 Urban Area
1949	90.64	21.68	405.66	103.69	4.48	4.78	381	941
1952	93.96	22.70	423.36	107.62	4.51	4.74	397	977
1957	102.56	27.41	482.28	134.76	4.70	4.92	453	1223
1962	106.11	29.29	462.74	137.86	4.36	4.71	434	1251
1965	105.31	29.64	490.17	146.74	4.65	4.95	460	1332
1970	113.07	32.14	539.19	150.81	4.77	4.69	506	1369
1975	123.18	36.56	574.22	161.13	4.66	4.41	539	1462
1978	131.27	40.08	585.33	168.00	4.46	4.19	549	1525
1980	138.44	43.03	596.11	175.27	4.31	4.07	560	1591
1985	157.06	53.43	626.72	190.87	3.99	3.57	588	1732
1988	169.72	58.95	651.69	201.38	3.84	3.42	612	1827
1989	177.47	61.57	657.16	203.63	3.70	3.31	617	1848
1990	186.79	63.94	666.65	205.78	3.57	3.22	626	1867
1991	192.46	67.15	670.93	207.22	3.49	3.09	630	1880
1992	199.08	68.94	673.11	209.28	3.38	3.04	632	1899
1993	201.36	70.13	675.35	212.06	3.35	3.02	634	1924
1994	204.05	71.24	678.53	214.97	3.33	3.02	637	1951
1995	208.13	72.53	684.63	218.38	3.29	3.01	643	1982
1996	212.40	75.11	690.27	223.86	3.25	2.98	648	2032
1997	215.12	76.39	695.44	227.22	3.23	2.97	653	2062
1998	218.59	77.90	699.57	229.58	3.20	2.95	657	2084
1999	222.61	79.27	702.97	231.94	3.16	2.93	660	2105
2000	224.73	80.46	706.65	234.60	3.14	2.92	664	2129
2001	227.43	81.41	710.49	237.60	3.12	2.92	667	2156
2002	229.67	82.85	715.65	241.74	3.12	2.92	672	2194
2003	232.26	84.15	720.68	246.77	3.10	2.93	677	2240
2004	235.29	86.93	731.12	258.40	3.11	2.97	686	2229
2005	237.35	87.99	740.91	265.43	3.12	3.02	695	2290
2006	239.33	89.12	749.38	271	3.13	3.04	703	2338
2007	241.55	90.21	757.99	275.55	3.14	3.05	711	2377
2008	243.18	91.22	761.56	276.25	3.13	3.03	715	2384
2009	244.74	92.15	762.92	275.47	3.12	2.99	676	1873
2010	246.11	93.30	763.64	275.50	3.10	2.95	677	1873
2011	247.94	94.69	766.36	277.09	3.09	2.93	679	1884
2012	249.27	95.87	769.56	279.57	3.09	2.92	682	1901

注：截至出书前，未从公安部门获得青岛市 2013—2022 年户籍人口信息。

Note：Data come from the Qingdao Municipal Public Security Bureau，and the Data of 2013—2022 are absent.

2-3 主要年份全市常住人口数
MAJOR YEAR'S TOTAL RESIDENT POPULATION

单位：万人（10000 persons）

年　份 Year	总人口 Total Population
2005	819.55
2006	829.42
2007	838.67
2008	845.61
2009	850.03
2010	871.51
2011	889.60
2012	903.20
2013	917.90
2014	934.50
2015	944.60
2016	961.00
2017	971.60
2018	981.40
2019	992.30
2020	1010.57
2021	1025.67
2022	1034.21

注：2011—2019年为山东省统计局根据第七次人口普查结果修订数据。
Note：From 2011 to 2019, the Shandong Provincial Statistics Bureau revised the feedback data based on the results of the seventh census.

2-4 青岛市常住人口
TOTAL RESIDENT POPULATION

单位：万人（10000 persons）

市、区名称	Region	2022年	2021年	2022年比2021年（±）2022/2021（±）
全　市	**Whole Municipality**	**1034.21**	**1025.67**	**8.54**
市南区	Shinan District	48.97	48.85	0.12
市北区	Shibei District	110.55	110.23	0.32
李沧区	Licang District	76.14	75.25	0.89
崂山区	Laoshan District	51.72	51.08	0.64
黄岛区	Huangdao District	199.35	196.42	2.93
城阳区	Chengyang District	116.92	114.78	2.14
即墨区	Jimo District	136.96	136.18	0.78
胶州市	Jiaozhou	103.36	102.19	1.17
平度市	Pingdu	118.45	118.78	-0.33
莱西市	Laixi	71.79	71.91	-0.12

2-5 主要年份常住人口城镇化率
THE URBANIZATION RATE OF THE MAIN YEAR PERMANENT RESIDENTS

单位：%

年　份 Year	城镇化率 Urbanization Rate
2005	63.20
2006	63.59
2007	63.90
2008	64.31
2009	64.68
2010	65.81
2011	66.04
2012	66.09
2013	66.23
2014	66.31
2015	68.04
2016	70.54
2017	71.87
2018	74.20
2019	74.85
2020	76.34
2021	77.17
2022	77.32

注：1. 城镇化率为城镇区域常住人口数量与全市常住总人口的比值。
2. 2011–2019 年为山东省统计局根据第七次人口普查结果修订数据。

Notes：1. The urbanization rate is the ratio of the number of permanent residents in urban areas to the total permanent population of the city.
2. From 2011 to 2019, the Shandong Provincial Statistics Bureau revised the feedback data based on the results of the seventh census.

2-6　分市、区土地面积（2022年底）
LAND AREA BY REGION（END OF 2022）

市、区名称	Region	土地面积（平方公里）Land Area（aq.km）
全　市	**Whole Municipality**	**11294.91**
市南区	Shinan District	32.22
市北区	Shibei District	66.13
李沧区	Licang District	99.10
崂山区	Laoshan District	395.76
黄岛区	Huangdao District	2129.09
城阳区	Chengyang District	583.65
即墨区	Jimo District	1921.39
胶州市	Jiaozhou	1323.67
平度市	Pingdu	3175.67
莱西市	Laixi	1568.23

注：2021年度土地变更调查结果。
Note：Survey results of land quality change in 2021.

2-7 第一、二、三、四、五、六、七次人口普查主要数据
MAIN DATA OF THE FIRST, SECOND, THIRD, FOURTH, FIFTH, SIXTH AND SEVENTH CENSUSES

项　目	Item	第一次人口普查 1st National Population Census	第二次人口普查 2nd National Population Census	第三次人口普查 3rd National Population Census	第四次人口普查 4th National Population Census	第五次人口普查 5th National Population Census	第六次人口普查 6th National Population Census	第七次人口普查 7th National Population Census
一、总人口（万人）	**Total Population (10000 persons)**	**91.68**	**138.34**	**422.76**	**666.40**	**749.42**	**871.51**	**1007.17**
按性别分	By Gender							
男（万人）	Male (10000 persons)	48.44	69.64	214.09	338.86	375.74	439.18	513.22
女（万人）	Female (10000 persons)	43.24	68.71	208.67	327.54	373.68	432.33	493.95
二、总户数（万户）	**Total Household (10000 households)**	**19.27**	**28.01**	**101.41**	**186.61**	**241.62**	**296.64**	**385.70**
家庭户（万户）	Family Household (10000 households)			101.09	185.56	232.70	282.43	362.32
平均家庭户规模（人）	Average Family Household Size (person)			4.07	3.49	2.97	2.79	2.55
三、民　族	**Ethnicity**							
民族个数（个）	Number of Ethnic Groups (unit)	14	16	25	41	51	53	56
汉族人口（万人）	Population of Han (10000 persons)	91.33	137.76	422.09	665.58	746.12	863.84	995.39
少数民族人口（万人）	Populaiton of Ethnic Minorities (10000 persons)	0.36	0.58	0.67	0.82	3.30	7.67	11.78
四、各种文化程度人口	**Population with Various Education Attainments**							
大学（万人）	College (10000 persons)		1.51	3.62	12.39	41.64	129.54	227.12
高中（万人）	Senior Secondary School (10000 persons)		4.86	34.82	68.42	111.40	150.82	176.69
初中（万人）	Junior Secondary School (10000 persons)		13.72	102.28	195.10	281.91	334.22	323.79
小学（万人）	Primary School (10000 persons)		51.25	144.52	236.34	206.91	170.77	187.26

2-8 计划生育情况（1978—2020 年）
FAMILY PLANNING SITUATION（1978 — 2020）

年 份 Year	已婚有生育能力的人数（人） Married and Fertile Persons（person）	节育人数（人） Persons under Birth Control（person）	节育率（%） Contraceptive Prevalence Rate（%）	四项手术人数（人） Persons Performed Four-operation（person）	#放环人数 Persons Set Rings
1978	694292	571077	82.25	125913	68475
1980	763226	673069	88.19	180979	70927
1985	1017649	929284	91.32	146742	67234
1990	1258232	1165216	92.61	149327	70964
1991	1319722	1219795	92.43	153970	77406
1992	1348503	1256271	93.16	90107	56226
1993	1380717	1271884	92.12	76783	45492
1994	1400425	1268378	90.57	73169	41482
1995	1427442	1285264	90.04	84099	52716
1996	1459465	1316516	90.21	84370	57648
1997	1482204	1340399	90.43	76579	55285
1998	1505499	1367648	90.84	74199	50526
1999	1523471	1378131	90.46	73663	44976
2000	1521331	1371447	90.15	74285	45999
2001	1514274	1360543	89.85	70205	43601
2002	1541855	1400145	90.81	50575	45453
2003	1518448	1354917	89.23	57458	47953
2004	1540706	1357703	88.04	52934	42859
2005	1590476	1417755	89.14	58097	49716
2006	1604665	1427785	88.98	51864	42457
2007	1595390	1426787	89.43	50074	41198
2008	1587344	1410426	88.85	120539	93291
2009	1623969	1418178	87.33	111084	100193
2010	1591103	1377726	86.59	78721	51794
2011	1581231	1355808	85.74	70823	48210
2012	1575996	1349572	85.63	62880	43021
2013	1527731	1293810	84.69	53252	30851
2014	1506274	1275142	84.66	34008	12827
2015	1475887	1226439	83.10	34879	9108
2016	1456953	1183221	81.21	36449	4474
2017	1439008	1188307	82.58	20905	4669
2018	1406047	1159775	82.48	17786	5097
2019	1375598	1141584	82.92	12582	3959
2020	1310212	1109885	84.71	342553	339219

注：2021 年起，卫健部门的省报表已不再统计以上指标。
Note：From 2021, the provincial report of the health department would have no longer counted the above indicators.

2-9 分市、区计划生育情况（2022年）
FAMILY PLANNING SITUATION BY REGION（2022）

市、区名称	Region	计划生育率（%）Fertility Rate（%）	计划内出生（人）Birth within the Plan（person）		计划外出生（人）Birth without the Plan（person）		多胎（人）Third Birth and Above（person）
			一胎 First Birth	二胎 Second Birth	一胎 First Birth	二胎 Second Birth	
全　市	**Whole Municipality**	**99.51**	**26726**	**21024**	**80**	**28**	**3690**
市南区	Shinan District	99.69	1605	864	5	2	87
市北区	Shibei District	99.78	2894	1561	3	4	145
李沧区	Licang District	99.74	1564	1382	1	2	127
崂山区	Laoshan District	99.68	1376	721	3	2	90
黄岛区	Huangdao District	99.52	4576	3951	11	4	322
城阳区	Chengyang District	99.76	3224	2326	5	1	678
即墨区	Jimo District	99.68	3599	2898	4	1	587
胶州市	Jiaozhou	99.33	2578	2255	11	2	594
平度市	Pingdu	99.25	3391	3361	18	3	727
莱西市	Laixi	98.85	1919	1705	19	7	333

主要统计指标解释

常住人口　指经常居住在某一地区的人口，主要包括居住在本乡镇街道且户口在本乡镇街道或户口待定的人，居住在本乡镇街道且离开户口登记地所在的乡镇街道半年以上的人，户口在本乡镇街道且外出不满半年或在境外工作学习的人。

户籍人口　指公民依照《中华人民共和国户口登记条例》已在其经常居住地的公安户籍管理机关登记了常住户口的人。

城镇化率　指一个国家（地区）城镇的常住人口占该国家（地区）常住总人口的比例。计算公式为：

$$城镇化率=\frac{城镇常住人口}{常住总人口}\times 100\%$$

Explanatory Notes on Main Statistical Indicators

Permanent Population　refers to the population that often resides in a certain place, mainly consisting of the people who live in the streets of the township and have registered in the streets or whose residence-registration is to be determined, the people who reside in the streets of the town and have been away from their registration areas for more than half a year, and the people who registered in the streets of the township and have gone out for less than half a year or have worked and studied abroad.

Registered Population　refers to those who have registered their permanent residence with the public security household registration management authority in the place of their habitual residence in accordance with the Regulations of the People's Republic of China on Household Registration.

Urbanization rate　refers to the proportion of the resident population of cities and towns in a country (region) to the total resident population of the country (region). The calculation formula is.

$$\text{Urbanization rate}=\frac{\text{Permanent Population of a Town}}{\text{Resident Population}}\times 100\%$$

就业与工资 3

EMPLOYMENT AND WAGES

简 要 说 明

一、本篇资料的主要内容

本篇资料主要反映全市单位从业人员、工资总额和平均工资等方面的资料。

二、本篇资料的来源

全市单位从业人员、工资总额和平均工资来源于劳动工资统计年报，由市统计局人口就业和社会科技文化统计处整理提供。

Brief Introduction

Ⅰ. Main Content

The data in this chapter mainly reflects the data on the employees, total wages and average wages of the city's units.

Ⅱ. Source of Data

The employees, total wages and average wages of the city's units are derived from the annual labor wage statistics report, which is compiled and provided by the Population Employment and Social Science, Technology and Culture Statistics Department of Qingdao Statistics Bureau.

3-1 社会就业人数（1978—2022 年）
SOCIAL EMPLOYMENT（1978—2022）

单位：万人（10000 persons）

年份 Year	合计 Total	第一产业 Primary Industry	第二产业 Secondary Industry	第三产业 Tertiary Industry
1978	256.7	157.4	65.6	33.7
1979	265.6	156.1	72.2	37.3
1980	270.1	153.0	77.3	39.8
1981	278.9	153.6	82.1	43.2
1982	282.7	151.1	86.2	45.4
1983	289.6	156.4	85.0	48.1
1984	304.2	149.2	97.7	57.4
1985	315.3	149.2	104.5	61.7
1986	326.4	149.6	112.1	64.6
1987	334.8	149.9	120.2	64.7
1988	336.5	147.6	123.2	65.7
1989	344.2	152.5	122.1	69.6
1990	352.8	156.5	123.3	73.1
1991	361.2	161.9	124.3	74.9
1992	370.3	161.7	127.8	80.8
1993	365.7	160.5	128.8	76.4
1994	367.6	157.1	129.4	81.2
1995	374.2	155.4	132.4	86.4
1996	381.5	152.2	137.1	92.2
1997	388.7	155.2	138.1	95.3
1998	393.1	154.8	138.6	99.7

注：第七次全国人口普查后，对 2000 年至 2020 年历年社会就业人数进行修订。
Note：The number of social employment in the calendar years from 2000 to 2020 has been revised after the seventh national census.

3-1 续表
Continued

年份 Year	合计 Total	第一产业 Primary Industry	第二产业 Secondary Industry	第三产业 Tertiary Industry
1999	396.1	150.3	142.0	103.8
2000	436.1	158.7	148.0	129.4
2001	439.5	146.9	156.2	136.4
2002	447.8	131.5	166.7	149.6
2003	450.8	123.1	168.4	159.3
2004	459.6	114.2	180.9	164.5
2005	467.4	103.7	195.3	168.4
2006	475.2	99.8	203.5	171.9
2007	481.5	97.4	207.3	176.8
2008	484.8	96.6	208.3	179.9
2009	489.3	98.3	205.1	185.9
2010	504.9	98.3	209.2	197.4
2011	510.8	98.2	210.4	202.2
2012	515.5	96.6	211.6	207.3
2013	517.5	97.4	210.3	209.8
2014	521.3	96.0	203.5	221.8
2015	523.7	94.9	201.8	227.0
2016	523.5	93.4	198.8	231.3
2017	524.3	88.4	198.1	237.8
2018	525.3	85.1	191.2	249.0
2019	523.6	82.2	200.5	240.9
2020	525.6	82.0	167.7	275.9
2021	527.7	82.3	168.3	277.1
2022	528.0	79.2	169.0	279.8

3-2　分市、区社会就业人数（2022年）
NUMBER OF EMPLOYED PERSONS BY REGION（2022）

单位：万人（10000 persons）

市、区名称	Region	2022年
全　市	**Whole Municipality**	**528.00**
市南区	Shinan District	25.39
市北区	Shibei District	57.51
李沧区	Licang District	38.71
崂山区	Laoshan District	26.28
黄岛区	Huangdao District	99.99
城阳区	Chengyang District	58.30
即墨区	Jimo District	70.15
胶州市	Jiaozhou	51.86
平度市	Pingdu	62.21
莱西市	Laixi	37.60

3-3 主要年份全市单位就业人员人数
MAJOR YEAR'S NUMBER OF EMPLOYEES IN THE CITY

单位：万人（10000 persons）

年份 Year	合计 Total	#市区 Urban Area	#国有单位 State-owned Units	#集体单位 Collective-owned Units	其他所有制单位 Other Ownership Units
1949	14.8	13.4	9.3	5.5	
1952	23.4	20.1	18.3	5.1	
1957	29.7	24.5	24.1	5.6	
1962	32.3	26.8	24.5	7.8	
1965	36.7	30.6	26.8	9.9	
1970	45.6	37.4	32.2	13.4	
1975	53.4	43.5	38.0	15.4	
1978	70.7	54.5	49.2	21.5	
1980	79.2	61.5	55.0	24.2	
1985	88.8	66.7	59.8	28.9	0.1
1988	98.2	70.0	66.7	31.2	0.3
1990	103.2	70.6	69.5	32.9	0.8
1991	105.4	78.4	71.5	32.5	1.4
1992	108.2	80.4	73.6	32.8	1.8
1993	109.4	80.8	75.3	29.5	4.6
1994	110.1	80.2	72.4	28.3	9.4
1995	111.6	80.2	72.4	27.5	11.7
1996	118.4	81.1	71.6	26.0	20.8
1997	117.1	78.1	69.0	22.6	25.5
1998	116.2	75.6	64.2	19.0	33.0

注：1. 2004 年以前为城镇单位职工人数。
2. 2013 年统计口径变化，国有单位、集体单位数据与上年不可比。
3. 2019 年统计口径变化，全市单位就业人员人数为全市城镇非私营口径。
4. 2020 年劳动工资改革，单位就业人数不再分登记注册类型。

Notes：1. Before 2004, the data refer to number of staff and workers in urban units.
2. Because of the adjustment about the statistics system, the data of State-owned Units and Collective-owned Units since 2013 are not fully comparable with historical statistics.
3. The statistical caliber changes in 2019, the number of employees in the city's units is the city's urban non-private caliber.
4. In 2020, the labor and wage reform will no longer divide the number of employees into registration types.

3-3 续表
Continued

年份 Year	合计 Total	#市区 Urban Area	#国有单位 State-owned Units	#集体单位 Collective-owned Units	其他所有制单位 Other Ownership Units
1999	119.0	78.3	60.4	16.6	42.0
2000	118.3	76.6	57.6	14.2	46.5
2001	117.5	75.1	53.2	12.2	52.1
2002	119.1	75.2	49.5	10.3	59.3
2003	118.0	74.3	47.2	8.9	61.9
2004	207.1	111.1	43.7	18.0	145.4
2005	224.3	122.3	43.9	18.2	162.2
2006	243.2	133.7	41.7	16.2	185.3
2007	249.8	137.3	45.1	17.9	186.8
2008	254.1	140.9	44.4	15.4	194.3
2009	260.5	145.6	44.4	14.6	201.5
2010	269.4	151.1	44.6	15.1	209.7
2011	275.9	156.5	44.3	14.7	216.9
2012	283.2	162.1	44.0	13.8	225.4
2013	293.7	184.1	37.8	5.4	250.5
2014	303.0	191.4	36.7	4.9	261.4
2015	309.2	192.4	35.8	4.6	268.8
2016	315.6	196.4	35.5	4.7	275.4
2017	321.4	249.1	35.1	4.6	281.7
2018	330.4	258.3	34.7	2.0	293.7
2019	146.6	118.5	34.1	1.1	111.4
2020	147.7				
2021	147.7				
2022	144.4				

3-4　全市城镇非私营单位国民经济各行业就业人员人数（2022 年）

NUMBER OF EMPLOYED PERSONS IN NON-PRIVATE UNITS OF THE CITY BY SECTOR（2022）

单位：万人（10000 persons）

行　业	Sector	2022 年		2021 年	
		合计 Total	女性 Female	合计 Total	女性 Female
总　计	**Total**	**144.4**	**58.8**	**147.7**	**61.2**
1. 农、林、牧、渔业	Agriculture，Forestry，Animal Husbandry and Fishery	0.0	0.0	0.1	0.0
2. 采矿业	Mining	0.0	0.0	0.0	0.0
3. 制造业	Manufacturing	44.1	15.1	45.0	15.6
4. 电力、热力、燃气及水生产和供应业	Electricity，Heat，Gas and Water Production and Supply Industry	2.1	0.5	2.2	0.6
5. 建筑业	Construction	11.9	1.9	12.2	2.0
6. 批发和零售业	Wholesale and Retail Trades	8.6	4.8	8.6	4.7
7. 交通运输、仓储和邮政业	Transport，Storage and Post	9.3	2.7	9.0	2.7
8. 住宿和餐饮业	Hotels and Catering Services	3.0	1.6	3.0	1.6
9. 信息传输、软件和信息技术服务业	Information Transmission, Software and Information Technology Services	3.0	1.3	2.8	1.2
10. 金融业	Financial Industry	8.8	5.5	11.3	7.3
11. 房地产业	Real Estate	4.9	2.0	5.1	2.1
12. 租赁和商务服务业	Leasing and Business Services	3.5	1.5	3.4	1.4
13. 科学研究和技术服务业	Scientific Research and Technical Services	5.4	1.8	5.5	1.8
14. 水利、环境和公共设施管理业	Management of Water Conservancy，Environment and Public Facilities	2.3	0.7	2.2	0.8
15. 居民服务、修理和其他服务业	Residents Service，RePair and Other Services	0.5	0.2	0.5	0.2
16. 教育	Education	13.2	8.6	14.2	9.0
17. 卫生和社会工作	Health and Social Work	8.9	6.2	8.6	6.1
18. 文化、体育和娱乐业	Culture，Sports and Entertainment Industry	1.2	0.5	1.3	0.6
19. 公共管理、社会保障和社会组织	Public Management，Social Security and Social Organization	13.4	3.8	12.6	3.5

3-5 全市就业人员工资总额、平均工资（1978—2022 年）

TOTAL WAGES AND AVERAGE WAGE OF CITYWIDE FULL-TIME EMPLOYEES（1978—2022）

年份 Year	工资总额（亿元） Total Wage Bill（100 million yuan）		平均工资（元） Average Wage（yuan）	
	全社会单位 All Units	其中：非私营单位 of which：Non-private Units	全社会单位 All Units	其中：非私营单位 of which：Non-private Units
1978		4.0		584
1979		4.8		662
1980		6.0		782
1981		6.3		778
1982		6.6		785
1983		6.9		809
1984		9.0		1041
1985		9.6		1103
1986		11.8		1311
1987		14.2		1519
1988		18.0		1862
1989		20.7		2120
1990		24.4		2400
1991		26.4		2553
1992		31.8		2970
1993		40.4		3694
1994		59.5		5455
1995		68.3		6164
1996		78.2		6640
1997		82.5		7030
1998		87.2		7518
1999		100.1		8405
2000		120.4		10072
2001		135.8		11426
2002		153.8		12839
2003	225.6	160.3	12597	15335
2004	280.5	193.4	13932	17190
2005	359.5	242.8	16015	20022
2006	445.6	292.0	18574	23457
2007	518.1	338.6	21419	27083
2008	578.7	371.9	23296	30233
2009	638.1	393.2	25396	33258
2010	738.0	446.8	28549	37805
2011	877.5	522.0	32763	43077
2012	1044.3	613.1	37399	49052
2013	1251.7	785.7	42688	55363
2014	1456.0	890.5	48453	62104
2015	1644.4	993.0	53715	69465
2016	1852.7	1088.5	58551	75803
2017	2034.7	1193.6	63047	82177
2018	2251.7	1290.8	68197	89525
2019		1438.3		98604
2020		1560.4		106011
2021		1700.4		116477
2022		1800.0		124061

注：1. 2003 年以前为职工工资总额、平均工资。
2. 2015 年以前为在岗职工工资总额、平均工资。
3. 自 2019 年统计口径变化，无全部单位工资数据。

Notes：1. The data before 2003 refer to the total wage bill and average wage of stall and workers.
2. It was the total salary and average salary of the on-spot staff before 2015.
3. Since the statistical caliber change in 2019, there is no wage data for all units.

3-6 全市就业人员工资总额、平均工资指数（1978-2022 年）

INDICES OF TOTAL WAGES AND AVERAGE WAGE OF CITYWIDE FULL-TIME EMPLOYEES（1978-2022）

年份 Year	工资总额指数 Total Wage Bill Indices		平均工资指数 Average Wage Indices	
	全社会单位 All Units	其中：非私营单位 of which：Non-private Units	全社会单位 All Units	其中：非私营单位 of which：Non-private Units
1978		120.80		104.66
1979		119.53		113.36
1980		123.95		118.13
1981		106.71		99.49
1982		103.80		100.90
1983		104.14		103.06
1984		130.64		128.68
1985		107.11		105.96
1986		123.22		118.86
1987		120.10		115.87
1988		126.48		122.58
1989		115.29		113.86
1990		117.66		113.21
1991		108.28		106.38
1992		120.26		116.33
1993		127.09		124.38
1994		147.46		147.67
1995		114.76		113.00
1996		114.54		107.72
1997		105.50		105.87
1998		105.64		106.94
1999		114.81		111.80
2000		120.29		119.83
2001		112.77		113.44
2002		113.31		112.37
2003		108.84		110.30
2004	124.34	120.65	110.60	112.10
2005	128.16	125.54	114.95	116.47
2006	123.95	120.26	115.98	117.16
2007	116.27	115.96	115.32	115.46
2008	111.70	109.83	108.76	111.63
2009	110.26	105.73	109.01	110.01
2010	115.66	113.63	112.42	113.67
2011	118.90	116.83	114.76	113.95
2012	119.01	117.45	114.15	113.87
2013	119.86	128.15	114.14	112.87
2014	116.32	113.34	113.50	112.18
2015	112.94	111.51	110.86	111.85
2016	110.25	106.49	109.71	110.33
2017	109.82	109.66	107.68	108.41
2018	110.66	108.14	108.17	108.94
2019		111.43		110.14
2020		108.49		107.51
2021		108.97		109.87
2022		105.85		106.51

注：1. 2004 年以前为职工工资总额、平均工资指数。
　　2. 2015 年以前为在岗职工工资总额、平均工资。
　　3. 自 2019 年统计口径变化，无全部单位工资数据。

Notes：1. The data before 2004 refer to the indices of total wage of stall and workers.
　　2. It was the total salary and average salary of the on-spot staff before 2015.
　　3. Since the statistical caliber change in 2019, there is no wage data for all units.

3-7 城镇非私营和城镇私营单位分行业就业人员平均工资（2022 年）

AVERAGE WAGES OF EMPLOYED PERSONS IN URBAN NON-PRIVATE AND URBAN PRIVATE UNITS BY SECTOR（2022）

行 业	Sector	非私营单位（元）Non-private Units（yuan）	私营单位（元）Private Units（yuan）
总 计	**Total**	**124061**	**64349**
（一）农、林、牧、渔业	Agriculture, Forestry, Animal Husbandry and Fishery	95806	49435
（二）采矿业	Mining	94447	57464
（三）制造业	Manufacturing	98175	66486
（四）电力、热力、燃气及水生产和供应业	Electricity, Heat, Gas and Water Production and Supply Industry	122696	71513
（五）建筑业	Construction	97981	67000
（六）批发和零售业	Wholesale and Retail Trades	100518	59169
（七）交通运输、仓储和邮政业	Transport, Storage and Post	122701	69860
（八）住宿和餐饮业	Hotels and Catering Services	64056	42987
（九）信息传输、软件和信息技术服务业	Information Transmission, Software and Information Technology Services	169403	85395
（十）金融业	Financial Industry	147522	89969
（十一）房地产业	Real Estate	112716	59653
（十二）租赁和商务服务业	Leasing and Business Services	95417	65746
（十三）科学研究和技术服务业	Scientific Research and Technical Services	152647	72783
（十四）水利、环境和公共设施管理业	Management of Water Conservancy, Environment and Public Facilities	69085	42308
（十五）居民服务、修理和其他服务业	Residents Service, RePair and Other Services	81913	48178
（十六）教育	Education	179110	64751
（十七）卫生和社会工作	Health and Social Work	169151	74837
（十八）文化、体育和娱乐业	Culture, Sports and Entertainment Industry	138352	59404
（十九）公共管理、社会保障和社会组织	Public Management, Social Security and Social Organization	164933	

3-8 城镇非私营和城镇私营单位分市区就业人员平均工资（2022年）
AVERAGE WAGES OF EMPLOYED PERSONS IN URBAN NON-PRIVATE AND URBAN PRIVATE UNITS BY DISTRICTS（2022）

市、区名称	Region	非私营单位（元） Non-private Units （yuan）	私营单位（元） Private Units （yuan）
全　市	**Whole Municipality**	**124061**	**64349**
市南区	Shinan District	135398	72887
市北区	Shibei District	136342	69469
李沧区	Licang District	107562	60809
崂山区	Laoshan District	159887	75553
黄岛区	Huangdao District	120499	62315
城阳区	Chengyang District	122392	68385
即墨区	Jimo District	98609	59302
胶州市	Jiaozhou	98777	61560
平度市	Pingdu	99216	53213
莱西市	Laixi	89331	60002

主要统计指标解释

单位从业人员 指报告期末最后一日24时在本单位中工作，并取得工资或其他形式劳动报酬的人员数。该指标为时点指标，不包括最后一日当天及以前已经与单位解除劳动合同关系的人员，是在岗职工、劳务派遣人员及其他就业人员之和。就业人员不包括：

（1）离开本单位仍保留劳动关系，并定期领取生活费的人员；

（2）在本单位实习的各类在校学生；

（3）本单位因劳务外包而使用的人员。

在岗职工 指在本单位工作且与本单位签订劳动合同，并由单位支付各项工资和社会保险、住房公积金的人员，以及上述人员中由于学习、病伤、产假等原因暂未工作仍由单位支付工资的人员。在岗职工还包括：

（1）应订立劳动合同而未订立劳动合同人员（如使用的农村户籍人员）；

（2）处于试用期人员；

（3）编制外招用的人员；

（4）派往外单位工作，但工资仍由本单位发放的人员（如挂职锻炼、外派工作等情况）。

工资总额 指根据《关于工资总额组成的规定》（1990年1月1日国家统计局发布的一号令）进行修订，在报告期内（季度或年度）直接支付给本单位全部就业人员的劳动报酬总额。包括计时工资、计件工资、奖金、津贴和补贴、加班加点工资、特殊情况下支付的工资，是在岗职工工资总额、劳务派遣人员工资总额和其他就业人员工资总额之和。

工资总额是税前工资，包括单位从个人工资中直接为其代扣或代缴的房费、水费、电费、住房公积金和社会保险基金个人缴纳部分等。

工资总额不论是计入成本的还是不计入成本的，不论是以货币形式支付的还是以实物形式支付的，均应列入工资总额的计算范围。

平均工资 指单位就业人员在一定时期内平均每人所得的工资额。它表明一定时期工资收入的高低程度，是反映就业人员工资水平的主要指标。

Explanatory Notes on Main Statistical Indicators

Employed Persons in Units refers to the number of employees who works in the institution or company and gets salary or other form of labor reward at 24:00 of the last day of the report period. This is a time-point indicator which is the total of on-spot staff, labor dispatched personnel and other employees, excluding persons that have released the employment contract with the institution or company on the last day or before. The following are not deemed as Jobholders：

（1）Persons that keep the employment relations and get regular living expenses after leaving the institution or company.

（2）All kinds of students who intern in our company.

（3）Personnel that uses by the institution or company in labour outsourcing.

On-spot staff refers to the employees that works for and signs the employment contract with the institution or company, and relevant salary, social insurance and house funding are paid by the institution or company, and the persons of the previous employees that are not working but still gets salary from the institution or company due to the reason of learning, injury, maternity leave, etc. It also includes the following:

(1) Employees who shall sign the employment contract with institution or company but not signed (for example, employees of rural household registration).

(2) Employees that are still in probation period.

(3) Employees that are recruited outside the authorized size.

(4) Employees that are sent to other institution or company but the salaries are still paid by the institution or company (such as onsite training and labour dispatching).

Total salary refers to total payment for labour made directly to all jobholders of the institution or company within the report period (quarterly or annually) revised according to Regulations on Constitution of Total Salary, Order No. 1 released by National Bureau of Statistics on January 1, 1990, including hourly wage, piece wage, bonus, allowance and subsidy, overtime wage, and wages paid under special situations. It is also the total volume of on-spot staff, labour dispatching staff and other employment.

Total salary is the pre-tax salary, including the expenses of housing, water, power and the personal part of house funding and social insurance funds, which has been withheld and paid by the institution or company from personal salaries.

No matter it is credited into cost or not, no matter it is paid in currency or in kind, all total salary shall be categorized as total salary.

Average salary refers to the total salary per capita of employees of the institution or company within the certain period, which is the major indicator of the salary level of employees and the level of salary income of the certain salary.

固定资产投资 4

INVESTMENT IN FIXED ASSETS

简 要 说 明

一、本篇资料的主要内容

本篇资料主要反映全市固定资产投资及房地产开发方面的情况，主要包括固定资产投资的规模、结构、资金来源和房地产开发投资、施竣工及销售情况等方面的资料

二、本篇资料的来源

本篇资料来源于固定资产投资及房地产开发投资统计年报，由市统计局固定资产投资统计处整理提供。

Brief Introduction

Ⅰ. Main Content

Data in this chapter show the basic conditions of investment in fixed assets and real estate development of the whole city, mainly including the total investment in fixed assets, the structure of investment, the resources of investment and investment in real estate development, construction, completion and sales, etc.

Ⅱ. Source of Data

Data in this chapter are based on the annual report on investment in fixed assets and real estate development, and provided by the Division of Investment and Construction Statistics of Qingdao Municipal Bureau of Statistics.

4-1 主要年份固定资产投资（不含农户）

MAJOP YEAP'S INVESTMENT IN FIXED ASSETS（EXCLUDING RURAL HOUSEHOLDS）

单位：万元（10000 yuan）

年 份 Year	固定资产投资总额（不含农户） Total Investment in Fixed Assets （Excluding Rural Households）	按用途分 Grouped by Use		
		生产性投资 Productive Investment	非生产性投资 Non-Productive Investment	#住宅投资 Investment in Residential Buildings
1949	16	12	4	3
1952	3097	1368	1729	1007
1957	5923	3947	1976	1151
1962	2747	2049	698	192
1965	5481	4155	1326	375
1970	6100	5813	287	154
1975	15839	13548	2381	1064
1978	29660	23499	6161	3203
1980	47499	33865	13634	9335
1985	107421	60643	73424	19058
1990	284576	210453	74123	38898
1991	349031	256633	92398	51898
1992	583068	420748	162320	83844
1993	953274	511684	441590	162419
1994	1329716	728532	601184	324094
1995	1648281	925194	723087	390206
1996	1610562	972398	638164	285412

注：1. 固定资产投资（不含农户）指城镇和农村各种登记注册类型的企业、事业、行政单位及城镇个体户进行的计划总投资 500 万元及 500 万元以上的建设项目投资和房地产开发投资，包含原口径的城镇固定资产投资加上农村企事业组织项目投资，该口径自 2011 年起开始使用。（以下相关表同）

2. 因 2004 年以来数据有调整，故表中数据不可比。

Notes：1. Investment in Fixed Assets（excluding rural households）refers to the construction project investment and real estate development investment with a planned total investment of 5 million yuan or more made by various registered enterprises, institutions, administrative units and urban self-employed individuals in both urban and rural areas, including the urban fixed asset investment plus project investment of rural enterprises and institutions according to the original statistical caliber that has been used since 2011.（The following related tables are the same.）

2. The data since 2004 are not comparable with other data because of the adjustment.

4-1 续表 1
Continued

单位：万元（10000 yuan）

年 份 Year	固定资产投资总额（不含农户）Total Investment in Fixed Assets (Excluding Rural Households)	按用途分 Grouped by Use		
		生产性投资 Productive Investment	非生产性投资 Non-Productive Investment	#住宅投资 Investment in Residential Buildings
1997	1611902	932207	679695	278951
1998	1909711	1125821	783890	316999
1999	2205891	1246328	959563	421151
2000	2426820	1311538	1115282	470963
2001	2934728	1487762	1446966	729181
2002	3683623	1962588	1721035	765030
2003	5475526	3023930	2451596	1038304
2004	9845646	6336279	3509367	1608738
2005	14032960	9172206	4860754	1841644
2006	14856894	9214578	5642316	2222733
2007	16353636	10231673	6121963	2720970
2008	20190098	12443179	7746919	3315538
2009	24588889	13852653	10736236	3831976
2010	30224785	16207885	14016900	5609189
2011	35025382	18622819	16402563	5707625
2012	41539146	24246803	17292343	6689114
2013	50278649	30996768	19281881	7220432
2014	57660308	32913906	24746402	7311090
2015	65556685	41402714	24153971	7569123
2016	74547006	44588200	29958806	9561782
2017	77770902	41719893	36051009	9255095

4-1 续表 2
Continued

单位：万元（10000 yuan）

年 份 Year	按构成分 Grouped by Composition of Funds			按资金来源分 Grouped by Sources of Funds			
	建筑安装工程 Construction and Installation	设备工器具购置 Purchase of Equipment and Instruments	其他费用 Others	国家投资 State Investment	国内贷款 Domestic Loans	利用外资 Foreign Investment	自筹及其他 Self-raising Fund and Others
1949	11	3	2	16			
1952	2146	870	81	1512			1585
1957	2853	2773	297	3816			2107
1962	1631	984	132	2205			542
1965	3346	1859	276	4451			1030
1970	3136	2835	129	2721			3379
1975	7489	8133	217	9378	1362		5099
1978	19968	9124	568	16828	1601		11231
1980	30993	15541	965	10371	12925	1420	22783
1985	64665	35100	7656	17377	35888	1136	53020
1990	167731	91305	25540	24687	91895	23688	144306
1991	196212	108929	43890	22615	131676	38325	156415
1992	304060	208384	70624	22660	213217	89130	258061
1993	600011	225555	127708	23736	208672	94469	626397
1994	842809	272126	214781	26062	318334	221265	764055
1995	1020484	385934	241863	25683	379198	328124	915276
1996	929735	458284	222543	35639	444443	310722	819758
1997	875057	485122	251723	27928	297089	363789	923096
1998	1034500	574852	300359	67762	491812	170709	1179428

4-1 续表 3
Continued

单位：万元（10000 yuan）

年 份 Year	按构成分 Grouped by Composition of Funds			按资金来源分 Grouped by Sources of Funds			
	建筑安装工程 Construction and Installation	设备工器具购置 Purchase of Equipment and Instruments	其他费用 Others	国家投资 State Investment	国内贷款 Domestic Loans	利用外资 Foreign Investment	自筹及其他 Self-raising Fund and Others
1999	1456473	459596	289822	128603	584120	145589	1347579
2000	1476397	652640	297783	75978	489697	164175	1806238
2001	1781235	744549	408944	93491	620562	217526	2157787
2002	2328492	796685	558446	78775	719677	411704	2831288
2003	3544790	1133333	797403	127861	989178	722644	4237643
2004	6413046	2312139	1120461	85549	1100297	1016145	8245272
2005	8949231	3141732	1941997	136632	1250343	1850921	11540604
2006	8818614	3668191	2370089	391315	2126523	1662897	11856506
2007	9981666	4171878	2200092	215649	2427031	1788056	13109824
2008	11795435	5907195	2487468	322484	3309471	1951468	15855082
2009	14911874	5869214	3807801	778090	4217265	1593287	21555685
2010	18725922	6362880	5135983	1305737	5881886	2135736	27898294
2011	22865421	7521441	4638520	1640702	5871709	1766278	33579182
2012	26080239	8601282	6857625	1324159	5484459	1561597	37356847
2013	33237368	9969777	7071504	1959340	8154829	1528585	49552883
2014	39006113	11640126	7014069	1404667	7452983	1181541	55024776
2015	42893643	15972153	6690889	2067396	7249574	1098178	62458544
2016	45915827	16425993	8789790	1788103	14203650	903773	66069945
2017	55647641	10977494	11145767	2257927	14569701	641216	65055089

4-2 主要年份固定资产投资构成(以投资总额为 100)

COMPOSITION OF MAJOR YEAR'S INVESTMENT IN FIXED ASSETS (TOTAL INVESTMENT=100)

年份 Year	按用途分 Grouped by Use		
	生产性投资 Productive Investment	非生产性投资 Non-Productive Investment	#住宅投资占非生产性比重 Percentage of Investment in Residential Buildings to Non-Productive Investment
1949	75.00	25.00	75.00
1952	44.17	55.83	58.24
1957	66.64	33.36	58.25
1962	74.59	25.41	27.51
1965	75.81	24.19	28.28
1970	95.30	4.70	53.66
1975	84.97	15.03	44.69
1978	79.23	20.77	51.99
1980	71.30	28.70	68.47
1985	56.45	43.55	40.74
1990	73.95	26.05	52.50
1991	73.53	26.47	56.17
1992	72.16	27.84	51.65
1993	53.68	46.32	36.78
1994	54.79	45.21	53.91
1995	56.10	43.90	54.00
1996	60.40	39.60	44.70
1997	57.80	42.20	41.00
1998	59.00	41.00	16.60

4-2 续表 1
Continued

年 份 Year	按用途分 Grouped by Use		
	生产性投资 Productive Investment	非生产性投资 Non-Productive Investment	#住宅投资占非生产性比重 Percentage of Investment in Residential Buildings to Non-Productive Investment
1999	56.50	43.50	19.10
2000	54.00	46.00	19.40
2001	50.70	49.30	50.40
2002	53.30	46.70	44.50
2003	55.20	44.80	42.40
2004	64.40	35.60	45.80
2005	65.40	34.60	37.90
2006	62.00	38.00	39.40
2007	62.60	37.40	44.40
2008	61.60	38.40	42.80
2009	56.30	43.70	35.70
2010	53.62	46.38	40.02
2011	53.17	46.83	34.80
2012	58.37	41.63	38.68
2013	61.65	38.35	37.45
2014	57.08	42.92	29.54
2015	63.16	36.84	31.34
2016	59.81	40.19	31.92
2017	53.64	46.36	25.67

4-2 续表 2
Continued

年份 Year	按构成分 Grouped by Composition of Funds			按资金来源分 Grouped by Sources of Funds			
	建筑安装工程 Construction and Installation	设备工器具购置 Purchase of Equipment and Instruction	其他费用 Others	国家投资 State Investment	国内贷款 Domestic Loans	利用外资 Foreign Investment	自筹及其他 Self-raising Fund and Others
1949	68.8	18.8	12.5	100.0			
1952	69.3	28.1	2.6	48.8			51.2
1957	48.2	46.8	5.0	64.4			35.6
1962	59.4	35.8	4.8	80.3			19.7
1965	61.1	33.9	5.0	81.2			18.8
1970	51.4	46.5	2.1	44.6			55.4
1975	47.3	51.4	1.4	59.2	8.6		32.2
1978	67.3	30.8	1.9	56.7	5.4		37.9
1980	65.3	32.7	2.0	21.8	27.2	3.0	48.0
1985	60.2	32.7	7.1	16.2	33.4	1.1	49.4
1990	58.9	32.1	9.0	8.7	32.3	8.3	50.7
1991	56.2	31.2	12.6	6.5	37.7	11.0	44.8
1992	52.2	35.7	12.1	3.9	36.6	15.3	44.3
1993	62.9	23.7	13.4	2.5	21.9	9.9	65.7
1994	63.4	20.5	16.2	2.0	23.9	16.6	57.5
1995	61.9	23.4	14.7	1.6	23.0	19.9	55.5
1996	57.7	28.5	13.8	2.2	27.6	19.3	50.9
1997	54.3	30.1	15.6	1.7	18.4	22.6	57.3
1998	54.2	20.8	15.7	3.5	25.8	8.9	61.8
1999	66.0	20.8	13.2	5.8	26.5	6.6	61.1
2000	60.8	26.9	12.3	3.1	20.2	6.8	74.4

4-2 续表 3
Continued

年　份 Year	按构成分 Grouped by Composition of Funds			按资金来源分 Grouped by Sources of Funds			
	建筑安装工程 Construction and Installation	设备工器具购置 Purchase of Equipment and Instruction	其他费用 Others	国家投资 State Investment	国内贷款 Domestic Loans	利用外资 Foreign Investment	自筹及其他 Self-raising Fund and Others
2001	60.7	25.4	13.9	3.0	20.1	7.0	69.9
2002	63.2	21.6	15.2	1.9	17.8	10.2	70.1
2003	64.7	20.7	14.6	2.1	16.3	11.9	69.7
2004	65.1	23.5	11.4	0.8	10.6	9.7	78.9
2005	63.8	22.4	13.8	0.9	8.5	12.5	78.1
2006	59.4	24.7	15.9	2.4	13.3	10.4	73.9
2007	61.0	25.5	13.5	1.2	13.8	10.2	74.8
2008	58.4	29.3	12.3	1.5	15.4	9.1	74.0
2009	60.6	23.9	15.5	2.8	15.0	5.6	76.6
2010	62.0	21.0	17.0	3.5	15.8	5.7	75.0
2011	65.3	21.5	13.3	3.8	13.7	4.1	78.4
2012	62.8	20.7	16.5	2.9	12.0	3.4	81.7
2013	66.1	19.8	14.1	3.2	13.3	2.5	81.0
2014	67.6	20.2	12.2	2.2	11.5	1.8	84.6
2015	65.4	24.4	10.2	2.8	10.0	1.5	85.7
2016	61.6	22.0	11.8	2.2	17.1	1.1	79.6
2017	71.6	14.1	14.3	2.7	17.7	0.8	78.8
2018	68.8	7.8	23.4	2.9	15.2	0.4	81.5
2019	65.3	7.0	27.7	1.8	16.2	1.3	80.7
2020	63.8	5.9	30.3	3.8	14.9	0.8	80.5
2021	71.5	6.2	22.3	4.0	11.2	0.2	84.6
2022	70.5	7.9	21.6	6.5	11.2	0.1	82.2

4-3 按三次产业分固定资产投资（不含农户）增速（2022 年）
GROWTH RATE OF INVESTMENT IN FIXED ASSETS （EXCLUDING RURAL HOUSEHOLDS） BY THREE INDUSTRIES（2022）

单位：%

指　标	Indicator	2022 年
总　计	**Total**	**4.5**
第一产业	Primary Industry	1.0
第二产业	Secondary Industry	15.6
#工业	Industry	15.5
第三产业	Tertiary Industry	0.8

4-4 分市、区固定资产投资（不含农户）增速(2022 年)
GROWTH RATE OF INVESTMENT IN FIXED ASSETS （EXCLUDING RURAL HOUSEHOLDS） BY REGION（2022）

单位：%

市、区名称	Region	固定资产投资（不含农户）增速 Growth Rate of Investment in Fixed Assets （Excluding Rural Households）	#房地产开发投资增速 Real Estate Development Investment Growth Rate
全　市	**Whole Municipality**	**4.5**	**-9.7**
市南区	Shinan District	4.5	63.3
市北区	Shibei District	15.9	-5.8
李沧区	Licang District	-8.6	8.2
崂山区	Laoshan District	18.2	1.0
黄岛区	Huangdao District	5.1	-5.4
城阳区	Chengyang District	-7.7	-12.4
即墨区	Jimo District	4.9	-14.9
胶州市	Jiaozhou	9.1	-30.5
平度市	Pingdu	10.2	-38.2
莱西市	Laixi	18.0	-18.5

4-5 固定资产投资（不含农户）(2022 年)
INVESTMENT IN FIXED ASSETS（EXCLUDING RURAL HOUSEHOLDS）（2022）

单位：%

项 目	Item	合计 Total	# 房地产开发 Investment in Real Estate Development
一、本年施工项目（个）	**Projects Under Construction This Year（unit）**	**7058**	**1380**
# 本年新开工（个）	Newly Started（unit）	3081	131
二、本年建成投产项目（个）	**Projects Completed and Put into Use This Year（unit）**	**2064**	
三、本年完成投资增速（%）	**Complete Investment Growth Rate This Year（%）**	**4.5**	**-9.7**
1. 按构成分	Grouped by Composition		
# 建筑安装工程	Construction Installation Project	3.1	-10.2
设备工器具购置	Purchase of Equipment and Instruments	33.6	37.1
2. 按建设性质分	Grouped by Type of Construction		
# 新建	New Construction	11.3	
扩建	Expansion	-7.9	
改建和技术改造	Reconstruction	33.6	
3. 按国民经济行业分	Grouped by Economic Sector		
（1）农、林、牧、渔业	Agriculture，Forestry，Animal Husbandry and Fishery	0.1	
农业	Agriculture	-13.7	
林业	Forestry	162.5	
畜牧业	Animal Husbandry	-51.3	
渔业	Fishery	11.4	
农、林、牧、渔服务业	Agriculture，Forestry，Animal Husbandry and Fishery Services	-4.2	
（2）采矿业	Mining	3.6	
煤炭开采和洗选业	Mining and Washing of Coal		
石油和天然气开采业	Extraction of Petroleum and Natural Gas		
黑色金属矿采选业	Mining of Ferrous Metal Ores	5.1	
有色金属矿采选业	Mining of Non-ferrous Metal Ores	-19.5	
非金属矿采选业	Mining and Processing of Non-metal Ores	409.1	
开采辅助活动	Auxiliary Activities of Mining		
其他采矿业	Mining of Other Ores		

4-5 续表 1
Continued

单位：%

项目	Item	合计 Total	#房地产开发 Investment in Real Estate Development
(3) 制造业	Manufacturing	13.2	
农副食品加工业	Processing of Food from Agricultural Products	-16.9	
食品制造业	Manufacture of Foods	-46.5	
酒饮料和精制茶制造业	Manufacture of Liquor, Beverages and Refined Tea	33.7	
烟草制品业	Manufacture of Tobacco	32.0	
纺织业	Manufacture of Textile	-11.0	
纺织服装服饰业	Manufacture of Textile Wearing Apparel	4.7	
皮革毛皮羽毛及其制品和制鞋业	Manufacture of Leather, Fur, Feather & Its Products and Footwear	-23.0	
木材加工和木竹藤棕草制品业	Processing of Timber, Manufacture of Wood, Bamboo, Rattan, Palm and Straw Products	-33.6	
家具制造业	Manufacture of Furniture	-7.0	
造纸和纸制品业	Manufacture of Paper and Paper Products	-20.8	
印刷和记录媒介复制业	Printing, Reproduction of Recording Media	-1.5	
文教工美体育和娱乐用品制造业	Manufacture of Articles for Culture, Arts & Crafts, Sports and Entertainment	9.4	
石油煤炭及其他燃料加工业	Processing of Petroleum, Coal and other Fuels	-62.7	
化学原料和化学制品制造业	Manufacture of Chemical Raw Material and Chemical Products	12.2	
医药制造业	Manufacture of Medicines	7.0	
化学纤维制造业	Manufacture of Chemical Fibres	-22.4	
橡胶和塑料制品业	Manufacture of Rubber and Plastic	-22.6	
非金属矿物制品业	Manufacture of Metallic Mineral Products	-17.8	
黑色金属冶炼和压延加工业	Smelting and Pressing of Ferrous Metals	-39.5	
有色金属冶炼和压延加工业	Smelting and Pressing of Non-ferrous Metals	-24.3	
金属制品业	Manufacture of Metal Products	-23.8	
通用设备制造业	Manufacture of General Purpose Machinery	28.3	
专用设备制造业	Manufacture of Special Purpose Machinery	12.7	
汽车制造业	Manufacture of Vehicle	-2.4	
铁路、船舶、航空航天和其他运输设备制造业	Manufacture of Transport Equipment for Railway, Shipping, Aerospace and other Uses	8.2	
电气机械和器材制造业	Manufacture of Electrical Machinery and Equipment	27.3	
计算机、通信和其他电子设备制造业	Manufacture of Computer, Communication Equipment and Other Electronic Equipment	105.7	
仪器仪表制造业	Manufacture of Measuring Instrument	24.3	
其他制造业	Manufacture of other Products	154.5	
废弃资源综合利用业	Recycling and Disposal of Waste Resources	247.5	
金属制品、机械和设备修理业	Maintenance of Metal Products, Machinery and Equipment		

4-5 续表 2
Continued

单位：%

项 目	Item	合计 Total	#房地产开发 Investment in Real Estate Development
（4）电力、热力、燃气及水生产和供应业	Electricity, Heat, Gas and Water Production and Supply Industry	52.5	
电力、热力生产和供应业	Electricity and Heat Production and Supply Industry	46.7	
燃气生产和供应业	Gas Production and Supply Industry	47.6	
水的生产和供应业	Water Production and Supply Industry	68.4	
（5）建筑业	Construction	444.6	
房屋建筑业	Housing Building Industry	22.0	
土木工程建筑业	Civil Engineering Construction Industry	1416.3	
建筑安装业	Construction and Installation Industry		
建筑装饰装、装修和其他建筑业	Building Decoration and Other Construction Industries		
（6）批发和零售业	Wholesale and Retail Trades	-49.3	
批发业	Wholesale Trade	-88.6	
零售业	Retails Trade	-27.5	
（7）交通运输、仓储和邮政业	Transport Storage and Post	5.7	
铁路运输业	Railway Transport	193.6	
道路运输业	Road Transport	15.0	
水上运输业	Water Transport	-13.2	
航空运输业	Air Transport	-68.4	
管道运输业	Pipeline Transport	71.4	
多式联运和运输代理业	Multi-dimensional Transportation & Transportation Forwarding Industry	115.2	
装卸搬运和仓储业	Handing, Carrying and Ware Houses and Storage	-2.8	
邮政业	Post	14.4	
（8）住宿和餐饮业	Hotels and Catering Services	-10.9	
住宿业	Hotels Services	2.7	
餐饮业	Catering Services	-75.1	
（9）信息传输、软件和信息技术服务业	Information Transmission, Software and Information Technology Services	3.2	
电信、广播电视和卫星传输服务	Telecommunications, Radio, Television and Satellite Transmission Services	-30.0	
互联网和相关服务	Internet and Related Services	7.0	
软件和信息技术服务业	Software and Information Technology Services	19.0	
（10）金融业	Financial Industry	-47.3	
货币金融服务	Monetary and Financial Services	-39.4	
资本市场服务	Capital Markets Services	-81.7	
保险业	Insurance Industry		
其他金融业	Other Financial Industries	-47.9	

4-5 续表 3
Continued

单位：%

项　目	Item	合计 Total	#房地产开发 Investment in Real Estate Development
（11）房地产业	Real Estate	-12.1	-9.7
（12）租赁和商务服务业	Leasing and Business Services	9.7	
租赁业	Leasing Services	-88.1	
商务服务业	Business Services	10.9	
（13）科学研究和技术服务业	Scientific Research and Technical Services	-4.7	
研究和实验进展	Research and Experimental Development	-32.0	
专业技术服务业	Professional Technical Service Industry	-10.7	
科技推广和应用服务业	Technology Promotion and Application Service Industry	92.2	
（14）水利、环境和公共设施管理业	Management of Water Conservancy，Environment and Pubic Facilities	40.2	
水利管理业	Management of Water Conservancy	64.8	
生态保护和环境治理业	Ecological Protection and Environmental Governance	51.6	
公共设施管理业	Management of Public Facilities	37.5	
土地管理业	Land Management	337.9	
（15）居民服务、修理和其他服务业	Residents Service, Repair and Other Services	4.3	
居民服务业	Serviced to Households	14.3	
机动车、电子产品和日用产品修理业	Maintenance of Vehicle，Electronic Products and Daily Articles	-85.5	
其他服务业	Other Services	-25.9	
（16）教育	Education	16.1	
（17）卫生和社会工作	Health and Social Work	48.3	
卫生	Health	28.7	
社会工作	Social Work	187.8	
（18）文化、体育和娱乐业	Culture，Sports and Entertainment Industry	-17.4	
新闻和出版业	Journalism and Publishing Activities		
广播、电视、电影和录音制作业	Broadcasting, Televisions, Movies and Audio Production Industry	-77.1	
文化艺术业	Cultural and Art Activities	0.8	
体育	Sports Activities	19.2	
娱乐业	Entertainment	-48.0	
（19）公共管理、社会保障和社会组织	Public Management，Social Security and Social Organzation	-50.1	
中国共产党机关	Communist Party of China		
国家机构	Government Agencies	-46.9	
人民政协、民主党派	People's Political Consultative Conference，Democratic Party		
社会保障	Social Security		
群众团体、社会团体和其他成员组织	Non-Governmental Institutions，Social Organizations and Other Organizations	-83.4	
基层群众自治组织及其他组织	Self-governing organizations and other organizations of Grassroots Level	-71.9	
（20）国际组织	International Organization		

4-5 续表 4
Continued

单位：%

项　目	Item	合计 Total	# 房地产开发 Investment in Real Estate Development
四、本年资金来源合计	**Total Funds This Year**	**2.9**	**-17.2**
上年末结余资金	Balance of Last Year	-5.2	-11.0
本年资金来源小计	Sub-total Funds This Year	4.7	-19.9
国家预算内资金	State Budget	70.6	
国内贷款	Domestic Loans	4.4	-8.9
债券	State Treasury Bond	257.8	
利用外资	Foreign Investment	-67.7	-100.0
自筹资金	Self-raising Funds	12.8	-6.4
其他资金来源	Others	-19.3	-27.8

4-6 主要年份房地产开发投资

MAJOR YEAR'S INVESTMENT IN REAL ESTATE DEVELOPMENT

单位：万元、万平方米（10000 yuan，10000 sq.m）

年　份 Year	房地产开发投资额 Investment in Real Estate Development	房屋施工面积 Floor Space Under Construction	房屋竣工面积 Floor Space Completed	房屋实际销售面积 Floor Space of Buildings Sold	房屋实际销售额 Sale of Buildings
1995	562861	1008	240	103	185384
1996	455765	748	203	80	125150
1997	426570	675	237	113	216311
1998	438059	742	259	178	351805
1999	629717	900	474	240	430123
2000	675142	1047	352	301	550401
2001	925153	1374	532	406	802364
2002	1036476	1417	537	427	933031
2003	1277969	1765	552	469	1121885
2004	1626965	2101	635	516	1530964
2005	2238370	2363	811	740	2666738
2006	2683631	2751	654	719	3054907
2007	3223547	3224	641	833	4333566
2008	3805652	3773	672	770	3924175
2009	4594829	4310	814	1262	7036744
2010	6024387	5058	1020	1360	8952942
2011	7827193	5693	925	1026	7702379
2012	9301099	6474	1212	951	7660684
2013	10485229	7073	957	1160	9786176
2014	11177297	8171	1136	1164	9708984
2015	11223458	8971	1523	1419	12628568
2016	13691425	9101	1426	1939	17899532
2017	13305432	9533	1487	1901	19992012
2018	14852089	10390	1625	1808	22824618
2019	18038081	11580	1602	1652	22469992
2020	20451153	12528	1154	1654	22168506
2021	19818480	13012	1657	1645	22672959
2022	17891221	12046	1610	1564	21808245

4-7 房地产开发投资情况(2022 年)
INVESTMENT IN REAL ESTATE DEVELOPMENT (2022)

单位:万元(10000 yuan)

指 标	Indicator	合计 Total	按经济类型分 Grouped by Economic Types		
			国有经济 State-owned	集体经济 Collective-owned	其他经济 Others
本年完成投资额	**Investment Completed This Year**	**17891221**	**875301**	**593230**	**16422690**
1. 住宅	Residential Buildings	13162138	552809	340780	12268549
2. 办公楼	Office Buildings	956765	59356	52601	844808
3. 商业营业用房	Houses for Business Use	1140884	81992	2539	1056353
4. 其他	Others	2631434	181144	197310	2252980

4-7 续表
Continued

单位:万元(10000 yuan)

指 标	Indicator	按资质等级分 Grouped by Qualification Criteria					
		一级 First Grade	二级 Second Grade	三级 Third Grade	四级 Fourth Grade	暂定 Provisional	其他 Others
本年完成投资额	**Investment Completed This Year**	**446268**	**2152856**	**261218**	**87455**	**12455462**	**2487962**
1. 住宅	Residential Buildings	391726	1463166	184072	61303	9210101	1851770
2. 办公楼	Office Buildings	9788	100855	6243	96	696463	143320
3. 商业营业用房	Houses for Business Use	12237	138931	13046	14479	845560	116631
4. 其他	Others	32517	449904	57857	11577	1703338	376241

4-8 房地产施工、竣工面积及竣工价值(2022 年)
FLOOR SPACE UNDER CONSTRUCTION AND COMPLETED AND COMPLETED VALUE OF REAL ESTATE (2022)

单位：万平方米(10000 sq.m)

施工、竣工房屋面积及竣工价值	Construction and Completed Housing Area and Completed Value	施工面积 Floor Space Under Construction	#新开工 Newly Started	竣工房屋 Floor Space Completed	竣工房屋价值(万元) Completed Value (10000 yuan)
房屋建筑面积总计	**Floor Space of Buildings**	**12046**	**1499**	**1610**	**7385603**
住宅	Residential Buildings	7953	1066	1092	5537923
办公楼	Office Buildings	777	40	64	273799
商业营业用房	Houses for Business Use	781	67	93	491807
其他	Others	2535	327	361	1082074

4-9 商品房屋销售情况(2022 年)
BASIC STATISTICS ON SALES OF COMMERCIALIZED BUILDINGS (2022)

商品房屋销售情况	Sales and Rental of Commercialized Buildings	实际销售(万平方米) Actual Sales (10000 sq.m)	实际销售额(万元) Actual Sales Volume (10000 yuan)	待售面积(万平方米) Area for Sale (10000 sq.m)
房屋面积总计	**Floor Space of Buildings**	**1564**	**21808245**	**656**
住宅	Residential Buildings	1264	18252662	322
办公楼	Office Buildings	143	1974327	97
商业营业用房	Houses for Business Use	110	1355238	161
其他	Others	46	226018	77

主要统计指标解释

固定资产投资 是以货币形式表现的在一定时期内建造和购置固定资产的工作量以及与此有关的费用的总称。

房地产开发投资 指各种登记注册类型的房地产开发法人单位统一开发的住宅、厂房、仓库、饭店、宾馆、度假村、写字楼、办公楼等房屋建筑物，配套的服务设施，土地开发工程（如道路、给水、排水、供电、供热、通讯、平整场地等基础设施工程）和土地购置的投资；不包括单纯的土地开发和交易活动。

固定资产投资的资金来源 根据固定资产投资的资金来源不同，分为国家预算资金、国内贷款、利用外资、自筹资金和其他资金。

固定资产投资 按建设性质分建设项目的性质一般分为新建、扩建、改建和技术改造、单纯建造生活设施、迁建、恢复、单纯购置。

固定资产投资 按构成分固定资产投资活动按其工作内容和实现方式分为建筑安装工程，设备、工具、器具购置，其他费用三个部分。

新增生产能力（或工程效益） 指建成投产项目或工程新增生产能力（或工程效益）的名称。

房屋施工面积 是指报告期内施工的全部房屋建筑面积。包括本期新开工的面积和上期开工跨入本期继续施工的房屋面积，以及上期已停缓建在本期恢复施工的房屋面积。本期竣工和本期施工后又停缓建的房屋，其建筑面积仍计入本期房屋施工面积中。

房屋竣工面积 是指在报告期内房屋建筑按照设计要求全部完工，达到住人和使用条件，经验收鉴定合格（或达到竣工验收标准），正式移交使用单位的各栋房屋建筑面积的总和。

本年新增固定资产 指在报告期已经完成建造和购置过程，并已交付生产或使用单位的固定资产的价值，包括已经建成投入生产或交付使用的工程投资和达到固定资产标准的设备、工具、器具的投资及有关应摊入的费用。

Explanatory Notes on Main Statistical Indicators

Fixed investment is a generic term of quantity of work from building and acquiring of fixed assets over a period of time and any relevant expenses incurred thereby in the form of currency.

Real estate development investment means investments in all kinds of registered housing & building, including residences, plants, warehouses, restaurants, hotels, resorts, office buildings and administrative buildings which are developed uniformly by real estate development corporation, supporting service facilities and land development projects (such as road, water supply & drainage, power supply, heat supply, telecommunication and ground leveling and other infrastructure projects) and land acquisition, excludes simple land development and transaction activities.

Source of funds for fixed–asset investment can be divided into national budget funds, domestic loans, utilization of foreign capital, self–raised funds and other funds in accordance with the different sources.

Construction items of fixed–asset investment can be divided into new construction, extension, reconstruction, technical reform, simply–constructed living facilities, relocation, restoration and simple acquisition by property of construction.

Fixed–asset investment activities can be divided into three parts, namely construction and installation project, acquisition of equipment, tools and appliances and other expenses by working content and method of achieving.

New productive capacity (or project benefit) means the completed projects or new productive capacity (or project benefit) of project.

Construction area means total areas of all buildings which are under construction in the report period, including the area which is newly constructed in this period and the areas of buildings which commence in the last period and carry forward to this period for continuing construction. and the areas of buildings which stop constructing in the last period and resume to be constructed in this period. The areas of the buildings which are completed in this period and stop constructing after this period' s construction are still reckoned in floor space under construction in this period.

Completed area means the sum total of areas of housings & buildings which are completed according to design requirements in the report period, reach conditions of living and using and are transferred to building users formally after checked and accepted (or reach the standards of completion and acceptance).

New fixed assets in this year means the value of fixed assets which are completed and acquired in the report period and delivered for production or use, including investment in constructions which are put into production or service, investment in equipment, tools and appliances which reach the standards of fixed asset, and the expenses which should be added into fixed assets.

对外经济贸易 5

INTERNATIONAL TRADE AND ECONOMIC COOPERATION

简 要 说 明

一、本篇资料的主要内容

本篇资料主要反映全市外经外贸和外资企业的基本情况，主要包括外贸进出口、利用外资、对外投资与经济合作等方面的资料。

二、本篇资料的来源

1. 口岸进出口数据来源于青岛海关。

2. 进出口、利用外资等资料、对外投资与经济合作来源于市商务局。

本篇资料由市统计局外经贸易统计处整理提供。

Brief Introduction

Ⅰ. Main Content

Data in this chapter show the basic conditions of foreign trade and foreign-funded enterprises, mainly including imports and exports, utilization of foreign capitals, production and operation condition of foreign-funded enterprises, etc.

Ⅱ. Source of Data

1. Port import and export data comes from Qingdao Customs.

2. Data on imports & exports and utilization of foreign capitals are provided by Qingdao Municipal Commerce Bureau.

Data in this chapter are prepared and compiled by the Division of Trade and External Economic Relations Statistics of Qingdao Municipal Bureau of Statistics.

5-1 青岛口岸进出口总额(1985—2022 年)

TOTAL VALUE OF IMPORTS AND EXPORTS OF QINGDAO PORT（1985—2022）

单位：万美元（10000 USD）、万元（10000 yuan）

年 份 Year	青岛口岸进出口总额 Total Value of Imports and Exports Qingdao Port	出口 Exports	进口 Imports
1985	414448	234652	179796
1986	382840	191926	190914
1987	445090	259458	185632
1988	474516	259176	215340
1989	506152	268397	237755
1990	477117	304011	173106
1991	519273	332949	186324
1992	581495	350163	231332
1993	678013	360297	317716
1994	888574	510760	377814
1995	1307508	705245	602263
1996	1391323	760566	629757
1997	1542284	936142	609142
1998	1463718	933392	530326
1999	1696514	1063768	632746
2000	2520420	1423266	1097154
2001	2797085	1636888	1160197
2002	3128048	1889612	1238436

注：2016 年起，统计单位为人民币万元。
Note：Statistic unit is RMB ten thousand Yuan as from 2016.

5-1 续表
Continued

单位：万美元（10000 USD）、万元（10000 yuan）

年 份 Year	青岛口岸进出口总额 Total Value of Imports and Exports Qingdao Port	出口 Exports	进口 Imports
2003	4088096	2366046	1722050
2004	5677570	3197697	2479873
2005	6932944	3959947	2972997
2006	8019198	4495731	3523467
2007	9257099	5263539	3993560
2008	11558079	5953501	5604578
2009	9049699	4694832	4354867
2010	11912702	5988254	5924448
2011	15095088	7294226	7800862
2012	14888716	7120813	7767903
2013	15662732	7696141	7966591
2014	16489966	8736358	7753608
2015	14448349	8776286	5672063
2016	94927180	56513317	38413863
2017	111024375	63298062	47726314
2018	121968146	67385279	54582867
2019	127239314	69443761	57795553
2020	116719854	66149587	50570266
2021	151615242	85492319	66122923
2022	184500182	105869323	78630860

5-2 进出口总额(1988—2022 年)

TOTAL VALUE OF IMPORTS AND EXPORTS（1988—2022）

单位：万美元（10000 USD）、万元（10000 yuan）

年 份 Year	进出口总额（含中央、省驻青公司） Total Value of Imports and Exports （including central and provincial companies）	出口 Exports	进口 Imports	进出口总额（不含中央、省驻青公司） Total Value of Imports and Exports （excluding central and provincial companies）	出口 Exports	进口 Imports
1988				28097	21731	6366
1989				39327	27797	11530
1990				41649	33529	8120
1991				54624	44746	9878
1992				88600	66291	22309
1993	517643	346288	171355	139048	100201	38847
1994	633213	434102	199111	234978	164135	70843
1995	858560	536386	322174	376372	245072	131300
1996	863521	516317	347204	461950	287123	174827
1997	916269	579261	377008	521967	338535	183432
1998	882042	573020	309022	595826	382657	213169
1999	1009885	631072	378813	775565	446260	329305
2000	1353222	826891	526331	1083133	611426	471707
2001	1541564	950160	591404	1235781	712024	523757
2002	1692567	1057141	635426	1409598	850420	559178
2003	2065912	1239199	826713	1784556	1035528	749028

注：1. 2012 年起，中央、省驻青公司外贸统计划归青岛，取消含中央、省驻青公司统计口径。
2. 2016 年起，统计单位为人民币万元。

Notes：1. Since 2012，the statistical calibre including central and provincial companies has been canclled.
2. Statistic unit is RMB ten thousand Yuan as from 2016.

5-2 续表
Continued

单位：万美元（10000 USD）、万元（10000 yuan）

年 份 Year	进出口总额（含中央、省驻青公司） Total Value of Imports and Exports (including central and provincial companies)	出口 Exports	进口 Imports	进出口总额（不含中央、省驻青公司） Total Value of Imports and Exports (excluding central and provincial companies)	出口 Exports	进口 Imports
2004	2698781	1578167	1120614	2433188	1391171	1042017
2005	3302230	1942242	1359988	3045542	1758834	1286708
2006	3911543	2346552	1564991	3655737	2164541	1491196
2007	4572534	2831004	1741530	4360499	2677596	1682903
2008	5363659	3262476	2101183	5215886	3146246	2069640
2009	4485115	2729865	1755250	4398639	2692197	1706442
2010	5705963	3391560	2314403	5614928	3335141	2279787
2011	7215217	4061309	3153908	7126310	4005572	3120738
2012				7320781	4081968	3238813
2013				7791217	4198605	3592612
2014				7988833	4577696	3411137
2015				7022243	4535015	2487228
2016				43506659	28219059	15287600
2017				50334973	30318103	20016870
2018				53212551	31722209	21490342
2019				59255880	34119000	25136880
2020				64070068	38767641	25302427
2021				84984331	49212763	35771568
2022				91171637	53610643	37560994

5-3 分国别（地区）外贸出口总额
TOTAL VALUE OF EXPORTS BY COUNTRIES（REGIONS）

单位：万美元（10000 USD）

国别（地区）	Country（Region）	2022 年	2022 年比 2021 年（±%） 2022/2021（±%）	占比（%） Ratio（%）
亚洲	Asia	3776506	5.6	47.0
中国香港	Hong Kong, China	192630	–46.4	2.4
日本	Japan	753223	6.0	9.4
韩国	Korea	699803	4.0	8.7
东盟	ASEAN	1249390	27.7	15.6
非洲	Africa	417004	13.9	5.2
南非	South Africa	67270	1.9	0.8
欧洲	Europe	1600049	3.2	19.9
欧盟	EU	1058356	0.0	13.2
南美洲	South America	275703	10.4	3.4
北美洲	North America	1401995	3.4	17.5
美国	USA	1142316	–4.8	14.2
大洋洲	Oceanica	232068	7.9	2.9
澳大利亚	Australia	192695	15.7	2.4

5-4 外贸出口商品分类
EXPORT COMMODITIES BY CATEGORY

单位：万元（10000 yuan）

项 目	Item	2022 年	2022 年比 2021 年（±%） 2022/2021（±%）	占比（%） Ratio（%）
合 计	**Total**	**53610643**	**9.0**	**100.0**
按企业性质划分	By Enterprises Nature			
国有企业	State-owned Enterprises	4439237	27.8	8.3
三资企业	Foreign-funded Enterprise	9652535	-9.8	18.0
其他企业	Other Enterprises	39518871	12.9	73.7
#集体企业	Collective-owned Enterprises	872374	2.9	1.6
私营企业	Private Enterprises	38622284	13.2	72.0
按贸易方式划分	By Customs Regime			
一般贸易	Ordinary Trade	39328790	9.1	73.4
加工贸易	Processing Trade	10220547	13.7	19.1
其他贸易	Others Trade	4061306	-1.9	7.6
按大类商品划分	By Category of Commodities			
纺织服装	Textile Garments	6203465	8.6	11.6
农产品	Agricultural Products	4326835	16.7	8.1
机电产品	Mechanical and Electrical Products	24329990	3.9	45.4
高新技术产品	High-tech Products	3405480	-13.1	6.4

5-5 外贸进口商品分类
IMPORT COMMODITIES BY CATEGORY

单位：万元（10000 yuan）

项　目	Item	2022年	2022年比2021年（±%） 2022/2021（±%）	占比（%） Ratio（%）
合　计	**Total**	**37560994**	**5.1**	**100.0**
按企业性质划分	By Enterprises Nature			
国有企业	State-owned Enterprises	7457233	7.9	19.9
三资企业	Foreign-funded Enterprise	5937174	-10.5	15.8
其他企业	Other Enterprises	24166586	8.9	64.3
#集体企业	Collective-owned Enterprises	101759	15.5	0.3
私营企业	Private Enterprises	24050083	9.4	64.0
按贸易方式划分	By Customs Regime			
一般贸易	Ordinary Trade	20970168	-3.2	55.8
加工贸易	Processing Trade	2648234	-14.6	7.1
其他贸易	Others Trade	13942591	27.1	37.1
按大类商品划分	By Category of Commodities			
纺织服装	Textile Garments	191382	-12.3	0.5
农产品	Agricultural Products	7664973	11.8	20.4
机电产品	Mechanical and Electrical Products	5574140	-9.5	14.8
高新技术产品	High-tech Products	3572224	-1.7	9.5

5-6 二十大出口商品出口情况

INFORMATION ON THE EXPORTATION OF TOP 20 PRODUCTS

单位：万美元（10000 USD）

商品名称	Name	2022 年	2022 年比 2021 年（±%） 2022/2021（±%）	占比（%） Ratio（%）
合　计	**Total**	**6702564**	**5.1**	**83.5**
机械设备	Machinery and Equipment	1259160	5.5	15.7
电器及电子产品	Electric Appliance and Electronic Products	758693	4.7	9.4
运输工具	Garments	683576	-12.7	8.5
服装及衣着附件	Clothing and Clothing Accessories	604499	11.3	7.5
金属制品	Metal Products	583097	28.5	7.3
化工产品	Chemical Products	481697	2.0	6.0
纺织纱线、织物及制品	Textile Yarns, Fabric and Textile Products	337424	17.7	4.2
汽车零配件	Automobile Parts	324624	-4.8	4.0
塑料制品	Plastic Articles	275969	4.6	3.4
钢材	Rolled Steel	223868	17.2	2.8
轮胎	Tyre	209902	-19.4	2.6
家具及其零件	Furniture	178232	0.7	2.2
水海产品	Aquatic and Seawater Products	175477	43.0	2.2
鞋类	Shoes	130829	10.1	1.6
仪器仪表	Instrumentation	113654	28.6	1.4
蔬菜	Vegetables	104891	17.2	1.3
箱包及类似容器	Bags and Similar Containers	91552	3.4	1.1
陶瓷产品	Ceramic Products	75186	-4.7	0.9
床垫、寝具及类似品	Mattresses，Bedding and Similar Products	64015	0.3	0.8
鲜、干水果及坚果	Fresh and Dried Fruits and Nuts	26221	-24.1	0.3

5-7 二十大进口商品进口情况
INFORMATION ON THE IMPORTATION OF TOP 20 PRODUCTS

单位：万美元（10000 USD）

商品名称	Name	2022 年	2022 年比 2021 年（±%） 2022/2021（±%）	占比（%） Ratio（%）
合　计	**Total**	**4538486**	**-2.0**	**80.7**
原油	Crude Oil	1155698	41.3	20.5
铁矿砂及其精矿	Iron Ore and Concentrate	403729	-49.3	7.2
以天然沥青等为基本成分的沥青混合物	Bituminous Mixtures Based on Natural Bitumen, etc	366339	23.1	6.5
机械设备	Machinery and Equipment	319949	-14.5	5.7
肉类	Meat	286701	-28.2	5.1
电器及电子产品	Electric Appliance and Electronic Products	254999	13.0	4.5
粮食	Grain	245995	-42.6	4.4
仪器仪表	Instruments and Meters	234196	65.0	4.2
集成电路	Integrated Circuits	218316	53.9	3.9
成品油	Refined Petroleum Products	202811	40.1	3.6
水海产品	Aquatic and Seawater Products	141689	55.1	2.5
初级形状的塑料	Plastic in Primary Form	132661	-1.3	2.4
铜矿砂及其精矿	Copper Ore and Concentrate	132291	-34.8	2.4
合成橡胶（包括胶乳）	Synthetic Rubber (including latex)	92360	28.4	1.6
铝矿砂及其精矿	Aluminum Ore and Concentrate	73879	17.0	1.3
天然橡胶（包括胶乳）	Natural Rubber (including latex)	71868	-38.5	1.3
棉花	Cotton	68335	9.2	1.2
纸浆	Pulp	66344	35.0	1.2
钢材	Rolled Steel	39797	123.8	0.7
纺织纱线、织物及制品	Textile Yarns, Fabric and Textile Products	30526	-23.5	0.5

5-8 利用外资情况（2000—2022 年）

UTILIZATION OF FOREIGN CAPITAL（2000 — 2022）

项　目	Item	单位	Unit	2000 年	2005 年
批准企业（项目）个数	**Number of Enterprises（Projects）Approved**	**个**	**unit**	**1132**	**2530**
一、外商直接投资	Foreign Direct Investments	个	unit	1128	2530
中外合资企业	Sino-foreign Joint Ventures	个	unit	303	274
中外合作企业	Sino-foreign Cooperative Enterprises	个	unit	57	18
外商独资企业	Foreign-owned Enterprises	个	unit	76	2236
外商投资股份制	Foreign–invested Joint–stock System	个	unit	1	2
合伙企业	Partnership	个	unit		
二、外商其他投资	Other Foreign Investments	个	unit	4	
合同外资金额	**Total Amount of Contracted Foreign Investment**	**万美元**	**10000 USD**	**269081**	**954486**
一、外商直接投资	Foreign Direct Investments	万美元	10000 USD	266221	954486
中外合资企业	Sino-foreign Joint Ventures	万美元	10000 USD	69889	112777
中外合作企业	Sino-foreign Cooperative Enterprises	万美元	10000 USD	26835	17588
外商独资企业	Foreign-owned Enterprises	万美元	10000 USD	169370	813485
外商投资股份制	Foreign–invested Joint–stock System	万美元	10000 USD	127	10636
合伙企业	Partnership	万美元	10000 USD		
二、外商其他投资	Other Foreign Investments	万美元	10000 USD	2860	
实际利用外资金额	**Total Amount of Foreign Investment Actually Utilized**	**万美元**	**10000 USD**	**128171**	**365625**
一、外商直接投资	Foreign Direct Investments	万美元	10000 USD	126132	365625
中外合资企业	Sino-foreign Joint Ventures	万美元	10000 USD	39224	77636
中外合作企业	Sino-foreign Cooperative Enterprises	万美元	10000 USD	3886	5654
外商独资企业	Foreign-owned Enterprises	万美元	10000 USD	82992	280130
外商投资股份制	Foreign–invested Joint–stock System	万美元	10000 USD	30	2205
合伙企业	Partnership	万美元	10000 USD		
二、外商其他投资	Other Foreign Investments	万美元	10000 USD	2039	

单位：万美元（10000 USD）

2010 年	2012 年	2013 年	2014 年	2015 年	2016 年	2017 年	2018 年	2019 年	2020 年	2021 年	2022 年
731	**553**	**645**	**619**	**763**	**680**	**650**	**956**	**954**	**882**	**908**	**693**
731	553	645	619	763	680	650	956	954	882	908	693
153	113	165	140	162	154	188	294	358	190	327	226
4	2	2	1	2		1	8	1			
574	438	478	475	597	523	457	653	586	661	531	427
			3	2	3	4	1	2	3	3	
								7	25	47	40
475723	**600231**	**758063**	**638637**	**827357**	**769101**	**909629**	**980231**	**1335551**	**1785353**	**2143457**	**2771377**
475723	600231	758063	638637	827357	769101	909629	980231	1335551	1785353	2143457	2771377
124148	102252	191172	126878	116013	207933	246280	195336	415708	431250	703368	237152
9179	122	4765	−849	1731	28	327	34333	1010		4567	
341977	490764	562208	506271	706172	554073	655377	756426	794686	1321040	1260406	1427911
419	7093	−82	6337	3441	7067	7645	−5864	93315	9547	32843	4972
								30832	23446	142273	1101342
284281	**460027**	**552227**	**608100**	**669062**	**700273**	**773500**	**869257**	**584193**	**585297**	**616897**	**551352**
284281	460027	552227	608100	669062	700273	773500	869257	584193	585297	616897	551352
84920	169469	159424	172180	135671	171051	195189	191040	215914	230342	258490	138781
3567	6262	2355	128	1570	251	220	19032	68		3000	
194500	275579	390210	435102	531544	520052	569461	658368	299610	352179	340031	402580
1294	8717	238	690	277	8918	8325	817	68585	441	15329	7156
								16	1275	47	2835

5-9 当年外商直接投资项目数和投资额（2022 年）
NUMBER OF PROJECTS AND TOTAL AMOUNT OF FOREIGN DIRECT INVESTMENT（2022）

项　目	Item	批准企业项目数（个）Number of Projects Approved（unit）	实际利用外资金额（万美元）Total Amount of Foreign Investment Actually Utilized（10000 USD）
外商直接投资	**Foreign Direct Investments**	**693**	**551352**
一、按投资方式分	**Grouped by Investment Form**		
#中外合资企业	Sino-foreign Joint Ventures	226	138781
中外合作企业	Sino-foreign Cooperative Enterprises		
外商独资企业	Foreign-owned Enterprises	427	402580
二、按主要行业分	**Grouped by Sector**		
#农、林、牧、渔业	Agriculture, Forestry, Animal Husbandry and Fishery	2	1428
制造业	Manufacturing	62	85474
电力、燃气及水的生产和供应业	Production and Supply of Electricity, Gas and Water	9	12351
建筑业	Construction	9	11572
信息传输、计算机服务和软件业	Information transmission, computer services and software industry	43	24545
批发和零售业	Wholesale and Retail Trades	258	145153
房地产业	Real Estate	9	34607
租赁和商务服务业	Leasing and Business Services	107	155286
科学研究、技术服务和地质勘查业	Scientific Research, Technical Service and Geological Survey	94	50147
三、按主要国别（地区）分	**Grouped by Countries（Regions）**		
#中国香港	Hong Kong, China	223	379573
韩国	Korea	156	95799
美国	USA	32	978
日本	Japan	64	26333
德国	Germany	5	1209
澳大利亚	Australia	6	583
新加坡	Singapore	33	14772

5-10　对外投资与经济合作
OUTBOUND INVESTMENT AND INTERNATIONAL ECONOMIC COOPERATION

名　称	Name	单位	Unit	2022 年	2022 年比 2021 年（±%） 2022/2021（±%）
对外投资项目数	Number of Outbound Investment Projects	个	unit	66	-1.5
对外投资中方投资额	The Amount of Investment by Chinese Sides in Outbound Investment	万美元	10000 USD	145354	-10.4
对外承包工程新签合同额	The Amount of New Contracts for Foreign Contracted Projects	万美元	10000 USD	218159	-30.1
对外承包工程完成营业额	The Completed Turnover of Foreign Contracted Projects	万美元	10000 USD	293426	-2.7
对外劳务合作	Number of Persons Sent Overseas for International Labor Service Cooperation	人	Person	10688	-9.5

5-11　对外投资分国别（地区）情况表（2022 年）
TABLE OF FOREIGN INVESTMENT BY COUNTRIES（REGIONS）（2022）

国别（地区）	Country（Region）	项目数量（个） Number of Projects （unit）	2022 年比 2021 年 （±%） 2022/2021 （±%）	中方投资额（万美元） Amount of Investment by Chinese Sides （10000 USD）	2022 年比 2021 年 （±%） 2022/2021 （±%）
总计	**Total**	**66**	**-1**	**145354.1**	**-10.4**
亚洲	Asia	50	35	68733.9	-47.5
中国香港	Hong Kong，China	20	25	2972.0	-37.5
新加坡	Singapore	6	50	484.1	-67.5
韩国	Korea	6	20	478.0	-61.5
泰国	Thailand	4	300	2187.8	-75.6
越南	Vietnam	4	300	11949.2	-84.3
阿拉伯联合酋长国	United Arab Emirates	2	100	25.0	150.0
马来西亚	Malaysia	2		43.8	
日本	Japan	1	-75	-170.2	-105.7
菲律宾	Philippines	1		20.0	
柬埔寨	Cambodia	1	0	10.0	-100.0
中国澳门	Macau, China	1		123.5	
乌兹别克斯坦	Uzbekistan	1		0.1	
印度尼西亚	Indonesia	1	0	50610.7	163265.7

5-11 续表
Continued

国别（地区）	Country（Region）	项目数量（个）Number of Projects（unit）	2022年比2021年（±%）2022/2021（±%）	中方投资额（万美元）Amount of Investment by Chinese Sides（10000 USD）	2022年比2021年（±%）2022/2021（±%）
非洲	Africa	6	-45	10830.7	4217.2
安哥拉	Angola	2		1.7	
南非	South Africa	1	0	37.0	19.4
尼日利亚	Nigeria	1		100.0	
塞舌尔	Seychelles	1		10.0	
埃及	Egypt	1		10682.0	
欧洲	Europe	2	-75	59277.1	222.2
俄罗斯联邦	Russia	1	-50	245.3	-47.2
西班牙	Spain	1		59031.8	
拉丁美洲	Latin America	1	-80	3367.8	-62.6
墨西哥	Mexico	1	-50	3186.8	-63.1
阿根廷	Argentina	0		181.0	-46.0
北美洲	North America	3	-40	1912.7	-40.4
美国	USA	2	-60	-231.3	-107.2
加拿大	Canada	1		2144.0	
大洋洲	Oceania	4	300	1231.9	252.4
澳大利亚	Australia	2	100	1021.9	192.3
萨摩亚	Samoa	1		50.0	
新西兰	New Zealand	1		160.0	

主要统计指标解释

批准企业（项目）个数　是指外商直接投资中批准设立的外商投资企业个数、批准的合作开发项目个数。

合同外资金额　是指外商投资企业（机构）的外放投资者认缴的注册资本、运营资金和投资者股权转让的溢折价。（摘自《外商投资统计调查制度（2022 年）》）包括新批准企业合同外资和原有企业的增资减资，增资减资不对企业（项目）个数进行调整。

实际使用外资金额　是指合同外资金额的实际执行金额。

外商直接投资　是指境外投资者在中国境内通过投资设立公司、合伙企业、分行（限境外银行）、分公司（限境外保险公司），单独或与境内投资者共同进行石油、天然气和煤层气等资源的勘探开发等方式进行的投资。上市公司中，单个境外投资者所占股权比例不低于 10%。（摘自《外商投资统计调查制度（2022 年）》）

外商其他投资　是指除外商直接投资以外其他方式吸收的外资。

进出口总额　指实际进出我国国境的货物总金额。包括对外贸易实际进出口货物，来料加工装配进出口货物，国家间、联合国及国际组织无偿援助物资和赠送品，华侨、港澳台同胞和外籍华人捐赠品，租赁期满归承租人所有的租赁货物，进料加工进出口货物，边境地方贸易及边境地区小额贸易进出口货物（边民互市贸易除外），中外合资企业、中外合作经营企业、外商独资经营企业进出口货物和公用物品，到、离岸价格在规定限额以上的进出口货样和广告品（无商业价值、无使用价值和免费提供出口的除外），从保税仓库提取在中国境内销售的进口货物，以及其他进出口货物。

Explanatory Notes on Main Statistical Indicators

Enterprises (Projects) Permitted　refers to number of foreign invested enterprises and developed projects under cooperation through the permission.

Contracted Foreign Investment　refers to the registered capital, operating capital and the premium and discount of investor's equity transfer subscribed by external investors of foreign-invested enterprises (institutions). (Excerpt *from Foreign Investment Statistical Survey System(2022)*) Itincludes newly approved enterprise contract foreign capital and capital increase and reduction of existing enterprises.The number of enterprises (projects) will not be adjusted for capital increase and reduction

Actual Utilization of Foreign Investment　refers to actual usage of contracted foreign investment, including cash, investment in kind and incorporeal agreed by the both sides as part of the investment, such as services and technology.

Foreign Direct Investment　refers to the investment made by foreign investors in the territory of China through the establishment of partnership branches (limited to overseas banks) branches (limited to overseas insurance companies), and the exploration and development of oil, natural gas, coal bed gas and other resources alone or jointly with domestic investors. Investments in resource exploration and development. In a listed company, the shareholding ratio of a single foreign investor shall not be less than 10%. (Excerpt *from Foreign Investment Statistical Survey System(2022))*

Other Investment by Foreign Entrepreneurs refers to all forms of utilization of foreign capitals other than foreign direct investment.

Total Imports and Exports refers to the real value of commodities imported into and exported from the boundary of China. They include the actual imports and exports through foreign trade, imported and exported goods under the processing and assembling trades and materials, supplies and gifts as aid given gratis between governments and by the United Nations and other international organizations, and contributions donated by overseas Chinese, compatriots in Hong Kong, Macao and Taiwan and Chinese with foreign citizenship, leasing commodities owned by tenant at the expiration of leasing period, the imported and exported commodities processed with imported materials, commodities trading in border areas (excluding mutual exchange goods), the imported and exported commodities and articles for public use of the Sino-foreign joint ventures, cooperative enterprises and ventures exclusively with foreign own investment. Also included are import or export of samples and advertising goods for whose CIF or FOB value are beyond the permitted ceiling (excluding goods of no trading or use value and free commodities for export), imported goods sold in China from bonded warehouses and other imported or exported goods.

城市建设、环境保护 6

CITY CONSTRUCTION AND ENVIRONMENTAL PROTECTION

简 要 说 明

一、本篇资料的主要内容

本篇资料主要反映全市城市基础设施基本情况，包括市政设施、供水、供电、公共交通、园林绿化、燃气供热、城市环卫、环境保护及工业“三废”排放情况等方面的资料。

二、本篇资料的来源

1. 本篇资料中市政设施、供水、公共交通、园林绿化、燃气供热、城市环卫相关资料来源于市住房和城乡建设局、市交通运输局，由市统计局固定资产投资统计处整理提供。

2. 本篇资料中供电资料来源于青岛供电公司，由市统计局能源统计处整理提供。

3. 本篇资料中环境保护、环境质量及工业“三废”排放情况来源于市生态环境局，由市统计局能源统计处整理提供。

Brief Introduction

Ⅰ. Main Content

The data in this chapter mainly reflects the basic conditions of the city' s urban infrastructure, including information on municipal facilities, water supply, power supply, public transportation, landscaping, gas heating, urban sanitation, environmental protection, and industrial “three wastes” emissions.

Ⅱ. Source of Data

1. The relevant information on municipal facilities, water supply, public transportation, landscaping, gas heating, and urban environmental sanitation in this article comes from the Municipal Housing and Urban-Rural Construction Bureau and the Municipal Transportation Bureau, and is provided by the Fixed Assets Investment Statistics Department of the Municipal Bureau of Statistics.

2. The power supply data in this data comes from Qingdao Power Supply Company, which is compiled and provided by the Energy Statistics Division of the Municipal Bureau of Statistics.

3. The environmental protection, environmental quality, and industrial “three wastes” emissions in this data come from the Municipal Ecological Environment Bureau and are compiled and provided by the Energy Statistics Division of the Municipal Bureau of Statistics.

6-1 主要年份城市建设和公用事业

MAJOR YEAR'S CITY CONSTRUCTION AND PUBLIC UTILITIES

年 份 Year	建成区面积 （平方公里） Developed Areas （sq.km）	年末道路长度 （公里） Length of Roads at Year-end（km）	年末道路面积 （万平方米） Area of Roads at Year-end（10000 sq.m）	公共汽车、电车线路网长度 （公里） Network Length of Bus and Trolley Bus（km）
1949	27	243	206	26.4
1952	29	245	213	124.4
1957	36	248	217	232.3
1962	55	266	235	252.8
1965	57	266	235	308.1
1970	59	374	346	358.5
1975	63	392	355	389.3
1978	66	408	368	422.1
1980	72	408	377	474.1
1985	79	462	464	611.3
1990	94.3	667	786	777
1991	94.7	673	826	922
1992	95.4	683	840	988
1993	99.9	764	944	1094
1994	103.9	811	985	1372
1995	106	936	1177	1101
1996	110	991	1339	1211
1997	112	1047	1436	1492
1998	114	1106	1436	1859
1999	116	1171	1698	2339

注：由于城市的发展变化，2022 年起，城市建设数据涵盖胶州市、平度市、莱西市数据。
Note：Due to the growth and changes of the city, from 2022, the data of urban development covers that of Jiaozhou, Pingdu and Laixi.

6-1　续表 1
Continued

年　份 Year	建成区面积 （平方公里） Developed Areas （sq.km）	年末道路长度 （公里） Length of Roads at Year-end（km）	年末道路面积 （万平方米） Area of Roads at Year-end（10000 sq.m）	公共汽车、电车线路网长度 （公里） Network Length of Bus and Trolley Bus（km）
2000	119.1	1192	1789	2711
2001	123	1248	2169	2521
2002	133	1426	2594	896
2003	145.9	1595	2816	973
2004	154.8	1755	3254	1185
2005	178.8	1862	3547	1159
2006	227.5	3160	5218	1362
2007	250.7	3288	5411	1480
2008	267.1	3318	5596	1470
2009	272.9	3402	5763	1216
2010	282.3	3409	5893	1383
2011	291.5	3705	6605	1719
2012	374.6	4281	7528	1978
2013	469.6	4334	7859	2002
2014	490.7	4393	7908	2023
2015	566.4	4375	7940	2106
2016	599.3	4484	8057	2116
2017	638.4	4865	8496	2220
2018	715.1	5770	9862	2400
2019	758.2	6315	10227	3973
2020	758.2	6374	10510	4044
2021	761.5	6352	11546	9377
2022	969.1	8474	15142	9455

6-1 续表 2
Continued

年份 Year	自来水供水管道长度（公里） Length of Tap Water Pipelines (km)	全年供水总量（万立方米） Annual Volume of Tap Water Supply (10000 cu.m)	#全年售水量（万立方米） Annual Volume of Tap Water Sale (10000 cu.m)	#居民家庭用水 Consumption for Residential Use	用水普及率（%） Coverage Rate of Population with Access to Tap Water (%)	排水管道长度（公里） Length of Sewage Pipes (km)	全年用电量（亿千瓦时） Annual Volume of Electricity Supply (100 million kW·h)	#居民生活用电 Consumption for Residential Use
1949	308	721	456	331	89	200	0.88	0.14
1952	341	778	612	310	90	227	1.85	0.14
1957	412	1392	1 296	606	93	273	2.61	0.26
1962	483	2700	2 512	937	98	290	3.77	0.57
1965	500	3220	2 979	929	98	295	5.92	0.68
1970	521	4503	4106	1085	99	350	9.83	1.02
1975	564	6726	6302	1950	99	361	12.41	1.43
1978	572	5334	4975	1314	99	382	16.34	1.62
1980	588	8224	7874	2577	99	394	21.48	2.78
1985	685	7557	7038	2628	99.9	505	26.39	2.87
1990	873	11896	10211	4270	96.9	645	41.08	4.32
1991	908	13865	11760	4990	96.6	649	44.51	5.34
1992	1035	16385	13070	5931	96.5	672	51.78	6.84
1993	1123	16137	14027	6124	99.1	734	55.02	7.66
1994	1124	17367	14716	6405	100	811	60.74	8.78
1995	1046	22513	15810	7050	100	990	67.23	10.16
1996	1182	23277	16566	7731	100	1051	72.87	12.23
1997	1266	24130	17215	8787	100	1167	77.82	13.73
1998	1390	23845	17271	9115	100	1210	79.65	14.28
1999	1471	23849	18558	10032	100	1301	88.12	15.31

注：由于城市的发展变化，2022 年起，城市建设数据涵盖胶州市、平度市、莱西市数据。
Note：Due to the growth and changes of the city, from 2022, the data of urban development covers that of Jiaozhou, Pingdu and Laixi.

6-1 续表 3
Continued

年份 Year	自来水供水管道长度（公里）Length of Tap Water Pipelines（km）	全年供水总量（万立方米）Annual Volume of Tap Water Supply（10000 cu.m）	#全年售水量（万立方米）Annual Volume of Tap Water Sale（10000 cu.m）	#居民家庭用水 Consumption for Residential Use	用水普及率（%）Coverage Rate of Population with Access to Tap Water（%）	排水管道长度（公里）Length of Sewage Pipes（km）	全年用电量（亿千瓦时）Annual Volume of Electricity Supply（100 million kW·h）	#居民生活用电 Consumption for Residential Use
2000	1524	25414	20642	11405	100	1460	106.80	16
2001	1665	22225	18556	10555	100	1539	116.10	17.62
2002	1781	27662	21684	10129	100	1641	131.44	18.31
2003	2060	27594	21483	10142	100	1884	147.68	19.88
2004	2566	30877	23864	11695	100	2002	167.95	23.63
2005	2876	33265	25874	12536	100	2309	193.81	33.76
2006	3984	30524	25572	10682	100	3994	215.35	34.87
2007	4187	31533	26454	11408	100	4079	236.42	37.40
2008	4642	32675	27396	11301	100	4229	250.07	40.31
2009	4767	33490	28274	12250	100	4555	259.42	43.29
2010	4926	34909	29617	12524	100	4708	292.97	49.50
2011	5121	34109	28837	10049	100	5187	313.44	50.13
2012	5243	38945	33039	12121	100	6814	318.36	51.64
2013	5522	38331	32418	11851	100	6536	339.27	57.52
2014	6177	46649	40612	14834	100	6840	337.82	59.95
2015	6142	46203	40202	15381	100	6993	342.29	64.71
2016	6132	43033	36748	14430	100	7146	367.26	69.52
2017	6498	45991	38963	17439	100	7367	401.06	74.84
2018	7531	53235	43298	18473	100	8854	431.82	77.39
2019	7997	52203	44597	19809	100	9350	457.9	81.95
2020	8207	55352	48408	21166	100	9713	476.59	81.36
2021	8249	55561	48155	21988	100	10213	552.65	91.21
2022	10299	65161	56298	28039	100	12435	576.47	103.93

6-1 续表 4
Continued

年 份 Year	公共汽车、电车营运车辆（辆） Number of Bus and Trolley Bus under Operation（unit）	全年客运量（万人次） Annual Passenger Traffic（10000 person-times）	出租汽车（辆） Number of Taxi（unit）	使用液化气、煤气、天然气人数（万人） Population with Access to Gas（10000 persons）	液化气 Liquefied Petroleum	煤气 Coal Gas	天然气 Natural Gas	液化气供气量（吨） Volume of Liquefied Petroleum Supply（ton）
1949	32	298						
1952	76	932						
1957	112	4110						
1962	127	4747						
1965	173	6092						
1970	224	13002						
1975	324	14426		2	2			184.9
1978	409	27351		17	17			3246
1980	485	38981	48	24	24			4345
1985	621	48852	219	42.1	42.1			10619
1990	801	63495	832	75.0	57.4	17.6		17512
1991	1372	67552	1070	76.2	57.4	18.8		17963
1992	1470	73529	1828	82.8	62.0	20.8		19565
1993	1875	72427	4874	88.4	64.6	23.8		22224
1994	1850	78231	5806	103.6	77.4	26.2		24684
1995	1891	71867	5887	116.2	82.9	33.3		32443
1996	2012	49077	6660	126.0	88.0	38.0		4065
1997	2148	55642	6861	133.6	92.9	40.7		38717
1998	2184	51042	7469	146.8	97.8	49.0		45381
1999	2470	55414	7839	154.9	98.3	56.6		40537

注：1. 1990 年以前公共营运车辆不包括系统外及个体。
2. 由于城市的发展变化，2022 年起，城市建设数据涵盖胶州市、平度市、莱西市数据。

Notes：1. Vehicles not belonging to system and individual vehicles are not contained in public operating vehicles before 1990.
2. Due to the growth and changes of the city, from 2022, the data of urban development covers that of Jiaozhou, Pingdu and Laixi.

6-1 续表 5
Continued

年 份 Year	公共汽车、电车营运车辆（辆）Number of Bus and Trolley Bus under Operation (unit)	全年客运量（万人次）Annual Passenger Traffic (10000 person-times)	出租汽车（辆）Number of Taxi (unit)	使用液化气、煤气、天然气人数（万人）Population with Access to Gas (10000 persons)	液化气 Liquefied Petroleum	煤气 Coal Gas	天然气 Natural Gas	液化气供气量（吨）Volume of Liquefied Petroleum Supply (ton)
2000	3141	59879	7933	164.1	93.3	70.8		46951
2001	3453	60167	8110	168.8	87.5	81.3		45295
2002	3681	61713	8376	224.2	133.8	90.4		60123
2003	3648	58792	8109	246.7	138.3	93.1	15.3	67803
2004	3848	66463	8144	258.4	140.6	78.8	39.0	58548
2005	4039	68776	8121	265.0	132.6	45.7	86.7	78000
2006	4167	73726	8146	271.0	112.5	49.5	109.0	97343
2007	4524	78702	8221	275.6	104.1	12.1	159.4	79715
2008	4701	82460	9241	276.3	91.9	10.5	173.9	81987
2009	4288	81768	9316	276.1	59.8	12.3	204.0	96721
2010	4664	85251	9539	276.3	36.7	12.6	227.0	80073
2011	5419	89614	9683	277.1	25.8	12.6	238.7	79812
2012	5640	97922	9693	313.7	36.7	13.1	263.9	54341
2013	6179	101108	9826	318.9	33.0		285.9	41302
2014	6515	105592	9720	325.4	33.0		292.4	39255
2015	6748	102402	10033	338.3	28.9		309.4	35255
2016	7210	99596	10048	441.6	29.0		412.6	32291
2017	7420	104898	10875	445.8	26.2		419.6	28309
2018	7795	104782	10867	512.7	29.9		482.8	30427
2019	8489	108339	10877	529.5	27.0		502.5	30210
2020	8553	65014	10877	550.1	23.8		526.3	29029
2021	10592	86073	11992	580.2	23.0		557.2	31287
2022	10509	64549	11997	731.6	44.2		687.4	44350

6-1 续表 6
Continued

年份 Year	煤气供气量（万立方米）Volume of Coal Gas Supply（10000 cu.m）	天然气供气量（万立方米）Volume of Natural Gas Supply（10000 cu.m）	燃气普及率（%）Coverage Rate of Population with Access to Gas（%）	绿地面积（公顷）Area of Green Areas（hectare）	公园绿地面积（公顷）Park Green Areas（hectare）	人均公园绿地面积（平方米）Per Capita Park Green Areas（sq.m）	建成区绿化覆盖率（%）Green Coverage Rate of Developed Areas（%）	公园（个）Number of Parks and Zoos（unit）	公园面积（公顷）Area of Parks and Zoos（hectare）
1949				133	42	0.7	4.9	3	43
1952				134	43	0.7	4.4	4	45
1957				245	132	1.7	6.9	10	122
1962				771	184	2.2	14.0	12	174
1965				777	184	2.1	13.7	12	174
1970				772	184	2.1	13.0	6	117
1975			2.3	465	162	1.8	7.6	5	134
1978			18.6	469	162	1.7	7.6	6	165
1980			24.5	625	206	2.1	10.4	6	152
1985			36.3	1072	255	2.3	17.3	7	153
1990	3073		56.2	2120	492	3.7	22.8	26	404
1991	3439		56.5	2318	500	3.7	24.4	28	443
1992	3824		60.0	2471	515	3.7	25.9	28	417
1993	4215		63.1	2488	543	3.9	26.5	31	453
1994	4116		63.1	2866	572	4.0	27.9	31	463
1995	4734		79.2	4547	771	5.3	30.1	33	675
1996	5447		83.9	4679	836	5.6	30.4	33	675
1997	5920		87.3	4717	924	6.0	31.3	34	730

注：1. 自 2002 年起人均公共绿地面积按辖区内全部人口计算。
2. 2005 年以前所用园林绿地面积；公共绿地面积；人均公共绿地面积；公园、动物园个数；公园、动物园面积指标分别改为现在的绿地面积；公共绿地面积；人均公园绿地面积；公园个数；公园面积。
3. 由于城阳区绿化指标进行了调整，部分绿地属性发生变化。导致 2017 年公园绿地面积及人均公园绿地面积的数据小于 2016 年。
4. 由于城市的发展变化，2022 年起，城市建设数据涵盖胶州市、平度市、莱西市数据。

Notes：1. Per capita public green areas is calculated at total population in the area under jurisdiction since 2002.
2. Before 2005, the corresponding indicators of greenbelt area, public greenbelt area, per capita public greenbelt area, coverage rate of green, number of parks and zoos, area of parks and zoos.
3. As the green index of Chengyang District has been adjusted, some green space properties have changed. As a result, the data of park green area and per capita park green area in 2017 are smaller than 2016.
4. Due to the growth and changes of the city, from 2022, the data of urban development covers that of Jiaozhou, Pingdu and Laixi.

6-1 续表 7
Continued

年 份 Year	煤气供气量（万立方米）Volume of Coal Gas Supply（10000 cu.m）	天然气供气量（万立方米）Volume of Natural Gas Supply（10000 cu.m）	燃气普及率(%) Coverage Rate of Population with Access to Gas（%）	绿地面积（公顷）Area of Green Areas（hectate）	公园绿地面积（公顷）Park Green Areas（hectare）	人均公园绿地面积(平方米) Per Capita Park Green Areas（sq.m）	建成区绿化覆盖率（%）Green Coverage Rate of Developed Areas（%）	公园(个) Number of Parks and Zoos（unit）	公园面积（公顷）Area of Parks and Zoos(hectare)
1998	5959		92.5	6812	1047	6.6	35.0	35	775
1999	7319		96.0	7007	1186	7.4	35.9	36	791
2000	9567		98.0	7439	1423	8.5	37.0	37	790
2001	11814		99.0	7688	1588	9.3	37.5	39	832
2002	13500		99.5	7967	1791	8.1	36.4	43	926
2003	14826	1181	100	8829	2305	9.3	37.5	45	1034
2004	15503	2710	100	10047	2842	11.0	38.0	48	1421
2005	16573	7456	100	11137	3132	11.8	38.8	47	1110
2006	9821	13876	100	11756	3198	11.8	39.2	47	1188
2007	9516	18103	100	15369	3661	13.3	37.8	73	1268
2008	8691	21780	100	15630	4014	14.5	41.5	77	1815
2009	7523	26948	100	16003	4003	14.5	43.4	71	1897
2010	9153	35681	100	16619	4027	14.6	43.4	72	1917
2011	9137	46147	100	18013	4041	14.6	44.7	74	1931
2012	8148	68397	100	21471	4573	14.6	44.7	78	2112
2013		70918	100	28007	4649	14.6	44.7	87	2698
2014		74823	100	28805	4741	14.6	44.7	91	2988
2015		70311	100	29117	4802	14.6	44.7	87	3163
2016		70586	100	34851	8194	18.6	38.6	151	4460
2017		91572	100	36209	7763	17.4	39.1	175	4727
2018		120089	100	39229	8587	16.3	39.2	191	5767
2019		131867	100	40844	8922	16.9	40.2	192	5773
2020		130745	100	41829	10508	19.0	41.0	212	8426
2021		147284	100	42661	10465	18.0	43.1	236	7943
2022		208205	100	52996	12719	17.4	45.2	318	9738

6-2 全年供电(2022年)
ANNUAL ELECTRICITY SUPPLY（2022）

项目	Item	单位	Unit	2022年
发电设备总容量	Total Capacity of Generation Equipment	万千瓦	10000 kW	500.00
全年发电量	Annual Electricity Generation	亿千瓦时	100 million kW·h	196.28
全年实际用电量	Annual Electricity Consumption	亿千瓦时	100 million kW·h	576.47
#工业	Industrial	亿千瓦时	100 million kW·h	302.09
农业	Agricultural	亿千瓦时	100 million kW·h	11.08
生活	Residential	亿千瓦时	100 million kW·h	103.93
平均每日用电量	Average Daily Consumption	万千瓦时	10000 kW·h	15793.58

6-3　分行业用电(2022 年)
ELECTRICITY CONSUMPTION BY SECTOR（2022）

单位：万千瓦时（10000 kW・h）

行　业	Sector	2022 年	2022 年比 2021 年增长（%）Growth Rate in 2022 over 2021（%）
全社会用电总计	**Total Electricity Consumption**	**5764655.95**	**4.31**
一、农、林、牧、渔业	Agriculture，Forestry，Animal Husbandry and Fishery	110761.99	12.51
二、工业	Industry	3020866.38	1.37
三、建筑业	Construction	123820.66	7.82
四、交通运输、仓储和邮政业	Transport，Storage and Post	279560.89	4.66
五、信息传输、计算机服务和软件业	Information Transmission，Computer Services and Software	98362.24	9.94
六、商业、住宿和餐饮业	Trade，Hotels and Catering Services	324912.32	4.66
七、金融、房地产、商务及居民服务业	Financial，Real Business and Residential Services	344345.70	5.88
八、公共事业及管理组织	Public Management and Social Organization	421756.26	-1.52
九、城乡居民生活用电	Household Consumption	1039289.02	13.86
城镇居民	Urban Area	657372.88	15.57
乡村居民	Rural Area	381813.60	10.99

6-4 城市供水
URBAN WATER SUPPLY

项 目	Item	单位	Unit	2022 年
自来水供水管道长度	Length of Tap Water Pipelines	公里	km	10299
综合生产能力	Synthesis Production Capacity	万立方米 / 日	10000 cu.m/day	248
全年供水总量	Annual Volume of Tap Water Supply	万立方米	10000 cu.m	65161
# 售水量	Volume of Tap Water Supply	万立方米	10000 cu.m	56298
# 生产运营用水	Consumption for Production Use	万立方米	10000 cu.m	18751
公共服务用水	Consumption for Public Services Use	万立方米	10000 cu.m	9487
居民家庭用水	Consumption for Residential Use	万立方米	10000 cu.m	28039
其他用水	Consumption for Other Uses	万立方米	10000 cu.m	21
平均每日供水量	Daily Volume of Tap Water Supply	万立方米	10000 cu.m	179
# 生产用	Consumption for Production Use	万立方米	10000 cu.m	57
生活用	Consumption for Residential Use	万立方米	10000 cu.m	77
用水户数	Households with Access to Water	户	household	2606231
用水人口	Population with Access to water	万人	10000 persons	732
工业用水量重复利用率	Recycle Rate of water for Industrial Use	%	%	92.5

注：由于城市的发展变化，2022 年起，城市建设数据涵盖胶州市、平度市、莱西市数据。
Note：Due to the growth and changes of the city, from 2022, the data of urban development covers that of Jiaozhou, Pingdu and Laixi.

6-5 城市公共交通
URBAN PUBLIC TRAFFIC

项　目	Item	单位	Unit	2022 年
公共汽车、电车线路网长度	Network Length of Bus and Trolley Bus	公里	km	9455
轨道交通线路长度	Rail Transit Line Length	公里	km	324
公共汽车、电车营运车辆	Number of Bus and Trolley Bus under Operation	辆	unit	10509
#汽车	Bus	辆	unit	3908
电车	Trolley Bus	辆	unit	5883
公共汽车、电车全年客运量	Annual Passenger Traffic of Bus and Trolley Bus	万人次	10000 person-times	64549
公共汽车、电车平均每日客运量	Daily Passenger Traffic of Bus and Trolley Bus	万人	10000 persons	176.8
出租汽车数	Number of Taxi	辆	unit	11997
轮渡运营船数	Number of Ferry Boat under Operation	艘	ship	3
轮渡客运总量	Passenger Traffic of Ferry Boat	万人次	10000 person-times	1.8
轮渡平均每日客运量	Daily Passenger Traffic of Ferry Boat	万人	10000 persons	
轨道交通客运总量	Total Passenger Traffic Of Rail Transit	万人次	10000 person-times	28404
轨道交通平均每日客运量	Average Daily Passenger Volume of Rail Transit	万人	10000 persons	78

注：由于城市的发展变化，2022 年起，城市建设数据涵盖胶州市、平度市、莱西市数据。
Note：Due to the growth and changes of the city, from 2022, the data of urban development covers that of Jiaozhou, Pingdu and Laixi.

6-6 城市供气
URBAN GAS SUPPLY

项 目	Item	单位	Unit	2022 年
煤气供应总量	Volume of Coal Gas Supply	万立方米	10000 cu.m	
#家庭用量	Household Consumption	万立方米	10000 cu.m	
煤气用气户数	Households with Access to Coal Gas	户	household	
#家庭用户	Household Users	户	household	
液化石油气供应总量	Volume of Liquefied Petroleum Supply	吨	ton	44350
#家庭用量	Household Consumption	吨	ton	26627
液化石油气用气户数	Households with Access to Liquefied Petroleum	户	household	228353
#家庭用户	Household Users	户	household	213678
天然气供应总量	Volume of Natural Gas Supply	万立方米	10000 cu.m	208205
#家庭用量	Household Consumption	万立方米	10000 cu.m	44768
天然气用气户数	Households with Access to Natural Gas	户	household	2977016
#家庭用户	Household Users	户	household	2955728
燃气普及率	Coverage Rate of Population with Access to Gas	%	%	100

注：由于城市的发展变化，2022 年起，城市建设数据涵盖胶州市、平度市、莱西市数据。
Note: Due to the growth and changes of the city, from 2022, the data of urban development covers that of Jiaozhou, Pingdu and Laixi.

6-7 城市环境卫生
URBAN ENVIRONMENTAL SANITATION

项　目	Item	单位	Unit	2022 年
市容环卫专用车辆总数	Number of Special Vehicles for Environmental Sanitation	辆	unit	6771
生活垃圾清运量	Volume of Garbage Disposal	万吨	10000 tons	402
生活垃圾无害化处理厂（场）数	Number of Bio-safety Disposal Plant of Garbage	座	unit	13
生活垃圾无害化处理能力	Bio-safety Disposal Capacity of Garbage	吨 / 日	ton/day	11797
生活垃圾无害化处理量	Bio-safety Disposal Volume of Garbage	万吨	10000 tons	402
道路清扫保洁面积	Area under Cleaning Program	万平方米	10000 sq.m	9981
# 机械化	Mechanization	万平方米	10000 sq.m	8931
公共厕所	Public Toilets	个	unit	2016

注：由于城市的发展变化，2022 年起，城市建设数据涵盖胶州市、平度市、莱西市数据。
Note：Due to the growth and changes of the city, from 2022, the data of urban development covers that of Jiaozhou, Pingdu and Laixi.

6-8 城市道路、下水道及绿化
URBAN ROAD，SEWAGE AND GREEN

项　目	Item	单位	Unit	2022 年
道路	**Road**			
年末道路长度	Length of Roads at Year-end	公里	km	8474
年末道路面积	Area of Roads at Year-end	万平方米	10000 sq.m	15142
#人行道面积	Area of Pavements	万平方米	10000 sq.m	3136
排水管道长度	Length of Sewage Pipes	公里	km	12435
园林绿化	**Greening**			
绿化覆盖面积	Area of Green Coverage Areas	公顷	hectare	58100
绿地面积	Area of Green Areas	公顷	hectare	52996
公园绿地面积	Area of Park Green Areas	公顷	hectare	12719
公园数	Number of Parks and Zoos	个	unit	318
公园面积	Area of Parks and Zoos	公顷	hectare	9738
城市每人平均公园绿地面积	Per Capita Public Green Areas	平方米	sq.m	17
建成区绿化覆盖率	Green Coverage Rate of Developed Areas	%	%	45

注：由于城市的发展变化，2022 年起，城市建设数据涵盖胶州市、平度市、莱西市数据。
Note：Due to the growth and changes of the city, from 2022, the data of urban development covers that of Jiaozhou, Pingdu and Laixi.

6-9 环境保护基本情况
BASIC CONDITIONS OF ENVIRONMENTAL PROTECTION

项 目	Item	单位	Unit	2022 年	2021 年
二氧化硫排放总量	Sulphur Dioxide Emission	吨	ton	5681.18	5777.14
氮氧化物排放总量	Discharge Amount of Nitrogen Oxides	吨	ton	69579.50	70774.38
烟（粉）尘排放总量	Soot（Dust）Emission	吨	ton	11707.24	11155.74
工业固体废物排放总量	Industrial Solid Wastes Discharged	吨	ton		
化学需氧量排放总量	Discharge Amount of Chemical Oxygen Demand	吨	ton	38059.60	41151.57
氨氮排放总量	Discharge Amount of Ammonia and Nitrogen	吨	ton	1868.06	2024.49
废水排放总量	Waste Water Discharged	万吨	10000 tons	33964.86	30841.15

注：2022 年生态环境统计数据为初报数据，氮氧化物、烟（粉）尘排放总量为工业源、生活源、移动源、集中式治理设施排放总量之和，二氧化硫排放总量为工业源、生活源、集中式治理设施排放总量之和。

Note：The ecological and environmental statistics for 2022 are preliminary data. The total emission of nitrogen oxide, smoke (powder) dust refers to the sum of the total emission of industrial sources, domestic sources, mobile sources, sources of centralized treatment facilities, and the sulfur dioxide emissions refers to the sum of the total emission of industrial sources, domestic sources, sources of centralized treatment facilities.

6-10 环境质量状况
ENVIRONMENT CONDITION

项 目	Item	单位	Unit	2022 年	2021 年	2022 年比 2021 年增（+）减（-）% 2022 Compared to 2021（+/-）%
市区空气质量优良率	Urban air quality good rate	%	%	88.50	84.90	3.60
一、二类海水水质面积比例	The proportion of Grade I and Ⅱ waters	%	%	99.00	99.00	0.00
市区区域环境噪声平均等效声级	The Average Equivalent Sound Level of the Urban Regional Environmental Noise	分贝（A）	db（A）	54.80	57.00	
市区道路交通噪声平均等效声级	The Average Equivalent Sound Level of the Urban Road Traffic Noise	分贝（A）	db（A）	69.30	68.60	

注：2022 年"市区区域环境噪声平均等效声级""市区道路交通噪声平均等效声级"指标统计区域增加即墨区，无法同比计算。

Note：In 2022, the "average equivalent sound level of environmental noise in urban areas" and "average equivalent sound level of road traffic noise in urban areas" will cover the statistical area of Jimo District, which cannot be calculated year-on-year.

6-11　工业“三废”排放情况
DISCHARGE CONDITIONS OF INDUSTRIAL WASTE WATER, WASTE GAS AND SOLID WASTE

项　目	Item	单位	Unit	2022 年	2021 年	2022 年比 2021 年增（+）减（-）% 2022 Compared to 2021（+/-）%
工业废水排放总量	Industrial Waste Water Discharged	万吨	10000 tons	6692.13	6513.76	2.74
废水治理设施数	Number of Facilities for Treatment of Waste Water	套	set	600	465	29.03
废水治理设施处理能力	Capacity of Facilities for Treatment of Waste Water	万吨 / 日	10000 tons/day	51.17	42.47	20.49
进入城市污水处理厂量	Volume Handled by Sewage Treatment Plant	万吨	10000 tons	5750.26	5768.10	-0.31
化学需氧量排放量	Discharge Amount of Chemical Oxygen Demand	吨	ton	1928.81	2015.04	-4.28
氨氮排放量	Discharge Amount of Ammonia and Nitrogen	吨	ton	40.59	47.94	-15.33
工业废气排放总量	Industrial Waste Air Discharged	亿标立方米	100 million cu.m	5102.70	4918.97	3.74
废气治理设施数	Number of Facilities for Treatment of Waste Air	套	set	3207	2555	25.52
其中：脱硫设施数	of which：Desulphurization Facilities	套	set	165	167	-1.20
废气治理设施处理能力	Capacity of Facilities for Treatment of Waste Air	万标立方米 / 时	10000 cu.m/hour	26044.22	23358.45	11.50
二氧化硫去除量	Sulphur Dioxide Removed	吨	ton	162758.38	149244.40	9.05
二氧化硫排放量	Sulphur Dioxide Emission	吨	ton	2467.74	2896.73	-14.81
烟（粉）尘排放量	Soot（Dust）Emission	吨	ton	2497.84	2723.53	-8.29
工业固体废物产生量	Industrial Solid Wastes Produced	万吨	10000 tons	935.34	828.46	12.90
其中：危险废物	of which: Hazardous Wastes	万吨	10000 tons	27.73	23.82	16.41
工业固体废物综合利用量	Industrial Solid Wastes Comprehensive Utilized	万吨	10000 tons	894.30	737.81	21.21
工业固体废物排放量	Industrial Solid Wastes Discharged	万吨	10000 tons			
其中：危险废物	of which: Hazardous Wastes	吨	ton			

注：1. 2022 年数据为初报数据。
2. 危险废物产生量为独立数据，不包括在“工业固体废物产生量”之中。“工业固体废物产生量”“工业固体废物综合利用量”仅指一般工业固废。

Notes：1. Data for 2022 are preliminary data.
2. The amount of hazardous waste generated is an independent data, which is not included in the "Generation of Industrial Solid Waste". "Generation of industrial solid waste" and "comprehensive utilization of industrial solid waste" refer only to general industrial solid waste.

主要统计指标解释

供水综合生产能力 指按供水设施取水、净化、送水、出厂输水干管等环节设计能力计算的综合生产能力。

年末供水管道长度 指从送水泵至用户水表之间所有管道的长度。不包括新安装尚未使用的管道。

用水普及率 指城市用水人口数与城市人口总数的比率。计算公式：

$$用水普及率=\frac{城市用水人口数}{城市人口总数}\times 100\%$$

全年供水总量 指报告期供水企业（单位）供出的全部水量。包括有效供水量和漏损水量。

全年供气总量 指全年燃气企业（单位）向用户供应的燃气数量。包括销售量和损失量。

用气普及率 指报告期末使用燃气的城市人口数与城市人口总数的比率。计算公式为：

$$用气普及率=\frac{城市用气人口数}{城市人口总数}\times 100\%$$

年末道路长度 指年末道路长度和与道路相通的广场、桥梁、隧道的长度，按车行道中心线计算。在统计时只统计路面宽度在3.5米（含3.5米）以上的各种铺装道路，包括开放型工业区和住宅区道路在内。

工业废气排放量 指报告期内企业厂区内燃料燃烧和生产工艺过程中产生的各种排入大气的含有污染物的气体的总量，以标准状态（273K，101325Pa）计算。

工业废水排放量 指经过企业厂区所有排放口排到企业外部的工业废水量。包括生产废水、外排的直接冷却水、超标排放的矿井地下水和与工业废水混排的厂区生活污水，不包括外排的间接冷却水（清污不分流的间接冷却水应计算在内）。

工业废水排放达标量 指各项指标都达到国家或地方排放标准的外排工业废水量，包括未经处理外排达标的和经过处理后外排达标的和两部分。国家排放标准见GB8978—88。

工业固体废物产生量 指企业在生产过程中产生的固体状、半固体状和高浓度液体状废弃物的总量，包括危险废物、冶炼废渣、粉煤灰、炉渣、煤矸渣、尾矿、放射性废物和其他废物等；不包括矿山开采的剥离废石和掘进废石（煤矸石和呈酸性或碱性的废石除外）酸性或碱性废石是指采掘的废石其流经水、雨淋水的pH值小于4或pH值大于10.5者。

工业粉尘排放量 指企业在生产工艺过程中排放的能在空气中悬浮一定时间的固体颗粒物排放量。如钢铁企业的耐火材料粉尘、焦化企业的筛焦系统粉尘、烧结机的粉尘、石灰窑的粉尘、建材企业的水泥粉尘等。不包括电厂排入大气的烟尘。

化学需氧量（COD） 测量有机和无机物质化学分解所消耗氧的质量浓度的水污染指数。

Explanatory Notes on Main Statistical Indicators

Production Capacity of Water Supply refers to the designed comprehensive production capacity of water facilities, covering the 4 links of water collection, purification, conveyance, and outflow through trunk pipelines.

Length of Water Supply Pipelines at the Year-end refers to the total length of all the pipelines between the water pumps and the user water meters, excluding pipelines newly installed but not used yet.

Coverage Rate of Urban Population with Access to Tap Water refers to the ratio of the urban population with access to tap water to the total urban population. The formula is :

Coverage rate of urban population with access to tap water = (Urban population with access to tap water) / (Urban population) × 100%

Annual Volume of Water Supply refers to the total volume of water supplied by water-works (units) during the reference period, including both the effective water supply and loss during the water supply.

Annual Volume of Gas Supply refers to the total volume of gas provided to users by gas-producing enterprises (units) in a year, including the volume sold and the volume lost.

Coverage Rate of Urban population with Access to Gas refers to the ratio of the urban population with access to gas to the total urban population at the end of the reference period. The formula is :

Coverage rate of urban population with access to gas = (Urban population with access to gas/Urban population) × 100%

Length of Paved Roads at the Year-end refers to the length of roads with paved surface including squares bridges and tunnels connected with roads by the end of the year. Length of the roads is measured by the central lines for vehicles for paved roads with a width of 3.5 meters and over, including roads in open-ended factory compounds and residential quarters.

Industrial Waste Air Emission refers to discharge into atmosphere of waste air containing pollutants generated from fuel burning and production process in enterprises within a given period of time. It is calculated at standard status (273K, 101325Pa) .

Waste Water Discharged by Industry refers to the volume of waste water discharged by industrial enterprises through all their outlets, including waste water from production process, directly cooled water, groundwater from mining wells which does not meet discharge standards and sewage from households mixed with waste water produced by industrial activities, but excluding indirectly cooled water discharged (It should be included if the discharge is not separated with waste water) .

Industrial Waste Water Meeting Discharge Standards refers to volume of industrial waste water discharge which, with or without treatment, reaches national or local standards with regard to all pollutants. National Discharge standards see GB8978-88.

Industrial Solid Wastes Produced refers to total volume of solid, semi-solid and high concentration liquid residues produced by industrial enterprises from production process in a given period of time, including hazardous wastes, slag, coal ash, gangue, tailings, radioactive residues and other wastes, but excluding stones stripped or dug out in mining (gangue and acid or alkaline stones not included), A stone is acid or alkaline depending on the pH value of the water below 4 or above 10.5 when the stone is in, or soaked by, the water.

Industrial Dust Emission refers to volume of dust emitted by production process of enterprises and suspended in the air for a given period of time, including dust from refractory material of iron and steel works, dust from coke-screening systems and sintering machines of coke plants, dust from lime kilns and dust from cement production in building material enterprises, but excluding soot and dust emitted from power plants.

Chemical Oxygen Demand (COD) refers to indices of water pollution measuring the mass concentration of oxygen consumed by the chemical breakdown of organic and inorganic matter.

能源消耗 7

CONSUMPTION OF ENERGY

简 要 说 明

一、本篇资料的主要内容

本篇资料主要反映全市规模以上工业主要能源消费与库存情况，主要包括规模以上工业主要能源消费与库存、规模以上工业主要能源分行业消费量、重点耗能工业企业能源加工转换、规模以上工业主要能源工业消费量等方面的资料。

二、本篇资料的来源

本篇资料来源于规模以上工业能源统计年报，由市统计局能源统计处整理提供。

Brief Introduction

Ⅰ. Main Content

Data in this chapter show the consumption and stock of major energy of industry above designated size，including consumption and stock of major energy of industry above designated size，major energy consumption of industry above designated size grouped by sector，energy conversion of major energy-consuming industrial enterprises and major energy consumption of industry above designated size，etc.

Ⅱ. Source of Data

Data in this chapter are based on the annual report of energy consumed by industrial enterprises above designated size. The data are provided by the Division of Energy Statistics of Qingdao Municipal Bureau of Statistics.

7-1 规模以上工业主要能源消费与库存（2022年）
CONSUMPTION AND STOCK OF MAJOR ENERGY OF INDUSTRY ABOVE DESIGNATED SIZE（2022）

名　称	Name	单位	Unit	年初库存 Stock at Year-beginning	工业生产消费量 Consumption for Industrial Production	年末库存 Stock at Year-end
原　煤	Raw Coal	吨	ton	1249119.25	11083023.35	1178743.96
焦　炭	Coke	吨	ton	70447.38	2044948.09	14685.19
焦炉煤气	Coking Gas	万立方米	10000 cu.m		29086.20	
高炉煤气	Blast Furnace Gas	万立方米	10000 cu.m		735912.50	
原　油	Crude Oil	吨	ton	420815.00	13958956.67	423941.00
汽　油	Petrol	吨	ton	1043.12	15110.27	123.50
煤　油	Kerosene	吨	ton		24.36	
柴　油	Diesel Oil	吨	ton	1080.06	55614.89	1026.41
燃料油	Fuel Oil	吨	ton	9726.70	197739.48	10029.23
液化石油气	Liquefied Petroleum Gas	吨	ton	55737.04	1047287.72	8098.51
炼厂干气	Refinery Dry Gas	吨	ton		391900.00	
热　力	Heat	百万千焦	million kJ		27174238.52	
电　力	Electricity	万千瓦时	10000 kW · h		2293724.52	

补充资料：2022年综合能源消费量1754.6万吨标准煤。
Supplementary Information : The comprehensive energy consumption in 2022 will be 1754.6 million tons of standard coal.

7-2 规模以上工业主要能源分行业消费量(2022年)
MAJOR ENERGY CONSUMPTION OF INDUSTRY ABOVE DESIGNATED SIZE BY SECTOR（2022）

名 称	Name	原煤（吨）Raw Coal（ton）	焦炭（吨）Coke（ton）	焦炉煤气（万立方米）Coking Cas（10000 cu.m）	原油（吨）Crude Oil（ton）	汽油（吨）Petrol（ton）
总　计	**Total**	**11083023**	**2044948**	**29086**	**13958957**	**15110**
采掘业	Mining					
制造业	Manufacturing	1634314	2044948	7401	13958957	14352
电力煤气及水生产供应业	Production and Supply of Electricity，Gas and Water	9448710		21685		758

7-2 续表
Continued

名 称	Name	煤油（吨）Kerosene（ton）	柴油（吨）Diesel Oil（ton）	燃料油（吨）Fuel Oil（ton）	液化石油气（吨）Liquefied Petroleum Gas（ton）	热 力（百万千焦）Heat（millon kJ）	电 力（万千瓦时）Electricity（10000 kW·h）
总　计	**Total**	**24**	**55615**	**197739**	**1047288**	**27174239**	**2293725**
采掘业	Mining		162				4434
制造业	Manufacturing	24	53734	196375	1047288	23082938	2008556
电力煤气及水生产供应业	Production and Supply of Electricity，Gas and Water		1719	1364		4091300	280734

7-3　重点耗能工业企业能源加工转换（2022 年）

ENERGY CONVERSION OF MAJOR ENERGY-CONSUMING INDUSTRIAL ENTERPRISES（2022）

名　称	Name	单　位	Unit	能源消费合　计 Total Energy Consumption	#加工转换投　入 Conversion Input	火　电 Thermal Power	供　热 Heating	炼　油 Petroleum Refining	制　气 Gas Production	能源加工转换产出 Conversion Output of Energy
原　煤	Raw Coal	吨	ton	10828592	9793567	5288398	4478167		27001	
洗精煤	Dressing Coal	吨	ton	2000074	2000074					
煤制品	Coal Products	吨	ton	68840	68840		68840			
焦　炭	Coke	吨	ton	2028006						1493469
其他焦化产品	Other Coking Products	吨	ton	305287						76715
焦炉煤气	Coking Gas	万立方米	10000 cu.m	21685	21685	21117	568			29086
高炉煤气	Blast Furnace GAS	万立方米	10000 cu.m	723244	266696	259750	6946			
原　油	Raw Oil	吨	ton	13958957	13953542			13953542		
汽　油	Petrol	吨	ton	220						3789326
煤　油	Kerosene	吨	ton							820355
柴　油	Diesel Oil	吨	ton	1841	498	131	367			3586142
燃料油	Fuel Oil	吨	ton	164278	164169	1103	152	162914		2124538
液化石油气	Liquefied Petroleum Gas	吨	ton	1041620	20			20		1073253
炼厂干气	Refinery Dry Gas	吨	ton	391900	5162	516	4646			391900
其他石油制品	Other Petroleum Products	吨	ton	1522229	847471			847471		1271943
热　力	Heat	百万千焦	million kJ	13273644	2779724	2779724				94561512
电　力	Electricity	万千瓦时	10000 kW · h	890446						1741267
其他燃料	Other Fuel	吨标准煤	ton SCE	23610	23610	9596	14015			
能源合计	**Total**	**吨标准煤**	**ton SCE**	**44140469**	**33365379**	**5378216**	**3912576**	**22100742**	**24973**	**28363539**

7-4 规模以上工业主要能源工业消费量（2022 年）
MAJOR ENERGY CONSUMPTION Of INDUSTRY ABOVE DESIGNATED SIZE（2022）

行 业	Sector
总 计	**Total**
煤炭开采和洗选业	Mining and Washing of Coal
石油和天然气开采业	Extraction of Petroleum and Natural Gas
黑色金属矿采选业	Mining of Ferrous Metal Ores
有色金属矿采选业	Mining of Non-ferrous Metal Ores
非金属矿采选业	Mining and Processing of Non-metal Ores
开采辅助活动	Auxiliary Activities of Mining
其他采矿业	Mining of Other Ores
农副食品加工业	Processing of Food from Agricultural Products
食品制造业	Manufacture of Foods
酒、饮料和精制茶制造业	Manufacture of Liquor，Beverages and Refined Tea
烟草制品业	Manufacture of Tobacco
纺织业	Manufacture of Textile
纺织服装、服饰业	Manufacture of Textile Wearing Apparel
皮革、毛皮、羽毛及其制品和制鞋业	Manufacture of Leather，Fur，Feathre & Its Products Footwear
木材加工和木、竹、藤、棕、草制品业	Processing of Timber, Manufacture of Wood, Bamboo, Rattan, Palm and Straw Products
家具制造业	Manufacture of Furniture
造纸和纸制品业	Manufacture of Paper and Paper Products
印刷和记录媒介复制业	Printing，Reproduction of Recording Media
文教、工美、体育和娱乐用品制造业	Manufacture of Articles for Culture，Arts&Crafts，Sports and Entertainment
石油加工、炼焦和核燃料加工业	Processing of Petroleum，Coking，Processing of Nucleus Fuel
化学原料和化学制品制造业	Manufacture of Chemical Raw Material and Chemical Products
医药制造业	Manufacture of Medicines
化学纤维制造业	Manufacture of Chemical Fibres
橡胶和塑料制品业	Manufacture of Rubber and Plastic
非金属矿物制品业	Manufacture of metallic Mineral Products
黑色金属冶炼和压延加工业	Smelting and Pressing of Ferrous Metals
有色金属冶炼和压延加工业	Smelting and Pressing of Non-ferrous Metals
金属制品业	Manufacture of Metal Products
通用设备制造业	Manufacture of General Purpose Machinery
专用设备制造业	Manufacture of Special Purpose Machinery
汽车制造业	Manufacture of Vehicle
铁路、船舶、航空航天和其他运输设备制造业	Manufacture of Transport Equipment for Railway，Shipping，Aerospace and other uses
电气机械和器材制造业	Manufacture of Electrical Machinery and Equipment
计算机、通信和其他电子设备制造业	Manufacture of Computer，Communication Equipment and Other Electronic Equipment
仪器仪表制造业	Manufacture of Measuring Instrument
其他制造业	Manufacture of Other Products
废弃资源综合利用业	Recycling and Disposal of Waste Resources
金属制品、机械和设备修理业	Manufacture of Metal Products，Machinery and Equipment
电力、热力生产和供应业	Production and Supply of Electric Power and Heat Power
燃气生产和供应业	Production and Supply of Gas
水的生产和供应业	Production and Supply of Water

原煤 （吨） Raw Coal （ton）	洗精煤 （吨） Dressing Coal （ton）	其他洗煤 （吨） Other Dressing Coal （ton）	煤制品 （吨） Coal Products （ton）	焦炭 （吨） Coke （ton）
11083023	**2000074**	**43510**	**68840**	**2044948**
60111				
18860				
9				
5				
20956				
526107		43510		
85350				
215913				16181
706952	2000074			2028006
3				761
47				
9448710			68840	

7-4 续表 1
Continued

行 业	Sector
总　计	**Total**
煤炭开采和洗选业	Mining and Washing of Coal
石油和天然气开采业	Extraction of Petroleum and Natural Gas
黑色金属矿采选业	Mining of Ferrous Metal Ores
有色金属矿采选业	Mining of Non-ferrous Metal Ores
非金属矿采选业	Mining and Processing of Non–metal Ores
开采辅助活动	Auxiliary Activities of Mining
其他采矿业	Mining of Other Ores
农副食品加工业	Processing of Food from Agricultural Products
食品制造业	Manufacture of Foods
酒、饮料和精制茶制造业	Manufacture of Liquor，Beverages and Refined Tea
烟草制品业	Manufacture of Tobacco
纺织业	Manufacture of Textile
纺织服装、服饰业	Manufacture of Textile Wearing Apparel
皮革、毛皮、羽毛及其制品和制鞋业	Manufacture of Leather，Fur，Feathre & Its Products Footwear
木材加工和木、竹、藤、棕、草制品业	Processing of Timber, Manufacture of Wood, Bamboo, Rattan, Palm and Straw Products
家具制造业	Manufacture of Furniture
造纸和纸制品业	Manufacture of Paper and Paper Products
印刷和记录媒介复制业	Printing，Reproduction of Recording Media
文教、工美、体育和娱乐用品制造业	Manufacture of Articles for Culture，Arts&Crafts，Sports and Entertainment
石油加工、炼焦和核燃料加工业	Processing of Petroleum，Coking，Processing of Nucleus Fuel
化学原料和化学制品制造业	Manufacture of Chemical Raw Material and Chemical Products
医药制造业	Manufacture of Medicines
化学纤维制造业	Manufacture of Chemical Fibres
橡胶和塑料制品业	Manufacture of Rubber and Plastic
非金属矿物制品业	Manufacture of metallic Mineral Products
黑色金属冶炼和压延加工业	Smelting and Pressing of Ferrous Metals
有色金属冶炼和压延加工业	Smelting and Pressing of Non-ferrous Metals
金属制品业	Manufacture of Metal Products
通用设备制造业	Manufacture of General Purpose Machinery
专用设备制造业	Manufacture of Special Purpose Machinery
汽车制造业	Manufacture of Vehicle
铁路、船舶、航空航天和其他运输设备制造业	Manufacture of Transport Equipment for Railway，Shipping，Aerospace and other uses
电气机械和器材制造业	Manufacture of Electrical Machinery and Equipment
计算机、通信和其他电子设备制造业	Manufacture of Computer，Communication Equipment and Other Electronic Equipment
仪器仪表制造业	Manufacture of Measuring Instrument
其他制造业	Manufacture of Other Products
废弃资源综合利用业	Recycling and Disposal of Waste Resources
金属制品、机械和设备修理业	Manufacture of Metal Products，Machinery and Equipment
电力、热力生产和供应业	Production and Supply of Electric Power and Heat Power
燃气生产和供应业	Production and Supply of Gas
水的生产和供应业	Production and Supply of Water

焦炉煤气 （万立方米） Coking Gas （10000 cu.m）	高炉煤气 （万立方米） Blast Furnace GAS （10000 cu.m）	原油 （吨） Crude Oil （ton）	汽油 （吨） Petrol （ton）	煤油 （吨） Kerosene （ton）
29086	**735912**	**13958957**	**15110**	**24**
			501	
			345	
			182	
			375	
			398	
			78	
			69	
			103	
			273	
			497	
			258	
		13958957	17	
			744	
			206	
			12	
			1385	
7401	12668		529	
	456548		44	
			66	
			1359	1
			1344	23
			1737	
			743	
			1075	
			772	
			420	
			681	
			51	
			89	
21685	266696		85	
			268	
			405	

7-4 续表 2
Continued

行 业	Sector
总 计	**Total**
煤炭开采和洗选业	Mining and Washing of Coal
石油和天然气开采业	Extraction of Petroleum and Natural Gas
黑色金属矿采选业	Mining of Ferrous Metal Ores
有色金属矿采选业	Mining of Non-ferrous Metal Ores
非金属矿采选业	Mining and Processing of Non-metal Ores
开采辅助活动	Auxiliary Activities of Mining
其他采矿业	Mining of Other Ores
农副食品加工业	Processing of Food from Agricultural Products
食品制造业	Manufacture of Foods
酒、饮料和精制茶制造业	Manufacture of Liquor，Beverages and Refined Tea
烟草制品业	Manufacture of Tobacco
纺织业	Manufacture of Textile
纺织服装、服饰业	Manufacture of Textile Wearing Apparel
皮革、毛皮、羽毛及其制品和制鞋业	Manufacture of Leather，Fur，Feathre & Its Products Footwear
木材加工和木、竹、藤、棕、草制品业	Processing of Timber, Manufacture of Wood, Bamboo, Rattan, Palm and Straw Products
家具制造业	Manufacture of Furniture
造纸和纸制品业	Manufacture of Paper and Paper Products
印刷和记录媒介复制业	Printing，Reproduction of Recording Media
文教、工美、体育和娱乐用品制造业	Manufacture of Articles for Culture，Arts&Crafts，Sports and Entertainment
石油加工、炼焦和核燃料加工业	Processing of Petroleum，Coking，Processing of Nucleus Fuel
化学原料和化学制品制造业	Manufacture of Chemical Raw Material and Chemical Products
医药制造业	Manufacture of Medicines
化学纤维制造业	Manufacture of Chemical Fibres
橡胶和塑料制品业	Manufacture of Rubber and Plastic
非金属矿物制品业	Manufacture of metallic Mineral Products
黑色金属冶炼和压延加工业	Smelting and Pressing of Ferrous Metals
有色金属冶炼和压延加工业	Smelting and Pressing of Non-ferrous Metals
金属制品业	Manufacture of Metal Products
通用设备制造业	Manufacture of General Purpose Machinery
专用设备制造业	Manufacture of Special Purpose Machinery
汽车制造业	Manufacture of Vehicle
铁路、船舶、航空航天和其他运输设备制造业	Manufacture of Transport Equipment for Railway，Shipping，Aerospace and other uses
电气机械和器材制造业	Manufacture of Electrical Machinery and Equipment
计算机、通信和其他电子设备制造业	Manufacture of Computer，Communication Equipment and Other Electronic Equipment
仪器仪表制造业	Manufacture of Measuring Instrument
其他制造业	Manufacture of Other Products
废弃资源综合利用业	Recycling and Disposal of Waste Resources
金属制品、机械和设备修理业	Manufacture of Metal Products，Machinery and Equipment
电力、热力生产和供应业	Production and Supply of Electric Power and Heat Power
燃气生产和供应业	Production and Supply of Gas
水的生产和供应业	Production and Supply of Water

柴油 （吨） Diesel Oil （ton）	燃料油 （吨） Fuel Oil （ton）	液化石油气 （吨） Liquefied Petroleum Gas （ton）	炼厂干气 （吨） Refinery Dry Gas （ton）
55615	**197739**	**1047288**	**391900**
15			
147			
1783	856	258	
246		664	
320		30	
127		413	
95			
455	222		
58			
38			
411			
540	652		
221		7	
354	162914	1130	391900
2268	632	1041600	
184			
21			
2345	347	385	
28518	30239	1896	
58		2	
855			
1829	66	443	
1522		92	
445			
1325		69	
8384	447	111	
834		180	
391		8	
12			
21			
73			
1553	1364		
22			
144			

7-4 续表 3
Continued

行　业	Sector
总　　计	**Total**
煤炭开采和洗选业	Mining and Washing of Coal
石油和天然气开采业	Extraction of Petroleum and Natural Gas
黑色金属矿采选业	Mining of Ferrous Metal Ores
有色金属矿采选业	Mining of Non-ferrous Metal Ores
非金属矿采选业	Mining and Processing of Non–metal Ores
开采辅助活动	Auxiliary Activities of Mining
其他采矿业	Mining of Other Ores
农副食品加工业	Processing of Food from Agricultural Products
食品制造业	Manufacture of Foods
酒、饮料和精制茶制造业	Manufacture of Liquor, Beverages and Refined Tea
烟草制品业	Manufacture of Tobacco
纺织业	Manufacture of Textile
纺织服装、服饰业	Manufacture of Textile Wearing Apparel
皮革、毛皮、羽毛及其制品和制鞋业	Manufacture of Leather, Fur, Feathre & Its Products Footwear
木材加工和木、竹、藤、棕、草制品业	Processing of Timber, Manufacture of Wood, Bamboo, Rattan, Palm and Straw Products
家具制造业	Manufacture of Furniture
造纸和纸制品业	Manufacture of Paper and Paper Products
印刷和记录媒介复制业	Printing, Reproduction of Recording Media
文教、工美、体育和娱乐用品制造业	Manufacture of Articles for Culture, Arts&Crafts, Sports and Entertainment
石油加工、炼焦和核燃料加工业	Processing of Petroleum, Coking, Processing of Nucleus Fuel
化学原料和化学制品制造业	Manufacture of Chemical Raw Material and Chemical Products
医药制造业	Manufacture of Medicines
化学纤维制造业	Manufacture of Chemical Fibres
橡胶和塑料制品业	Manufacture of Rubber and Plastic
非金属矿物制品业	Manufacture of metallic Mineral Products
黑色金属冶炼和压延加工业	Smelting and Pressing of Ferrous Metals
有色金属冶炼和压延加工业	Smelting and Pressing of Non-ferrous Metals
金属制品业	Manufacture of Metal Products
通用设备制造业	Manufacture of General Purpose Machinery
专用设备制造业	Manufacture of Special Purpose Machinery
汽车制造业	Manufacture of Vehicle
铁路、船舶、航空航天和其他运输设备制造业	Manufacture of Transport Equipment for Railway, Shipping, Aerospace and other uses
电气机械和器材制造业	Manufacture of Electrical Machinery and Equipment
计算机、通信和其他电子设备制造业	Manufacture of Computer, Communication Equipment and Other Electronic Equipment
仪器仪表制造业	Manufacture of Measuring Instrument
其他制造业	Manufacture of Other Products
废弃资源综合利用业	Recycling and Disposal of Waste Resources
金属制品、机械和设备修理业	Manufacture of Metal Products, Machinery and Equipment
电力、热力生产和供应业	Production and Supply of Electric Power and Heat Power
燃气生产和供应业	Production and Supply of Gas
水的生产和供应业	Production and Supply of Water

其他石油制品（吨）Other Petroleum Products (ton)	热　力（百万千焦）Heat (million kJ)	电　力（万千瓦时）Electricity (10000 kW·h)	其他燃料（吨标准煤）Other Fuel (ton SCE)
1522854	**27174239**	**2293725**	**24805**
		3620	
		814	
	3360969	97903	22091
	659157	47161	66
	1829252	19659	
	1652173	43267	
	253865	9589	
		5937	161
		5166	
		7735	110
	64775	9008	
	262054	18335	
		14112	
1458394	2343	122255	
64437	6114372	374441	
	366621	18687	
	9532	6182	
	3016029	199102	
	201507	158566	
	3309573	240325	
		23755	
2	107690	105080	
	118872	81585	
	102137	39126	
21	389819	102502	
	753544	78326	
	346383	80436	
	162271	88922	
		4626	
		3012	
		3376	
		380	
	4091300	206755	2376
		10756	
		63223	

主要统计指标解释

工业企业能源消费量 工业企业能源消费包括工业企业在生产过程中作为燃料、动力、原料、辅助材料使用的能源以及工艺用能、非生产用能；作为能源加工转换企业，还要包括能源加工转换的投入量。工业企业能源消费量具体包括：

（1）用于本企业产品生产、工业性作业和其他生产性活动的能源。

（2）用于技术更新改造措施、新技术研究和新产品试制以及科学试验等方面的能源。

（3）用于经营维修、建筑及设备大修理、机电设备和交通运输工具等方面的能源。

（4）用于劳动保护的能源。

（5）其他非生产消费的能源。

不包括：

（1）由仓库发到车间，但在报告期最后一天没有消费的能源。这部分能源应在办理假退料手续后计入库存量。

（2）拨到外单位，委托外单位加工用的能源。

（3）调出本单位或借给外单位的能源。

工业生产能源消费 是指工业企业为进行工业生产活动所使用的能源。主要包括：

（1）用于本企业产品生产、工业性作业的能源，包括用作原料、材料、燃料、动力：作为能源加工转换企业，还包括用作加工转换的能源。

（2）产品生产过程中作为辅助材料使用的能源。

（3）生产工艺过程使用的能源。

（4）新技术研究、新产品试制、科学试验使用的能源。

（5）为了工业生产活动而在进行的各种修理过程中使用的能源。

（6）生产区内的劳动保护用能等。

Explanatory Notes on Main Statistical Indicators

Energy Consumption of Industrial Enterprises include energy in the production process as fuel, power, raw materials, supplementary materials, and for use of technology and non-production. As energy processing and conversion enterprises, also include energy processing and conversion of inputs. These specifically include：(1) Energy for the enterprise product, industrial production operations and other activities. (2) Energy for technical upgrading measures and new technology research and new product production and scientific experiments. (3) Energy for operation maintenance, construction and equipment overhaul, electrical and mechanical equipment and transport, and other aspects. (4) Energy for the protection of labor. (5) Energy for Other non-production and consumption. And these exclude：(1) Energy from the warehouse to the workshop, but out of consumption on the last day of the reporting period. This part of the energy should leave retreat materials handling procedures included stock. (2) Energy transferred to other units, entrusted with the processing. (3) Energy transferred out of the unit or loans to other units.

Energy Consumption for Industrial Production refers to energy for industrial enterprises in industrial production activities. These mainly include：(1) Energy for the enterprise products, industrial operations, including energy as raw materials, materials, fuels, and Power. As energy processing and conversion enterprises, also include energy for processing and conversion. (2) Energy as supplementary material in product process. (3) Energy used in production process. (4) Energy for new technologies, new product production, and scientific experiment. (5) Energy in process of repairing for industrial production activities. (6) Energy for labor protection in production areas and so on.

财政、金融和保险业 8

GOVERNMENT FINANCE, FINANCIAL AND INSURANCE

简要说明

一、本篇资料的主要内容

本篇资料主要反映全市财政收支、金融和保险方面的情况，主要包括财政收入、财政支出、金融机构存贷款、保险业务开展等方面的资料。

二、本篇资料的来源

1. 财政部分的资料来源于市财政局。

2. 金融方面的资料来源于中国人民银行青岛市分行。

3. 保险方面的资料来源于国家金融监督管理总局青岛监管局。

本篇资料由市统计局国民经济核算处整理提供。

Brief Introduction

Ⅰ. Main Content

Data in this chapter mainly reflects the city's fiscal revenue and expenditure, finance and insurance, mainly including fiscal revenue, fiscal expenditure, deposits and loans of financial institutions, and insurance business development.

Ⅱ. Source of Data

1. The financial information comes from the Qingdao Municipal Finance Bureau.

2.The financial information comes from the People's Bank of China Qingdao Branch .

3. Information on insurance is from National Financial Regulatory Administration Qingdao Bureau.

The data in this article is compiled and provided by the National Economic Accounting Office of Qingdao Statistics Bureau.

8-1 主要年份地方财政收支
MAJOR YEAR'S REVENUE AND EXPENDITURE OF LOCAL GOVERNMENT FINANCE

单位：万元（10000 yuan）

年份 Year	财政收入 Revenue of Government Finance	财政支出 Expenditure of Government Finance
1949	1527	306
1952	19809	2226
1957	29875	3556
1962	32869	4327
1965	47682	6280
1970	95778	7825
1975	90220	11966
1978	130749	19427
1980	124835	20064
1985	165155	41996
1988	201206	93931
1990	242303	133875
1991	259377	137716
1992	275589	155696
1993	182348	211938
1994	227490	277331
1995	294771	376982
1996	379674	469569
1997	476804	564787
1998	580434	678575
1999	680089	740937
2000	800120	878702
2001	987080	1097848
2002	1006616	1243880
2003	1201398	1471747
2004	1305136	1646214
2005	1763412	2030622
2006	2257663	2367875
2007	2925798	3211777
2008	3424359	3694111
2009	3769896	4335754
2010	4526138	5323888
2011	5661400	6580605
2012	6701820	7659801
2013	7889313	10142273
2014	8952450	10747138
2015	10063220	12228664
2016	11000303	13528516
2017	11572389	14030252
2018	12319138	15597764
2019	12417359	15759729
2020	12538548	15846485
2021	13682971	17067635
2022	12733096	16961652

注：1. 1993 年以后实行新制度，财政收入数与历年不可比。
2. 2002 年以后，财政收入、支出为一般预算数。

Notes：1. Since 1993，new regulations have been adopted in calculating revenue of government finance，the figures are not comparable with those over the years.
2. Since 2002，revenue of government finance and expenditure of government finance refer to general budgetary revenue and expenditure.

8-2 分市、区公共财政预算收入（2022年）
PUBLIC FINANCE BUDGET REVENUE BY REGION（2022）

单位：万元（10000 yuan）

市、区名称	Region	一般公共预算收入 Public Finance Budget Revenue	#增值税 Value-added Tax	#营业税 Business Tax	#企业所得税 Enterprise Income Tax
全　市	**Whole Municipality**	**12733096**	**2572486**		**1830525**
市南区	Shinan District	923523	262925		135419
市北区	Shibei District	742610	26552		176097
李沧区	Licang District	511092	41158		69115
崂山区	Laoshan District	2036659	463708		483046
黄岛区	Huangdao District	2545402	303583		480009
城阳区	Chengyang District	1461027	270165		164194
即墨区	Jimo District	995479	154408		72520
胶州市	Jiaozhou	1129809	262873		65692
平度市	Pingdu	612927	90519		48827
莱西市	Laixi	576992	171395		60656

8-2 续表
Continued

单位：万元（10000 yuan）

市、区名称	Region	#个人所得税 Personal Income Tax	#城市维护建设税 Urban Maintenance and Development Tax	#基金预算收入 Funds Budgetary Revenue
全　市	**Whole Municipality**	**726050**	**587365**	**8963050**
市南区	Shinan District	124534	40644	
市北区	Shibei District	44945	52920	
李沧区	Licang District	20486	26179	
崂山区	Laoshan District	182095	134380	768087
黄岛区	Huangdao District	125118	131232	2351139
城阳区	Chengyang District	50378	58366	1092683
即墨区	Jimo District	27661	46806	582610
胶州市	Jiaozhou	25602	48126	661556
平度市	Pingdu	22829	22789	169280
莱西市	Laixi	102402	25923	271175

8-3 分市、区公共财政预算支出（2022年）
PUBLIC FINANCE BUDGET EXPENDITURE BY REGION（2022）

单位：万元（10000 yuan）

市、区名称	Region	一般公共预算支出 Public Finance Budget Revenue	#一般公共服务支出 General Public Services	#公共安全 Public Security	#教育 Education	#科学技术 Science and Technology	#文化旅游体育与传媒 Culture, Tourism, Sports and Media
全　市	**Whole Municipality**	**16961652**	**1828211**	**998752**	**3321126**	**494822**	**274867**
市南区	Shinan District	570310	77332	24627	121840	6570	4552
市北区	Shibei District	590976	92304	17935	193915	19993	2767
李沧区	Licang District	423434	68295	11178	134211	4673	3745
崂山区	Laoshan District	1417820	135355	38721	203002	106158	8252
黄岛区	Huangdao District	2724689	343668	86296	616652	130985	28364
城阳区	Chengyang District	1478539	138534	30219	402180	82609	34754
即墨区	Jimo District	1329000	156974	48838	369225	16051	10904
胶州市	Jiaozhou	1395272	182696	60759	350705	20762	19875
平度市	Pingdu	1130679	113067	49872	312757	8303	6454
莱西市	Laixi	894353	106764	39184	160423	2919	6486

8-3 续表
Continued

单位：万元（10000 yuan）

市、区名称	Region	#社会保障和就业 Social Security and Employment	#卫生健康 Health and Hygiene	#节能环保 Environment Protection	#城乡社区 Urban and Rural Communities	#农林水 Agriculture, Forestry and Water Conservancy	#基金预算支出 Funds Budgetary Expenditure
全　市	**Whole Municipality**	**2525402**	**1424188**	**320918**	**1853260**	**864015**	**13317639**
市南区	Shinan District	120397	62895	7143	69105	7115	60704
市北区	Shibei District	87329	31010	11561	75220	2766	173242
李沧区	Licang District	56015	45038	15233	63391	1157	361131
崂山区	Laoshan District	78105	75285	27917	319049	63473	770451
黄岛区	Huangdao District	374425	235834	24501	238980	118101	3605502
城阳区	Chengyang District	145167	93758	2671	70184	70533	1989959
即墨区	Jimo District	294369	127282	10746	53963	90235	1059670
胶州市	Jiaozhou	186647	143603	31117	149166	90605	1112163
平度市	Pingdu	240071	116573	7162	27241	183414	483732
莱西市	Laixi	193262	98031	18597	41390	105102	691032

8-4 主要年份金融系统人民币存贷款（年末余额）

MAJOR YEAR'S DEPOSITS AND LOANS OF FINANCIAL INSTITUTIONS（YEAR-END BALANCE）

单位：万元（10000 yuan）

年份 Year	存款合计 Total Deposits	#企业存款 Deposits by Enterprises	#储蓄存款 Savings Deposits	贷款合计 Total Loans
1949	693	239	28	278
1952	9093	4308	1838	3322
1957	10372	3359	4037	30690
1962	20040	8579	3279	73601
1965	27331	11830	6347	64555
1970	38264	13024	7576	126382
1975	60622	22568	15637	207006
1978	66523	21004	21455	297184
1980	120644	38105	38609	379666
1985	344760	99736	155604	452142
1990	1235562	321542	655895	1535751
1991	1553564	411417	824428	1871462
1992	2076667	612868	1044165	2352449
1993	2747294	835617	1372239	2940658
1994	3769019	1399110	1918734	3610564
1995	5324026	2030382	2687888	4777864
1996	6991289	2630958	3499219	5941281
1997	7385092	2885632	4060259	6508776
1998	8183471	3018063	4591012	7239231
1999	9160001	3454570	4978045	8945730
2000	10560624	4386316	5353215	9564293
2001	12323942	4955336	6187409	10798871
2002	15225733	5819655	7449408	13044792
2003	18920868	7027227	9084693	16783917
2004	22462592	7924690	10894941	18472613
2005	26975372	8226661	13431016	20394792
2006	32453583	10144296	15676197	25779442
2007	38915882	13213434	17020383	30970553
2008	47353803	14641948	21233637	37483209
2009	63019764	21001185	25278658	48735326
2010	76592065	27271963	29123256	58862263
2011	86384994	49189415	31985099	69477500
2012	94348924	50978985	37576007	79465532
2013	109695588	60367185	41405946	88607439
2014	113703085	60791933	44358964	97200532
2015	125330268	45526577	50235905	107718528
2016	140071344	50912759	53263262	118916821
2017	143877550	53835435	53941843	132647913
2018	155321863	57270448	59137089	151941934
2019	172829678	66873600	67552370	173318261
2020	198218001	76209031	80309469	202109625
2021	215823413	82945990	90282352	232534611
2022	241662892	90856152	109482351	260447258

注：本表数据来源于人民银行，自 2015 年起，人民银行报表指标变化，企业存款指标暂用非金融企业存款，储蓄存款指标暂用住户存款，口径与以前年度不一致。

Note：The data in this table comes from the People's Bank of China. Since 2015, the report index of the People's Bank of China has changed, the enterprise deposit index is temporarily used as the deposit of the enterprise, the savings deposit index is temporarily used for household deposit, the caliber is not consistent with the previous year.

8-5　金融系统人民币存贷款（年末余额）
DEPOSITS AND LOANS OF FINANCIAL INSTITUTIONS（YEAR-END BALANCE）

单位：万元（10000 yuan）

项　目	Item	2022 年	比年初增减数 Incremental/Reductions Compared to the Beginning of the Year
一、存款总计	Total Deposits	241662892	25839479
住户存款	Household Deposits	109482351	19199803
非金融企业存款	Non-Financial Corporate Deposits	90856152	7921498
广义政府存款	General Government Deposits	27339983	-617764
非银行业金融机构存款	Non-Banking Financial Institutions's Deposits	12021637	-98097
二、贷款总计	Total Loans	260447258	27912647
住户贷款	Household Loans	78471983	1702784
#短期贷款	Short-Term Loans	10061600	-333603
中长期贷款	Medium And Long-Term Loans	68410383	2036387
非金融企业及机关团体贷款	Non-Financial Enterprises and Institutions/ Organizations' Loans	181428974	25979658
#短期贷款	Short-Term Loans	51803541	6511141
中长期贷款	Medium & Long-term Loans	112627227	15920846
票据融资	Notes Financing	15096330	3159978
非银行业金融机构贷款	Non-Banking Financial Institution's Loans		

注：自 2015 年起，人民银行报表中指标发生变化，本表数据按照新指标提供。
Note：Since 2015, the indexes in the People's Bank of China's statements have changed, the data in the table are provided according to the new indexes.

8-6 国内保险业务（2000—2022 年）

DOMESTIC INSURANCE BUSINESS（2000—2022）

项　目	Item	2000 年	2005 年	2010 年	2012 年	2013 年
风险保障金额	**Total Domestic Insurance Value**	**38357485**	**91691581**	**309244255**	**447476690**	**491953749**
国内业务收入	**Domestic Business Income**	**220780**	**495701**	**1538526**	**1602881**	**1789854**
1. 保费收入	Premium Income	218714	495701	1538526	1602881	1789854
#财产险	Property Insurance	85161	159746	492190	644269	744470
农业险	Agriculture Insurance	18	12	3261	5046	6824
人身险	Personal Insurance	133535	335943	1043075	953566	1038560
国内业务支出	**Domestic Business Expenditure**	**94877**	**214148**	**497832**	**592167**	**757404**
1 . 赔款支出	Indemnity Expenditure	62275	111385	279019	360085	432494
#财产险	Property Insurance	58361	92700	250966	328877	392860
农业险	Agriculture Insurance	5	11	2808	1833	3820
人身险	Personal Insurance	3909	18674	25245	29375	35814
2 . 给付支出	Mature Payment	27955	32739	109318	154922	194592
3 . 退保	Surrender	4647	70024	109496	77159	130318

注：1. 本表由国家金融监督管理总局青岛监管局提供，风险保障金额 2012 年之前为国内保险总值。
2. 因部分保险机构正在进行风险处置，2021 年后保险业相关数据暂不包括这部分机构。

Notes：1. This table is provided by the National Financial Regulatory Administration Qingdao Bureau. The amount of risk protection before 2012 was the total value of domestic insurance.
2. As some insurance institutions are in the process of risk disposal, insurance industry data after 2021 do not include those of these institutions.

单位：万元（10000 yuan）

2014 年	2015 年	2016 年	2017 年	2018 年	2019 年	2020 年	2021 年	2022 年
611632799	**836499657**	**1687559828**	**2232390824**	**2337365406**	**2759993215**	**3149621411**	**4706405207**	**6464309268**
2031421	**2441172**	**3359013**	**3967170**	**4393970**	**4868673**	**5183142**	**4618400**	**5024708**
2031421	2441172	3359013	3967170	4393970	4868673	5183142	4618400	5024708
872805	920229	1046908	1062116	1269489	1243160	1451301	1404366	1496425
8395	12100	12734	15670	18043	24523	28263	37427	47263
1150220	1508843	2299371	2889384	3106438	3600989	3703578	3176607	3481019
1031415	**1236281**	**1522375**	**1704218**	**1919252**	**1882881**	**1788966**	**1949551**	**2112128**
492693	539320	681211	733493	917964	937025	1045920	1194932	1353211
442168	492573	526586	554513	756987	706639	831317	935922	1003148
5519	9724	16337	18232	10985	14019	24474	19531	30531
45006	37023	138288	160749	149992	216368	190129	239478	319532
274790	340786	455300	470266	493511	498555	379492	428880	439748
263932	356175	376777	500459	507777	447301	363553	325739	319169

主要统计指标解释

财政收入 指国家财政参与社会产品分配所取得的收入，是实现国家职能的财力保证。财政收入所包括的内容几经变化，目前主要包括：

（1）税收收入:包括增值税、企业所得税、个人所得税、资源税、城市维护建设税、房产税、印花税、城镇土地使用税、土地增值税、车船税、耕地占用税、契税、烟叶税、其他税收收入。

（2）非税收入:包括专项收入、行政事业性收费收入、罚没收入、国有资本经营收入、国有资源有偿使用收入、捐赠收入、政府住房基金收入、其他收入。

财政支出 国家财政将筹集起来的资金进行分配使用，以满足经济建设和各项事业的需要，主要包括：

（1）一般公共服务支出：反映政府提供一般公共服务的支出。

（2）公共安全:反映政府维护社会公共安全方面的支出,有关事务包括武装警察、公安、国家安全、检察、法院、司法行政、监狱、劳教、国家保密、缉私警察等。

（3）教育支出：反映政府教育事务支出。有关具体教育事务包括教育行政管理、学前教育、小学教育、初中教育、普通高中教育、普通高等教育、初等职业教育、中专教育、技校教育、职业高中教育、高等职业教育、广播电视教育、留学生教育、特殊教育、干部继续教育、教育机关服务等。

（4）科学技术：反映政府用于科学技术方面的支出。

（5）文化旅游体育与传媒：反映政府在文化、旅游、文物、体育、广播电视、新闻出版等方面的支出。

（6）社会保障和就业:反映政府在社会保障与就业方面的支出。有关事项包括社会保障与就业管理事务、民政管理事务、财政对社会保险基金的补助、补充全国社会保障基金、行政事业单位离退休、企业改革补助、就业补助、抚恤、退役安置、社会福利、残疾人事业、城市居民最低生活保障、其他城镇社会救济、农村社会救济、自然灾害生活补助、红十字事务等。

（7）卫生健康支出：反映政府卫生健康方面的支出。

（8）节能环保：反映政府节能环保支出。

（9）城乡社区：反映政府城乡社区事务支出。具体包括：城乡社区管理事务支出、城乡社区规划与管理支出、城乡社区公共设施支出、城乡社区住宅支出、城乡社区环境卫生支出、建设市场管理与监督支出等。

（10）农林水：反映政府农林水事务方面的支出。具体包括农业、林业、水利、扶贫支出、农业综合开发支出等。

存款 指企业、机关、团体或居民根据资金必须收回的原则，把货币资金存入银行或其他信贷机构保管并取得一定利息的一种信用活动形式。根据存款对象或性质的不同可划分为住户存款、非金融企业存款、财政性存款、机关团体存款、非银行业金融机构存款等科目。它是银行信贷资金的主要来源。

贷款 指银行或其他信贷机构根据资金必须归还的原则，按一定利率，为企业、个人等提供资金的一种信用活动形式。我国银行贷款分为短期贷款、中长期贷款、融资租赁、票据融资、各项垫款等。

保费 指投保人为取得保险人在约定范围内所承担赔偿责任而支付给保险人的费用。

Explanatory Notes on Main Statistical Indicators

Government Revenue refers to the revenue of the government finance by means of participating in the distribution of the social products, which is the financial resources for ensuring the government to function. The contents of government revenue have been changed several times. Now it includes the following main items:

(1) Various tax revenues, including value added tax, enterprise income tax, personal income tax, resources tax, fixed assets investment direction regulating tax, tax on city maintenance and construction, real estate tax, stamp tax, tax on use of urban land, land

value added tax, vehicle and vessel tax, tax on occupancy of cultivated land, property tax, tobacco leaf tax, and other tax revenues.

(2) Non–tax income: including special income, administrative fee income, fine and confiscated income, state–owned capital operating income, income from the paid use of state–owned resources, donation income, government housing fund income, and other income.

Government Expenditure refers to the distribution and use of the funds the government finance has raised, so as to meet the needs of economic construction and various causes. It includes the following main items:

(1) Expenditure for general public services: It reflects the expenditure from the government for general public services.

(2) Expenditure on public security: It reflects the expenditure from the government towards safeguarding the public security, including the related affairs of armed police, public security, state security, procuratorial administration, law court, judicial administration, jail , reeducation through labor, state confidentiality, anti-smuggling Patrol, etc.

(3) Expenditure on education: It reflects the expenditure from the government on education, including the related affairs of educational administration management, preschool education, primary education, junior secondary educate, regular senior secondary educate, regular higher education, primary vocational education, specialized secondary educate, technical educate, vocational senior secondary educate, vocational higher education, radio and television education, foreign student educate, special education, cadre continuing education, education institution services,etc.

(4) Expenditure on science and technology: It reflects the expenditure from the government on science and technology.

(5) Cultural tourism, sports and media: reflecting government expenditures on culture, tourism, cultural relics, sports, radio and television, press and publication, etc.

(6) Expenditure on social security and employment:It reflects the expenditure from the government on social security and employment, including the related affairs of management of social security and employment, civil administration, subsidies to social insurance funds, supplement to national social security funds, retirees of government agencies and institutions, subsidies to enterprises reform, subsidies to employment, pension, settling down demobilized servicemen, social security, disabled person administration, minimum living allowance in urban area, other social relief in urban area, social relief in rural area, subsidies to natural disaster, Red Cross business, etc.

(7) Health expenditure: reflecting government's expenditure on health.

(8) Expenditure on energy saving and environmental protection: reflecting the government's expenditure on energy saving and environmental protection.

(9) Urban and rural community: It reflects the expenditure from the government on urban and rural community affairs, including expenditure on management of urban and rural community affairs, plan and management of urban and rural community, public utility of urban and rural community, residential buildings of urban and rural community, environmental sanitation of urban and rural community, management and supervision of markets construction, etc.

(10) Agriculture, forestry and water conservancy: reflecting the government's expenditure on agriculture, forestry and water conservancy, poverty alleviation, and comprehensive agricultural development, etc.

Deposit refers to a form of credit activity in which enterprises, agencies, organizations or residents deposit monetary funds in banks or other credit institutions for safekeeping and obtain a certain amount of interest based on the principle that funds must be recovered. According to the different deposit objects or nature, it can be divided into accounts such as household deposits, non–financial enterprise deposits, fiscal deposits, government agency deposits, and non–banking financial institutions deposits. It is the main source of bank credit funds.

Loan refers to a form of credit activity in which banks or other credit institutions provide funds for enterprises and individuals at a certain interest rate based on the principle that funds must be returned. Bank loans in my country are divided into short–term loans, medium and long–term loans, financial leasing, bill financing, and various advances.

Premium is the fee paid by the insurant to the insurer to obtain the obligation of compensation from the insurance within the agreed terms.

价格指数 9

PRICE INDICES

简要说明

一、本篇资料的主要内容

本篇资料主要包括工业生产者出厂、工业生产者购进、固定资产投资、房地产、居民消费、商品零售等价格指数。

二、本篇资料的来源

1. 工业生产者出厂、工业生产者购进、固定资产投资、房地产价格指数分别来源于生产、投资、房地产价格统计调查月报，由国家统计局青岛调查队生产价格调查处整理提供。

2. 居民消费、商品零售价格指数来源于消费价格统计调查月报，由国家统计局青岛调查队消费价格调查处整理提供。

Brief Introduction

Ⅰ. Main Content

Data in this chapter mainly include producer price indices for manufactured goods, purchasing price indices for industrial producers, price indices of investment in fixed assets, real estate price indices, consumer price indices and retail price indices.

Ⅱ. Source of Data

1. Data on producer price indices for manufactured goods, purchasing price indices for industrial producers price indices of investment in fixed assets, real estate price indices are based on monthly report of price survey on production, investment, real estate, and provided by the Division of Production Price Survey of NBS Survey Office in Qingdao.

2. Data on consumer price indices and retail price indices are based on monthly report of consumer price survey, and provided by the Division of Consumer Price Survey of NBS Survey Office in Qingdao.

9-1 主要年份居民消费和商品零售价格指数（以上年价格为 100）
MAJOR YEAR'S CONSUMER AND RETAIL PRICE INDICES（PRECEDING YEAR=100）

年 份 Year	居民消费价格指数 Consumer Price Indices	#食品类 Food	#衣着类 Clothing	#服务项目价格指数 Services Price Indices	商品零售价格指数 Retail Price Indices
1951	110.5	105.2	112.4		110.5
1952	99.8	99.6	98.7		99.8
1957	101.4	101.3	101.4	99.3	101.4
1962	102.6	102.0	100.2	99.9	102.6
1965	101.2	101.3	98.8	96.9	101.2
1970	98.9	99.7	100.0	99.5	98.9
1975	100.3	100.1	100.0	100.0	100.3
1978	100.5	100.2	99.8	100.0	100.5
1980	105.2	108.5	100.3	100.6	105.5
1985	110.4	115.2	102.3	102.7	110.9
1988	120.7	125.2	117.3	118.3	120.9
1990	104.5	103.4	103.4	118.8	103.6
1991	107.0	107.0	112.1	109.6	106.8
1992	111.4	115.1	108.6	119.9	110.8
1993	123.9	120.9	119.0	158.5	119.8
1994	126.9	135.2	130.1	117.9	122.8
1995	116.2	118.1	122.8	123.2	114.2
1996	112.6	110.1	104.3	130.4	106.0
1997	104.0	101.2	102.3	120.8	100.2
1998	100.0	93.7	94.5	136.2	94.9
1999	100.2	96.7	97.1	115.6	96.6

注：1.2016 年起，食品类统计口径有变化，不包括“茶及饮料”和“在外餐饮”两项内容。
2.2016 年起，统计分类“服务项目价格指数”改为“服务价格指数”，增加“养老服务”和“金融服务”两项内容。

Notes：1. Statistical caliber of food category has changed since 2016. The two sections of “Tea and Drinks” and “Catering Service” are not included.
2. The statistical category of “Price Indices of Service Item” has been revised to “Price Indices of Service” as of 2016 with two additional sections of “Elderly Care Service” and “Financial Service”.

9-1 续表
Continued

年 份 Year	居民消费价格指数 Consumer Price Indices	#食品类 Food	#衣着类 Clothing	#服务项目价格指数 Services Price Indices	商品零售价格指数 Retail Price Indices
2000	103.3	100.0	108.3	112.0	99.7
2001	101.0	100.6	98.0	108.7	98.9
2002	98.9	97.8	100.2	101.0	99.5
2003	101.4	104.3	98.4	101.7	98.3
2004	102.1	104.0	103.6	104.7	99.0
2005	102.3	102.1	108.3	101.4	99.3
2006	100.9	101.7	99.4	100.8	99.7
2007	104.5	111.6	99.4	102.4	102.7
2008	104.7	111.7	103.9	99.8	103.9
2009	100.5	101.6	101.4	100.6	98.6
2010	102.2	106.4	101.0	100.4	101.4
2011	105.0	111.1	108.2	103.1	104.5
2012	102.7	104.3	106.3	102.1	101.7
2013	102.5	105.3	104.9	100.7	101.4
2014	102.6	104.4	103.2	101.9	102.3
2015	101.2	101.7	102.8	101.3	100.0
2016	102.5	105.0	100.3	101.8	102.0
2017	102.0	99.6	100.5	103.4	100.8
2018	102.1	103.1	103.8	101.6	101.8
2019	103.3	111.6	100.6	101.7	102.4
2020	102.4	109.8	99.9	100.7	101.5
2021	101.5	99.7	100.6	102.0	101.4
2022	102.0	103.4	100.8	100.8	102.8

9-2 主要年份居民消费和商品零售价格指数(以1950年价格为100)
MAJOR YEAR'S CONSUMER AND RETAIL PRICE INDICES（1950 = 100）

年 份 Year	居民消费价格指数 Consumer Price Indices	#食品类 Food	#衣着类 Clothing	#服务项目价格指数 Services Price Indices	商品零售价格指数 Retail Price Indices
1951	110.5	105.2	112.4		110.5
1952	110.3	104.8	110.9		110.3
1957	119.5	120.7	115.3	91.6	119.5
1962	127.4	128.8	115.1	94.2	127.4
1965	133.3	138.7	108.4	81.5	133.3
1970	129.0	137.6	110.3	76.8	129.0
1975	128.8	138.2	110.0	75.7	128.8
1978	129.1	138.7	109.8	75.7	129.1
1980	137.6	154.1	109.3	76.1	138.1
1985	160.8	196.1	103.8	80.5	162.5
1988	223.8	295.2	133.2	100.8	227.6
1990	269.7	333.3	166.8	155.9	269.7
1991	288.6	356.7	187.0	170.9	288.1
1992	321.5	410.5	203.1	204.9	319.2
1993	398.3	496.3	241.7	324.8	382.4
1994	505.4	671.1	314.4	382.9	469.5
1995	587.3	792.5	386.1	471.8	536.2
1996	661.3	872.6	402.7	615.2	568.4
1997	687.8	883.0	412.0	743.1	569.5
1998	687.8	827.4	389.3	1012.1	540.5
1999	689.2	800.1	378.0	1170.0	522.1

注：1. 2016 年起，食品类统计口径有变化，不包括“茶及饮料”和“在外餐饮”两项内容。
2. 2016 年起，统计分类“服务项目价格指数”改为“服务价格指数”，增加“养老服务”和“金融服务”两项内容。

Notes：1. Statistical caliber of food category has changed since 2016. The two sections of "Tea and Drinks" and "Catering Service" are not included.
2. The statistical category of "Price Indices of Service Item" has been revised to "Price Indices of Service" of 2016 with two additional sections of "Elderly Care Service" and "Financial Service".

9-2 续表
Continued

年 份 Year	居民消费价格指数 Consumer Price Indices	#食品类 Food	#衣着类 Clothing	#服务项目价格指数 Services Price Indices	商品零售价格指数 Retail Price Indices
2000	711.9	800.1	409.4	1310.4	520.5
2001	719.0	804.9	401.2	1424.4	514.8
2002	711.1	787.2	402.0	1438.7	512.2
2003	721.1	821.0	395.6	1463.1	503.5
2004	736.2	853.9	409.8	1531.9	498.5
2005	753.1	871.8	443.8	1553.4	495.0
2006	759.9	886.6	441.2	1565.8	493.5
2007	794.1	989.5	438.5	1603.4	506.8
2008	831.4	1105.3	455.6	1600.2	526.6
2009	835.6	1123.0	462.0	1609.8	519.2
2010	854.0	1194.9	466.6	1616.2	526.5
2011	896.7	1327.5	504.9	1666.3	550.2
2012	920.9	1384.6	536.7	1701.3	559.6
2013	943.9	1458.0	563.0	1713.2	567.4
2014	968.4	1522.2	581.0	1745.8	580.5
2015	980.0	1548.1	597.3	1768.5	580.5
2016	1004.5	1625.5	599.1	1800.3	592.1
2017	1024.6	1619.0	602.1	1861.5	596.8
2018	1046.1	1669.2	625.0	1891.3	607.6
2019	1080.6	1862.8	628.7	1923.4	622.2
2020	1106.5	2045.4	628.1	1936.9	631.5
2021	1123.1	2039.3	631.9	1975.6	640.3
2022	1145.6	2108.6	637.0	1991.4	658.2

9-3 主要年份生产投资价格指数（以上年价格为 100）

MAJOR YEAR'S PRICE INDICES FOR PRODUCTION AND INVESTMENT（PRECEDING YEAR=100）

年 份 Year	工业生产者出厂价格指数 Producer Price Indices for Industrial Producers	工业生产者购进价格指数 Purchasing Price Indices for Industrial Producers	房屋销售价格指数 Sales Price Indices of Houses	房屋租赁价格指数 Renting Price Indices of Houses	物业管理价格指数 Property Management Price Indices	固定资产投资价格指数 Price Indices for Investment in Fixed Assets
1990	104.33	108.64				
1991	101.68	108.10				
1992	105.46	107.13				
1993	115.49	126.91				
1994	121.62	120.30				
1995	112.70	114.25				
1996	103.81	103.25				
1997	100.22	101.93				
1998	94.96	92.77	100.1	94.0		
1999	96.93	95.88	103.7	104.3		
2000	101.89	106.81	102.3	95.8		
2001	98.00	97.81	104.1	107.0		
2002	97.37	96.78	107.6	94.4		
2003	100.97	106.51	114.6	99.4		
2004	102.92	113.62	115.2	98.6		105.8
2005	101.39	106.52	110.9	103.3	100.2	103.1
2006	101.08	105.80	106.9	110.1	99.8	102.6
2007	101.50	106.69	106.5	108.3	100.4	104.1
2008	105.33	115.91	105.1	106.5	102.1	111.0
2009	95.78	90.35	100.3	103.5	100.4	94.6
2010	103.75	112.21		103.0	100.5	104.9
2011	104.90	109.39				107.0
2012	98.61	97.00				100.0
2013	98.82	96.53				100.1
2014	99.20	97.40				99.9
2015	97.04	94.24				97.1
2016	98.77	97.28				99.8
2017	104.40	110.73				107.3
2018	104.22	105.22				106.6
2019	100.0	98.4				

注：2010 年之前工业生产者出厂价格为工业品出厂价格；工业生产者购进价格为主要原材料、燃料、动力购进价格；根据国家制度规定 2019 年起不编制固定资产投资价格指数；根据国家有关规定 2020 年起不再编制工业生产者价格指数。

Note：Producers Prices at works were the prices of industrial products at words before 2010. Producers purchasing price refers to the purchasing price of main raw materials, fuels and power.According to the national system, the fixed asset investment price indices will not be compiled from 2019；according to the relevant national regulations, the industrial producer price indices will no longer be compiled from 2020.

9-4 工业生产者出厂价格指数（以上年价格为 100）
PRODUCER PRICE INDICES FOR INDUSTRIAL PRODUCERS（PRECEDING YEAR=100）

类　别	Item	2000 年	2005 年	2009 年	2010 年
总指数	**General Indices**	**101.89**	**101.39**	**95.78**	**103.75**
其中：轻工业	Light Industry	98.50	99.78	97.21	100.80
重工业	Heavy Industry	105.62	104.32	93.45	107.57
其中：生产资料	**Means of Production**	**105.03**	**103.24**	**94.25**	**106.43**
采掘	Excavation	95.67	114.74	93.44	130.94
原料	Raw Materials	113.82	106.91	90.67	115.24
加工	Processing	97.58	101.45	95.34	103.50
生活资料	**Means of Livelihood**	**98.25**	**99.13**	**97.45**	**99.61**
食品	Food	96.59	98.80	98.21	105.06
衣着	Clothing	99.37	101.48	102.03	101.56
一般日用品	Articles for Daily Use	104.52	101.97	99.39	99.96
耐用消费品	Durable Consumer Goods	97.70	97.43	94.52	93.23

注：根据国家有关规定 2020 年起不再编制工业生产者价格指数。
Note：According to relevant national regulations, the industrial producer price indices will no longer be compiled from 2020.

2011 年	2012 年	2013 年	2014 年	2015 年	2016 年	2017 年	2018 年	2019 年
104.90	**98.61**	**98.82**	**99.20**	**97.04**	**98.77**	**104.40**	**104.22**	**100.0**
103.46	99.70	99.11	99.62	99.85	98.74	101.13	101.27	101.6
105.89	97.87	98.62	98.91	95.10	98.79	106.46	106.01	98.9
105.54	**97.55**	**98.58**	**98.87**	**95.23**	**98.60**	**106.34**	**105.86**	**99.0**
132.07	93.35	91.72	100.65	95.12				
111.52	99.05	99.26	98.87	88.59	93.92	112.92	114.50	95.8
103.49	97.20	98.50	98.84	97.06	99.60	104.96	103.95	99.8
103.82	**100.42**	**99.21**	**99.76**	**100.07**	**99.12**	**100.69**	**100.95**	**101.8**
109.71	99.91	95.34	98.34	102.53	102.59	100.55	100.55	104.8
107.44	102.03	102.74	100.34	100.39	100.93	101.54	100.14	101.6
108.02	101.64	101.42	101.01	99.59	100.12	101.63	101.54	100.3
94.34	98.79	98.41	99.65	98.26	94.58	99.78	101.32	100.3

9-5 工业生产者购进价格指数（以上年价格为 100）
PURCHASING PRICE INDICES FOR INDUSTRIAL PRODUCERS（PRECEDING YEAR=100）

类　别	Item	2000 年	2005 年	2010 年	2011 年
总指数	**General Indices**	**106.81**	**106.52**	**112.21**	**109.39**
燃料、动力类	Fuel and Power	113.82	117.34	115.43	111.29
黑色金属材料类	Ferrous Metals	102.66	107.84	111.97	113.08
#钢材	Rolled-steel	105.44	106.57	108.67	107.95
其他	Others	101.1	112.88	122.64	129.01
有色金属材料及电线类	Non-ferrous Metals and Electric Wire	106.75	108.06	122.65	108.45
化工原料类	Raw Chemical Materials	106.9	112.47	111.04	113.79
木材及纸浆类	Timber and Paper Pulp	108.98	103.8	117.06	103.78
建筑材料及非金属矿类	Building Materials and Nonmetals	99.5	115.54	107.61	116.71
其他工业原材料及半成品	Other Industrial Raw Materials and Semi-finished Goods	105.32	97.87	106.41	103.31
农副产品	Agricultural Products	92.73	101.55	121.30	115.04
纺织原料类	Textile Materials	104.03	98.15	112.90	111.11

注：根据国家有关规定 2020 年起不再编制工业生产者价格指数。
Note：According to relevant national regulations, the industrial producer price indices will no longer be compiled from 2020.

2012 年	2013 年	2014 年	2015 年	2016 年	2017 年	2018 年	2019 年
97.00	**96.53**	**97.40**	**94.24**	**97.28**	**110.73**	**105.22**	**98.4**
100.64	95.18	97.65	88.51	89.94	112.91	112.55	95.3
93.20	93.76	95.81	87.26	97.23	117.41	104.02	100.0
92.33	92.87	96.87	89.99	96.89	119.10	108.75	99.1
94.64	96.57	92.49	78.70	98.41	110.30	86.82	103.4
93.64	96.23	96.24	92.34	96.29	114.82	103.94	97.7
96.72	96.47	99.51	96.44	101.00	107.63	101.55	94.2
93.12	98.79	102.42	98.33	99.93	125.23	111.21	89.3
102.48	100.13	97.36	95.52	100.91	115.06	115.97	107.8
98.05	96.65	96.25	96.95	97.50	106.42	102.41	100.5
98.21	98.54	97.62	99.75	101.53	105.92	99.70	103.6
95.61	99.60	97.38	95.86	99.81	110.09	105.80	97.1

9-6 按工业行业分工业生产者出厂价格指数（以上年价格为 100）
PRODUCER PRICE INDICES FOR INDUSTRIAL PRODUCERS BY SECTOR（PRECEDING YEAR=100）

行 业	Sector
工业生产者出厂价格指数	**Producer Price Indices for Manufactured Manufactured Goods**
黑色金属矿采选业	Mining of Ferrous Metal Ores
有色金属矿采选业	Mining of Non-ferrous Metal Ores
非金属矿采选业	Mining and Processing of Non–metal Ores
农副食品加工业	Processing of Food from Agricultural Products
食品制造业	Manufacture of Foods
酒、饮料和精制茶制造业	Manufacture of Liquor，Beverages and Refined Tea
纺织业	Manufacture of Textile
纺织服装、服饰业	Manufacture of Textile Wearing Apparel
皮革、毛皮、羽毛及其制品和制鞋业	Industry of Leather，Furs，Down and Related Products，and Shoes Making
木材加工和木、竹、藤、棕、草制品业	Processing of Timber, Manufacture of Wood, Bamboo, Rattan, Palm and Straw Products
家具制造业	Manufacture of Furniture
造纸和纸制品业	Manufacture of Paper and Paper Products
印刷和记录媒介复制业	Printing，Reproduction of Recording Media
文教、工美、体育和娱乐用品制造业	Industry of Culture and Education，Arts and Crafts，and Entertainment Products Manufacturing
石油、煤炭及其他燃料加工业	Oil, Coal and Other Fuel Processing Industries
化学原料和化学制品制造业	Manufacture of Chemical Raw Material and Chemical Products
医药制造业	Manufacture of Medicines
化学纤维制造业	Manufacture of Chemical Fibres
橡胶和塑料制品业	Industry of Rubber and Plastic Products
非金属矿物制品业	Manufacture of metallic Mineral Products
黑色金属冶炼和压延加工业	Smelting and Pressing of Ferrous Metals
有色金属冶炼和压延加工业	Smelting and Pressing of Non-ferrous Metals
金属制品业	Manufacture of Metal Products
通用设备制造业	Manufacture of General Purpose Machinery
专用设备制造业	Manufacture of Special Purpose Machinery
汽车制造业	Vehicle Manufacturing Industry
铁路、船舶、航空航天和其他运输设备制造业	Maufacturing Industry of Railroads，Vessels，Aerospace and Other Transportation Equipment
电气机械和器材制造业	Manufacture of Electrical Machinery and Equipment
计算机、通信和其他电子设备制造业	Computer，Communications and Other Electronic Equipment Manufacturing
仪器仪表制造业	Instruments Manufacturing Industry
其他制造业	Other Manufacturing Industry
金属制品、机械和设备修理业	Industry of Metal Products，and Repair of Machinery and Equipment
电力、热力生产和供应业	Production and Supply of Electric Power and Heat Power
燃气生产和供应业	Production and Supply of Gas
水的生产和供应业	Production and Supply of Water

注：1. 2019 年国民经济行业分类调整，本表中 2011—2019 年数据采用新国民经济行业分类 GB/T 4754–2017。
2. 根据国家有关规定 2020 年起不再编制工业生产者价格指数。

Notes：1. Classification of national economic industries was adjusted in 2019. The new national economic industries classification by GB/T 4754–2017 applies to data from 2011 to 2019 in this table.
2. According to relevant national regulations, the industrial producer price indices will no longer be compiled from 2020.

2011年	2012年	2013年	2014年	2015年	2016年	2017年	2018年	2019年
104.90	**98.61**	**98.82**	**99.20**	**97.04**	**98.77**	**104.40**	**104.22**	**100.0**
104.33	99.93	100.00	99.86	100.00				
111.39	102.48	98.72	95.57	89.94				
145.13	89.33	87.06	102.14	94.85				
111.34	98.69	93.46	97.58	102.47	102.80	101.12	101.41	104.8
112.52	103.11	103.08	101.78	100.66	100.30	101.40	98.67	99.4
104.14	105.89	100.48	98.76	99.01	99.97	99.54	100.85	107.2
105.09	96.15	100.18	100.27	99.41	97.60	103.84	103.58	101.0
105.43	101.66	104.17	101.74	100.84	100.83	102.17	100.28	102.5
104.79	102.59	101.83	98.56	99.72	99.81	100.15	99.82	99.6
108.13	103.21	99.67	100.96	100.35				
101.11	102.00	100.02	100.00	99.91	98.46	98.72	100.48	99.3
105.71	95.59	96.13	101.96	99.78	99.58	115.83	104.86	96.7
110.06	107.10	108.65	96.97	95.96	98.45	101.11	102.77	97.5
100.61	101.47	100.47	100.00	99.96	99.88	101.90	100.54	101.2
114.95	104.26	99.49	97.38	76.03	91.60	114.48	121.44	97.8
114.60	89.61	98.04	99.70	96.53	95.20	119.17	113.72	94.2
107.33	95.05	105.08	127.56	100.73	104.83	101.06	100.95	102.6
123.72	92.56	95.65	96.69	90.31	89.56	117.03	98.53	96.4
114.68	99.67	95.40	95.50	94.93	97.60	100.62	100.10	99.4
108.19	98.39	99.82	100.91	101.62	99.08	114.14	120.19	100.1
111.00	86.47	93.52	94.45	83.44	99.13	117.16	108.23	99.7
108.26	89.14	93.87	94.43	87.95	95.29	125.17	102.35	98.0
99.79	99.82	104.14	96.62	96.59	103.64	106.15	105.34	99.4
101.39	100.07	103.87	101.02	100.37	98.78	103.45	104.80	103.4
101.69	101.26	99.99	99.81	99.72	98.36	100.00	101.23	101.0
99.27	98.97	98.59	102.49	101.04	101.46	100.93	99.83	100.9
99.17	99.66	97.65	100.96	100.03	99.29	100.16	99.79	97.3
103.10	98.40	98.82	99.24	98.61	98.96	102.82	102.36	99.8
84.65	95.43	94.31	98.88	96.31	90.16	102.17	100.06	97.7
102.01	98.72	98.01	98.43	97.05	100.00	100.09	100.15	100.2
95.16	98.52	99.94	100.12	99.89	100.87	104.20	105.84	108.8
102.17	98.43	88.75	91.69	90.21				
101.49	104.36	99.81	99.15	98.10	97.59	97.05	97.83	96.6
107.34	103.32	102.54	109.38	98.88	101.26	96.32	108.74	104.7
100.15	100.25	100.05	100.34	103.46	108.78	100.00	113.81	100.0

9-7 固定资产投资价格指数（以上年价格为 100）
PRICE INDICES FOR INVESTMENT IN FIXED ASSETS（PRECEDING YEAR=100）

项目名称	Item	2005	2009	2010	2011	2012	2013	2014	2015	2016	2017	2018
总　计	**Total**	**103.1**	**94.6**	**104.9**	**107.0**	**100.0**	**100.1**	**99.9**	**97.1**	**99.8**	**107.3**	**106.6**
建筑安装、装饰工程	Construction and Installation Project	103.7	92.1	107.5	110.1	99.8	100.0	99.6	95.5	99.6	110.7	109.5
其中：人工费	Labor Cost	112.7	104.9	112.0	115.9	110.4	107.8	104.8	103.1	101.6	103.0	104.9
材料费	Materials Expenses	101.0	87.5	107.0	109.6	96.7	97.6	97.7	92	98.8	114.9	112.4
机械使用费	Expenses on Machinery Use	104.2	100.0	104.3	105.0	102.3	101.0	100.8	100.9	100.1	101.2	102.0
设备、工器具购置	Purchase of Equipment, Tools and Instruments	99.7	98.0	100.2	101.8	99.2	99.3	99.9	99.2	98.7	100.6	101.5
其他费用	Others	105.5	98.5	102.2	103.0	102.0	101.4	101.4	101.2	102.2	102.0	99.9

注：根据国家制度规定 2019 年起不编制固定资产投资价格指数。

Note：According to national regulations, starting from 2019, no fixed asset investment price indices will be compiled.

9-8 住宅销售价格指数 (2022 年)(上年同期 =100)
SALES PRICE INDICES FOR RESIDENCE（2022）（PRECEDING YEAR=100）

项　目	Item	2022
新建住宅销售价格指数	**Sales Price Indices for Newly Constructed Residence**	
一月	January	103.7
二月	February	103.4
三月	March	103.3
四月	April	102.6
五月	May	102.0
六月	June	101.9
七月	July	100.8
八月	August	100.3
九月	September	100.1
十月	October	100.1
十一月	November	100.2
十二月	December	100.6
二手住宅销售价格指数	**Sales Price Indices for Second-hand Residence**	
一月	January	101.1
二月	February	100.8
三月	March	100.5
四月	April	99.4
五月	May	98.7
六月	June	99.0
七月	July	98.4
八月	August	97.9
九月	September	97.5
十月	October	97.0
十一月	November	96.8
十二月	December	96.6

9-9 居民消费价格分类指数(2022 年)(上年同期 =100)
CONSUMER PRICE INDICES BY CATEGORY（2022）（PRECEDING YEAR=100）

项　　目	Item	指数 Indices
居民消费价格总指数	**Consumer Price Indices**	**102.0**
非食品烟酒价格指数	Price Indices of Non-food Cigarettes and Alcohol	101.7
服务价格指数	Price Indices of Services	100.8
鲜活食品价格指数	Price Indices of Fresh Food	103.1
消费品价格指数	Consumer Goods Price Indices	102.9
扣除鲜菜鲜果价格指数	Price Indices Without Fresh Vegetables and Fresh Fruits	101.8
一、食品烟酒	**Food，cigarettes and liquor**	**103.0**
1. 食品	Food	103.4
（1）粮食	Grain	106.2
（2）薯类	Potatoes	111.6
（3）豆类	Beans	108.3
（4）食用油	Cooking Oil	100.0
（5）菜及食用菌	Vegetables and Edible Fungi	105.7
（6）畜肉类	Livestock Products	93.8
（7）禽肉类	Poultry Products	103.6
（8）水产品	Aquatic Products	105.5
（9）蛋类	Eggs	105.5
（10）奶类	Dairy Products	99.6
（11）干鲜瓜果类	Dried and Fresh Melons and Fruits	109.4
（12）糖果糕点类	Candy and Pastry	103.9
（13）调味品	Flavoring	100.9
（14）其他食品类	Other Foods	105.2
2. 茶及饮料	Tea and Beverages	107.2
3. 烟酒	Tobacco Liquor	102.1
4. 在外餐饮	Catering service	101.7

注：2021 年起，居民消费价格调查目录进行了调整，新调查目录与国际标准更为接近。
Note：Since 2021, the consumption price investigation directory has been adjusted, and the new investigation directory is basically consistent with the household consumption expenditure catalogue.

9-9 续表
Continued

项　目	Item	指数 Indices
二、衣着	**Clothing**	**100.8**
1. 服装	Garments	101.0
2. 鞋类	Shoes	99.5
三、居住	**Residence**	**100.8**
1. 租赁房房租	Rents	100.4
2. 住房保养维修及管理	Maintenance and Management of House	104.5
3. 水电燃料	Water, Electricity and Fuels	100.5
4. 自有住房	Private Housing	100.2
四、生活用品及服务	**Article of Daily Use and Service**	**101.4**
1. 家具及室内装饰品	Furniture and Interior Decoration	98.6
2. 家用器具	Home Appliances	100.8
3. 家用纺织品	Home Textile	98.4
4. 家庭日用杂品	Daily Use Household Articles	101.4
5. 个人护理用品	Personal–care Supply	104.3
6. 家庭服务	Household Services	103.8
五、交通通信	**Transportation and Communication**	**105.8**
1. 交通	Transportation	107.8
2. 通信	Communication	99.3
六、教育文化娱乐	**Education, Culture and Entertainment**	**100.3**
1. 教育	Education	100.5
2. 文化娱乐	Culture and Entertainment	99.9
七、医疗保健	**Health Care**	**100.7**
1. 药品及医疗器具	Medicine and Medical Apparatus	101.7
2. 医疗服务	Medical Service	100.2
八、其他用品及服务	**Other Articles and Services**	**101.5**
1. 其他用品	Other Articles	101.9
2. 其他服务	Other Services	101.0

9-10 商品零售价格分类指数（2022 年）(上年同期 =100)

RETAIL PRICE INDICES BY CATEGORY（2022）（PRECEDING YEAR=100）

项　　目	Item	指数 Indices
商品零售价格总指数	**Retail Price Indices**	**102.8**
一、食品	**Food**	**102.9**
1. 粮食	Grain	106.2
2. 薯类	Potatoes	111.6
3. 豆类	Beans	108.3
4. 食用油	Edible oil	100.0
5. 菜及食用菌	Vegetables and Edible Fungi	105.7
6. 畜肉类	Stock meat	93.8
7. 禽肉类	Poultry meat	103.6
8. 水产品	Aquatic Products	105.5
9. 蛋类	Eggs	105.5
10. 奶类	Dairy	99.6
11. 干鲜瓜果类	Dried and Fresh Melon, and Fruits	109.4
12. 糖果糕点类	Sweets and cakes	103.9
13. 调味品	Flavoring	100.9
14. 其他食品类	Other food	105.2
15. 餐饮业零售	Catering Services and Retail Trades	101.7
二、饮料、烟酒	**Beverages, Tobacco and Liquor**	**103.2**
1. 茶及饮料	Tea and Beverages	107.2
2. 卷烟	Cigarettes	100.9
3. 酒类	Liquor	103.3
三、服装、鞋帽	**Clothing**	**100.7**
1. 服装	Garments	101.0
2. 鞋帽袜	Footgear and Hats	99.8
3. 其他衣着配件	Other Clothing and Accessories	100.4
四、纺织品	**Textiles**	**97.1**
1. 服装材料	Clothing Material	92.0
2. 床上用品	Blend Cloth	97.9
五、家用电器及音像器材	**Household Appliances, Music and Video Equipment**	**100.0**
1. 家庭设备	Household Facilities	100.9
2. 文娱用耐用消费品	Durable Consumer Goods for Cultural and Recreational Use and Services	97.1
3. 专业音像器材	Professional Audio and Video Equipment	109.8

注：2021 年起，居民消费价格调查目录进行了调整，新调查目录与国际标准更为接近。

Note：Since 2021, the consumption price investigation directory has been adjusted, and the new investigation directory is basically consistent with the household consumption expenditure catalogue.

9-10 续表
Continued

项　目	Item	指数 Indices
六、文化办公用品	**Culture and Office Articles**	**102.1**
七、日用品	**Articles for Daily Use**	**102.1**
1. 日用百货	General Merchandise for Daily Use	103.6
2. 厨具餐具茶具	Kitchen ware, Tableware, Tea set	103.2
3. 清洗用品	Cleaning Products	98.4
4. 其他日用品	Other Articles for Daily Use	102.1
八、体育娱乐用品	**Sports and Recreation Articles**	**102.2**
1. 体育户外用品	Sports and Outdoors	103.0
2. 娱乐用品	Recreation Articles	102.2
九、交通、通信用品	**Transportation and Communication Appliances**	**98.7**
1. 交通运输机械	Transportation Machines	98.7
2. 通信器材	Communication Equipment	98.8
十、家具	**Furniture**	**98.3**
十一、化妆品	**Cosmetics**	**105.1**
十二、金银饰品	**Gold, Silver and Jewelry**	**102.2**
十三、中西药品及医疗保健用品	**Traditional Chinese and Western Medicals and Health Care Articles**	**101.7**
1. 医疗卫生器具	Medical Apparatus	101.2
2. 中药	Herbal Medicine	107.0
3. 西药	Western Medicines	100.2
4. 保健器具及用品	Health Care Articles	100.0
十四、书报杂志及电子出版物	**Books, Newspapers, Magazines and Electronic Publications**	**101.7**
1. 教材及参考书	Teaching Material and Reference Books	102.0
2. 书报杂志及音像制品	Books, Newspapers, Magazines and Audio-Video Products	104.4
3. 计算机办公软件	Computer Office Software	98.6
十五、燃料	**Fuels**	**119.3**
1. 煤炭及制品	Coal and Its Products	117.0
2. 石油及制品	Petroleum and Its Products	119.4
十六、建筑材料及五金电料	**Building Materials and Hardware**	**101.3**
1. 建筑装潢材料	Building Decoration Materials	101.6
2. 五金水暖	Hardware	100.4

主要统计指标解释

居民消费价格指数 是反映一定时期内城乡居民所购买的生活消费品价格和服务项目价格变动趋势和程度的相对数，是对城市居民消费价格指数和农村居民消费价格指数进行综合汇总计算的结果。该指数可以观察和分析消费品的零售价格和服务价格变动对城乡居民实际生活费支出的影响程度。

商品零售价格指数 是反映一定时期内城乡商品零售价格变动趋势和程度的相对数。商品零售价格的变动直接影响到城乡居民的生活支出和国家的财政收入，影响居民购买力和市场供需的平衡，影响到消费与积累的比例关系。因此，该指数可以从一个侧面对上述经济活动进行观察和分析。

工业生产者出厂价格指数 是反映一定时期内全部工业产品出厂价格总水平的变动趋势和程度的相对数，包括工业企业售给本企业以外所有单位的各种产品和直接售给居民用于生活消费的产品。该指数可以观察出厂价格变动对工业总产值及增加值的影响。

工业生产者购进价格指数 是反映工业企业作为生产投入，而从物资交易市场和能源、原材料生产企业购买原材料、燃料和动力产品时，所支付的价格水平变动趋势和程度的统计指标，是扣除工业企业物质消耗成本中的价格变动影响的重要依据。

房地产价格指数 是反映一定时期内房地产价格变动趋势和程度的相对数，包括新建住宅销售价格指数、二手住宅销售价格指数。

Explanatory Notes on Main Statistical Indicators

Consumer Price Indices reflect the trend and degree of changes in prices of consumer goods and services purchased by urban and rural households during a given period. They are obtained by combining the Urban Consumer Price Indices and the Rural Consumer Price Indices. The Indices enable the observation and analysis of the degree of impact of the changes in the prices of retailed goods and services on the actual living expenses of urban and rural residents.

Retail Price Indices reflect the trend and degree of change in retail prices of commodities during a given period. The change in retail prices of commodities directly affect the living expenditure of urban and rural residents, government revenue, purchasing power of residents and the equilibrium of market supply and demand, and the ratio of consumption to accumulation. Therefore, the retail price indices are useful to analyze the changes of the above economic activities.

Producer Price Indices for Industrial Producers reflect the trend and degree of changes in general ex–factory prices of all industrial products during a given period, including sales of industrial products by an industrial enterprise to all units outside the enterprise, as well as sales of consumer goods to residents. It can be used to analyze the impact of ex–factory prices on gross output value and value–added of the industrial sector.

Purchasing Price Indices for Industrial Producers reflect changes in the level and degree of prices paid by industrial enterprises when they purchase production input such as raw materials, fuels and power from the market or from other energy or raw materials producing enterprises. These indices provide important basis for measuring the material consumption of industrial enterprises after removing influence of price changes.

Price Indices for Real Estate reflect the trend and degree of changes in prices of real estate during a given period, including sales price indices for newly constructed residential buildings and secondhand residential buildings.

人民生活 10

PEOPLE'S LIVELIHOODS

简要说明

一、本篇资料的主要内容

本篇资料主要反映全市居民的家庭收支、居住、家庭消费构成、耐用消费品拥有量等方面的情况。

二、本篇资料的来源

本篇资料中相关数据来源于住户收支与生活状况调查年报，由国家统计局青岛调查队住户调查处整理提供。

Brief Introduction

Ⅰ. Main Content

This section mainly reflects the residents' household income and expenditure, housing. household consumption structure, quantity of durable consumer goods possessed and other information.

Ⅱ. Source of Data

The relevant data in this article comes from the annual survey of household income and expenditure and living conditions, compiled and provided by the Household Survey Division of NBS Survey office in Qingdao.

10-1 城镇居民收支(1978—2014 年)
INCOME AND EXPENDITURE OF URBAN RESIDENTS（1978—2014）

年 份 Year	城镇居民人均可支配收入（元） Annual Per Capita Disposable Income of Urban Households（yuan）	城镇居民人均消费支出（元） Per Capita Consumption Expenditure of Urban Households（yuan）	城镇居民恩格尔系数（%） Engel Coefficient of Urban Residents（%）
1978	336	321	
1979	380	360	
1980	537	495	53.5
1981	500	490	57.8
1982	528	484	61.5
1983	549	510	63.7
1984	665	580	62.8
1985	733	681	58.6
1986	882	806	59.2
1987	1089	996	58.1
1988	1225	1278	55.9
1989	1455	1439	57.8
1990	1624	1507	58.4
1991	1856	1767	57.4
1992	2138	1956	57.0
1993	2668	2445	51.8
1994	3880	3479	53.2
1995	5357	4606	52.5
1996	5602	5079	51.8
1997	6222	5525	48.2
1998	6542	5567	46.4
1999	7255	5985	44.3
2000	7971	6684	42.1
2001	8665	6858	41.5
2002	8641	7356	39.8
2003	9962	8072	38.4
2004	10944	9023	36.7
2005	12725	9909	35.9
2006	15066	11981	33.9
2007	17516	13421	33.7
2008	20034	15055	33.4
2009	21857	16145	33.7
2010	24380	17608	30.9
2011	27861	19382	31.1
2012	31349	20481	30.4
2013	34356	22157	30.8
2014	37346	24122	30.2

注：自 2015 年开始，全市城乡住户调查统一使用一体化改革后的数据，与原数据相比，城乡居民收支指标的调查范围和口径均存在较大变化。原“城市居民人均可支配收入”调整为“城镇居民人均可支配收入”；原“农民人均纯收入”调整为“农村居民人均可支配收入”。

Note：Since 2015, the city's urban and rural household surveys have uniformly used the data after the integration reform. Compared with the original data, the survey scope and caliber of the income indicators of urban and rural residents have changed significantly. The"per capita disposable income of residents in cities" was changed to" per capita disposable income of urban residents" , the "per capita net income of farmers" was changed to "per capita disposable income of rural residents".

10-2 农村居民收支(1978—2014 年)

INCOME AND EXPENDITURE OF RURAL RESIDENTS(1978—2014)

年 份 Year	农村居民人均可支配收入(元) Annual Per Capita Net Income of Rural Households(yuan)	农村居民人均消费支出(元) Per Capita Consumption Expenditure of Rural Households(yuan)	农村居民恩格尔系数(%) Engel Coefficient of Rural Residents(%)
1978	146	109	59.2
1979	153	129	58.3
1980	209	142	55.0
1981	218	163	44.2
1982	273	199	53.0
1983	399	277	52.8
1984	452	304	50.0
1985	567	376	47.8
1986	647	474	46.4
1987	730	462	42.9
1988	820	439	38.8
1989	876	510	38.9
1990	952	494	41.5
1991	1021	546	41.3
1992	1029	572	41.7
1993	1255	743	42.7
1994	1694	1384	54.5
1995	2225	1641	55.7
1996	2625	2173	50.5
1997	2599	2150	52.9
1998	3144	2112	49.5
1999	3349	2135	47.2
2000	3534	2354	42.9
2001	3756	2579	40.8
2002	4003	2768	38.3
2003	4283	2921	37.0
2004	4757	3266	37.6
2005	5384	3625	36.3
2006	6013	4061	35.2
2007	6801	4557	35.6
2008	7666	5083	35.9
2009	8255	5568	34.4
2010	9326	6335	32.8
2011	10934	7285	33.7
2012	12366	8228	33.3
2013	13905	9305	32.1
2014	15434	10277	31.0

注:自 2015 年开始,全市城乡住户调查统一使用一体化改革后的数据,与原数据相比,城乡居民收支指标的调查范围和口径均存在较大变化。原"城市居民人均可支配收入"调整为"城镇居民人均可支配收入";原"农民人均纯收入"调整为"农村居民人均可支配收入"。

Note: Since 2015, the city's urban and rural household surveys have uniformly used the data after the integration reform. Compared with the original data, the survey scope and caliber of the income indicators of urban and rural residents have changed significantly. The"per capita disposable income of residents in cities" was changed to" per capita disposable income of urban residents" , the "per capita net income of farmers" was changed to "per capita disposable income of rural residents".

10-3 城乡居民住房面积（1990—2014 年）
HOUSING AREA OF URBAN AND RURAL RESIDENTS（1990—2014）

年 份 Year	城市居民人均现住房建筑面积（平方米） Per Capita Home Floor Area of Urban Residents（sq. m）	农村居民人均居住面积（平方米） Per Capita Housing Area of Rural Residents（sq. m）
1990	14.16	19.60
1995	17.12	23.03
2000	20.76	25.88
2001	21.86	26.59
2002	22.76	27.00
2003	23.73	27.00
2004	24.22	27.99
2005	22.96	29.54
2006	23.73	30.82
2007	23.72	30.95
2008	26.83	30.73
2009	26.71	31.39
2010	27.42	30.97
2011	27.67	31.73
2012	27.86	32.32
2013	29.12	33.50
2014	29.80	34.20

10-4 全体居民家庭基本情况（2014—2022年）

BASIC INFORMATION ON ALL HOUSEHOLDS（2014—2022）

指 标	Indicator	单位	Unit	2014年	2015年
人均可支配收入	**Per Capita Disposable Income**	**元**	**yuan**	**30273**	**32885**
（一）工资性收入	Income from Wages and Salaries	元	yuan	18348	20068
（二）经营净收入	Net Income from Household Operations	元	yuan	6035	6480
（三）财产净收入	Income from Properties	元	yuan	2396	2522
（四）转移净收入	Income from Transfers	元	yuan	3494	3815
人均消费支出	**Per Capita Consumption Expenditure**	**元**	**yuan**	**19653**	**21326**
（一）食品烟酒	Food，Tobacco and Liquor	元	yuan	5970	6459
（二）衣着	Clothing	元	yuan	1944	2096
（三）居住	Residence	元	yuan	4316	4584
（四）生活用品及服务	Household Facilities，Articles and Services	元	yuan	1374	1485
（五）交通通信	Transportation and Communication	元	yuan	2905	3226
（六）教育文化娱乐	Education，Cultural and Recreation Services	元	yuan	1654	1830
（七）医疗保健	Health Care and Medical Services	元	yuan	1002	1115
（八）其他用品和服务	Other Goods and Services	元	yuan	488	531
城镇居民人均现住房建筑面积	**Per Capita Building Space in Urban Areas**	**平方米**	**sq.m**		**31.5**
农村居民人均现住房建筑面积	**Per Capita Living Space in Rural Areas**	**平方米**	**sq.m**		**32.4**

注：自2015年开始，全市城乡住户调查统一使用一体化改革后的数据，与原数据相比，城乡居民收支指标的调查范围和口径均存在较大变化。原“城市居民人均可支配收入”调整为“城镇居民人均可支配收入”；原“农民人均纯收入”调整为“农村居民人均可支配收入”。本表2014年数据为新口径，与2015年年鉴数据不一致。2014年农村居民住房为拥有面积，2015年后改为现住房建筑面积。

Note：Since 2015, the city's urban and rural household surveys have uniformly used the data after the integration reform. Compared with the original data, the survey scope and caliber of the income indicators of urban and rural residents have changed significantly. The"per capita disposable income of residents in cities" was changed to" per capita disposable income of urban residents" , the "per capita net income of farmers" was changed to "per capita disposable income of rural residents". Data in 2014 were counted by new gauge and they are different from the data in last year' s yearbook. As for the statistics of rural resident homes, the owned house area was taken in 2014, but in 2015, the construction area was counted.

2016 年	2017 年	2018 年	2019 年	2020 年	2021 年	2022 年
35680	**38763**	**42019**	**45452**	**47156**	**51223**	**53735**
21700	23514	25303	27164	28082	30491	31911
7011	7485	8027	8685	8816	9701	10081
2781	3082	3475	3850	4008	4319	4450
4188	4682	5214	5753	6250	6712	7292
23256	**25232**	**27316**	**29501**	**30294**	**32878**	**32497**
6983	7489	7787	8325	8520	9204	9140
2271	2467	2538	2657	2706	2973	2775
5018	5454	6365	6969	7173	7707	7515
1607	1747	1837	1957	1998	2192	2042
3479	3753	4084	4369	4477	4873	4932
2075	2347	2571	2904	3012	3363	3480
1233	1350	1480	1600	1679	1789	1883
590	625	654	720	729	777	730
31.7	**32.7**	**32.9**	**31.9**	**33.4**	**32.1**	**34.0**
33.2	**34.8**	**35.9**	**37.0**	**38.0**	**37.4**	**38.7**

10-5 城镇居民家庭基本情况（2014—2022 年）
BASIC CONDITIONS OF URBAN HOUSEHOLDS（2014—2022）

指 标	Indicator	单位	Unit	2014 年	2015 年
人均可支配收入	**Per Capita Disposable Income**	**元**	**yuan**	**37346**	**40370**
（一）工资性收入	Income from Wages and Salaries	元	yuan	23034	25040
（二）经营净收入	Net Income from Household Operations	元	yuan	5818	6277
（三）财产净收入	Income from Properties	元	yuan	3436	3580
（四）转移净收入	Income from Transfers	元	yuan	5058	5473
人均消费支出	**Per Capita Consumption Expenditure**	**元**	**yuan**	**24122**	**26052**
（一）食品烟酒	Food，Tobacco and Liquor	元	yuan	7295	7856
（二）衣着	Clothing	元	yuan	2497	2685
（三）居住	Residence	元	yuan	5302	5607
（四）生活用品及服务	Household Facilities，Articles and Services	元	yuan	1686	1819
（五）交通通信	Transportation and Communication	元	yuan	3455	3810
（六）教育文化娱乐	Education，Cultural and Recreation Services	元	yuan	2057	2264
（七）医疗保健	Health Care and Medical Services	元	yuan	1227	1352
（八）其他用品和服务	Other Goods and Services	元	yuan	603	659

注：本表数据为新口径，2014 年数据与 2015 年统计年鉴数据不一致。
Note：The data in this sheet is in line with new statistic caliber，which leads to the inconsistency between the data of 2014 and of 2015's yearbook.

2016 年	2017 年	2018 年	2019 年	2020 年	2021 年	2022 年
43598	**47176**	**50817**	**54484**	**55905**	**60239**	**62584**
26898	28992	30955	32921	33641	36222	37635
6846	7299	7836	8455	8479	9416	9793
3909	4297	4789	5234	5365	5706	5805
5945	6588	7237	7874	8420	8895	9352
28285	**30569**	**32890**	**35266**	**35936**	**38574**	**37592**
8473	9059	9318	9877	10025	10727	10512
2882	3117	3168	3276	3306	3596	3290
6105	6605	7751	8449	8626	9152	8812
1962	2121	2207	2333	2365	2571	2336
4089	4399	4765	5062	5154	5556	5568
2553	2875	3122	3503	3608	3972	4051
1490	1624	1764	1893	1977	2079	2175
731	769	795	873	876	920	847

10-6 农村居民家庭基本情况（2014—2022 年）

BASIC CONDITIONS OF RURAL HOUSEHOLDS（2014—2022）

指　标	Indicator	单位	Unit	2014 年	2015 年
人均可支配收入	**Per Capita Disposable Income**	**元**	**yuan**	**15434**	**16730**
（一）工资性收入	Income from Wages and Salaries	元	yuan	8517	9337
（二）经营净收入	Net Income from Household Operations	元	yuan	6489	6919
（三）财产净收入	Income from Properties	元	yuan	216	236
（四）转移净收入	Income from Transfers	元	yuan	212	238
人均消费支出	**Per Capita Consumption Expenditure**	**元**	**yuan**	**10277**	**11127**
（一）食品烟酒	Food，Tobacco and Liquor	元	yuan	3188	3442
（二）衣着	Clothing	元	yuan	784	826
（三）居住	Residence	元	yuan	2248	2377
（四）生活用品及服务	Household Facilities，Articles and Services	元	yuan	720	765
（五）交通通信	Transportation and Communication	元	yuan	1751	1965
（六）教育文化娱乐	Education，Cultural and Recreation Services	元	yuan	809	895
（七）医疗保健	Health Care and Medical Services	元	yuan	532	604
（八）其他用品和服务	Other Goods and Services	元	yuan	245	253

注：本表数据为新口径，2014 年数据与 2015 年统计年鉴数据不一致。
Note：The data in this sheet is in line with new statistic caliber，which leads to the inconsistency between the data of 2014 and of 2015's yearbook.

2016 年	2017 年	2018 年	2019 年	2020 年	2021 年	2022 年
17969	**19364**	**20820**	**22573**	**23656**	**26125**	**27701**
10074	10882	11684	12580	13151	14536	15074
7381	7913	8487	9270	9720	10495	10931
256	280	310	344	365	458	463
258	289	339	379	421	636	1233
12006	**12928**	**13885**	**14899**	**15138**	**17021**	**17508**
3651	3869	4098	4393	4476	4965	5103
905	971	1020	1091	1096	1237	1258
2586	2801	3024	3222	3269	3685	3700
814	885	945	1004	1011	1138	1178
2113	2262	2445	2611	2659	2972	3059
1004	1129	1245	1389	1412	1668	1801
658	717	794	856	880	980	1025
275	294	314	333	336	377	386

10-7 全体居民家庭消费构成（2014—2022 年）
HOUSEHOLDS CONSUMPTION STRUCTURE（2014—2022）

单位：%

项　目	Item	2014 年	2015 年	2016 年	2017 年	2018 年	2019 年	2020 年	2021 年	2022 年
消费支出	**Consumption Expenditure**	**100**	**100**	**100**	**100**	**100**	**100**	**100**	**100**	**100**
（一）食品烟酒	Food，Tobacco and Liquor	30.4	30.3	30.0	29.7	28.5	28.2	28.1	28.0	28.1
（二）衣着	Clothing	9.9	9.8	9.8	9.8	9.3	9.0	8.9	9.0	8.5
（三）居住	Residence	21.9	21.5	21.6	21.6	23.3	23.6	23.7	23.5	23.1
（四）生活用品及服务	Household Facilities，Articles and Services	7.0	7.0	6.9	6.9	6.7	6.6	6.6	6.7	6.3
（五）交通通信	Transportation and Communication	14.8	15.1	15.0	14.9	15.0	14.8	14.8	14.8	15.2
（六）教育文化娱乐	Education，Cultural and Recreation Services	8.4	8.6	8.9	9.3	9.4	9.9	10.0	10.2	10.7
（七）医疗保健	Health Care and Medical Services	5.1	5.2	5.3	5.4	5.4	5.4	5.5	5.4	5.8
（八）其他用品和服务	Other Goods and Services	2.5	2.5	2.5	2.4	2.4	2.5	2.4	2.4	2.3

10-8 城镇居民家庭消费构成（2014—2022年）

COMPOSITION OF URBAN HOUSEHOLDS CONSUMPTION（2014—2022）

单位：%

项 目	Item	2014年	2015年	2016年	2017年	2018年	2019年	2020年	2021年	2022年
消费支出	**Consumption Expenditure**	**100**	**100**	**100**	**100**	**100**	**100**	**100**	**100**	**100**
（一）食品烟酒	Food，Tobacco and Liquor	30.2	30.2	30.0	29.6	28.3	28.0	27.9	27.8	28.0
（二）衣着	Clothing	10.4	10.3	10.2	10.2	9.6	9.3	9.2	9.3	8.8
（三）居住	Residence	22.0	21.5	21.6	21.6	23.6	24.0	24.0	23.7	23.4
（四）生活用品及服务	Household Facilities，Articles and Services	7.0	7.0	6.9	6.9	6.7	6.6	6.6	6.7	6.2
（五）交通通信	Transportation and Communication	14.3	14.6	14.4	14.4	14.5	14.3	14.4	14.4	14.8
（六）教育文化娱乐	Education，Cultural and Recreation Services	8.5	8.7	9.0	9.4	9.5	9.9	10.0	10.3	10.8
（七）医疗保健	Health Care and Medical Services	5.1	5.2	5.3	5.3	5.4	5.4	5.5	5.4	5.8
（八）其他用品和服务	Other Goods and Services	2.5	2.5	2.6	2.6	2.4	2.5	2.4	2.4	2.2

10-9 农村居民家庭消费构成（2014—2022年）
COMPOSITION OF RURAL HOUSEHOLDS CONSUMPTION（2014—2022）

单位：%

项 目	Item	2014年	2015年	2016年	2017年	2018年	2019年	2020年	2021年	2022年
消费支出	**Consumption Expenditure**	**100**	**100**	**100**	**100**	**100**	**100**	**100**	**100**	**100**
（一）食品烟酒	Food，Tobacco and Liquor	31.0	30.9	30.4	29.9	29.5	29.5	29.6	29.2	29.1
（二）衣着	Clothing	7.6	7.4	7.5	7.5	7.3	7.3	7.2	7.3	7.2
（三）居住	Residence	21.9	21.4	21.5	21.7	21.8	21.6	21.6	21.6	21.1
（四）生活用品及服务	Household Facilities，Articles and Services	7.0	6.9	6.8	6.8	6.8	6.8	6.7	6.7	6.7
（五）交通通信	Transportation and Communication	17.0	17.7	17.6	17.5	17.6	17.5	17.6	17.5	17.5
（六）教育文化娱乐	Education，Cultural and Recreation Services	7.9	8.0	8.4	8.7	9.0	9.3	9.3	9.8	10.3
（七）医疗保健	Health Care and Medical Services	5.2	5.4	5.5	5.5	5.7	5.8	5.8	5.7	5.9
（八）其他用品和服务	Other Goods and Services	2.4	2.3	2.3	2.4	2.3	2.2	2.2	2.2	2.2

10-10 城镇住户每百户家庭主要耐用品拥有量(1980—2022年)
OWNERSHIP OF MAJOR DURABLE CONSUMER GOODS PER 100 URBAN HOUSEHOLDS(1980—2022)

年份 Year	家用电脑(台) Computer (set)	钢琴(架) Piano (set)	空调器(台) Air Conditioner (set)	热水器(台) Water Heater (unit)	洗衣机(台) Washing Machine (set)	电冰箱(台) Household Refrigerator (set)	家用汽车(辆) Automobile (unit)	彩色电视机(台) Color TV (set)	移动电话(部) Cell Phone (unit)	照相机(架) Camera (set)
1980										2
1981					12			1		2
1982					22			2		4
1983					27	1		6		6
1984					30	2		8		8
1985					36	4		18		14
1986					40	5		25		15
1987					52	18		34		18
1988					61	33		47		21
1989					67	50		59		22
1990					66	62		68		26
1991					70	76		82		33
1992		1	0	13	73	83		81		39
1993		2	1	18	83	86		88		50
1994		4	1	17	81	89		92		51
1995		4	3	34	82	89		100		61
1996		5	7	40	83	92		105		63
1997	1	5	9	47	83	93		111	3	63
1998	8	5	17	53	83	92		111	7	69
1999	11	4	22	61	83	94		117	15	69
2000	19	2	25	66	83	94		120	30	70
2001	20	2	24	66	84	93		128	36	69
2002	32	2	38	75	89	93	1	123	80	73
2003	41	3	48	76	91	93	0	125	106	70
2004	46	3	55	79	93	93	2	124	128	68
2005	55	4	69	84	92	95	4	118	153	72
2006	71	8	89	88	97	99	6	125	187	82
2007	75	7	98	93	100	107	8	122	194	83
2008	75	5	94	90	95	103	13	116	191	67
2009	82	7	98	91	96	105	18	118	199	71
2010	86	8	99	91	97	107	20	119	208	71
2011	95	8	103	92	98	108	22	117	219	77
2012	101	9	104	93	98	108	29	115	231	79
2013	105	10	104	93	98	107	32	118	232	79
2014	105	10	104	98	99	105	34	109	235	79
2015	80	9	91	91	91	94	50	101	215	57
2016	86		98	93	90	96	58	100	212	63
2017	80		101	94	91	95	60	100	205	
2018	81		120	101	100	108	62	107	228	
2019	89		126	99	100	111	64	110	233	
2020	82		127	101	100	111	62	105	235	
2021	72		129	99	103	108	67	104	245	
2022	71		134	101	109	112	72	103	237	

10-11 农村住户每百户家庭主要耐用品拥有量（1985—2022 年）
OWNERSHIP OF MAJOR DURABLE CONSUMER GOODS PER 100 RURAL HOUSEHOLDS（1985—2022）

年 份 Year	家用电脑（台）Computer (set)	空调器（台）Air Conditioner (set)	热水器（台）Water Heater (unit)	自行车（辆）Bicycle (unit)	洗衣机（台）Washing Machine (set)	电冰箱（台）Household Refrigerator (set)	彩色电视机（台）Color TV (set)	移动电话（部）Cell Phone (unit)	照相机（架）Camera (set)	家用汽车（辆）Automobile (unit)
1985				147	0.3		3		1	
1986				165	1.1	0.3	4.5		1	
1987				148	2.4	0.5	7		2	
1988				154	2.4	1	9		2	
1989				170	3	1	12		2	
1990				164	4	2	13		2	
1991				173	5	4	16		2	
1992				178	5	7	20		2	
1993				203	7	14	26		2	
1994				204	9	21	35		7	
1995				203	16	28	43		6	
1996				198	13	33	46		8	
1997				191	15	36	56		13	
1998				184	17	39	63		15	
1999				185	20	42	74		10	
2000				165	28	47	86		13	
2001				153	28	53	92		13	
2002				152	36	58	98		16	
2003	6	5	33	137	39	60	100	45	16	2
2004	8	8	39	142	48	68	105	68	21	2
2005	14	14	53	138	57	77	109	91	21	5
2006	17	15	54	116	63	87	112	114	14	7
2007	19	19	63	118	70	94	113	132	17	8
2008	25	23	68	124	76	97	114	148	19	9
2009	28	25	71	127	79	99	115	160	21	11
2010	34	30	75	128	82	102	117	170	21	12
2011	44	32	76	114	85	100	112	202	18	15
2012	55	37	85	119	91	102	114	216	21	16
2013	61	45	88	111	93	105	116	221	26	23
2014	61	49	85		93	102	106	225	24	26
2015	46	54	86		92	105	110	219	21	41
2016	56	70	89		96	107	113	226	21	45
2017	52	78	90		98	106	110	223		48
2018	45	93	88		97	109	105	232		43
2019	42	98	96		98	108	104	227		40
2020	45	97	94		98	107	108	231		49
2021	49	101	95		92	109	101	244		55
2022	45	104	98		99	109	105	245		59

主要统计指标解释

常住成员 指住户成员中，经常在家居住，或者调查期内居住时间超过一半的人员，以及本住户供养的学生。

可支配收入 指调查户在调查期内获得的、可用于最终消费支出和储蓄的总和，即调查户可以用来自由支配的收入。可支配收入既包括现金，也包括实物收入。按照收入的来源，可支配收入包含四项，分别为：工资性收入、经营净收入、财产净收入和转移净收入。计算公式为：

可支配收入 = 工资性收入 + 经营净收入 + 财产净收入 + 转移净收入

居民人均可支配收入是按居民家庭常住人口计算的平均每人可支配收入

消费支出 指住户用于满足家庭日常生活消费需要的全部支出。根据用途不同，消费支出可划分为食品烟酒、衣着、居住、生活用品及服务、交通通信、教育文化娱乐、医疗保健、其他用品及服务八大类。根据来源不同，消费支出可划分为现金消费支出、实物消费支出（含自产自用、来自单位、来自政府和其他社会组织）。

Explanatory Notes on Main Statistical Indicators

Permanent resident refers to residents that live usually in home or more than half of the survey period and students that are supported by them.

Disposable income refers to sum of all income earned within the survey period that can be used for deposit and expense on final consumption，which means the income that can be disposed freely by residents. The disposable income includes not only cash，but also income in kinds，which shall be categorized into four kinds according to source of incomes：salary income，net operating income，net property income，net transfer income. Computing formula is as follows：

Disposable income = salary income + net operating income + net property income + net transfer income

Disposable income per capita of residents is the average disposable income per person calculated based on the number of permanent residents of the family.

Consumer spending refers to all spending of residents to cover daily life consumption demands. According to different usages，the consumer spending shall be classified into eight categories：food，cigarettes and alcohol，clothing，housing，daily use articles and services，transportation & communication，education，culture & entertainment，medical and health care，other articles and services. According to sources，the consumer spending shall be classified as cash consumer spending，consumer spending in kinds（including self-produced，from the unit，from government and other social organization）.

11 农 业

AGRICULTURE

简 要 说 明

一、本篇资料的主要内容

本篇资料主要反映全市农业生产和农村经济的基本情况，主要包括农林牧渔业总产值、中间消耗、增加值、农村劳动力、耕地、主要农产品产量、农业机械年末拥有量、农业机械化和电气化以及农田水利建设等方面的资料。

二、本篇资料的来源

1. 本篇资料中耕地面积资料来源于市自然资源和规划局。

2. 水产品产量等相关资料来源于市海洋发展局。

3. 农业机械化、农田水利灌溉等相关资料等相关资料来源于市农业农村局。

4. 植树造林等相关资料来源于市园林和林业局。

三、说明

本篇按照国家统计局规定，根据 2016 年第三次全国农业普查结果对 2007 年至 2017 年历史数据进行了核定和修正。

本篇资料由市统计局农村统计处、市统计局国民经济核算处、国家统计局青岛调查队农业农村调查处整理提供。

Brief Introduction

Ⅰ. Main Content

The information in this part mainly reflects the basic situation of the city′s agricultural production and rural economy, mainly including the total output value of agriculture, forestry, animal husbandry and fishery, intermediate consumption, added value, rural labor force, cultivated land, output of major agricultural products, agricultural machinery owned at the end of the year, agricultural mechanization and electrification, and information on farmland water conservancy construction and other aspects.

Ⅱ. Source of Data

1. Data on area of cultivated land are provided by Qingdao Natural Resources and Planning Bureau.

2. Data on output of aquatic products are provided by Qingdao Marine Development Bureau.

3. Agricultural mechanization, farmland water conservancy irrigation and other related data are from Qingdao Municipal Agriculture and Rural Affairs Bureau.

4. Relevant materials of afforestation are from Qingdao Municipal Gardening and Forestry Bureau.

Ⅲ. Explain

This chapter is in accordance with the provisions of the State Statistical Bureau. According to the results of the third national agricultural census in 2016, the historical data from 2007 to 2017 were verified and revised.

The information in this article was compiled and provided by the Rural Statistics Division of the Qingdao Municipal Bureau of Statistics, the National Economic Accounting Division of the Qingdao Municipal Bureau of Statistics, and the Agricultural and Rural Investigation Division of NBS Survey Office in Qingdao.

11-1　农村基本情况（2000-2022 年）
BASIC STATISTICS ON RURAL AREA（2000-2022）

项目	Item	单位	Unit	2000 年	2005 年	2010 年	2012 年	2013 年	2014 年
一、年末实有耕地面积	**Year-end Area of Cultivated Land**	**万公顷**	**10000 hectares**	**48**	**42**		**53**	**53**	**52**
二、农用机械总动力	**Total Agricultural Machinery Power**	**万千瓦**	**10000 kW**	**459**	**620**	**764**	**798**	**809**	**827**
拖拉机	Tractors	台	unit	126981	163032	200208	206290	206300	205065
三、农村用电量	**Electricity Consumed in Rural Areas**	**万千瓦时**	**10000 kW · h**	**189651**	**372645**	**426819**	**426815**	**359139**	**404380**
四、农用化肥施用量（折纯）	**Consumption of Chemical Fertilizer（convert to pure amount）**	**万吨**	**10000 tons**	**33**	**33**	**30**	**29**	**29**	**29**
五、农药使用量	**Pesticide Usage**	**吨**	**ton**						
六、耕地机电灌溉面积	**Cultivated Land Electromechanical Irrigation Area**	**万公顷**	**10000 hectares**	**30**	**30**	**33**	**33**	**30**	**32**

11-1 续表
Continued

项　目	Item	单位	Unit	2015年	2016年	2017年	2018年	2019年	2020年	2021年	2022年
一、年末实有耕地面积	**Year-end Area of Cultivated Land**	万公顷	**10000 hectares**	**52**	**52**	**52**	**52**	**52**	**52**	**43**	**43**
二、农用机械总动力	**Total Agricultural Machinery Power**	**万千瓦**	**10000 kW**	**854**	**698**	**728**	**738**	**751**	**754.8**	**757.3**	**760.0**
拖拉机	Tractors	台	unit	207809	211689	214799	215668	216496	214845	210358	205607
三、农村用电量	**Electricity Consumed in Rural Areas**	**万千瓦时**	**10000 kW·h**	**401122**	**385434**	**382437**	**377858**	**388484**	**359584**	**328106**	
四、农用化肥施用量（折纯）	**Consumption of Chemical Fertilizer（convert to pure amount）**	**万吨**	**10000 tons**	**28**	**28**	**28**	**27**	**27**	**26**	**25**	**25**
五、农药使用量	**Pesticide Usage**	**吨**	**ton**					**5401**	**5273**	**5107**	**4979**
六、耕地机电灌溉面积	**Cultivated Land Electromechanical Irrigation Area**	**万公顷**	**10000 hectares**	**32**	**33**	**33**	**33**	**33**	**36**	**33**	**33**

注：1. 农机机械总动力 2016 年为新统计口径，扣除农用运输汽车数据。
2. 2020 年起有效灌溉面积改为耕地机电灌溉面积，数据由农业农村局提供。
3. 根据国家统计局 2022 年农林牧渔业统计报表制度取消农村用电量指标。

Notes：1. Data of total power of agricultural machinery of 2016 is based on the new statistic caliber, deducted by the data of agricultural vehicle.
2. Starting from 2020, the effective irrigation area will be changed to the electromechanical irrigation area of arable land. The data is provided by the Agriculture and Rural Bureau.
3. According to the Agricultural, Forestry, Animal husbandry and Fishery Statistical Report System(2022) issued by National Bureau of Statistics, the rural electricity consumption index will be canceled.

11-2 分市、区农药、化肥使用量
AMOUNT OF PESTICIDES AND FERTILIZERS USED BY REGION

单位：吨（ton）

市、区名称	Region	农药使用量 Pesticide Usage		化肥施用量（折纯） Fertilizer Application Amount（convert to pure amounte）	
		2022 年	2021 年	2022 年	2021 年
全 市	**Whole Municipality**	**4979**	**5106**	**246113**	**248970**
崂山区	Laoshan District	15	16	299	324
黄岛区	Huangdao District	463	474	22778	23057
城阳区	Chengyang District	15	15	461	469
即墨区	Jimo District	522	546	30997	31559
胶州市	Jiaozhou	982	1001	32749	32879
平度市	Pingdu	1599	1643	108800	109617
莱西市	Laixi	1385	1411	50028	51065

11-3 主要年份农、林、牧、渔业总产值（按现价计算）
MAJOR YEAR'S GROSS OUTPUT VALUE OF AGRICULTURE, FORESTRY, ANIMAL HUSBANDRY AND FISHERY (CURRENT PRICE)

单位：万元（10000 yuan）

年份 Year	农、林、牧、渔业总产值 Gross Output Value of Agriculture, Forestry, Animal Husbandry and Fishery	农业产值 Agriculture	林业产值 Forestry	畜牧业产值 Animal Husbandry	渔业产值 Fishery
1949	16511	14755	325	1200	231
1952	24428	21353	479	1888	708
1957	26189	22717	644	2218	610
1962	15356	13257	230	1243	626
1965	25123	21488	854	2110	671
1970	44078	36889	1851	3817	1521
1975	93213	79208	2144	7923	3938
1978	121497	94397	3112	17293	6695
1980	149436	117547	2953	22215	6721
1985	299139	215729	8986	53894	20530
1987	378981	263066	5949	73271	36695
1989	463952	303679	19134	91885	49254
1990	579877	381287	13801	119208	65581
1991	664779	417111	12875	144909	89884
1992	703433	400471	15252	150942	136768
1993	989763	509601	20845	232143	227174
1994	1424074	763366	23101	356734	280873
1995	1923771	1021413	26765	503999	371594
1996	2317434	1145399	29100	692362	450573
1997	2047712	939922	24052	578443	505295
1998	2386303	1198043	16760	633735	537765

注：2007—2017 年数据为根据第三次农业普查结果核定修正后数据。
Note: The 2007—2017 data are the approved revised data based on the results of the third agricultural census.

11-3 续表
Continued

年份 Year	农、林、牧、渔业总产值 Gross Output Value of Agriculture，Forestry，Animal Husbandry and Fishery	农业产值 Agriculture	林业产值 Forestry	畜牧业产值 Animal Husbandry	渔业产值 Fishery
1999	2382320	1169596	17122	618020	577582
2000	2483256	1116397	19102	692782	654975
2001	2615228	1135816	20433	758313	700666
2002	2688532	1110671	23157	796007	758697
2003	2759692	1062576	36183	859915	801018
2004	2967389	1181009	32831	937494	816055
2005	3205057	1265695	25246	1070831	843285
2006	3396096	1360755	23546	1076254	855131
2007	3665342	1460800	20801	1143644	916648
2008	3995027	1723855	24356	1195857	907793
2009	4070777	1771982	22133	1133732	980995
2010	4802184	2197935	19090	1225222	1181911
2011	5345885	2188072	19049	1500469	1426786
2012	5672486	2270097	20221	1510234	1633469
2013	6105875	2547805	21875	1553621	1711549
2014	6279086	2644851	22266	1559709	1739234
2015	6123485	2469656	21789	1529587	1814625
2016	6690910	2844023	27741	1621935	1777293
2017	6978980	3003367	30891	1663278	1830324
2018	7369968	3290651	36575	1631422	1920519
2019	7781197	3600911	43066	1671765	1936932
2020	8071003	3732576	44453	1800325	1933437
2021	8970590	4228955	41462	1836006	2247619
2022	9256086	4430675	41715	1768677	2340543

11-4 分市、区农、林、牧、渔业总产值(2022年，现价)

GROSS OUTPUT VALUE OF AGRICULTURE，FORESTRY，ANIMAL HUSBANDRY AND FISHERY BY REGION (2022, CURRENT PRICE)

单位：万元（10000 yuan）

市、区名称	Region	农、林、牧、渔业总产值 Gross Output Value of Agriculture，Forestry，Animal Husbandry and Fishery	农业 Agriculture	林业 Forestry	畜牧业 Animal Husbandry	渔业 Fishery	服务业 Services
全 市	**Whole Municipality**	**9256086**	**4430675**	**41715**	**1768677**	**2340543**	**674476**
崂山区	Laoshan District	152366	34262	42		90669	27393
黄岛区	Huangdao District	1765968	552853	13017	211849	867488	120761
城阳区	Chengyang District	373750	48766	1800	17598	298570	7016
即墨区	Jimo District	1738457	540504	148	285162	751627	161016
胶州市	Jiaozhou	1302498	632108	9911	208230	321619	130630
平度市	Pingdu	2371178	1748379	14804	488926	2354	116715
莱西市	Laixi	1551869	873803	1993	556912	8216	110945

11-5 分市、区农、林、牧、渔业增加值(2022 年，现价)

VALUE-ADDED OF AGRICULTURE, FORESTRY, ANIMAL HUSBANDRY AND FISHERY BY REGION (2022，CURRENT PRICE)

单位：亿元 (100 million yuan)

市、区名称	Region	农、林、牧、渔业增加值 Added Value Of Agriculture, Forestry, Animal Husbandry and Fishery	农、林、牧、渔专业及辅助性活动 Agriculture, Forestry, Animal Husbandry, Fishery and Supporting Activities
全　市	**Whole Municipality**	**512.64**	**34.59**
崂山区	Laoshan District	8.85	1.39
黄岛区	Huangdao District	98.50	6.04
城阳区	Chengyang District	21.26	0.35
即墨区	Jimo District	97.05	8.33
胶州市	Jiaozhou	72.70	6.72
平度市	Pingdu	133.26	6.21
莱西市	Laixi	81.00	5.56

11-6 主要年份耕地面积与播种面积
MAJOR YEAR'S CULTIVATED AND SOWN AREA

单位：万公顷（10000 hectares）

年份 Year	年末实有耕地面积 Year-end Area of Cultivated Land	农作物播种面积 Sown Area of Farm Crops	#粮食作物 Grain Crops	#经济作物 Economic Crops
1949		93.47	84.00	7.20
1952		97.53	85.07	10.80
1957		97.87	87.07	10.53
1962		81.47	72.53	5.80
1965		82.80	71.80	8.33
1970		80.73	68.27	10.07
1975		79.82	65.84	11.01
1978		77.60	63.60	10.40
1980		75.87	60.33	12.00
1985		78.27	57.33	15.73
1987		76.67	55.87	15.93
1989		74.78	54.28	16.06
1990		76.85	56.99	15.53
1991		76.98	56.89	15.69
1992		76.96	56.37	15.64
1993	56.90	77.75	56.22	15.71
1994		76.61	54.08	16.20
1995		76.54	53.71	15.65
1996	55.01	77.26	54.81	14.90
1997		75.04	52.32	14.40

注：1. 2009 年前本表数据由市统计局提供。
2. 2010 年起，粮食作物面积由青岛调查队提供，经济作物面积由市统计局提供。
3. 2007—2017 年农作物播种面积为根据第三次农业普查结果核定修正后数据。

Notes：1. Those of before 2009 were provided by the National Bureau of Statistics.
2. Since 2010, the area of grain crops has been provided by NBS survey office in Qingdao , and the area of cash crops has been provided by the Municipal Statistics Bureau.
3. Sown Area of Farm Crops from 2007 to 2017 is revised according to the results of the third agricultural census.

11-6 续表
Continued

年份 Year	年末实有耕地面积 Year-end Area of Cultivated Land	农作物播种面积 Sown Area of Farm Crops	#粮食作物 Grain Crops	#经济作物 Economic Crops
1998		77.18	53.05	14.54
1999		77.56	50.61	13.24
2000		76.47	45.07	13.98
2001		73.69	41.91	14.54
2002		72.32	40.83	13.95
2003		67.82	36.05	14.50
2004		71.33	41.40	14.11
2005	42.10	75.02	49.93	11.89
2006	41.29	74.86	49.79	11.75
2007	41.31	64.13	39.16	24.98
2008	41.79	65.29	42.56	22.73
2009	41.87	63.72	42.01	21.72
2010		64.10	42.65	21.45
2011		64.53	43.84	20.70
2012	52.81	64.36	43.95	20.40
2013	52.55	66.16	45.69	20.48
2014	52.42	66.70	46.75	19.95
2015	52.22	67.10	47.93	19.17
2016	52	68.19	48.49	19.70
2017	51.86	67.32	47.79	19.54
2018	51.86	68.37	48.11	20.26
2019	51.62	66.73	47.50	19.23
2020	51.62	66.40	46.95	19.45
2021	43.21	66.80	48.01	18.79
2022	42.76	66.39	48.16	18.23

11-7　分市、区耕地面积（2022年）
AREA OF CULTIVATED LAND BY REGION（2022）

单位：公顷（hectare）

市、区名称	Region	年末耕地面积 Year-end Area of Cultivated Land	#旱田 Dry Farmland
全　市	**Whole Municipality**	**427606**	**196221**
崂山区	Laoshan District	583	563
黄岛区	Huangdao District	50179	42894
城阳区	Chengyang District	3588	2438
即墨区	Jimo District	75830	59282
胶州市	Jiaozhou	46165	17070
平度市	Pingdu	171328	9109
莱西市	Laixi	79863	64799

11-8 分市、区农作物播种面积（2022年）
SOWN AREA OF FARM CROPS BY REGION（2022）

单位：万公顷（10000 hectares）

市、区名称	Region	总播种面积 Total Sown Area	#粮食 Grain	#棉花 Cotton	#花生 Peanut	#烟叶 Tobacco	#蔬菜 Vegetable
全　市	**Whole Municipality**	**66.39**	**48.16**	**0.00**	**6.49**	**0.04**	**10.81**
崂山区	Laoshan District	0.04			0.00		0.03
黄岛区	Huangdao District	7.49	4.86		1.73	0.03	0.81
城阳区	Chengyang District	0.19	0.09		0.00		0.09
即墨区	Jimo District	9.94	7.84		0.84		1.14
胶州市	Jiaozhou	9.01	6.36	0.00	0.56	0.00	2.05
平度市	Pingdu	27.12	20.22	0.00	1.84	0.00	4.70
莱西市	Laixi	12.61	8.78		1.50		1.98

11-9　分市、区部分农作物产量（2022 年）

OUTPUT OF FARM CROPS BY REGION（2022）

单位：吨（ton）

市、区名称	Region	粮食 Grain	棉花 Cotton	花生 Peanut	烟叶 Tobacco	蔬菜 Vegetable
全　市	**Whole Municipality**	**3112959**	**25**	**311678**	**939**	**6598713**
崂山区	Laoshan District			106		9807
黄岛区	Huangdao District	258840		86048	823	567869
城阳区	Chengyang District	5716		138		32312
即墨区	Jimo District	442375		34521		680833
胶州市	Jiaozhou	386256	1	23831	46	1118284
平度市	Pingdu	1456494	24	89825	70	2904633
莱西市	Laixi	563278		77209		1284975

11-10 分市、区部分农作物单位面积产量（2022年）
OUTPUT OF FARM CROPS PER HECTARE BY REGION（2022）

单位：千克/公顷（kg/hectares）

市、区名称	Region	粮食 Grain	棉花 Cotton	花生 Peanut	烟叶 Tobacco	蔬菜 Vegetable
全　市	**Whole Municipality**	**6464**	**1215**	**4800**	**2460**	**61065**
崂山区	Laoshan District			4680		29865
黄岛区	Huangdao District	5331		4965	2430	70215
城阳区	Chengyang District	6113		4515		37035
即墨区	Jimo District	5642		4095		59685
胶州市	Jiaozhou	6072	1395	4245	2880	54420
平度市	Pingdu	7202	1200	4875	2715	61770
莱西市	Laixi	6415		5130		64950

11-11　主要年份农作物总产量
MAJOR YEAR'S OUPTUT OF FARM CROPS

单位：吨（ton）

年份 Year	粮食 Grain	#小麦 Wheat	#玉米 Corn	棉花 Cotton	花生 Peanut	水果 Fruit	蔬菜 Vegetable
1949	723190	158815	25810	1280	71080	9955	356015
1952	967640	200380	58130	6025	115585	13468	284050
1957	921920	210690	141540	3520	90445	18869	625220
1962	628930	104340	53010	1280	35470	8366	524455
1965	917635	180610	135595	6090	88390	16034	465850
1970	1175985	243945	244530	16490	96280	33907	541145
1975	1899540	430135	420095	15390	98495	59206	693970
1978	1900850	514570	510635	8720	114370	82819	921140
1980	2164415	520045	819930	19630	160670	80840	996565
1985	2331060	961055	739455	19335	475270	200515	1253075
1987	2626029	996165	1030926	13819	394296	249655	1489250
1989	2654334	993406	1084441	14638	391782	288757	1664238
1990	2998246	1265157	1210687	17490	413636	292366	1786041
1991	3180893	1421143	1285043	25965	446880	294349	1837265
1992	2675641	1235755	981490	8160	321145	341415	2030327
1993	3164812	1463759	1248780	15344	419109	383368	2705349
1994	3106562	1392977	1252952	8326	494827	423024	3002318
1995	3291587	1480385	1365167	8177	510662	478685	3221507
1996	3390033	1513479	1466668	4001	486574	505711	3405056
1997	2523064	1584478	743199	2000	308233	438398	3333181
1998	3469821	1627261	1484182	4159	546786	529592	4036992
1999	3331124	1501182	1499775	3668	572941	606800	5459140

注：2007—2017年数据为根据第三次农业普查结果核定修正后数据。

Note：Agricultural data from 2007 to 2017 are revised according to the results of the third agricultural census.

11-11 续表 1
Continued

年份 Year	粮食 Grain	# 小麦 Wheat	# 玉米 Corn	棉花 Cotton	花生 Peanut	水果 Fruit	蔬菜 Vegetable
2000	2780481	1353445	1169649	2077	534174	651591	6649322
2001	2539257	1143679	1178851	3409	579441	675244	6250361
2002	2383802	1085936	1094731	3755	557714	579703	6847570
2003	2221697	931787	1117704	5324	568798	677361	7305618
2004	2650952	1301791	1202063	7216	580290	748516	6720886
2005	3150203	1535471	1478616	4042	503941	737300	5792110
2006	3039266	1548928	1372166	3954	471853	827755	6051239
2007	2319354	1118044	1106106	3546	495458	1366106	6180515
2008	2602592	1234264	1279002	3163	470424	1276385	6164760
2009	2590287	1276029	1228485	3213	467937	1294706	5743437
2010	2553744	1206593	1272970	2411	439872	1267226	5895190
2011	2678626	1213908	1386365	2375	441237	1262896	5948249
2012	2707295	1242299	1396704	2334	456372	1201836	5826702
2013	2791826	1295227	1432355	2057	440426	1217969	5906625
2014	2780244	1302282	1418469	1392	394461	1188690	6134061
2015	2878062	1332125	1497121	1279	342034	1189312	5988945
2016	2940668	1345273	1551200	408	365207	1207498	5915380
2017	2968896	1264073	1670338	420	383668	1187041	6277779
2018	3100964	1376646	1690817	977	384918	1092176	6443615
2019	3026054	1426280	1544645	434	342424	1185951	6261517
2020	3045755	1334205	1635225	136	360029	1164739	6558479
2021	3127743	1429566	1631325	79	339448	1198348	6617749
2022	3112959	1415271	1637987	25	311678	1219414	6598713

11-11　续表 2　分市、区部分蔬菜产量（2022 年）
Continued　OUTPUT OF SOME VEGETABLES BY REGION（2022）

单位：吨（ton）

市、区名称	Region	蔬菜 Vegetable	#大白菜 Cabbage	#芹菜 Celery	#胡萝卜 Carrot
全　市	**Whole Municipality**	**6598713**	**1371902**	**150499**	**701813**
崂山区	Laoshan District	9807	4451	12	11
黄岛区	Huangdao District	567868	263830	21331	1223
城阳区	Chengyang District	32312	5761	830	629
即墨区	Jimo District	680832	159909	13309	73258
胶州市	Jiaozhou	1118284	289953	57284	5916
平度市	Pingdu	2904634	485261	26354	382850
莱西市	Laixi	1284976	162737	31379	237926

11-11　续表 3　分市、区部分蔬菜产量（2022 年）
Continued　OUTPUT OF SOME VEGETABLES BY REGION（2022）

单位：吨（ton）

市、区名称	Region	#黄瓜 Cucumber	#西红柿 Tomato	#大葱 Green onion	#蒜头 Garlic	#食用菌 Edible fungi
全　市	**Whole Municipality**	**393140**	**510003**	**784072**	**89860**	**42478**
崂山区	Laoshan District	416	138	211	13	24
黄岛区	Huangdao District	13263	60999	4234	1443	6800
城阳区	Chengyang District	6626	6066	354	70	650
即墨区	Jimo District	48674	27478	95047	1209	18161
胶州市	Jiaozhou	24509	21999	57878	774	1924
平度市	Pingdu	44301	152267	613637	76284	10936
莱西市	Laixi	255351	241056	12711	10067	3983

11-12　分市、区猪、羊及家禽存养量（2022年）
HOGS，SHEEP，GOATS AND POULTRY IN STOCK BY REGION（2022）

单位：万头、万只（10000 head）

市、区名称	Region	年末生猪存养量 Hogs in Stock（year-end）	#母猪 Sow	牛 Cattle and Buffaloes	#奶牛 Cows	年末羊存养量 Sheep and Goats in Stock（year-end）	年末家禽存栏 Poultry stock at the end of the year	#蛋禽 Poultry
全　市	**Whole Municipality**	**159.44**	**16.84**	**14.20**	**8.30**	**17.42**	**4420.07**	**1342.82**
崂山区	Laoshan District							
黄岛区	Huangdao District	21.72	1.87	0.91	0.02	2.42	407.44	153.76
城阳区	Chengyang District	0.79	0.08	0.12	0.12	0.10	22.34	18.56
即墨区	Jimo District	29.71	1.86	2.53	1.62	1.65	1096.86	441.58
胶州市	Jiaozhou	22.34	2.73	0.81	0.14	2.68	353.88	185.44
平度市	Pingdu	42.92	4.44	1.05	0.30	7.68	1248.27	219.18
莱西市	Laixi	41.97	5.87	8.78	6.11	2.89	1291.29	324.31

11-13　分市、区肉、蛋、奶产量（2022年）
OUTPUT OF MEAT，EGGS AND MILK BY REGION（2022）

单位：万吨（10000 tons）

市、区名称	Region	肉类产量 Output of Meat	#猪肉 Port	#禽肉 Poultry Meat	禽蛋 Poultry Egg	牛奶 Milk
全　市	**Whole Municipality**	**51.96**	**21.27**	**28.73**	**26.90**	**29.57**
崂山区	Laoshan District					
黄岛区	Huangdao District	5.40	3.07	2.02	2.83	0.06
城阳区	Chengyang District	0.16	0.12	0.04	0.37	0.42
即墨区	Jimo District	8.37	3.77	4.37	8.86	5.55
胶州市	Jiaozhou	4.08	2.99	0.82	3.66	0.50
平度市	Pingdu	15.34	5.83	9.06	4.57	1.09
莱西市	Laixi	18.62	5.49	12.42	6.61	21.96

11-14 分市、区渔业养殖面积
AQUACULTURE AREA BY REGION

单位：公顷（hectare）

市、区名称	Region	2022年 养殖面积 Aquaculture Area	2022年 #海水 Seawater	2022年 #淡水 Fresh Water	2021年 养殖面积 Aquaculture Area	2021年 #海水 Seawater	2021年 #淡水 Fresh Water
全　市	**Whole Municipality**	**37849**	**34869**	**2980**	**37254**	**34286**	**2968**
崂山区	Laoshan District	986	986		986	986	
黄岛区	Huangdao District	14051	13674	377	12866	12458	408
城阳区	Chengyang District	5490	5379	111	6165	6012	153
即墨区	Jimo District	13339	13079	260	13339	13079	260
胶州市	Jiaozhou	2442	1751	691	2442	1751	691
平度市	Pingdu	593		593	509		509
莱西市	Laixi	948		948	947		947

11-15 分市、区水产品总产量（2022年）
OUTPUT OF AQUATIC PRODUCTS BY REGION（2022）

单位：吨（ton）

市、区名称	Region	水产品总产量 Output of Aquatic Products	按生产方式分 By Bode of Production: #养殖产量 Aquaculture Output	按生产方式分 By Bode of Production: #捕捞产量 Catch	按品种分 By Species: #鱼类 Fish	按品种分 By Species: #甲壳类 Crust	按品种分 By Species: #贝类 Shellfish	按品种分 By Species: #藻类 Algae	按品种分 By Species: #其他 Others
全　市	**Whole Municipality**	**993208**	**793060**	**200148**	**139577**	**59215**	**729203**	**2178**	**63035**
崂山区	Laoshan District	32484	3343	29141	18809	6374	3833		3468
黄岛区	Huangdao District	326024	260981	65043	66459	15756	217408	1258	25143
城阳区	Chengyang District	228173	197347	30826	9985	6792	193947		17449
即墨区	Jimo District	300175	249015	51160	15932	23126	244923	920	15274
胶州市	Jiaozhou	102857	78994	23863	24970	7097	69092		1698
平度市	Pingdu	1210	1210		1137	70			3
莱西市	Laixi	2285	2170	115	2285				

11-16 分市、区植树及造林面积（2022年）
AREA OF TREE PLANTING AND AFFORESTATION BY REGION（2022）

市、区名称	Region	当年造林面积（公顷）Area of Afforestation in the Year（hectare）	育苗数量（万株）Number of Seedlings（10000 trees）	森林抚育作业面积（公顷）Forest Tending Area（hectare）	零星（四旁）植树（万株）Surrounding Tree Planting（10000 trees）
全　市	**Whole Municipality**	**754**	**7874.6**	**3918**	**189.9**
崂山区	Laoshan District		15.0	467	15.0
黄岛区	Huangdao District	421	3800.0	634	
城阳区	Chengyang District	86	400.0	1585	41.2
即墨区	Jimo District		1460.0	699	
胶州市	Jiaozhou		860.0	133	3.0
平度市	Pingdu	180	1339.6	200	130.7
莱西市	Laixi	67		200	

11-17 分市、区水果产量（2022年）
OUTPUT OF FRUITS BY REGION（2022）

单位：吨（ton）

市、区名称	Region	水果总产量 Output of Fruits（ton）	#园林水果 Garden Fruits	#瓜果类水果 Melon Fruits
全　市	**Whole Municipality**	**1219414**	**831310**	**388104**
崂山区	Laoshan District	6254	6184	70
黄岛区	Huangdao District	127036	104028	23008
城阳区	Chengyang District	19342	18251	1091
即墨区	Jimo District	51336	34434	16902
胶州市	Jiaozhou	76464	59930	16534
平度市	Pingdu	414283	233975	180308
莱西市	Laixi	524700	374509	150191

11-17　续表
Continued

单位：吨（ton）

市、区名称	Region	# 苹果 Apple	# 梨 Pear	# 桃 Peach	# 葡萄 Grape	# 杏 Apricot	# 山楂 Hawthorn	# 西瓜 Watermelon	# 甜瓜 Muskmelon
全　市	**Whole Municipality**	**249399**	**160989**	**174104**	**155468**	**6205**	**2278**	**199201**	**117454**
崂山区	Laoshan District	73	67	1979	42	1481			
黄岛区	Huangdao District	37932	3808	22708	6460	241	46	14759	1691
城阳区	Chengyang District	845	186	4533	4369	4064	1		5
即墨区	Jimo District	8555	2934	16192	2676	188	18	11972	1785
胶州市	Jiaozhou	13949	4312	29366	2834	222	9	14347	643
平度市	Pingdu	57074	39841	45811	61831	10	485	136241	784
莱西市	Laixi	130970	109841	53513	77257		1719	21882	112546

11-18　分市、区果园、茶园面积和茶叶产量（2022 年）
AREA OF ORCHARD AND TEA GARDEN AND PRODUCTION OF TEA BY REGION （2022）

单位：公顷（hectare），吨（ton）

市、区名称	Region	果园面积 Area of Orchards	# 苹果园 Apple Orchard	# 梨园 Pear Orchard	# 葡萄园 Vineyard	# 桃园 Peach Orchard	茶园面积 Area of Tea Plantations	茶叶产量 Tea Yield
全　市	**Whole Municipality**	**32752**	**7937**	**4132**	**4780**	**7023**	**4776**	**5000**
崂山区	Laoshan District	611	2	3	2	58	1233	1399
黄岛区	Huangdao District	5465	1088	140	229	1226	3083	3011
城阳区	Chengyang District	910	21	7	127	181	38	49
即墨区	Jimo District	1928	306	235	132	1042	321	517
胶州市	Jiaozhou	2701	600	173	103	1206	45	10
平度市	Pingdu	11126	2232	1218	2075	1608	15	6
莱西市	Laixi	10012	3688	2357	2112	1702	40	8

11-19 主要年份主要农业机械拥有量
MAJOR YEAR'S OWNERSHIP OF AGRICULTURAL MACHINERY

年份 Year	农业机械总动力（万千瓦） Total Agricultural Machinery Power（10000 kW）	农用拖拉机 Agricultural Tractors		大、中型机引农具（万台） Large and Medium Towing Farm Machinery（10000 sets）	排灌机械 Drainage and Irrigation Machinery	
		台 set	千瓦 kW		台 set	万千瓦 10000 kW
1949						
1952						
1957	0.22	59	2.2	0.01		
1962	2.47	254	11.47	0.06		
1965	3.49	296	13.2	0.08		
1970	10.40	602	7 963	0.07		
1975	43.94	6447	103 476	0.48		
1978	75.45	15576	309 287	1.02		
1980	110.44	24278	502 731	1.72		
1985	174.76	33097	506 217	1.71	67794	54.92
1990	253.52	55363	680 903	2.03	105574	74.63
1991	250.58	57404	691 332	2.20	134900	73.77
1992	253.94	57182	684 182	2.28	124800	82.68
1993	261.24	56335	678 161	2.34	144460	78.96
1994	278.41	58698	688 886	2.39	147259	80.81
1995	289.23	56391	657 025	2.28	138625	73.98
1996	303.57	59698	680 447	2.32	148313	81.53
1997	326.72	66841	744 424	2.42	155629	88.09
1998	364.21	87226	894 985	2	156565	86.68
1999	411.44	105743	1 075 907	3	170875	96.20
2000	459.21	126981	1 253 210	3	182646	108.26
2001	496.27	141409	1 394 114	4	178437	104.18
2002	534.92	152920	1 537 544	5	182799	107.35

11-19 续表
Continued

年份 Year	农业机械总动力（万千瓦）Total Agricultural Machinery Power (10000 kW)	农用拖拉机 Agricultural Tractors		大、中型机引农具（万台）Large and Medium Towing Farm Machinery (10000 sets)	排灌机械 Drainage and Irrigation Machinery	
		台 set	千瓦 kW		台 set	万千瓦 10000 kW
2003	560.94	160676	1 666 185	5	192930	109.44
2004	599	168061	1 818 276	5	192144	110
2005	620	163032	1757177	6	188689	112
2006	651	171155	1890402	6	192010	116
2007	680	173326	1958047	7	195050	118
2008	697	176156	2034453	8	208711	134
2009	719	180171	2266697	9	207648	134
2010	764	200208	2331867	10	190770	123
2011	784	202022	2649283	10	189834	127
2012	798	206290	2759004	10	190134	127
2013	809	206309	2968332	10	190433	127
2014	827	205065	2960438	10	190584	128
2015	854	207809	3176870	10	191152	128
2016	698	211689	3372681	10	191283	128
2017	728	214799	3550005	11	191417	128
2018	738	215668	3668505	0.8	232943	
2019	752	216496	3769281	1.7	232952	
2020	755	214845	3789730			
2021	757	210358				
2022	760	205607				

注：1. 大、中型机引农具 2018 年为新统计口径，只统计功率 58.8 千瓦以上机引农具。
2. 2020 年起，市农业农村局不再提供大、中型机引农具及排灌机械数据。
3. 2021 年起，市农业农村局不再提供农用拖拉机的功率数据。

Notes：1. Large and medium type agricultural tools are the new statistical caliber in 2018, and only the statistical power is 58.8 kilowatts or more.
2. Starting in 2020, Qingdao Bureau of Agriculture and Rural Affairs will no longer provide data on large and medium-sized mechanically-introduced agricultural tools and irrigation and drainage machinery.
3. Starting in 2020, Qingdao Bureau of Agriculture and Rural Affairs would have no longer provided data of power on agricultural tractors.

11-20 主要年份农业机械化用电量、化肥施用量
MAJOR YEAR'S MECHANIZATION, ELECTRICITY AND CHEMICAL FERTILIZER CONSUMPTION

年份 Year	耕地机电灌溉面积（公顷）Cultivated Land Electromechanical Irrigation Area (hectare)	配套机电井（眼）Number of Electromechanical Well (unit)	机耕面积（公顷）Area of Motorized Cultivation (hectare)	机播面积（公顷）Area of Motorized Planting (hectare)	机收面积（公顷）Area of Motorized Harvesting (hectare)	农村用电量（万千瓦时）Electricity Consumption in Rural Area (10000 kW·h)	化肥施用量（折纯万吨）Chemical Fertilizer Consumption (convert to 10000 tons)
1949	8340						
1952	14980						
1957	59353		12800	13			0.19
1962	55213	191	65680	927	927	55	0.10
1965	80000	125	11433	573	247	128	0.55
1970	147613	3947	143700	2527	133	1208	1.76
1975	233980	12820	248867	54507	953	2522	2.77
1978	276660	21017	329213	178533	15060	13975	3.64
1980	296606	22472	444800	187980	55333	20492	12.06
1985	302647	42925	366786	148433	56447	41524	11.66
1990	274680	56821	426680	220593	143133	67616	20.47
1991	281500	58987	431293	254266	192946	81200	22.53
1992	281610	62100	438533	270453	207780	88024	22.60
1993	284080	63954	439300	260287	225807	102501	28.04
1994	286750	64877	436820	262846	238693	121307	28.73
1995	287020	64651	435213	271707	250267	134284	31.45
1996	289320	65237	438947	280480	235933	143740	31.36
1997	292130	66783	442213	308267	266147	150971	28.99
1998	294120	64109	442920	359447	285513	153113	32.0
1999	294790	64734	440967	396180	286367	169337	32.6
2000	295190	65179	439980	346480	292787	189651	32.5
2001	296980	65547	436576	382870	265730	228069	31.7
2002	294310	65588	433660	364680	267690	256453	31.1

11-20 续表
Continued

年份 Year	耕地机电灌溉面积（公顷）Cultivated Land Electromechanical Irrigation Area (hectare)	配套机电井（眼）Number of Electromechanical Well (unit)	机耕面积（公顷）Area of Motorized Cultivation (hectare)	机播面积（公顷）Area of Motorized Planting (hectare)	机收面积（公顷）Area of Motorized Harvesting (hectare)	农村用电量（万千瓦时）Electricity Consumption in Rural Area (10000 kW·h)	化肥施用量（折纯万吨）Chemical Fertilizer Consumption (convert to 10000 tons)
2003	292410	65406	415790	404980	256600	299425	31.9
2004	292520	65501	415220	454800	314680	330609	32.5
2005	296450	65303	409610	493240	367740	372644	33.0
2006	303070	65981	403980	493750	398700	413762	32.6
2007	305760	66400	400480	499590	429630	425715	33.9
2008	313920	66828	404080	517540	455120	424292	31.1
2009	322710	67027	404080	538220	481176	426306	30.2
2010	328960	67242	578726	558611	499248	426819	29.9
2011	331690	62104	600451	567947	547108	431646	29.4
2012	333850	62112	610382	627701	566653	426815	29.1
2013	302790	170008	410601	627701	566653	359138	29.1
2014	321670	169491	411355	590798	545360	404380	28.9
2015	323400	155074	417991	640022	600696	401122	28.5
2016	327600	135057	362912	561022	511000	385434	28.37
2017	329620	139342	360085	566264	516763	382437	27.83
2018	331240	136785	359238	578082	531733	377858	27.05
2019	329390	136963	353624	563689	527199	388484	26.71
2020	355077		334148	563410	516895	359584	26.28
2021	332085		325956	571213	515677	328106	24.90
2022	328670		322859	566648	528425		24.61

注：1. 2020 年起有效灌溉面积改为耕地机电灌溉面积，数据由农业农村局提供。
2. 2020 年起，部门不再提供配套机电井数据。
3. 根据国家统计局 2022 年农林牧渔业统计报表制度取消农村用电量指标。

Notes：1. Starting from 2020, the effective irrigation area will be changed to the electromechanical irrigation area of arable land. The data is provided by the Agriculture and Rural Bureau.
2. Starting from 2020, the department will no longer provide supporting electromechanical well data.
3. According to the Agricultural, Forestry, Animal husbandry and Fishery Statistical Report System 2022 issued by National Bureau of Statistics, the rural electricity consumption index will be canceled.

11-21 分市、区农业机械化和电气化（2022年）
MECHANIZATION AND ELECTRIFICATION IN AGRICULTURE BY REGION（2022）

市、区名称	Region	机耕作业面积 Area of Motorized Cultivation	机播地面积 Area of Motorized Planting	机收面积 Area of Motorized Harvesting
		面积（公顷）Area（hectare）		
全　市	**Whole Municipality**	**322859**	**566648**	**528425**
崂山区	Laoshan District			
黄岛区	Huangdao District	33048	62850	55580
城阳区	Chengyang District	953	953	952
即墨区	Jimo District	51836	88889	82662
胶州市	Jiaozhou	28345	68182	65300
平度市	Pingdu	144706	239346	224071
莱西市	Laixi	63971	106428	99860

11-22 分市、区农用化肥施用量（2022年）
CONSUMPTION OF CHEMICAL FERTILIZERS BY REGION（2022）

单位：吨（ton）（折纯）（convert to pure amount）

市、区名称	Region	农用化肥施用量 Consumption of Chemical Fertilizers	氮肥 Nitrogenous Fertilizer	磷肥 Phosphate Fertilizer	钾肥 Potash Fertilizer	复合肥 Compound Fertilizer	附：平均每公顷耕地施用化肥量（折纯千克）Annotation：Consumption of Chemical Fertilizer Per Hectare（convert to pure volume）
全　市	**Whole Municipality**	**246113**	**28132**	**8844**	**13753**	**195384**	**576**
崂山区	Laoshan District	299	3		1	296	514
黄岛区	Huangdao District	22778	3306	1752	4572	13148	454
城阳区	Chengyang District	461	51	25	24	362	129
即墨区	Jimo District	30997	5851	1223	1101	22822	409
胶州市	Jiaozhou	32749	4909	789	3335	23715	709
平度市	Pingdu	108800	5346	1896	2814	98743	635
莱西市	Laixi	50028	8667	3158	1906	36298	626

11-23　分市、区农田水利情况（2022 年）
FARMLAND WATER CONSERVANCY BY REGION（2022）

市、区名称	Region	耕地机电灌溉面积（公顷） Cultivated Land Electromechanical Irrigation Area（hectare）	机电灌溉面积占耕地面积比重（%） Proportion of Electromechanical Irrigation Area in Cultivated Land Area（%）
全　市	**Whole Municipality**	**328670**	**100.0**
崂山区	Laoshan District	520	100.0
黄岛区	Huangdao District	41470	100.0
城阳区	Chengyang District	1150	100.0
即墨区	Jimo District	59990	100.0
胶州市	Jiaozhou	39760	100.0
平度市	Pingdu	131110	100.0
莱西市	Laixi	54670	100.0

11-24　分市、区主要农业机械拥有量（2022年）

OWNERSHIP OF MAJOR AGRICULTURAL MACHINERY BY REGION（2022）

市、区名称	Region	农业机械总动力（万千瓦）Agricultural Machinery Power（10000 kW）	平均每公顷耕地拥有量（千瓦）Power Per Hectare of Cultivated Land（kW）	大中型拖拉机（台）Large and Medium Tractors（set）	小型拖拉机（台）Small Tractors（set）
全　市	**Whole Municipality**	**760.0**	**17.8**	**47458**	**158149**
崂山区	Laoshan District				
黄岛区	Huangdao District	84.6	16.9	2972	42924
城阳区	Chengyang District	26.2	73.0	55	189
即墨区	Jimo District	114.6	15.1	4954	31997
胶州市	Jiaozhou	112.6	24.4	5570	17624
平度市	Pingdu	283.0	16.5	25400	33723
莱西市	Laixi	139.0	17.4	8507	31692

11-24　续表

Continued

市、区名称	Region	机引犁（部）Towing Ploughs（unit）	机引耙（部）Towing Rakes（unit）	粮食加工机械（台）Grain Processing Machinery（set）	油料加工机械（部）Oil Processing Machinery（unit）	棉花加工机械（部）Cotton Processing Machinery（unit）	饲草料加工机械（台套）Forage processing machinery（unit）
全　市	**Whole Municipality**	**160685**	**32245**	**25632**	**9092**	**131**	**22804**
崂山区	Laoshan District						
黄岛区	Huangdao District	32944	109	1125	256		3000
城阳区	Chengyang District	1196	197	1472	465	16	338
即墨区	Jimo District	19974	1680	3305	1472		1481
胶州市	Jiaozhou	15171	5242	3074	2125		3599
平度市	Pingdu	21967	16515	4374	1424		7663
莱西市	Laixi	69433	8502	12282	3350	109	6723

主要统计指标解释

农业总产值　是以货币表现的农、林、牧、渔业全部产品的总量，它反映一定时期内农业生产的总规模和总成果。

农、林、牧、渔业的统计范围是：

（1）农业包括农作物种植业和其他农业。农作物种植业包括谷物、豆类、薯类、棉、油料、糖料、麻类、烟叶、蔬菜、药材、瓜类和其他农作物的种植，以及茶园、桑园、果园的生产经营。其他农业包括采集野生植物的果实、纤维、树胶、树脂、油料以及柴草、野生药材、菌类等及农民家庭兼营的商品性工业。

（2）林业包括林木的栽培（不包括茶园、桑园和果园的栽培、管理和收获等活动）、林产品的采集和村及村以下合作经济组织和农户的竹木采伐。

（3）畜牧业包括除渔业养殖以外的一切动物饲养和放牧，以及野生动物的捕猎和饲养。

（4）渔业包括水生动物和海藻类植物的养殖和捕捞。

（5）农、林、牧、渔专业及辅助性活动指对农业提供的各种专业及辅助性生产活动，不包括各种科学技术和专业技术服务。

粮食作物　指一般用作人类主食，种植在耕地或非耕地上的农作物。根据我国产品目录分类标准，粮食包括谷物、豆类、薯类。

粮食作物播种面积　指本年度内收获的粮食作物在全部土地（耕地或非耕地）上的播种或移植面积。凡是本年内收获的粮食作物，无论是本年还是上年播种，都算为当年播种面积，但不包括本年播种、下年收获的粮食作物面积。移植的粮食作物面积按移植后的面积计算，不计算移植前的秧田面积。如果因灾害等原因，应该收获却未能收获，也要按原播种面积计算，新补或改种，并在本年收获的，也要按复种作物计算面积。间种、混种的作物面积按比例折算各个作物的面积，如果完全混合、同步生长、收获的作物，按混合面积平均分配。复种、套种的作物，按次数计算面积，每种一次计算一次。再生稻、再生高粱等，因其没有经过播种或移植，不计入播种面积。

粮食作物产量　指本年度内生产的全部粮食作物数量。其中，谷物产量按脱粒后的原粮计算，豆类按去豆荚后的干豆计算，薯类按鲜薯重量统计上报，统一按 5∶1 折算粮食产量。

经济作物　指除粮食作物之外，种植在耕地或非耕地上的农作物。包括油料、棉花、生麻、糖料、烟叶、中草药材、蔬菜、瓜果等。

经济作物播种面积　指农业生产经营者应在日历年度内收获的经济作物在全部土地（耕地或非耕地）上的播种或移植面积。凡是本年内收获的经济作物，无论是本年还是上年播种，都算为本年播种面积，但不包括本年播种，下年收获的作物面积。移植的作物面积按移植后的面积计算，不计算移植前在育苗田、棚等的面积。多年生作物，即播种后可连续生长多年的宿根性草本植物，如有些麻类、中药等作物的播种面积，按本年新增面积加往年的连续累计面积计算。如果因灾害等原因，应该收获却未能收获，也要按原播种面积计算，新补或改种，并在本年收获的，要按复种作物计算面积。间种、混种的作物面积按比例折算各个作物的面积，如果完全混合、同步生长、收获的作物，按混合面积平均分配。复种、套种的作物，按次数计算面积，每种一次计算一次。再生烟等，因其没有经过播种或移植，不计入播种面积。莲藕等水生蔬菜类生长在湖泊、水塘等水域的面积占比重较大，不仅难以统计，而且因非耕地面积过大对统计口径产生影响，因此在湖泊、水塘等水域的莲藕等水生蔬菜无论是野生还是人工种植均不计算面积，只计算其在耕地上种植的面积。

经济作物产量　指除粮食外，各经济作物在日历年度内生产的数量。经济作物产量按作物计算，不计算总产量。各主要经济作物的产量计算方法如下：

（1）棉花按去籽后的皮棉计算。

（2）麻类除亚麻以麻秆计算，苎麻以刮皮后的干麻计算，茼麻和线麻以熟麻皮计算外，其余一律以生麻皮计算。一般情况是一公斤熟麻皮可折为二公斤生麻皮，如果原来就习惯按熟麻皮计算的，亦要按比例折成生麻皮后上报。为了准确地统计黄红麻产量，由基层填报的报表，可分别统计生麻皮产量和熟麻皮产量，再由综合部门统一折成生麻皮产量。

（3）烤烟与晒烟均以干烟叶计算。

（4）花生以带壳的干花生计算。

（5）甜菜以块根计算。

（6）瓜果按鲜果计算。

水产品产量 指人工养殖的水产品和天然生长的水产品的捕捞量。包括海水的鱼类、虾蟹类、贝类和藻类以及内陆水域的鱼类、虾蟹类和贝类，不包括淡水生植物。

猪、牛、羊肉产量 指当年出栏并已屠宰、除去头蹄下水后带骨头肉（即胴体重）的重量。其统计范围为全社会。

农用化肥施用量 指本年内实际用于农业生产的化肥数量，包括氮肥、磷肥、钾肥和复合肥。化肥施用量要求按折纯量计算数量。折纯量是指把氮肥、磷肥、钾肥分别按含氮、含五氧化二磷、含氧化钾的百分之百成分进行折算后的数量。复合肥按其所含主要成分折算。

公式：折纯量 = 实物量 × 某种化肥有效成分含量的百分比

农业机械总动力 指用于农、林、牧、渔业生产的各种动力机械的动力总和。动力机械包括耕作、排灌、种植、植物保护、收获、农产品加工、运输、畜牧、渔业、农田水利等各种机械。不包括专门用于乡办工业、基本建设、非农业运输、科学试验和教学等非农业生产方面用的动力机械与作业机械的数量。

Explanatory Notes on Main Statistical Indicators

Gross Output Value of Agriculture refers to the total volume of products of Agriculture, forestry, animal husbandry, and fishery expressed in the monetary terms. It reflects the overall scale and achievements of agricultural production during a given period of time.

The scope of statistics on Agriculture, forestry, animal husbandry, and fishery are as follows:

(1) Agriculture includes cultivation of farm crops and other agricultural activities. Cultivation of farm crops include cultivation of grain crops, legume crops, tuber-crops, cotton, oil-bearing crops, sugar crops, and cultivation and management of tea plantations, mulberry fields and orchards. Other agricultural activities include harvesting wild fruits, fiber, tree gum, resin, oil-bearing plants, firewood, wild medicinal herbs, fungus, and rural-household commodity industries.

(2) Forestry refers to planting trees of various kinds (excluding tea plantations, mulberry fields and orchards), collection of forestry products and cutting and felling of bamboo and trees by villages and other cooperative organizations under village level.

(3) Animal husbandry refers to raising and grazing of all kinds of farm animals except fishing and aquatic cultivating, and hunting and rising of wild animals.

(4) Fishery refers to cultivation and catching of fish and other aquatic products and cultivation and collection of seaweed and other aquatic plants.

(5) Agriculture, forestry, animal husbandry, and fishery professions and auxiliary activities refer to various professional and

auxiliary production activities provided to agriculture, excluding various scientific and technical and professional technical services.

Grain Crops refer to crops that are generally used as the staple food for humans and grown on arable or non–arable land. According to the classification standard of China's product catalog, food crops include grains, beans, and potatoes.

The Sown Area of Grain Crops refers to the sown or transplanted area of grain crops harvested in the current year on all land (arable or non–arable land). All grain crops harvested in the current year, whether sown in the current year or the previous year, are counted as the sown area of the current year, but the area of grain crops sown in the current year and to be harvested in the next year is not included. The area of transplanted grain crops is calculated according to the area after transplantation, excluding the area of seedling field before transplantation. If, due to disasters or other reasons, the crops should be harvested but failed to harvest, the original planting area should be used for calculation, and those newly planted or replanted and harvested in the current year should also be calculated as multi–crop crops. The area of inter–planting and mixed–planting crops shall be converted into the area of each crop in proportion. If the crops are completely mixed, grown synchronously and harvested, they shall be evenly distributed according to the mixed area. For multiple crops and interplanted crops, the area is calculated according to the number of times, and each type is calculated once. Regenerated rice, regenerated sorghum, etc., are not included in the sown area because they have not been sown or transplanted.

Grain Crops Output refers to the total amount of grain crops produced in the current year. Among them, the grain output is calculated according to the raw grain after threshing, the beans are calculated according to the dried beans after removing pods, and the potatoes are reported according to the weight of fresh potatoes, and the grain output is uniformly converted at 5:1.

Economic Crops refer to crops grown on arable land or non–arable land except food crops,including oilseeds, cotton, raw hemp, sugar crops, tobacco leaves, Chinese medicinal herbs, vegetables, melons and fruits, etc.

The Sown Area of Economic Crops refers to the sown or transplanted area of cash crops that should be harvested by agricultural producers and operators within the calendar year on all land (arable land or non–arable land). All cash crops harvested in the current year, whether sown in the current year or the previous year, are counted as the sown area of the current year, but it does not include the area of crops sown in the current year and to be harvested in the next year. The area of transplanted crops is calculated according to the area after transplantation, excluding the area in nursery fields and sheds before transplantation. The planting area of perennial crops, that is, perennial herbaceous plants that can grow continuously for many years after sowing, such as some hemp and traditional Chinese medicines, is calculated by adding the newly added area of this year to the cumulative area of previous years. If, due to disasters or other reasons, the crops should be harvested but fail to be harvested, the original sown area should be used for calculation, and those newly replanted or replanted and harvested in the current year should be calculated as multi–planted crops. The area of inter–planting and mixed–planting crops shall be converted into the area of each crop in proportion. If the crops are completely mixed, grown synchronously and harvested, they shall be evenly distributed according to the mixed area. For multiple crops and interplanted crops, the area is calculated according to the number of times, and each type is calculated once. Regenerated tobacco, etc., are not included in the sowing area because they have not been sown or transplanted. The proportion of aquatic vegetables such as lotus root in lakes, ponds and other waters, is relatively large, which is not only difficult to count, but also has an impact on the statistical caliber due to the large area of non–cultivated land. Therefore, aquatic vegetables such as lotus root in lakes, ponds and other waters is not counted, whether it is wild or artificial cultivation, but only the area cultivated on the arable land is counted.

The Output of Economic Crops cash crops refers to the quantity of allcash crops produced in a calendar year except grain. The output of cash crops is calculated by crops, not the total output. The calculation methods for the output of each major cash crop are as follows:

(1) Cotton is calculated as lint after seed removal.

(2) Flax is counted as hemp stalks, ramie is counted as dry hemp after being scraped; china jute and twine are counted as cooked hemp bark, and the rest are all counted as raw hemp bark. Generally, one kilogram of cooked hemp bark can be converted into two kilograms of raw hemp bark. If calculating is based on cooked hemp bark, it is necessary to convert them into raw hemp bark in proportion and report. In order to accurately count the output of jute and kenaf, the reports filled out by the grassroots can separately count the output of raw hemp bark and the output of cooked hemp bark, and then the comprehensive departments will uniformly convert it into the output of raw hemp bark.

(3) Both flue–cured and sun–cured tobacco are calculated as dry tobacco leaves.

(4) Peanuts are calculated as dry peanuts with shells.

(5) Beets are counted as tubers.

(6) Melons and fruits are calculated as fresh fruits

Output of Aquatic Products refers to catches of both artificially cultured and naturally grown aquatic products, including fish, shrimps, crabs and shellfish in sea and inland water as well as seaweed. Freshwater plants are not included.

Output of Pork, Beef, and Mutton refers to the meat of slaughtered hogs, cattle, sheep and goats with head, feet, and offal taken away. Data refers to the production of the whole country.

Consumption of Chemical Fertilizers in Agriculture refers to the quantity of chemical fertilizers applied in agriculture in the year, including nitrogenous fertilizer, phosphate fertilizer, potash fertilizer, and compound fertilizer. The consumption of chemical fertilizers in required in calculation to convert the gross weight into weight containing 100% effective component (e. g. 100% nitrogen content in nitrogenous fertilizer, 100% phosphorous pent oxide contents in phosphate fertilizer, 100% potassium oxide contents in potash fertilizer). Compound fertilizer is converted with its major component. The formula is:

Volume of effective component = physical quantity × effective component of certain chemical fertilizer (%)

Total Power of Agriculture Machinery Refers to the total mechanical power of machinery used in Agriculture forestry animal husbandry and fishery, including machines used for ploughing, irrigation and drainage, crop growing, plant protection, harvesting, farm product processing, transport, stock breeding, fishery and water conservancy, Machinery employed for non agricultrual purposes such as township industry, capital construction, non-agricultrual transport, scientific experiments and for teaching is excluded.

工　业　12

INDUSTRY

简要说明

一、本篇资料的主要内容

本篇资料主要反映全市工业生产和基本效益情况，主要包括工业企业单位数、历年工业总产值、规模以上工业、国有控股工业、国有工业、集体工业、外商投资和港澳台投资工业、大中型工业企业的主要经济指标、相关的财务分析指标和主要工业产品产量等方面的内容。

二、本篇资料的来源

本篇中规模以上工业资料来源于工业统计年报，由市统计局工业统计处整理提供。

Brief Introduction

Ⅰ. Main Content

Data in this chapter show the basic condition of industrial production and benefit in Qingdao, mainly including the number of industrial enterprises, gross industrial output value and indices, the output of major industrial products and major economic and relevant financial indicators of industrial enterprises. Industrial enterprises include enterprises above designated size, state share-holding enterprises, state owned enterprises, collective owned enterprises, foreign funded enterprises, enterprises with funds from Hong Kong, Macao and Taiwan, large and medium sized enterprises.

Ⅱ. Source of Data

Data on industry above designated size are based on the annual report of industrial statistics, and prepared by the Division of Industry Statistics of Qingdao Municipal Bureau of Statistics.

12-1 规模以上工业企业单位数
NUMBER OF INDUSTRIAL ENTERPRISES ABOVE DESIGNATED SIZE

单位：个（unit）

项　目	Item	1985年	1990年	1995年	2000年	2005年	2006年
总　计	**Total**	**2411**	**2997**	**4987**	**1504**	**3697**	**4567**
一、按经济类型分	**Grouped by Economic Types**						
国有企业	State-owned Enterprises	502	568	1084	179	76	74
集体企业	Collective-owned Enterprises	1907	2386	2731	226	87	72
其他经济类型企业	Other Economic Types Enterprises	2	43	1172	1099	3534	4421
#外商及港澳台商投资企业	Foreign Funded Enterprises and Enterprises with Funds from Hong Kong，Macao and Taiwan		35	1027	593	1658	1952
二、按轻重工业分	**Grouped by Light and Heavy Industries**						
轻工业	Light Industry	1398	1730	2858	891	1942	2313
重工业	Heavy Industry	1013	1267	2129	613	1755	2254
三、按企业规模分	**Grouped by Size of Enterprises**						
大型企业	Large Enterprises	26	42	89	202	51	51
中型企业	Medium Enterprises	80	168	216	229	441	469
小型企业	Small Enterprises	2305	2787	4480	1073	3205	4047
四、按行业分	**Grouped by sectors**						
黑色金属矿采选业	Miring of Ferrous Metal Ores		4	6	1	2	5
有色金属矿采选业	Mining of Non-ferrous Metal Ores	2	7	9	7	5	5
非金属矿采选业	Mining and Processing of Non-metal Ores	43	70	87	29	34	31
食品制造业	Manufacture of Foods	244	324	437	170	121	137
#粮食及饲料加工	Processing of Gren and Feed	62	57	60	27		
饮料制造业	Manufacture of Beverage	31	44	74	23	29	28
#饮料酒	Beverage Liquor	20	28	27	19	20	25

12-1　续表 1
Continued

单位：个（unit）

项　目	Item	2007 年	2008 年	2009 年	2010 年	2011 年
总　计	**Total**	**5032**	**5628**	**5895**	**5674**	**4727**
一、按经济类型分	**Grouped by Economic Types**					
国有企业	State-owned Enterprises	63	65	163	61	147
集体企业	Collective-owned Enterprises	72	61	59	53	31
其他经济类型企业	Other Economic Types Small Enterprises	4897	5502	5673	5560	4549
#外商及港澳台商投资企业	Foreign Funded Enterprises and Enterprises with Funds from Hong Kong, Macao and Taiwan	2091	2217	2244	2037	1618
二、按轻重工业分	**Grouped by Light and Heavy Industries**					
轻工业	Light Industry	2489	2704	2805	2635	2131
重工业	Heavy Industry	2543	2924	3090	3039	2596
三、按企业规模分	**Grouped by Size of Enterprises**					
大型企业	Large Enterprises	53	48	50	52	50
中型企业	Medium Enterprises	489	519	502	525	516
小型企业	Small Enterprises	4490	5061	5343	5097	4161
四、按行业分	**Grouped by sectors**					
黑色金属矿采选业	Miring of Ferrous Metal Ores	7	23	22	12	12
有色金属矿采选业	Mining of Non-ferrous Metal Ores	5	6	6	4	
非金属矿采选业	Mining and Processing of Non-metal Ores	33	30	26	26	23
食品制造业	Manufacture of Foods	156	158	174	167	127
#粮食及饲料加工	Processing of Gren and Feed					
饮料制造业	Manufacture of Beverage	33	40	42	42	36
#饮料酒	Beverage Liquor					

12-1 续表 2
Continued

单位：个（unit）

项　目	Item	1985年	1990年	1995年	2000年	2005年	2006年
烟草制品业	Manufacture of Tobacco	2	2	5	3	2	2
纺织业	Manufacture of Textile	169	225	330	132	300	327
纺织服装、鞋、帽制造业	Manufacture of Textile Wearing Apparel. Footware and Caps	171	194	322	95	272	339
皮革、毛皮、羽毛(绒)及其制品业	Manufacture of Leather，Fur，Feather and Related Products	56	64	161	64	167	194
木材加工制品业	Processing of Wood and Wood Products	71	89	116	19	40	53
家具制造业	Manufacture of Furniture	61	72	88	10	72	103
造纸及纸制品业	Manufacture of Paper and Paper Products	66	74	110	56	102	128
印刷业和记录媒介的复制	Printing，Reproduction of Recording Media	61	81	215	23	44	59
文教体育用品制造业	Manufacture of Articles For Culture，Education and Sport Activities	31	27	93	48	89	91
石油、煤炭及其他燃料加工业	Oil, Coal and Other Fuel Processing Industries	2	3	13	5	10	6
化学原料及制品	Manufacture of Raw Chemical Materials and Chemical Products	106	156	278	81	178	233
医药制造业	Manufacture of Medicines	16	14	39	20	30	46
化学纤维制造业	Manufacture of Chemical Fibres	2	4	26	15	14	13
橡胶制品业	Manufacture of Rubber	53	57	143	48	116	170
塑料制品业	Manufacture of Plastics	103	131	237	64	153	179
非金属矿物制品业	Manufacture of Metallic Mineral Products	230	245	275	62	161	218
黑色金属压延加工业	Smelting and Pressing of Ferrous Metals	11	13	31	15	41	45
有色金属压延加工业	Smelting and Pressing of Non-ferrous Metals	6	8	19	9	28	40
金属制品业	Manufacture of Metal Products	161	186	372	88	186	250
通用设备制造业	Manufacture of General Purpose Machinery	320	398	320	94	299	397
交通运输制造业	Manufacture of Electrical Machinery and Equipment	104	114	358	52	151	194
电气机械及器材制造业	Manufacture of Electrical tion Machinery and Equipment	86	96	211	79	214	249
通信设备、计算机及其他电子设备制造业	Manufacture of Communication Equipment，Computers and Other Electronic Equipment	32	31	79	34	123	140
仪器仪表及文化、办公用机械制造业	Manufacture of Measuring Instruments and Machinery for Cultural Activity and Office Work	28	33	70	20	40	44
水的生产和供应业	Production and Supply of Water	8	12	12	8	10	10
电力、热力的生产和供应业	Production and Supply of Electric Power and Heat Power	10	16	20	17	27	32
燃气生产和供应业	Production and Supply of Gas	1	4	3	2	5	6
其他工业	Other Industrial Sectors	46	48	209	63	166	534

12-1 续表 3
Continued

单位：个（unit）

项　目	Item	2007 年	2008 年	2009 年	2010 年	2011 年
烟草制品业	Manufacture of Tobacco	2	2	2	1	1
纺织业	Manufacture of Textile	340	330	322	287	229
纺织服装、鞋、帽制造业	Manfacture of Testilee Wearing Apparel. Footware and Caps	362	418	434	392	295
皮革、毛皮、羽毛(绒)及其制品业	Manufacture of Leather，Fur，Feather and Related Products	197	209	210	211	160
木材加工制品业	Processing of Woon and Wood Products	64	66	68	68	49
家具制造业	Manufacture of Furniture	119	130	133	117	97
造纸及纸制品业	Manufacture of Paper and Paper Products	126	133	133	138	101
印刷业和记录媒介的复制	Printing，Reproduction of Recording Media	63	74	79	92	58
文教体育用品制造业	Manufacture of Articles For Culture，Education and Sport Activities	97	96	99	90	75
石油、煤炭及其他燃料加工业	Oil, Coal and Other Fuel Processing Industries	7	7	9	8	7
化学原料及制品	Manufacture of Raw Chemical Materials and Chemical Products	261	276	275	262	231
医药制造业	Manufacture of Medicines	48	49	56	52	44
化学纤维制造业	Manufacture of Chemical Fibres	12	13	14	12	10
橡胶制品业	Manufacture of Rubber	183	211	214	196	187
塑料制品业	Manufacture of Plastics	199	227	234	233	169
非金属矿物制品业	Manufacture of Metallic Mineral Products	259	311	320	327	303
黑色金属压延加工业	Smelting and Pressing of Ferrous Metals	39	24	27	31	29
有色金属压延加工业	Smelting and Pressing of Non-ferrous Metals	40	41	40	35	34
金属制品业	Manufacture of Metal Products	271	347	376	361	294
通用设备制造业	Manufacture of General Purpose Machinery	473	535	592	597	521
交通运输制造业	Manufacture of Electrical Machinery and Equipment	217	264	290	296	263
电气机械及器材制造业	Manufacture of Electrication Machinery and Equipment	274	303	300	281	230
通信设备、计算机及其他电子设备制造业	Manufacture of Communication Equipment，Computers and Other Electronic Equipment	152	163	168	167	124
仪器仪表及文化、办公用机械制造业	Manufacture of Measuring Instruments and Machinery for Cultural Activity and Office Work	47	47	55	54	39
水的生产和供应业	Production and Supply of Water	10	13	14	14	11
电力、热力的生产和供应业	Production and Supply of Electric Power and Heat Power	34	36	39	38	36
燃气生产和供应业	Production and Supply of Gas	7	13	13	14	11
其他工业	Other Industrial Sectors	895	1033	1109	1049	921

12-1 续表 4
Continued

单位：个（unit）

项 目	Item	2012 年	2013 年	2014 年	2015 年	2016 年
总 计	**Total**	**4817**	**4917**	**4790**	**4876**	**4431**
一、按经济类型分	**Grouped by Economic Types**					
国有企业	State-owned Enterprises	144	140	132	141	128
集体企业	Collective-owned Enterprises	28	24	19	15	11
其他经济类型企业	Other Economic Types	4645	4753	4639	4720	4292
#外商及港澳台商投资企业	Foreign Funded Enterprises and Enterprises with Funds from Hong Kong，Macao and Taiwan	1599	1551	1445	1361	1205
二、按轻重工业分	**Grouped by Light and Heavy Industries**					
轻工业	Light Industry	2153	2190	2080	2095	1875
重工业	Heavy Industry	2664	2727	2710	2781	2556
三、按企业规模分	**Grouped by Size of Enterprises**					
大型企业	Large Enterprises	98	97	91	89	85
中型企业	Medium Enterprises	596	599	568	566	516
小微型企业	Small & Micro–Enterprises	4123	4221	4131	4221	3830
四、按行业分	**Grouped by sectors**					
黑色金属矿采选业	Mining of Ferrous Metal Ores	10	11	8	7	1
有色金属矿采选业	Mining of Non–ferrous Metal Ores					
非金属矿采选业	Mining and Processing of Non–metal Ores	14	13	7	6	5
农副食品加工业	Processing of Food from Agricultural Products	454	468	444	458	419
食品制造业	Manufacture of Foods	129	123	109	116	115
酒、饮料和精制茶制造业	Manufacture of Liquor，Beverages and Refined Tea	34	35	34	38	33
烟草制品业	Manufacture of Tobacco	1	1	1	1	
纺织业	Manufacture of Textile	181	175	146	133	111
纺织服装、服饰业	Manufacture of Textile Wearing Apparel	312	283	249	244	206
皮革、毛皮、羽毛及其制品和制鞋业	Manufacture of Leather, Fur, Feather & Its Products Footwear	177	148	124	116	89
木材加工和木、竹、藤、棕、草制品业	Processing of Timbers, Manufacture of Wood, Bamboo, Rattan, Palm and Straw Products	34	40	32	34	31
家具制造业	Manufacture of Furniture	103	107	96	98	88
造纸和纸制品业	Manufacture of Paper and Paper Producls	100	71	54	52	50
印刷和记录媒介复制业	Printing, Reproduction of Recording Media	80	121	150	156	137

注：国家统计局根据《国民经济行业分类》（GB/T 4754–2017），对《三次产业划分规定（2012）》中行业类别进行了对应调整，其中“石油加工、炼焦和核燃料加工业”更名为“石油、煤炭及其他燃料加工业”，并将 2011 版《国民经济行业分类》4500 中部分内容和 4120 全部内容调到此类。

Note：According to the national economic industry classification (GB/ T 4754–2017), the National Bureau of Statistics carries out a corresponding adjustment to the three industries according to the classification of the national economy (GB/ T 4754–2017), in which the petroleum processing, coking and nuclear fuel processing industry is changed to petroleum, coal and other fuel processing industries, and the content of part of the content and 4120 of the 2011 edition of the national economy industry category 4500 are transferred to this category.

12-1 续表 5
Continued

单位：个（unit）

项 目	Item	2017 年	2018 年	2019 年	2020 年	2021 年	2022 年
总 计	**Total**	**3569**	**3508**	**3536**	**3856**	**4280**	**4613**
一、按经济类型分	**Grouped by Economic Types**						
国有企业	State-owned Enterprises	131	145	175	189	226	243
集体企业	Collective-owned Enterprises	5	4	5	5	4	4
其他经济类型企业	Other Economic Types	3433	3359	3356	3662	4050	4366
#外商及港澳台商投资企业	Foreign Funded Enterprises and Enterprises with Funds from Hong Kong，Macao and Taiwan	1037	938	868	825	817	815
二、按轻重工业分	**Grouped by Light and Heavy Industries**						
轻工业	Light Industry	1522	1448	1400	1469	1597	1722
重工业	Heavy Industry	2047	2060	2136	2387	2683	2891
三、按企业规模分	**Grouped by Size of Enterprises**						
大型企业	Large Enterprises	78	76	86	77	73	76
中型企业	Medium Enterprises	459	383	386	396	391	378
小微型企业	Small & Micro-Enterprises	3032	3049	3064	3383	3816	4159
四、按行业分	**Grouped by sectors**						
黑色金属矿采选业	Miring of Ferrous Metal Ores						1
有色金属矿采选业	Mining of Non-ferrous Metal Ores		1	1	2	2	2
非金属矿采选业	Mining and Processing of Non-metal Ores	2	1	2	2	1	1
农副食品加工业	Processing of Food from Agricultural Products	338	331	304	295	319	321
食品制造业	Manufacture of Foods	111	115	123	142	159	171
酒、饮料和精制茶制造业	Manufacture of Liquor，Beverages and Refined Tea	18	17	13	13	18	18
烟草制品业	Manufacture of Tobacco						
纺织业	Manufacture of Textile	91	93	103	134	140	156
纺织服装、服饰业	Manufacture of Texitile Wearing Apparel	152	144	132	121	126	131
皮革、毛皮、羽毛及其制品和制鞋业	Manufacture of Leather, Fur, Feather & Its Products Footwear	58	47	39	36	31	30
木材加工和木、竹、藤、棕、草制品业	Processing of Timbers, Manufacture of Wood, Bamboo, Rattan, Palm and Straw Products	27	22	28	43	52	52
家具制造业	Manufacture of Furniture	65	64	59	61	64	64
造纸和纸制品业	Manufacture of Paper and Paper Products	40	40	43	64	57	62
印刷和记录媒介复制业	Printing, Reproduction of Recording Media	110	101	88	66	97	104

12-1 续表 6
Continued

单位：个（unit）

项 目	Item	2012 年	2013 年	2014 年	2015 年	2016 年
文教、工美、体育和娱乐用品制造业	Manufacture of Articles for Culture, Arts & Crafts, Sports and Entertainment	263	335	348	345	310
石油、煤炭及其他燃料加工业	Oil, Coal and Other Fuel Processing Industries	8	8	9	9	9
化学原料和化学制品制造业	Manufacture of Chemical Raw Material and Chemical Products	224	240	246	249	223
医药制造业	Manufacture of Medicines	45	49	50	54	47
化学纤维制造业	Manufacture of Chemical Fibres	9	8	8	8	6
橡胶和塑料制品业	Manufacture of Rubber and Plastic	350	345	331	310	281
非金属矿物制品业	Manufacture of Metallic Mineral Products	325	333	330	338	315
黑色金属冶炼和压延加工业	Smelting and Pressing of Ferrous Metals	105	93	87	83	73
有色金属冶炼和压延加工业	Smelting and Pressing of Non-ferrous Metals	37	36	38	39	30
金属制品业	Manufacture of Metal Products	399	389	380	388	348
通用设备制造业	Manufacture of General Purpose Machinery	362	382	395	402	383
专用设备制造业	Manufacture of Special Purpose Machinery	312	322	314	336	311
汽车制造业	Manufacture of Vehicle	136	141	145	158	154
铁路、船舶、航空航天和其他运输设备制造业	Manufacture of Transport Equipment for Railway, Shipping, Aerospace and other uses	145	146	152	168	156
电气机械和器材制造业	Manufacture of Electrical Machinery and Equipment	202	212	217	226	211
计算机、通信和其他电子设备制造业	Manufactute of Computer, Communication Equipment and Other Electronic Equipment	137	136	141	147	140
仪器仪表制造业	Manufacture of Measuring Instrument	41	49	52	58	50
其他制造业	Manufacture of Other Products	18	17	13	15	16
废弃资源综合利用业	Recycling and Disposal of Waste Resources	4	6	6	5	6
金属制品、机械和设备修理业	Maintenance of Metal Products, Machinery and Equipment	7	7	7	6	5
电力、热力生产和供应业	Production and Supply of Electric Power and Heat Power	36	39	40	43	42
燃气生产和供应业	Production and Supply of Gas	12	13	12	14	14
水的生产和供应业	Production and Supply of Water	11	15	15	16	16

12-1 续表 7
Continued

单位：个（unit）

项　目	Item	2017 年	2018 年	2019 年	2020 年	2021 年	2022 年
文教、工美、体育和娱乐用品制造业	Manufacture of Articles for Culture, Arts & Crafts, Sports and Entertainment	222	179	131	103	107	126
石油、煤炭及其他燃料加工业	Oil, coal and other fuel processing industries	9	8	10	10	13	16
化学原料和化学制品制造业	Manufacture of Chemical Raw Material and Chemical Products	176	171	165	164	172	188
医药制造业	Manufacture of Medicines	35	34	40	43	50	61
化学纤维制造业	Manufacture of Chemical Fibres	7	8	7	8	8	9
橡胶和塑料制品业	Manufacture of Rubber and Plastic	250	252	268	331	362	386
非金属矿物制品业	Manufacture of metallic Mineral Products	228	218	234	296	344	398
黑色金属冶炼和压延加工业	Smelting and Pressing of Ferrous Metals	27	30	25	31	32	39
有色金属冶炼和压延加工业	Smelting and Pressing of Non-ferrous Metals	23	24	29	31	33	34
金属制品业	Manufacture of Metal Products	289	278	295	343	402	438
通用设备制造业	Manufacture of General Purpose Machinery	301	316	318	325	369	397
专用设备制造业	Manufacture of Special Purpose Machinery	233	245	243	275	320	351
汽车制造业	Manufacture of Vehicle	156	168	200	236	253	254
铁路、船舶、航空航天和其他运输设备制造业	Manufacture of Transport Equipment for Railway, Shipping, Aerospace and other uses	150	155	164	168	191	189
电气机械和器材制造业	Manufacture of Electrical Machinery and Equipment	184	186	184	197	211	225
计算机、通信和其他电子设备制造业	Manufactute of Computer, Communication Equipment and Other Electronic Equipment	128	114	117	114	130	152
仪器仪表制造业	Manufacture of Measuring Instrument	46	49	59	67	73	79
其他制造业	Manufacture of Other Products	10	11	11	16	14	12
废弃资源综合利用业	Recycling and Disposal of Waste Resources	3	3	3	2	5	9
金属制品、机械和设备修理业	Maintenance of Metal Products, Machinery and Equipment	6	6	3	7	8	11
电力、热力生产和供应业	Production and Supply of Electric Power and Heat Power	43	44	58	64	71	78
燃气生产和供应业	Production and Supply of Gas	14	15	14	17	17	17
水的生产和供应业	Production and Supply of Water	17	18	23	29	29	31

12-2 分市、区规模以上工业企业数（2022 年）
NUMBER OF ALL INDUSTRIAL ENTERPRISES BY REGION（2022）

单位：个（unit）

市、区名称	Region	规模以上 Above Designated	按轻重工业分 Grouped by Light and Heavy Ind		按企业规模分 Grouped by Size of Enterprises		
			轻工业 Light Industry	重工业 Heavy Industry	大型企业 Large Enterprises	中型企业 Medium Enterprises	小微型企业 Small & Micro-Enterprises
全 市	**Whole Municipality**	**4613**	**1722**	**2891**	**76**	**378**	**4159**
市南区	Shinan District	13	6	7	1	3	9
市北区	Shibei District	53	13	40	2	12	39
李沧区	Licang District	124	31	93		6	118
崂山区	Laoshan District	113	48	65	4	17	92
黄岛区	Huangdao District	1070	296	774	31	94	945
城阳区	Chengyang District	881	340	541	11	74	796
即墨区	Jimo District	594	255	339	10	60	524
胶州市	Jiaozhou	903	365	538	6	56	841
平度市	Pingdu	500	210	290	6	34	460
莱西市	Laixi	361	157	204	4	22	335

12-2 续表
Continued

单位：个（unit）

市、区名称	Region	按经济类型分 Grouped by Economic Types			
		国有企业 State-owned Enterprises	集体企业 Collective-owned Enterprises	其他经济 Others	#外资及港澳台商企业 Foreign Funded Enterprises and Enterprises with Funds from Kong Kong，Macao and Taiwan
全 市	**Whole Municipality**	**243**	**4**	**4366**	**815**
市南区	Shinan District	3		10	
市北区	Shibei District	17	1	35	10
李沧区	Licang District	11		113	12
崂山区	Laoshan District	13		100	23
黄岛区	Huangdao District	91		979	204
城阳区	Chengyang District	40		841	207
即墨区	Jimo District	16		578	103
胶州市	Jiaozhou	14		889	121
平度市	Pingdu	24	3	473	80
莱西市	Laixi	13		348	55

12-3 历年全部工业总产值
GROSS INDUSTRIAL OUTPUT VALUE OVER THE YEARS

单位：万元（10000 yuan）

年 份 Year	工业总产值 Gross Industrial Output Value	轻工业产值 Light Industry	重工业产值 Heavy Industry
1949	21605	18494	3111
1950	34010	28720	5290
1951	53538	44600	8938
1952	84295	69258	15037
1953	115222	74716	40506
1954	126064	80604	45460
1955	118935	86956	31979
1956	144833	93809	51024
1957	142920	101202	41718
1958	217648	92407	125241
1959	282610	84376	198234
1960	291451	77043	214408
1962	120738	64233	56505
1963	139542	83630	55912
1964	177273	108884	68389
1965	215536	141765	73771
1966	252896	152304	100592
1967	287739	163627	124112
1968	299814	175791	123489
1969	296814	188860	107954
1970	345212	202903	142309

注：本表按当年价格计算，1995 年开始工业总产值按新规定计算。
Note：The data in this form are calculated at current price. Since 1995，new regulations have been adopted in calculating gross industrial output value.

12-3 续表 1
Continued

单位：万元（10000 yuan）

年 份 Year	工业总产值 Gross Industrial Output Value	轻工业产值 Light Industry	重工业产值 Heavy Industry
1971	365770	216172	149598
1972	378266	230309	147957
1973	377943	245371	132572
1974	237219	154054	83165
1975	402541	261418	141123
1976	439793	278514	161279
1977	490669	296728	193941
1978	565503	336817	228686
1979	625227	379276	245951
1980	677690	442078	235612
1981	707434	479954	227480
1982	732705	474767	257938
1983	816793	513759	303034
1984	918364	569080	349284
1985	1113891	699524	414367
1986	1316230	833864	482366
1987	1703830	1065873	637957
1988	2481594	1451215	1030379
1989	3191643	1857019	1334624
1990	3571845	2057968	1513878

12-3 续表 2
Continued

单位：万元（10000 yuan）

年 份	Year	工业总产值 Gross Industrial Output Value	轻工业产值 Light Industry	重工业产值 Heavy Industry
1991	1991	3986427	2318257	1668170
1992	1992	4826834	2835728	1991106
1993	1993	5929236	3422107	2507129
1994	1994	8456974	4931262	3525712
1995	1995	9412635	5579637	3832998
1996	1996	11173672	6793007	4380665
1997	1997	13704735	8620710	5084025
1998	1998	15794106	10153634	5640472
1999	1999	16822436	10918827	5903609
2000	2000	19408338	12433214	6975124
2001	2001	22398464	14368582	8029882
2002	2002	25794324	14811106	10983218
2003	2003	31195595	17306539	13889056
2004	2004	39590783	21473202	18117581
2005	2005	50017829	24697792	25320037
2006	2006	59188120	28686826	30501294
2007	2007	74306364	33463071	40843293
2008	2008	89467300	37871227	51596073
2009	2009	102556155	42715781	59840374
2010	2010	116148345	44954630	71193715
2011	2011	132779629	50854938	81924691

12-3 续表 3
Continued

单位：万元（10000 yuan）

年　份	Year	工业总产值 Gross Industrial Output Value	轻工业产值 Light Industry	重工业产值 Heavy Industry
2012	2012	153102565	60516341	92546833
2013	2013	168971805	66799317	102172488
2014	2014	174442125	67683545	106758580
2015	2015	180194299	71176748	109017551
2016	2016	174157133	68552071	105605062
2017	2017	130197343	48954201	81243142
2018	2018	113897787	39054621	74843166
“一五”时期合计	“First Five-Year Plan” Period	647974	437287	210687
“二五”时期合计	“Second Five-Year Plan” Period	1077075	388406	688669
1963-1965 年合计	1963-1965	532351	334279	198072
“三五”时期合计	“Third Five-Year Plan” Period	1481941	883485	598456
“四五”时期合计	“Fourth Five-Year Plan” Period	1761739	1107324	654415
“五五”时期合计	“Fifth Five-Year Plan” Period	2798882	1733413	1065469
“六五”时期合计	“Sixth Five-Year Plan” Period	4289187	2737084	1552103
“七五”时期合计	“Seventh Five-Year Plan” Period	12265142	7265939	4999204
“八五”时期合计	“Eighth Five-Year Plan” Period	32612106	19087323	13524783
“九五”时期合计	“Ninth Five-Year Plan” Period	76903287	48919392	27983895
“十五”时期合计	“Tenth Five-Year Plan” Period	168996995	92657221	76339774
“十一五”时期合计	“Eleventh Five-Year Plan” Period	175336465	73641456	101695009
“十二五”时期合计	“Twelfth Five-Year Plan” Period	809490422	317030889	492420143

12-4 规模以上工业企业主要指标（2022年）
MAIN INDICATORS OF INDUSTRIAL ENTERPRISES ABOVE DESIGNATED SIZE（2022）

项 目	Item	企业单位数（个）Number of Enterprises（unit）
总 计	**Total**	**4613**
按注册登记类型分	**Grouped by Status of Registration**	
国有及国有控股企业	State-owned and State-holding Enterprises	283
集体企业	Collective-owned Enterprises	4
股份有限公司	Share-holding Corporations Ltd	104
外商投资企业	Foreign Funded Enterprises	630
港澳台商投资企业	Invested by HongKong, Macao and Taiwan	185
按轻重工业分	**Grouped by Light and Heavy Industries**	
轻工业	Light Industry	1722
重工业	Heavy Industry	2891
按企业规模分	**Grouped by Size of Enterprises**	
大型企业	Large Enterprises	76
中型企业	Medium Enterprises	378
小微型企业	Small & Micro-Enterprises	4159
按所在地分	**Grouped by Location**	
市南区	Shinan District	13
市北区	Shibei District	53
李沧区	Licang District	124
崂山区	Laoshan District	113
黄岛区	Huangdao District	1070
城阳区	Chengyang District	881
即墨区	Jimo District	594
胶州市	Jiaozhou	903
平度市	Pingdu	500
莱西市	Laixi	361
按行业分	**Grouped by sector**	
煤炭开采和洗选业	Mining and Washing of Coal	
石油和天然气开采业	Extraction of Petroleum and Natural Gas	
黑色金属矿采选业	Mining of Ferrous Metal Ores	1
有色金属矿采选业	Mining of Non-ferrous Metal Ores	2
非金属矿采选业	Mining and Processing of Non-metal Ores	1
开采辅助活动	Auxiliary Activities of Mining	
其他采矿业	Mining of Other Ores	

单位：万元（10000 yuan）

资产合计 Total Assets	流动资产年合计 Total Current Assets	固定资产净值 Net Value of Fixed Assets
140450622	**88347112**	**25265417**
58156693	31713155	12465240
241229	160454	42402
29102730	18221078	2659176
23217052	16412203	3886625
7980100	5335126	1492280
33551713	33551713	4715271
106898909	106898909	20550146
51438052	30236422	8887549
39707598	25099780	7012829
49304973	33010910	9365039
1036284	348522	513893
4759933	2667909	894176
3736408	2234734	487402
6758798	4530851	563599
51220507	29930973	10954859
25667307	17874078	3421806
15692117	10256342	2654797
14475414	10268361	1943408
9278264	5038564	2154982
7825590	5196779	1676497

12-4 续表 1
Continued

项　目	Item	营业收入 Revenue from Principal Business
总　计	**Total**	**122775552**
按注册登记类型分	**Grouped by Status of Registration**	
国有及国有控股企业	State-owned and State-holding Enterprises	41976436
集体企业	Collective-owned Enterprises	907445
股份有限公司	Share-holding Corporations Ltd	18149606
外商投资企业	Foreign Funded Enterprises	25563430
港澳台商投资企业	Invested by HongKong, Macao and Taiwan	6706653
按轻重工业分	**Grouped by Light and Heavy Industries**	
轻工业	Light Industry	38900179
重工业	Heavy Industry	83875373
按企业规模分	**Grouped by Size of Enterprises**	
大型企业	Large Enterprises	40069404
中型企业	Medium Enterprises	37606050
小微型企业	Small & Micro-Enterprises	45100097
按所在地分	**Grouped by Location**	
市南区	Shinan District	378975
市北区	Shibei District	5045999
李沧区	Licang District	4661181
崂山区	Laoshan District	5096208
黄岛区	Huangdao District	46765737
城阳区	Chengyang District	17845438
即墨区	Jimo District	13725852
胶州市	Jiaozhou	12844819
平度市	Pingdu	10304529
莱西市	Laixi	6106814
按行业分	**Grouped by sector**	
煤炭开采和洗选业	Mining and Washing of Coal	
石油和天然气开采业	Extraction of Petroleum and Natural Gas	
黑色金属矿采选业	Mining of Ferrous Metal Ores	
有色金属矿采选业	Mining of Non-ferrous Metal Ores	
非金属矿采选业	Mining and Processing of Non-metal Ores	
开采辅助活动	Auxiliary Activities of Mining	
其他采矿业	Mining of Other Ores	

单位：万元（10000 yuan）

营业成本 Cost of Principal Business	营业税金及附加 Taxes and Extra Charges on Principal Business	利润总额 Total Profits	全部从业人员年平均人数（人） Annual Average Employed Persons（person）
104786826	**1932390**	**5664677**	**701041**
36360856	1528072	1757509	132862
795260	3800	-12901	3566
14944136	130012	1269064	79249
21537704	218692	1917761	154785
5702021	28061	339432	41595
32467020	215062	2090254	274564
72319806	1717328	3574423	426477
33907690	347224	2372186	172604
31615516	1412084	1719564	202614
39263620	173082	1572927	325823
372781	10669	-19033	2998
4725442	21629	78400	13981
3914266	347239	181961	15860
4200565	26046	309735	24537
39644360	1152514	2222667	192468
14500770	84276	1140635	139581
12021349	151708	744592	96548
11204519	48530	473229	97397
8985431	63354	349121	72194
5217345	26426	183371	45477

12-4　续表 2
Continued

项　目	Item	企业单位数（个）Number of Enterprises (unit)
农副食品加工业	Processing of Food from Agricultural Products	321
食品制造业	Manufacture of Foods	171
酒、饮料和精制茶制造业	Manufacture of Liquor，Beverages and Refined Tea	18
烟草制品业	Manufacture of Tobacco	
纺织业	Manufacture of Textile	156
纺织服装、服饰业	Manufacture of Textile Wearing Apparel	131
皮革、毛皮、羽毛及其制品和制鞋业	Processing of Leather, Fur, Feather & Its Products Footwear	30
木材加工和木、竹、藤、棕、草制品业	Processing of Timber, Manufacture of Wood, Bamboo, Rattan, Palm and Straw Products	52
家具制造业	Manufacture of Furniture	64
造纸和纸制品业	Manufacture of Paper and Paper Products	62
印刷和记录媒介复制业	Printing, Reproduction of Recording Media	104
文教、工美、体育和娱乐用品制造业	Manufacture of Articles for Culture, Arts & Crafts, Sports and Entertainment	126
石油、煤炭及其他燃料加工业	Oil, Coal and Other Fuel Processing Industries	16
化学原料和化学制品制造业	Manufacture of Chemical Raw Material and Chemical Products	188
医药制造业	Manufacture of Medicines	61
化学纤维制造业	Manufacture of Chemical Fibres	9
橡胶和塑料制品业	Manufacture of Rubber and Plastic	386
非金属矿物制品业	Manufacture of metallic Mineral Products	398
黑色金属冶炼和压延加工业	Smelting and Pressing of Ferrous Metals	39
有色金属冶炼和压延加工业	Smelting and Pressing of Nonferrous Metals	34
金属制品业	Manufacture of Metal Products	438
通用设备制造业	Manufacture of General Purpose Machinery	397
专用设备制造业	Manufacture of Special Purpose Machinery	351
汽车制造业	Manufacture of Vehicle	254
铁路、船舶、航空航天和其他运输设备制造业	Manufacture of Transport Equipment for Railway, Shipping, Aerospace and other uses	189
电气机械和器材制造业	Manufacture of Electrical Machinery and Equipment	225
计算机、通信和其他电子设备制造业	Manufacture of Compute, Communication Equipment and Other Electronic Equipment	152
仪器仪表制造业	Manufacture of Measuring Instrument	79
其他制造业	Manufacture of Other Products	12
废弃资源综合利用业	Recycling and Disposal of Waste Resources	9
金属制品、机械和设备修理业	Manufacture of Metal Products, Machinery and Equipment	11
电力、热力生产和供应业	Production and Supply of Electric Power and Heat Power	78
燃气生产和供应业	Production and Supply of Gas	17
水的生产和供应业	Production and Supply of Water	31

单位：万元（10000 yuan）

资产合计 Total Assets	流动资产合计 Total Current Assets	固定资产净值 Net Value of Fixed Assets
5763339	4556584	668955
3949250	2660838	779906
4013809	2195148	351633
1119607	835072	201304
1822422	1068751	172370
221643	160774	45263
280905	192558	52817
508792	401152	51893
457626	299498	98052
865288	576186	214769
805227	566132	147317
2932437	2350695	417621
9363769	4673929	2325275
2411563	1484489	404798
91492	53475	17919
6939516	4141046	1658649
7000161	5419235	1035458
3021418	1306319	1309568
748522	332786	213793
6403536	3969553	954485
7769658	5462692	1195308
9364519	7133414	926464
12169359	9237648	1985860
15823101	10717580	1993591
11227554	7640298	1050363
11814682	5734299	2063840
1638100	1141552	123162
164239	104758	34308
49307	24969	9798
120056	84293	24587
7464019	2471100	2886006
1690645	356230	1024694
2215394	950426	776043

12-4 续表 3
Continued

项　目	Item	营业收入 Revenue from Principal Business
农副食品加工业	Processing of Food from Agricultural Products	10526371
食品制造业	Manufacture of Foods	3213006
酒、饮料和精制茶制造业	Manufacture of Liquor， Beverages and Refined Tea	2922898
烟草制品业	Manufacture of Tobacco	
纺织业	Manufacture of Textile	1708175
纺织服装、服饰业	Manufacture of Textile Wearing Apparel	1674171
皮革、毛皮、羽毛及其制品和制鞋业	Processing of Leather, Fur, Feather & Its Products Footwear	339916
木材加工和木、竹、藤、棕、草制品业	Processing of Timber, Manufacture of Wood, Bamboo, Rattan, Palm and Straw Products	302674
家具制造业	Manufacture of Furniture	528777
造纸和纸制品业	Manufacture of Paper and Paper Products	602205
印刷和记录媒介复制业	Printing, Reproduction of Recording Media	951615
文教、工美、体育和娱乐用品制造业	Manufacture of Articles for Culture, Arts & Crafts, Sports and Entertainment	933285
石油、煤炭及其他燃料加工业	Oil, Coal and Other Fuel Processing Industries	9412920
化学原料和化学制品制造业	Manufacture of Chemical Raw Material and Chemical Products	8792240
医药制造业	Manufacture of Medicines	1377810
化学纤维制造业	Manufacture of Chemical Fibres	79007
橡胶和塑料制品业	Manufacture of Rubber and Plastic	5376496
非金属矿物制品业	Manufacture of metallic Mineral Products	4635151
黑色金属冶炼和压延加工业	Smelting and Pressing of Ferrous Metals	3915903
有色金属冶炼和压延加工业	Smelting and Pressing of Non-ferrous Metals	1046624
金属制品业	Manufacture of Metal Products	5981017
通用设备制造业	Manufacture of General Purpose Machinery	6605161
专用设备制造业	Manufacture of Special Purpose Machinery	6109611
汽车制造业	Manufacture of Vehicle	10976886
铁路、船舶、航空航天和其他运输设备制造业	Manufacture of Transport Equipment for Railway, Shipping, Aerospace and other uses	7244232
电气机械和器材制造业	Manufacture of Electrical Machinery and Equipment	13566909
计算机、通信和其他电子设备制造业	Manufacture of Compute, Communication Equipment and Other Electronic Equipment	8784839
仪器仪表制造业	Manufacture of Measuring Instrument	1101029
其他制造业	Manufacture of Other Products	147300
废弃资源综合利用业	Recycling and Disposal of Waste Resources	121545
金属制品、机械和设备修理业	Manufacture of Metal Products, Machinery and Equipment	82493
电力、热力生产和供应业	Production and Supply of Electric Power and Heat Power	2051288
燃气生产和供应业	Production and Supply of Gas	1166962
水的生产和供应业	Production and Supply of Water	447125

单位：万元（10000 yuan）

营业成本 Cost of Principal Business	营业税金及附加 Taxes and Extra Charges on Principal Business	利润总额 Total Profits	全部从业人员年平均人数（人） Annual Average Employed Persons (person)
9911043	16749	145283	44926
2563489	16317	147654	18511
2311573	75374	290551	15383
1539028	6463	36786	17113
1470029	9722	61369	31988
293367	1625	13247	9772
270012	1779	129	3227
455510	2488	-3883	8308
548471	1678	7304	4626
797414	4471	49597	11268
776399	4896	50549	16276
7783029	1277346	303189	2360
7654064	30861	388123	24066
693284	13389	251247	11263
68403	434	3358	805
4547316	25577	214138	49730
3942930	23032	215828	28849
3651544	15042	116769	8482
959744	5319	21929	2911
5175079	24012	265887	43608
5328367	29898	396122	59167
4830401	28752	504246	45129
9709706	145181	611928	49992
6043916	47572	401274	51252
10811449	54383	954728	58144
7912181	28878	198335	46823
747854	6962	135626	10808
130714	994	79	3693
117125	408	2032	252
66065	707	4628	1861
2210850	13319	-244237	12886
1013919	2034	82568	2624
417590	15423	32792	4512

12-5 按行业分国有控股工业企业主要指标（2022年）
MAIN INDICATORS OF STATE-HOLDING INDUSTRIAL ENTERPRISES BY INDUSTRIAL SECTOR（2022）

项 目	Item	企业单位数（个）Number of Enterprises（unit）
总 计	**Total**	**243**
煤炭开采和洗选业	Mining and Washing of Coal	
石油和天然气开采业	Extraction of Petroleum and Natural Gas	
黑色金属矿采选业	Mining of Ferrous Metal Ores	
有色金属矿采选业	Mining of Non-ferrous Metal Ores	2
非金属矿采选业	Mining and Processing of Non-metal Ores	1
开采辅助活动	Auxiliary Activities of Mining	
其他采矿业	Mining of Other Ores	
农副食品加工业	Processing of Food from Agricultural Products	2
食品制造业	Manufacture of Foods	6
酒、饮料和精制茶制造业	Manufacture of Liquor， Beverages and Refined Tea	4
烟草制品业	Manufacture of Tobacco	
纺织业	Manufacture of Textile	
纺织服装、服饰业	Manufacture of Textile Wearing Apparel	2
皮革、毛皮、羽毛及其制品和制鞋业	Manufacture of Leather, Fur, Feather & Its Products Footwear	
木材加工和木、竹、藤、棕、草制品业	Processing of Timber, Manufacture of Wood, Bamboo, Rattan, Palm and Straw Products	2
家具制造业	Manufacture of Furniture	
造纸和纸制品业	Manufacture of Paper and Paper Products	1
印刷和记录媒介复制业	Printing, Reproduction of Recording Media	2
文教、工美、体育和娱乐用品制造业	Manufacture of Articles for Culture, Arts & Crafts, Sports and Entertainment	
石油、煤炭及其他燃料加工业	Oil, Coal and Other Fuel Processing Industries	2
化学原料和化学制品制造业	Manufacture of Chemical Raw Material and Chemical Products	11
医药制造业	Manufacture of Medicines	4
化学纤维制造业	Manufacture of Chemical Fibres	
橡胶和塑料制品业	Manufacture of Rubber and Plastic	6
非金属矿物制品业	Manufacture of metallic Mineral Products	17
黑色金属冶炼和压延加工业	Smelting and Pressing of Ferrous Metals	7
有色金属冶炼和压延加工业	Smelting and Pressing of Non-ferrous Metals	5
金属制品业	Manufacture of Metal Products	9
通用设备制造业	Manufacture of General Purpose Machinery	17
专用设备制造业	Manufacture of Special Purpose Machinery	17
汽车制造业	Manufacture of Vehicle	9
铁路、船舶、航空航天和其他运输设备制造业	Manufacture of Transport Equipment for Railway, Shipping, Aerospace and other uses	16
电气机械和器材制造业	Manufacture of Electrical Machinery and Equipment	9
计算机、通信和其他电子设备制造业	Manufacture of Computer, Communication Equipment and Other Electronic Equipment	13
仪器仪表制造业	Manufacture of Measuring Instrument	3
其他制造业	Manufacture of Other Products	
废弃资源综合利用业	Recycling and Disposal of Waste Resources	1
金属制品、机械和设备修理业	Manufacture of Metal Products, Machinery and Equipment	3
电力、热力生产和供应业	Production and Supply of Electric Power and Heat Power	47
燃气生产和供应业	Production and Supply of Gas	6
水的生产和供应业	Production and Supply of Water	19

单位：万元（10000 yuan）

资产合计 Total Assets	流动资产合计 Total Current Assets	固定资产净值 Net Value of Fixed Assets
54842719	**29901157**	**11760255**
290951	205979	54665
3696058	1964299	284039
2557970	666860	1031135
871862	496699	156559
702302	340314	312699
551051	436849	70524
2571729	966993	1230998
408633	50932	183303
830962	526531	223406
532597	369750	125624
2128998	1573620	224480
4121030	3393146	396359
12973445	8694440	1617354
2941437	1773743	206712
7393368	2969864	1324784
50758	36198	7314
59400	28400	21791
5940068	2006388	2343582
1063540	114368	715388
2008012	856761	732136

12-5 续表
Continued

项　目	Item	营业收入 Revenue from Principal Business
总　计	**Total**	**39794703**
煤炭开采和洗选业	Mining and Washing of Coal	
石油和天然气开采业	Extraction of Petroleum and Natural Gas	
黑色金属矿采选业	Mining of Ferrous Metal Ores	
有色金属矿采选业	Mining of Non-ferrous Metal Ores	
非金属矿采选业	Mining and Processing of Non-metal Ores	
开采辅助活动	Auxiliary Activities of Mining	
其他采矿业	Mining of Other Ores	
农副食品加工业	Processing of Food from Agricultural Products	
食品制造业	Manufacture of Foods	147167
酒、饮料和精制茶制造业	Manufacture of Liquor， Beverages and Refined Tea	2674085
烟草制品业	Manufacture of Tobacco	
纺织业	Manufacture of Textile	
纺织服装、服饰业	Manufacture of Textile Wearing Apparel	
皮革、毛皮、羽毛及其制品和制鞋业	Manufacture of Leather, Fur, Feather & Its Products Footwear	
木材加工和木、竹、藤、棕、草制品业	Processing of Timber, Manufacture of Wood, Bamboo, Rattan, Palm and Straw Products	
家具制造业	Manufacture of Furniture	
造纸和纸制品业	Manufacture of Paper and Paper Products	
印刷和记录媒介复制业	Printing, Reproduction of Recording Media	
文教、工美、体育和娱乐用品制造业	Manufacture of Articles for Culture, Arts & Crafts, Sports and Entertainment	
石油、煤炭及其他燃料加工业	Oil, Coal and Other Fuel Processing Industries	
化学原料和化学制品制造业	Manufacture of Chemical Raw Material and Chemical Products	1842767
医药制造业	Manufacture of Medicines	349979
化学纤维制造业	Manufacture of Chemical Fibres	
橡胶和塑料制品业	Manufacture of Rubber and Plastic	462833
非金属矿物制品业	Manufacture of metallic Mineral Products	342978
黑色金属冶炼和压延加工业	Smelting and Pressing of Ferrous Metals	2917608
有色金属冶炼和压延加工业	Smelting and Pressing of Non-ferrous Metals	159792
金属制品业	Manufacture of Metal Products	926991
通用设备制造业	Manufacture of General Purpose Machinery	443821
专用设备制造业	Manufacture of Special Purpose Machinery	1310306
汽车制造业	Manufacture of Vehicle	4304868
铁路、船舶、航空航天和其他运输设备制造业	Manufacture of Transport Equipment for Railway, Shipping, Aerospace and other uses	5737702
电气机械和器材制造业	Manufacture of Electrical Machinery and Equipment	2144380
计算机、通信和其他电子设备制造业	Manufacture of Computer, Communication Equipment and Other Electronic Equipment	4076995
仪器仪表制造业	Manufacture of Measuring Instrument	28966
其他制造业	Manufacture of Other Products	
废弃资源综合利用业	Recycling and Disposal of Waste Resources	
金属制品、机械和设备修理业	Manufacture of Metal Products, Machinery and Equipment	27822
电力、热力生产和供应业	Production and Supply of Electric Power and Heat Power	1734292
燃气生产和供应业	Production and Supply of Gas	379571
水的生产和供应业	Production and Supply of Water	384778

单位：万元（10000 yuan）

营业成本 Cost of Principal Business	营业税金及附加 Taxes and Extra Charges on Principal Business	利润总额 Total Profits	全部从业人员年平均人数（人） Annual Average Employed Persons (person)
34380323	**1507016**	**1721126**	**123284**
120207	1227	14202	1130
2139415	70742	243151	12935
1532368	8531	159374	4402
133783	4235	79116	2668
445152	2084	-27567	3576
303549	1973	10058	1248
2698222	13091	114802	6232
114231	4208	20425	1108
766181	3574	77137	5386
395051	1990	5414	3266
1127234	4988	46870	6126
3936241	20755	206937	9007
4798874	37620	353223	26515
1707896	11658	307770	8057
3697147	15346	13764	10949
21367	238	3298	190
24429	288	-1221	159
1968767	10547	-272251	10930
320049	1072	37704	1058
380153	14664	15493	4048

12-6 按行业分规模以上外商投资和港澳台商投资工业企业主要指标（2022年）
MAIN INDICATORS OF FOREIGN FUNDED ENTERPRISES AND ENTERPRISES WITH FUNDS FROM HONG KONG, MACAO AND TAIWAN ABOVE DESIGNATED SIZE BY INDUSTRIAL SECTOR（2022）

项　目	Item	企业单位数（个）Number of Enterprises（unit）
总　计	**Total**	**815**
煤炭开采和洗选业	Mining and Washing of Coal	
石油和天然气开采业	Extraction of Petroleum and Natural Gas	
黑色金属矿采选业	Mining of Ferrous Metal Ores	1
有色金属矿采选业	Mining of Non-ferrous Metal Ores	
非金属矿采选业	Mining and Processing of Non-metal Ores	
开采辅助活动	Auxiliary Activities of Mining	
其他采矿业	Mining of Other Ores	
农副食品加工业	Processing of Food from Agricultural Products	70
食品制造业	Manufacture of Foods	38
酒、饮料和精制茶制造业	Manufacture of Liquor， Beverages and Refined Tea	5
烟草制品业	Manufacture of Tobacco	
纺织业	Manufacture of Textile	40
纺织服装、服饰业	Manufacture of Textile Wearing Apparel	38
皮革、毛皮、羽毛及其制品和制鞋业	Manufacture of Leather, Fur, Feather & Its Products Footwear	11
木材加工和木、竹、藤、棕、草制品业	Processing of Timber, Manufacture of Wood, Bamboo, Rattan, Palm and Straw Products	5
家具制造业	Manufacture of Furniture	14
造纸和纸制品业	Manufacture of Paper and Paper Products	12
印刷和记录媒介复制业	Printing, Reproduction of Recording Media	16
文教、工美、体育和娱乐用品制造业	Manufacture of Articles for Culture, Arts & Crafts, Sports and Entertainment	32
石油、煤炭及其他燃料加工业	Oil, Coal and Other Fuel Processing Industries	1
化学原料和化学制品制造业	Manufacture of Chemical Raw Material and Chemical Products	42
医药制造业	Manufacture of Medicines	11
化学纤维制造业	Manufacture of Chemical Fibres	2
橡胶和塑料制品业	Manufacture of Rubber and Plastic	52
非金属矿物制品业	Manufacture of metallic Mineral Products	37
黑色金属冶炼和压延加工业	Smelting and Pressing of Ferrous Metals	7
有色金属冶炼和压延加工业	Smelting and Pressing of Non-ferrous Metals	3
金属制品业	Manufacture of Metal Products	57
通用设备制造业	Manufacture of General Purpose Machinery	66
专用设备制造业	Manufacture of Special Purpose Machinery	49
汽车制造业	Manufacture of Vehicle	60
铁路、船舶、航空航天和其他运输设备制造业	Manufacture of Transport Equipment for Railway, Shipping, Aerospace and other uses	27
电气机械和器材制造业	Manufacture of Electrical Machinery and Equipment	33
计算机、通信和其他电子设备制造业	Manufacture of Computer, Communication Equipment and Other Electronic Equipment	46
仪器仪表制造业	Manufacture of Measuring Instrument	12
其他制造业	Manufacture of Other Products	4
废弃资源综合利用业	Recycling and Disposal of Waste Resources	
金属制品、机械和设备修理业	Manufacture of Metal Products, Machinery and Equipment	2
电力、热力生产和供应业	Production and Supply of Electric Power and Heat Power	7
燃气生产和供应业	Production and Supply of Gas	9
水的生产和供应业	Production and Supply of Water	6

单位：万元（10000 yuan）

资产合计 Total Assets	流动资产合计 Total Current Assets	固定资产净值 Net Value of Fixed Assets
31197152	**21747330**	**5378906**
2086456	1694621	201334
2390245	1638362	477970
145850	109398	26857
387232	297051	70124
430180	337402	37911
125378	88008	31915
58832	48294	8651
134608	105211	21868
162081	114397	37365
264826	189258	50867
447517	309347	89547
2534024	1374413	526975
419360	325329	77345
1088330	663035	379394
850947	550301	234335
181231	135211	36422
33829	30362	3333
1133338	739793	254500
1885767	1352545	380056
1780172	1354155	246064
6394930	5295143	918579
2351992	1797729	246453
2568120	1219664	236784
1747079	1141398	363025
477500	384212	28423
121797	66882	30437
282352	66173	148337
364940	186449	139353
177462	74019	60942

12-6 续表
Continued

项　目	Item	营业收入 Revenue from Principal Business
总　计	**Total**	**32270083**
煤炭开采和洗选业	Mining and Washing of Coal	
石油和天然气开采业	Extraction of Petroleum and Natural Gas	
黑色金属矿采选业	Mining of Ferrous Metal Ores	
有色金属矿采选业	Mining of Non-ferrous Metal Ores	
非金属矿采选业	Mining and Processing of Non-metal Ores	
开采辅助活动	Auxiliary Activities of Mining	
其他采矿业	Mining of Other Ores	
农副食品加工业	Processing of Food from Agricultural Products	3850900
食品制造业	Manufacture of Foods	1766450
酒、饮料和精制茶制造业	Manufacture of Liquor, Beverages and Refined Tea	174083
烟草制品业	Manufacture of Tobacco	
纺织业	Manufacture of Textile	502745
纺织服装、服饰业	Manufacture of Textile Wearing Apparel	650744
皮革、毛皮、羽毛及其制品和制鞋业	Manufacture of Leather, Fur, Feather & Its Products Footwear	199783
木材加工和木、竹、藤、棕、草制品业	Processing of Timber, Manufacture of Wood, Bamboo, Rattan, Palm and Straw Products	35056
家具制造业	Manufacture of Furniture	178485
造纸和纸制品业	Manufacture of Paper and Paper Products	182259
印刷和记录媒介复制业	Printing, Reproduction of Recording Media	343068
文教、工美、体育和娱乐用品制造业	Manufacture of Articles for Culture, Arts & Crafts, Sports and Entertainment	431769
石油、煤炭及其他燃料加工业	Oil, Coal and Other Fuel Processing Industries	
化学原料和化学制品制造业	Manufacture of Chemical Raw Material and Chemical Products	2855790
医药制造业	Manufacture of Medicines	255230
化学纤维制造业	Manufacture of Chemical Fibres	
橡胶和塑料制品业	Manufacture of Rubber and Plastic	1039510
非金属矿物制品业	Manufacture of metallic Mineral Products	650525
黑色金属冶炼和压延加工业	Smelting and Pressing of Ferrous Metals	428047
有色金属冶炼和压延加工业	Smelting and Pressing of Non-ferrous Metals	13747
金属制品业	Manufacture of Metal Products	1348423
通用设备制造业	Manufacture of General Purpose Machinery	1954061
专用设备制造业	Manufacture of Special Purpose Machinery	1445178
汽车制造业	Manufacture of Vehicle	5945455
铁路、船舶、航空航天和其他运输设备制造业	Manufacture of Transport Equipment for Railway, Shipping, Aerospace and other uses	779279
电气机械和器材制造业	Manufacture of Electrical Machinery and Equipment	3848839
计算机、通信和其他电子设备制造业	Manufacture of Computer, Communication Equipment and Other Electronic Equipment	2061622
仪器仪表制造业	Manufacture of Measuring Instrument	434217
其他制造业	Manufacture of Other Products	97857
废弃资源综合利用业	Recycling and Disposal of Waste Resources	
金属制品、机械和设备修理业	Manufacture of Metal Products, Machinery and Equipment	
电力、热力生产和供应业	Production and Supply of Electric Power and Heat Power	52679
燃气生产和供应业	Production and Supply of Gas	632316
水的生产和供应业	Production and Supply of Water	55273

单位：万元（10000 yuan）

营业成本 Cost of Principal Business	营业税金及附加 Taxes and Extra Charges on Principal Business	利润总额 Total Profits	全部从业人员年平均人数（人） Annual Average Employed Persons (person)
27239724	**246754**	**2257194**	**196380**
3640416	6383	66848	14337
1333468	10482	106561	6640
125377	1446	32723	1536
438514	2863	17873	6351
591694	3355	2757	11466
178568	955	2642	5717
30650	203	199	402
157544	1156	1350	3291
161576	808	5478	1332
281780	1883	25798	4072
362564	2500	23924	8106
2523761	11108	75405	7079
144442	2748	61837	1433
855313	9378	52298	10941
547887	3520	42044	4067
415694	967	–3301	1091
12958	45	–242	182
1127690	8245	116103	11820
1589638	9669	133117	15439
1153073	7829	128714	10465
5092817	123727	568017	20676
579583	6537	103507	8465
3053864	17982	435911	14508
1786601	6818	120843	19071
270106	2913	74048	2468
90745	811	–4106	3221
29417	572	18020	268
582537	769	35420	939
34556	708	10785	347

12-7　按行业分大中型工业企业主要指标（2022 年）

MAIN INDICATORS OF LARGE AND MEDIUM-SIZED INDUSTRIAL ENTERPRISES BY INDUSTRIAL SECTOR（2022）

项　目	Item	企业单位数（个） Number of Enterprises （unit）
总　计	**Total**	**454**
煤炭开采和洗选业	Mining and Washing of Coal	
石油和天然气开采业	Extraction of Petroleum and Natural Gas	
黑色金属矿采选业	Mining of Ferrous Metal Ores	
有色金属矿采选业	Mining of Non-ferrous Metal Ores	
非金属矿采选业	Mining and Processing of Non-metal Ores	
开采辅助活动	Auxiliary Activities of Mining	
其他采矿业	Mining of Other Ores	
农副食品加工业	Processing of Food from Agricultural Products	35
食品制造业	Manufacture of Foods	11
酒、饮料和精制茶制造业	Manufacture of Liquor，Beverages and Refined Tea	4
烟草制品业	Manufacture of Tobacco	
纺织业	Manufacture of Textile	12
纺织服装、服饰业	Manufacture of Textile Wearing Apparel	24
皮革、毛皮、羽毛及其制品和制鞋业	Manufacture of Leather, Fur, Feather & Its Products Footwear	8
木材加工和木、竹、藤、棕、草制品业	Processing of Timber, Manufacture of Wood, Bamboo, Rattan, Palm and Straw Products	2
家具制造业	Manufacture of Furniture	6
造纸和纸制品业	Manufacture of Paper and Paper Products	2
印刷和记录媒介复制业	Printing, Reproduction of Recording Media	5
文教、工美、体育和娱乐用品制造业	Manufacture of Articles for Culture, Arts & Crafts, Sports and Entertainment	10
石油、煤炭及其他燃料加工业	Oil, Coal and Other Fuel Processing Industries	2
化学原料和化学制品制造业	Manufacture of Chemical Raw Material and Chemical Products	17
医药制造业	Manufacture of Medicines	8
化学纤维制造业	Manufacture of Chemical Fibres	
橡胶和塑料制品业	Manufacture of Rubber and Plastic	25
非金属矿物制品业	Manufacture of metallic Mineral Products	12
黑色金属冶炼和压延加工业	Smelting and Pressing of Ferrous Metals	4
有色金属冶炼和压延加工业	Smelting and Pressing of Non-ferrous Metals	2
金属制品业	Manufacture of Metal Products	22
通用设备制造业	Manufacture of General Purpose Machinery	45
专用设备制造业	Manufacture of Special Purpose Machinery	32
汽车制造业	Manufacture of Vehicle	34
铁路、船舶、航空航天和其他运输设备制造业	Manufacture of Transport Equipment for Railway, Shipping, Aerospace and other uses	29
电气机械和器材制造业	Manufacture of Electrical Machinery and Equipment	39
计算机、通信和其他电子设备制造业	Manufacture of Computer, Communication Equipment and Other Electronic Equipment	37
仪器仪表制造业	Manufacture of Measuring Instrument	6
其他制造业	Manufacture of Other Products	1
废弃资源综合利用业	Recycling and Disposal of Waste Resources	
金属制品、机械和设备修理业	Manufacture of Metal Products, Machinery and Equipment	1
电力、热力生产和供应业	Production and Supply of Electric Power and Heat Power	14
燃气生产和供应业	Production and Supply of Gas	2
水的生产和供应业	Production and Supply of Water	3

单位：万元（10000 yuan）

资产合计 Total Assets	流动资产合计 Total Current Assets	固定资产净值 Net Value of Fixed Assets
91145649	**55336202**	**15900378**
2123953	1666107	225962
2251532	1590823	409880
3747666	2014892	296619
362984	276959	47285
1093635	613268	87714
140953	95575	33509
229438	193970	11352
183614	129096	37673
342693	248081	57310
6546935	2698439	1885917
1584473	993739	242453
4570430	2448706	1179968
953497	649992	203861
2511639	901428	1237809
3288133	1767564	417907
4872924	3297614	732573
5171697	4064563	427136
9175961	7106864	1459423
13677654	9326923	1717976
8700638	5678556	831554
9987237	4474233	1836492
926179	604200	62565
3713485	1446548	1130283
1218539	614283	472543

12-7 续表
Continued

项　目	Item	营业收入 Revenue from Principal Business
总　计	**Total**	**77675455**
煤炭开采和洗选业	Mining and Washing of Coal	
石油和天然气开采业	Extraction of Petroleum and Natural Gas	
黑色金属矿采选业	Mining of Ferrous Metal Ores	
有色金属矿采选业	Mining of Non-ferrous Metal Ores	
非金属矿采选业	Mining and Processing of Non-metal Ores	
开采辅助活动	Auxiliary Activities of Mining	
其他采矿业	Mining of Other Ores	
农副食品加工业	Processing of Food from Agricultural Products	3834981
食品制造业	Manufacture of Foods	1592162
酒、饮料和精制茶制造业	Manufacture of Liquor, Beverages and Refined Tea	2819182
烟草制品业	Manufacture of Tobacco	
纺织业	Manufacture of Textile	649203
纺织服装、服饰业	Manufacture of Textile Wearing Apparel	1035415
皮革、毛皮、羽毛及其制品和制鞋业	Manufacture of Leather, Fur, Feather & Its Products Footwear	256681
木材加工和木、竹、藤、棕、草制品业	Processing of Timber, Manufacture of Wood, Bamboo, Rattan, Palm and Straw Products	
家具制造业	Manufacture of Furniture	249521
造纸和纸制品业	Manufacture of Paper and Paper Products	
印刷和记录媒介复制业	Printing, Reproduction of Recording Media	224306
文教、工美、体育和娱乐用品制造业	Manufacture of Articles for Culture, Arts & Crafts, Sports and Entertainment	319776
石油、煤炭及其他燃料加工业	Oil, Coal and Other Fuel Processing Industries	
化学原料和化学制品制造业	Manufacture of Chemical Raw Material and Chemical Products	5570095
医药制造业	Manufacture of Medicines	816025
化学纤维制造业	Manufacture of Chemical Fibres	
橡胶和塑料制品业	Manufacture of Rubber and Plastic	2442038
非金属矿物制品业	Manufacture of metallic Mineral Products	635970
黑色金属冶炼和压延加工业	Smelting and Pressing of Ferrous Metals	2718967
有色金属冶炼和压延加工业	Smelting and Pressing of Non-ferrous Metals	
金属制品业	Manufacture of Metal Products	2742906
通用设备制造业	Manufacture of General Purpose Machinery	4023261
专用设备制造业	Manufacture of Special Purpose Machinery	3181252
汽车制造业	Manufacture of Vehicle	8649582
铁路、船舶、航空航天和其他运输设备制造业	Manufacture of Transport Equipment for Railway, Shipping, Aerospace and other uses	6154666
电气机械和器材制造业	Manufacture of Electrical Machinery and Equipment	11133321
计算机、通信和其他电子设备制造业	Manufacture of Computer, Communication Equipment and Other Electronic Equipment	6990508
仪器仪表制造业	Manufacture of Measuring Instrument	569432
其他制造业	Manufacture of Other Products	
废弃资源综合利用业	Recycling and Disposal of Waste Resources	
金属制品、机械和设备修理业	Manufacture of Metal Products, Machinery and Equipment	
电力、热力生产和供应业	Production and Supply of Electric Power and Heat Power	1218246
燃气生产和供应业	Production and Supply of Gas	
水的生产和供应业	Production and Supply of Water	152047

单位：万元（10000 yuan）

营业成本 Cost of Principal Business	营业税金及附加 Taxes and Extra Charges on Principal Business	利润总额 Total Profits	全部从业人员年平均人数（人） Annual Average Employed Persons (person)
65523206	**1759309**	**4091750**	**375218**
3607657	6534	55340	25948
1197911	8216	100449	5600
2247613	70822	270785	14138
583333	2491	21307	5489
901611	6698	71213	20410
218990	1416	12964	7937
208885	1451	−5454	3264
181935	1229	20977	2583
257990	2000	28326	5931
4953175	18388	192219	10937
338903	9671	197413	5901
2043411	15708	92731	21843
535250	2503	37219	4919
2505391	13008	110014	6382
2334214	11687	217698	16371
3207640	18913	286740	29662
2465631	16613	285057	19860
7662955	134492	541607	27491
5137115	41379	366135	38760
8671145	47662	862430	42629
6309058	24428	140910	35974
379128	3995	86364	3915
1405910	6877	−222646	7503
185429	12077	−7689	2450

12-8　按行业分规模以上工业企业主要经济效益指标（2022 年）
MAIN INDICATORS ON ECONOMIC BENEFIT OF INDUSTRIAL ENTERPRISES ABOVE DESIGNATED SIZE BY INDUSTRIAL SECTOR （2022）

项　目	Item	总资产贡献率（%）Ratio of Total Assets to Industrial Output Value（%）
总　计	**Total**	**7.16**
煤炭开采和洗选业	Mining and Washing of Coal	
石油和天然气开采业	Extraction of Petroleum and Natural Gas	
黑色金属矿采选业	Mining of Ferrous Metal Ores	-0.59
有色金属矿采选业	Mining of Non-ferrous Metal Ores	9.17
非金属矿采选业	Mining and Processing of Non-metal Ores	4.19
开采辅助活动	Auxiliary Activities of Mining	
其他采矿业	Mining of Other Ores	
农副食品加工业	Processing of Food from Agricultural Products	4.71
食品制造业	Manufacture of Foods	6.51
酒、饮料和精制茶制造业	Manufacture of Liquor，Beverages and Refined Tea	10.83
烟草制品业	Manufacture of Tobacco	
纺织业	Manufacture of Textile	6.21
纺织服装、服饰业	Manufacture of Textile Wearing Apparel	5.2
皮革、毛皮、羽毛及其制品和制鞋业	Manufacture of Leather, Fur, Feather & Its Products Footwear	8.3
木材加工和木、竹、藤、棕、草制品业	Processing of Timber, Manufacture of Wood, Bamboo, Rattan, Palm and Straw Products	3.77
家具制造业	Manufacture of Furniture	2.87
造纸和纸制品业	Manufacture of Paper and Paper Products	4.21
印刷和记录媒介复制业	Printing, Reproduction of Recording Media	9.81
文教、工美、体育和娱乐用品制造业	Manufacture of Articles for Culture, Arts & Crafts, Sports and Entertainment	8.8
石油、煤炭及其他燃料加工业	Oil, Coal and Other Fuel Processing Industries	54.89
化学原料和化学制品制造业	Manufacture of Chemical Raw Material and Chemical Products	5.96
医药制造业	Manufacture of Medicines	14.94
化学纤维制造业	Manufacture of Chemical Fibres	5.78
橡胶和塑料制品业	Manufacture of Rubber and Plastic	4.98
非金属矿物制品业	Manufacture of metallic Mineral Products	5.51
黑色金属冶炼和压延加工业	Smelting and Pressing of Ferrous Metals	6.12
有色金属冶炼和压延加工业	Smelting and Pressing of Non-ferrous Metals	4.64
金属制品业	Manufacture of Metal Products	6.37
通用设备制造业	Manufacture of General Purpose Machinery	6.97
专用设备制造业	Manufacture of Special Purpose Machinery	7.24
汽车制造业	Manufacture of Vehicle	8.77
铁路、船舶、航空航天和其他运输设备制造业	Manufacture of Transport Equipment for Railway, Shipping, Aerospace and other uses	3.57
电气机械和器材制造业	Manufacture of Electrical Machinery and Equipment	11.61
计算机、通信和其他电子设备制造业	Manufacture of Computer, Communication Equipment and Other Electronic Equipment	2.78
仪器仪表制造业	Manufacture of Measuring Instrument	11.4
其他制造业	Manufacture of Other Products	2.74
废弃资源综合利用业	Recycling and Disposal of Waste Resources	14.11
金属制品、机械和设备修理业	Manufacture of Metal Products, Machinery and Equipment	9.48
电力、热力生产和供应业	Production and Supply of Electric Power and Heat Power	-0.95
燃气生产和供应业	Production and Supply of Gas	6.35
水的生产和供应业	Production and Supply of Water	3.39

单位：万元（10000 yuan）

资产负债率（%） Assets-Liability Ratio（%）	流动资产周转次数（次/年） Number of Times of Annual of Turnover Current Assets（time/year）	工业成本费用利润率（%） Ratio of Profits to Industrial Costs（%）
57.58	**1.39**	**4.86**
55.59	0.81	-4.33
48.4	2.29	24.87
83.75	0.4	4.22
70.56	2.31	1.4
63.07	1.21	4.82
50.16	1.33	10.58
57.29	2.05	2.2
52.43	1.57	3.78
61.27	2.11	4.07
73.35	1.57	0.04
69.13	1.32	-0.75
66.77	2.01	1.23
65.65	1.65	5.46
47.98	1.65	5.73
46.46	4	3.87
53.02	1.88	4.62
41.04	0.93	22.29
64.25	1.48	4.45
56.68	1.3	4.15
67.2	0.86	4.89
66.11	3	3.05
63.49	3.15	2.14
50.74	1.51	4.68
52.72	1.21	6.33
59.63	0.86	8.88
63.45	1.19	5.89
60.21	0.68	5.83
49.42	1.78	7.53
46.66	1.53	2.27
43.46	0.96	13.84
69.05	1.41	0.05
69.46	4.87	1.69
39.14	0.98	5.96
75.75	0.83	-10.22
53.62	3.28	7.46
64.62	0.47	6.76

12-9 按行业分国有控股工业企业主要经济效益指标（2022年）
MAIN INDICATORS ON ECONOMIC BENEFIT OF STATE-OWNED AND STATE-HOLDING INDUSTRIAL ENTERPRISES BY INDUSTRIAL SECTOR （2022）

项　目	Item	总资产贡献率（%）Ratio of Total Assets to Industrial Output Value（%）
总　计	**Total**	**7.21**
煤炭开采和洗选业	Mining and Washing of Coal	
石油和天然气开采业	Extraction of Petroleum and Natural Gas	
黑色金属矿采选业	Mining of Ferrous Metal Ores	
有色金属矿采选业	Mining of Non-ferrous Metal Ores	9.17
非金属矿采选业	Mining and Processing of Non-metal Ores	4.19
开采辅助活动	Auxiliary Activities of Mining	
其他采矿业	Mining of Other Ores	
农副食品加工业	Processing of Food from Agricultural Products	-1.09
食品制造业	Manufacture of Foods	6.46
酒、饮料和精制茶制造业	Manufacture of Liquor，Beverages and Refined Tea	10.10
烟草制品业	Manufacture of Tobacco	
纺织业	Manufacture of Textile	
纺织服装、服饰业	Manufacture of Textile Wearing Apparel	-2.64
皮革、毛皮、羽毛及其制品和制鞋业	Manufacture of Leather, Fur, Feather & Its Products Footwear	
木材加工和木、竹、藤、棕、草制品业	Processing of Timber, Manufacture of Wood, Bamboo, Rattan, Palm and Straw Products	3.33
家具制造业	Manufacture of Furniture	
造纸和纸制品业	Manufacture of Paper and Paper Products	1.37
印刷和记录媒介复制业	Printing, Reproduction of Recording Media	14.21
文教、工美、体育和娱乐用品制造业	Manufacture of Articles for Culture, Arts & Crafts, Sports and Entertainment	
石油、煤炭及其他燃料加工业	Oil, Coal and Other Fuel Processing Industries	58.46
化学原料和化学制品制造业	Manufacture of Chemical Raw Material and Chemical Products	8.46
医药制造业	Manufacture of Medicines	12.66
化学纤维制造业	Manufacture of Chemical Fibres	
橡胶和塑料制品业	Manufacture of Rubber and Plastic	-2.09
非金属矿物制品业	Manufacture of metallic Mineral Products	4.87
黑色金属冶炼和压延加工业	Smelting and Pressing of Ferrous Metals	6.47
有色金属冶炼和压延加工业	Smelting and Pressing of Non-ferrous Metals	6.65
金属制品业	Manufacture of Metal Products	13.09
通用设备制造业	Manufacture of General Purpose Machinery	2.73
专用设备制造业	Manufacture of Special Purpose Machinery	4.14
汽车制造业	Manufacture of Vehicle	7.80
铁路、船舶、航空航天和其他运输设备制造业	Manufacture of Transport Equipment for Railway, Shipping, Aerospace and other uses	3.43
电气机械和器材制造业	Manufacture of Electrical Machinery and Equipment	13.21
计算机、通信和其他电子设备制造业	Manufacture of Computer, Communication Equipment and Other Electronic Equipment	0.87
仪器仪表制造业	Manufacture of Measuring Instrument	10.98
其他制造业	Manufacture of Other Products	
废弃资源综合利用业	Recycling and Disposal of Waste Resources	9.18
金属制品、机械和设备修理业	Manufacture of Metal Products, Machinery and Equipment	2.30
电力、热力生产和供应业	Production and Supply of Electric Power and Heat Power	-2.28
燃气生产和供应业	Production and Supply of Gas	4.85
水的生产和供应业	Production and Supply of Water	2.68

单位：万元（10000 yuan）

资产负债率（%） Assets-Liability Ratio（%）	流动资产周转次数（次/年） Number of Times of Annual of Turnover Current Assets（time/year）	工业成本费用利润率（%） Ratio of Profits to Industrial Costs（%）
59.14	**1.33**	**4.61**
48.40	2.29	24.87
83.75	0.40	4.22
124.60	0.75	-4.30
39.43	0.71	10.56
49.16	1.36	9.63
7.69	0.28	-10.68
88.54	0.39	-0.37
62.98	2.83	0.34
63.76	1.56	10.64
45.22	4.11	3.99
64.77	2.76	9.44
35.97	0.70	29.59
78.50	1.36	-5.63
70.76	0.79	3.06
67.85	3.02	4.06
55.23	3.14	14.93
61.01	1.76	9.31
74.27	1.20	1.23
71.79	0.83	3.61
64.66	1.27	4.97
61.58	0.66	6.51
42.90	1.21	16.14
44.43	1.37	0.33
50.44	0.80	13.00
61.28	4.77	-0.54
37.17	0.98	-4.22
77.43	0.86	-12.96
50.12	3.32	10.71
65.73	0.45	3.51

12-10 按行业分规模以上外商及港澳台商投资工业企业主要经济效益指标（2022年）

MAIN INDICATORS ON ECONOMIC BENEFIT OF FOREIGN FUNDED ENTERPRISES AND ENTERPRISES WITH FUNDS FROM HONG KONG, MACAO AND TAIWAN ABOVE DESIGNATED SIZE BY INDUSTRIAL SECTOR（2022）

项　目	Item	总资产贡献率（%） Ratio of Total Assets to Industrial Output Value（%）
总　计	**Total**	**10.09**
煤炭开采和洗选业	Mining and Washing of Coal	
石油和天然气开采业	Extraction of Petroleum and Natural Gas	
黑色金属矿采选业	Mining of Ferrous Metal Ores	-0.59
有色金属矿采选业	Mining of Non-ferrous Metal Ores	
非金属矿采选业	Mining and Processing of Non-metal Ores	
开采辅助活动	Auxiliary Activities of Mining	
其他采矿业	Mining of Other Ores	
农副食品加工业	Processing of Food from Agricultural Products	5.83
食品制造业	Manufacture of Foods	7.40
酒、饮料和精制茶制造业	Manufacture of Liquor，Beverages and Refined Tea	26.83
烟草制品业	Manufacture of Tobacco	
纺织业	Manufacture of Textile	7.08
纺织服装、服饰业	Manufacture of Textile Wearing Apparel	2.61
皮革、毛皮、羽毛及其制品和制鞋业	Manufacture of Leather, Fur, Feather & Its Products Footwear	4.25
木材加工和木、竹、藤、棕、草制品业	Processing of Timber, Manufacture of Wood, Bamboo, Rattan, Palm and Straw Products	3.32
家具制造业	Manufacture of Furniture	5.57
造纸和纸制品业	Manufacture of Paper and Paper Products	6.36
印刷和记录媒介复制业	Printing, Reproduction of Recording Media	14.57
文教、工美、体育和娱乐用品制造业	Manufacture of Articles for Culture, Arts & Crafts, Sports and Entertainment	7.23
石油、煤炭及其他燃料加工业	Oil, Coal and Other Fuel Processing Industries	-1.49
化学原料和化学制品制造业	Manufacture of Chemical Raw Material and Chemical Products	4.22
医药制造业	Manufacture of Medicines	20.24
化学纤维制造业	Manufacture of Chemical Fibres	6.96
橡胶和塑料制品业	Manufacture of Rubber and Plastic	7.12
非金属矿物制品业	Manufacture of metallic Mineral Products	6.88
黑色金属冶炼和压延加工业	Smelting and Pressing of Ferrous Metals	2.78
有色金属冶炼和压延加工业	Smelting and Pressing of Non-ferrous Metals	0.21
金属制品业	Manufacture of Metal Products	12.20
通用设备制造业	Manufacture of General Purpose Machinery	8.87
专用设备制造业	Manufacture of Special Purpose Machinery	9.27
汽车制造业	Manufacture of Vehicle	13.81
铁路、船舶、航空航天和其他运输设备制造业	Manufacture of Transport Equipment for Railway, Shipping, Aerospace and other uses	5.67
电气机械和器材制造业	Manufacture of Electrical Machinery and Equipment	20.87
计算机、通信和其他电子设备制造业	Manufacture of Computer, Communication Equipment and Other Electronic Equipment	7.97
仪器仪表制造业	Manufacture of Measuring Instrument	20.02
其他制造业	Manufacture of Other Products	-1.12
废弃资源综合利用业	Recycling and Disposal of Waste Resources	
金属制品、机械和设备修理业	Manufacture of Metal Products, Machinery and Equipment	11.99
电力、热力生产和供应业	Production and Supply of Electric Power and Heat Power	9.28
燃气生产和供应业	Production and Supply of Gas	11.40
水的生产和供应业	Production and Supply of Water	8.71

单位：万元（10000 yuan）

资产负债率（%） Assets-Liability Ratio（%）	流动资产周转次数（次/年） Number of Times of Annual of Turnover Current Assets（time/year）	工业成本费用利润率（%） Ratio of Profits to Industrial Costs（%）
51.09	**1.48**	**7.52**
55.59	0.81	-4.33
69.57	2.27	1.77
65.67	1.08	6.44
60.47	1.59	20.25
33.66	1.69	3.70
52.01	1.93	0.43
54.33	2.27	1.35
74.63	0.73	0.57
57.52	1.70	0.76
51.36	1.59	3.10
57.89	1.81	8.11
35.29	1.40	5.86
58.27	1.35	-2.05
46.36	2.08	2.72
40.58	0.78	31.93
64.09	1.08	7.93
36.67	1.57	5.33
39.54	1.18	6.90
24.45	3.17	-0.77
71.86	0.45	-1.74
44.39	1.82	9.54
43.52	1.44	7.28
52.75	1.07	9.77
52.77	1.12	10.66
53.09	0.43	15.31
46.74	3.16	12.51
47.04	1.81	6.20
46.11	1.13	20.71
78.39	1.46	-4.03
27.15	0.82	11.92
44.36	0.80	49.82
56.23	3.39	5.82
51.85	0.75	24.54

12-11 按行业分大中型工业企业主要经济效益指标（2022 年）

MAIN INDICATORS ON ECONOMIC BENEFIT OF LARGE AND MEDIUM-SIZED INDUSTRIAL ENTERPRISES BY INDUSTRIAL SECTOR（2022）

项　目	Item	总资产贡献率（%）Ratio of Total Assets to Industrial Output Value（%）
总　计	**Total**	**7.97**
煤炭开采和洗选业	Mining and Washing of Coal	
石油和天然气开采业	Extraction of Petroleum and Natural Gas	
黑色金属矿采选业	Mining of Ferrous Metal Ores	
有色金属矿采选业	Mining of Non-ferrous Metal Ores	
非金属矿采选业	Mining and Processing of Non-metal Ores	
开采辅助活动	Auxiliary Activities of Mining	
其他采矿业	Mining of Other Ores	
农副食品加工业	Processing of Food from Agricultural Products	4.52
食品制造业	Manufacture of Foods	7.38
酒、饮料和精制茶制造业	Manufacture of Liquor, Beverages and Refined Tea	10.81
烟草制品业	Manufacture of Tobacco	
纺织业	Manufacture of Textile	8.83
纺织服装、服饰业	Manufacture of Textile Wearing Apparel	8.26
皮革、毛皮、羽毛及其制品和制鞋业	Manufacture of Leather, Fur, Feather & Its Products Footwear	12.09
木材加工和木、竹、藤、棕、草制品业	Processing of Timber, Manufacture of Wood, Bamboo, Rattan, Palm and Straw Products	5.23
家具制造业	Manufacture of Furniture	2.43
造纸和纸制品业	Manufacture of Paper and Paper Products	1.76
印刷和记录媒介复制业	Printing, Reproduction of Recording Media	15.73
文教、工美、体育和娱乐用品制造业	Manufacture of Articles for Culture, Arts & Crafts, Sports and Entertainment	10.27
石油、煤炭及其他燃料加工业	Oil, Coal and Other Fuel Processing Industries	58.46
化学原料和化学制品制造业	Manufacture of Chemical Raw Material and Chemical Products	4.56
医药制造业	Manufacture of Medicines	17.23
化学纤维制造业	Manufacture of Chemical Fibres	
橡胶和塑料制品业	Manufacture of Rubber and Plastic	3.44
非金属矿物制品业	Manufacture of metallic Mineral Products	5.74
黑色金属冶炼和压延加工业	Smelting and Pressing of Ferrous Metals	6.35
有色金属冶炼和压延加工业	Smelting and Pressing of Non-ferrous Metals	5.39
金属制品业	Manufacture of Metal Products	8.49
通用设备制造业	Manufacture of General Purpose Machinery	7.48
专用设备制造业	Manufacture of Special Purpose Machinery	7.01
汽车制造业	Manufacture of Vehicle	10.15
铁路、船舶、航空航天和其他运输设备制造业	Manufacture of Transport Equipment for Railway, Shipping, Aerospace and other uses	3.49
电气机械和器材制造业	Manufacture of Electrical Machinery and Equipment	13.17
计算机、通信和其他电子设备制造业	Manufacture of Computer, Communication Equipment and Other Electronic Equipment	2.37
仪器仪表制造业	Manufacture of Measuring Instrument	12.35
其他制造业	Manufacture of Other Products	-2.48
废弃资源综合利用业	Recycling and Disposal of Waste Resources	
金属制品、机械和设备修理业	Manufacture of Metal Products, Machinery and Equipment	51.63
电力、热力生产和供应业	Production and Supply of Electric Power and Heat Power	-3.67
燃气生产和供应业	Production and Supply of Gas	6.23
水的生产和供应业	Production and Supply of Water	1.07

单位：万元（10000 yuan）

资产负债率（%） Assets-Liability Ratio （%）	流动资产周转次数（次/年） Number of Times of Annual of Turnover Current Assets（time/year）	工业成本费用利润率（%） Ratio of Profits to Industrial Costs （%）
55.32	**1.40**	**5.62**
71.22	2.30	1.46
67.06	1.00	6.69
49.70	1.40	10.17
44.81	2.34	3.40
41.22	1.69	7.21
68.59	2.69	5.36
61.24	1.68	3.10
71.56	1.29	−2.27
67.87	2.49	0.31
59.98	1.74	10.28
34.18	1.29	9.71
45.22	4.11	3.99
55.68	2.06	3.57
32.64	0.82	31.88
55.75	1.00	3.97
58.91	0.98	6.25
65.33	3.02	4.17
35.44	6.07	19.82
37.12	1.55	8.75
51.82	1.22	7.60
59.60	0.78	9.78
62.32	1.22	6.69
61.47	0.66	6.28
50.54	1.96	8.34
44.76	1.56	2.02
43.27	0.94	17.74
84.60	1.42	−6.61
43.34	3.65	0.64
73.57	0.84	−14.89
56.54	3.11	7.16
62.82	0.25	−3.62

12-12 主要年份规模以上工业主要产品产量

OUTPUT OF MAIN PRODUCTS OF INDUSTRIES ABOVE DESIGNATED SIZE IN MAJOR YEARS

年份 Year	原盐（万吨）Salt (10000 tons)	发电量（亿千瓦时）Electricity (100 million kW·h)	饮料酒（万吨）Beverage Liquor (10000 tons)	#啤酒 Beer	卷烟（万箱）Cigarettes (10000 cases)	罐头（吨）Canned Food (ton)	化学纤维（吨）Chemical Fiber (ton)	纱（吨）Yarn (ton)
1949	15.16	1.21	0.18	0.12	2.36			27447
1952	35.08	2.11	0.37	0.18	12.27			59674
1957	44.34	2.92	0.96	0.58	23.41			50699
1962	38.60	3.86	1.58	0.79	16.59		28	17939
1965	41.34	6.80	2.04	1.34	31.34		205	68082
1970	29.96	10.57	3.39	2.55	42.16		621	85591
1975	34.52	10.98	5.30	2.98	36.00		357	79516
1978	60.68	13.63	6.25	3.75	44.00	4743	1413	85233
1980	41.19	12.50	8.49	4.84	48.79	3521	2116	83389
1985	47.34	26.97	13.76	10.05	51.81	6400	1747	91839
1988	53.28	29.35	26.61	15.58	57.01	27200	3393	107720
1990	35.70	40.22	29.18	19.61	61.94		2900	100381
1991	31.39	54.60	36.75	27.38	56.19	130510	5200	96271
1992	46.24	58.63	44.59	37.01	59.37	3200	6000	99043
1993	48.88	59.39	54.74	45.92	63.46	1900	27100	91351
1994	53.02	59.62	60.00	50.92	69.20	2300	21400	86744
1995	50.84	64.69	60.85	54.16	70.96	4609	20973	79492
1996	41.39	83.02	61.79	54.40	73.04	1719	22945	66832
1997	34.11	95.12	66.64	56.06	88.32	554	26300	70402
1998	19.08	79.65	47.33	42.79	77.10		23858	66504
1999	30.30	82.00	126.21	120.10	149.00	379	29967	56431
2000	41.83	90.84	211.47	206.50	148.10	225	65362	69561
2001	31.40	85.73	279.37	274.28	142.95	99	89989	72933
2002	42.50	89.70	323.20	320.60	138.10	11690	91394	70888
2003	36.85	87.69	353.90	351.80	148.00		101752	65919
2004	34.36	89.01	393.30	390.60	147.10	10889	115187	71931
2005	10.00	98.63	439.70	435.20	150.70	10097	95887	72140
2006	15.30	124.54	101.60（本地）	95.60（本地）	95.16（本地）	1668	72381	56128
2007	19.23	155.30	118.10（本地）	112.50（本地）	100.08（本地）	1850	68746	47850
2008	15.90	164.58	132.07（本地）	124.75（本地）	100.02（本地）	1510	51751	43102
2009	5.90	172.66	137.21（本地）	127.12（本地）	100.08（本地）	4706	59852	38566
2010	11.25	181.93	144.66（本地）	141.65（本地）	102.55（本地）	1092	68654	35278
2011		173.69	164.04（本地）	156.50（本地）	104.51（本地）	41204	38640	18556
2012		174.72	174.03（本地）	163.95（本地）	106.03（本地）	35026	32371	19404
2013	1.28	180.11	194.22（本地）	185.17（本地）	108.36（本地）	30203	23647	33687
2014		178.29	169.85（本地）	164.59（本地）	112.06（本地）	23970	22053	32336
2015		173.53	162.66（本地）	157.83（本地）	111.48（本地）	36179	17419	27721
2016		175.40	168.82（本地）	164.27（本地）		53139	14839	33416
2017		181.80	163.41（本地）	159.97（本地）		85942	11565	26493
2018		192.40	165.81（本地）	162.44（本地）		43893	5545	28948
2019		181.03	177.82（本地）	174.80（本地）		5940	39091	40562
2020		172.47	180.84（本地）	178.17（本地）		2699	11855	30269
2021		187.90	202.46（本地）	199.17（本地）		1398.32	155	60779
2022		196.28	208.45（本地）	205.45（本地）		1243.01	13114	40842

注：1998 年以前为乡及乡以上工业。

Note：Before 1998，the data refer to those at and above county level.

12-12 续表 1
Continued

年 份 Year	布 （万米） Cloth （10000 m）	印染布 （万米） Printed Fabric （10000 m）	机制纸及纸板（万吨） Machine-made Paper and Paperboards （10000 tons）	硫酸 （万吨） Sulfuric Acid （10000 tons）	烧碱 （万吨） Caustic Soda （10000 tons）	纯碱 （万吨） Soda Ash （10000 tons）
1949	10608	2947	0.98		0.01	
1952	30069	13658	0.44		0.17	
1957	27806	16053	1.54		0.74	
1962	7444	7375	1.45	0.06	0.89	
1965	29538	13670	2.22		1.66	5.32
1970	33660	21994	3.14	0.04	2.14	12.01
1975	31242	22828	3.10	0.53	2.36	9.15
1978	36877	25797	4.55	1.32	3.61	14.04
1980	34937	22900	5.25	4.11	4.33	18.18
1985	34998	17679	6.20	3.34	5.52	26.03
1988	35890	21213	7.42	4.88	6.62	31.12
1990	34066	21446	6.02	4.86	6.73	30.48
1991	34076	19999	5.99	5.62	5.99	29.50
1992	33682	21534	5.95	6.70	5.62	34.60
1993	35912	16606	8.84	6.96	6.07	40.43
1994	43241	16387	12.36	8.33	6.48	43.36
1995	41170	17864	11.06	9.69	7.90	43.20
1996	39023	16881	11.31	10.12	7.30	46.91
1997	43615	15722	7.78	10.16	8.45	50.55
1998	40440	9864	6.91	10.33	9.25	52.80
1999	39576	4340	7.77	12.56	8.96	53.70
2000	41783	3526	10.96	12.96	10.24	56.20
2001	40640	3402	23.05	13.03	11.44	58.47
2002	47609	5592	29.92	5.00	13.80	60.70
2003	35922	10131	31.76	4.50	13.53	62.50
2004	50111	7718	36.38	14.70	14.86	60.80
2005	51307	16027	31.95	14.80	16.10	62.50
2006	55093	20867	15.50	7.00	15.90	63.95
2007	44251	18708	24.04	9.22	14.91	71.02
2008	48399	58907	22.41	13.02	12.78	72.03
2009	31048	27998	34.59	1.40	12.24	68.21
2010	17457	29631	35.43	4.07	13.87	69.35
2011	49617	28449	32.28	5.06	13.20	70.07
2012	48987	32478	22.27	7.22	13.71	63.35
2013	51646	34381	17.95	4.32	11.06	61.66
2014	44593	33653	18.26			67.85
2015	28040	25458	18.29			68.95
2016	24973	28661	18.17		11.33	
2017	23550	21530	17.39		33.89	
2018	46737	22647	14.58		35.36	
2019	11354	27528	11.52		35.11	
2020	16207	31116	26.21		39.17	
2021	23090	35830	19.44		69.01	
2022	24347	28242	4.03		67.54	

12-12 续表 2
Continued

年 份 Year	合成氨 （万吨） Synthetic Ammonia （10000 tons）	化学肥料 （万吨） Chemical Fertilizer （10000 tons）	化学农药 （吨） Chemical Pesticide （ton）	油漆 （吨） Paint （ton）	染料 （吨） Dye （ton）
1949				30	599
1952				480	2855
1957			1226	1247	4307
1962		0.45	213	910	3560
1965		1.42	2	4727	8667
1970	0.98	5.89	2313	6380	9347
1975	3.46	12.46	4439	7016	5967
1978	7.17	23.66	9714	8786	5877
1980	7.24	7.82	8333	14556	2159
1985	6.31	5.16	2000	26055	4448
1988	8.72	9.41	2400	28943	5527
1990	7.56	7.55	2500	29075	5119
1991	8.52	8.04	2800	33548	5263
1992	10.45	7.85	3400	35058	4821
1993	10.70	8.02	3600	33054	4550
1994	13.04	12.39	3600	29437	5097
1995	14.98	12.62	4934	37772	7185
1996	18.67	12.62	4976	26762	7668
1997	16.94	12.52	4600	19743	11189
1998	22.36	15.30	6755	17594	8274
1999	26.09	20.19	4480	3730	7866
2000	24.64	20.04	3758	693	9306
2001	35.53	28.07	3915	1349	9757
2002	20.30	9.80	4020	1701	9826
2003	21.55	9.70	2039	2106	10734
2004	30.30	19.60	5061	1955	3961
2005	33.80	22.10	6524	1687	13979
2006	33.30	21.30	12544		26544
2007	28.22	25.70	16433	2957	28269
2008	17.93	21.51	12848	12105	18263
2009	17.71	21.23	49684		24893
2010	16.84	14.10	16450		41383
2011	10.78	9.26	23286		
2012	7.71	6.98	28801		
2013	6.48	5.10	27715		
2014			27160		
2015			36853		
2016		14.33	34993		
2017		7.38	18911		
2018		8.08	8507		
2019		8.50	17524		
2020		8.60	11938		
2021		8.65	14167		
2022		14.52	16806		

12-12 续表 3

Continued

年 份 Year	化学药品原药 （吨） Chemical API （ton）	水泥 （万吨） Cement （10000 tons）	平板玻璃 （万重量箱） Plate Glass （10000 wt. cases）	耐火材料 （万吨） Refractory Material （10000 tons）	粗钢 （万吨） Crude Steel （10000 tons）	钢材 （万吨） Rolled-steel （10000 tons）
1949						0.06
1952				0.78	0.36	0.41
1957				3.39	1.77	4.30
1962		2.09		2.41	4.59	2.94
1965		6.59		2.91	11.72	8.43
1970		7.35	16.31	3.23	19.38	14.56
1975	55	20.93	19.44	4.88	21.25	20.01
1978	185	35.40	8.86	5.93	31.06	27.61
1980	123	44.66	70.13	5.38	37.14	32.82
1984	7228	70.27	91.25	7.98	37.81	32.43
1985	4222	82.70	77.00	4.35	37.51	32.68
1988	7655	141.00	108.81	4.56	50.17	38.26
1990	6913	139.48	83.13	3.91	54.55	38.04
1991	4754	165.66	96.90	3.71	56.96	39.02
1992	5743	191.50	120.00	3.86	63.75	50.09
1993	6566	221.30	148.71	3.55	61.75	44.88
1994	4238	246.50	145.12	3.06	60.82	46.95
1995	1993	213.82	426.40	3.88	67.27	49.60
1996	5505	181.45	423.60	3.54	72.02	50.60
1997	1693	208.04	570.85	2.45	75.71	51.06
1998	910	131.51	509.38	0.99	84.02	64.93
1999	1691	149.41	576.50	0.59	108.10	86.58
2000	2131	137.52	556.58	0.62	101.17	93.35
2001	2534	148.67	421.51	0.51	124.45	119.77
2002	2712	140.30	405.40	0.45	145.90	142.20
2003	3288	154.90	361.40	0.47	204.80	204.30
2004	4394	181.19	163.30	0.69	225.70	230.97
2005	4430	210.80	297.50	1.04	309.70	330.30
2006	32232	232.72	418.74	1.21	325.82	375.52
2007	14139	425.53	397.79	2.38	327.00	365.55
2008	17910	363.57	599.87	3.65	300.19	350.14
2009	19086	397.66	681.02	18.46	307.89	349.63
2010	26170	442.66	662.04	8.17	300.04	333.46
2011	29337	588.08	510.05	20.02	318.27	325.89
2012	49290	556.57	494.54	33.44	252.78	274.67
2013	49081	575.66	610.21	42.34	235.53	230.39
2014	50713	597.35	612.40	39.37	214.43	212.79
2015	45923	532.36	534.99	41.13	154.56	140.63
2016	2248	600.56	576.16	108.76	188.04	191.37
2017	2775	525.42	557.44	109.84	280.97	291.85
2018	1809	284.47	561.51	27.97	309.70	319.90
2019	2616	442.47	393.64	12.18	319.25	336.19
2020	745	414.03	1003.97	19.54	335.19	389.20
2021	806	522.43	998.18	25.53	325	544.82
2022	847	456.69	853.05	21.58	435.02	564.42

12-12 续表 4
Continued

年 份 Year	金属切削机床（台） Metal-cutting Machine Tools （unit）	锻压机械（台） Metal Forming Machinery （unit）	交流电动机（万千瓦） AC Motors （10000 kW）
1949			0.02
1952	105		0.50
1957	76		3.61
1962	167	77	3.85
1965	526	111	6.48
1970	2353	531	14.53
1975	3213	788	15.56
1978	2558	379	21.72
1980	595	444	20.11
1985	900	607	26.08
1988	1336	737	39.60
1990	1049	440	34.28
1991	869	764	44.17
1992	1018	982	61.08
1993	1532	919	64.13
1994	1505	860	37.71
1995	972	2563	39.18
1996	1084	584	22.65
1997	449	416	20.74
1998	280		6.43
1999	251		11.10
2000	384		38.70
2001	472	2477	42.72
2002	588		68.25
2003	990		95.63
2004	1287		96.13
2005	1347		63.50
2006	3636		702.02
2007	3392	1869	119.23
2008	8381	1230	96.89
2009	668		728.03
2010	1120		101.10
2011	1194		74.08
2012	1014		104.48
2013	2689		126.82
2014	2563		114.46
2015	618		104.30
2016	588		98.70
2017	610		202.79
2018	204		230.86
2019	584		110.03
2020	466		173.94
2021	387		243.72
2022	358		194.81

12-12 续表 5
Continued

年 份 Year	钢芯铝绞线（吨） Steel-cored Aluminum Stranded Wire （ton）	家用电冰箱（万台） Home Refrigerators （10000 sets）	家用洗衣机（万台） Home Washing Machines （10000 sets）	彩色电视机（万台） Color TV Sets （10000 sets）
1949				
1952				
1957				
1962				
1965	250			
1970	34			
1975	188			
1978	684			
1980	1232			
1985	2327	1.66	0.48	6.60
1988	1571	15.22	42.38	17.00
1990	1880	27.41	45.86	18.50
1991	2463	31.51	45.70	22.27
1992	2248	54.84	46.31	28.07
1993	1144	50.48	56.59	36.08
1994	287	62.50	71.34	60.15
1995	1659	107.91	64.34	60.53
1996	2265	193.80	100.94	56.68
1997	2616	257.10	171.95	124.86
1998	1725	219.23	183.67	96.83
1999	2805	259.60	256.30	285.20
2000	4202	311.10	318.50	379.40
2001	4498	396.30	367.89	455.40
2002	5825	518.20	408.6	593.20
2003	4940	598.30	471.5	671.70
2004	6608	815.03	575.06	957.90
2005	116592	908.80	614.9	1324.30
2006	46974	1290.00	649.4	1205.60
2007	22564	1421.40	769.4	1243.10
2008	29507	723.19	407.54	836.66
2009		827.21	488.72	1064.70
2010		801.22	580.87	1111.19
2011		718.54	604.55	1154.20
2012		575.01	583.6	1439.98
2013		524.35	606.65	1512.05
2014		610.07	590.95	1714.93
2015		872.09	595.11	1736.20
2016		882.22	606.74	2111.71
2017		818.65	603.4	1703.01
2018		886.58	601.72	1695.18
2019		731.81	513.71	1580.42
2020		822.01	575.41	1774.86
2021		888.81	730.78	1986.73
2022		832.13	776.06	2545.61

12-13　规模以上工业主要产品产量
OUTPUT OF MAJOR INDUSTRIAL PRODUCTS OF INDUSTRY ABOVE DESIGNATED SIZE

产品名称	Name	计量单位	Unit	2022 年	增长（±%） Increase（±%）
冶金工业产品	**Products of Metallurgical Industry**				
粗钢	Crude Steel	万吨	10000 tons	435.02	33.85
钢材	Rolled-steel	万吨	10000 tons	564.42	4.14
耐火材料制品	Refractory Material	万吨	10000 tons	21.58	-15.73
电力工业产品	**Products of Electricity Industry**				
发电量	Electricity	亿千瓦时	100 million kW·h	196.28	4.58
化学工业产品	**Products of Chemical Industry**				
原油加工量	Processing Amount of Crude Oil	万吨	10000 tons	1395.35	-5.31
汽油	Petrol	万吨	10000 tons	378.93	-13.05
柴油	Diesel Oil	万吨	10000 tons	358.61	0.92
燃料油	Fuel Oil	万吨	10000 tons	212.45	14.24
化学农药	Chemical Pesticides	万吨	10000 tons	1.68	14.22
塑料制品	Plastic	万吨	10000 tons	49.41	-3.10
化学药品原药	Chemical API	万吨	10000 tons	0.08	5.07

12-13　续表 1
Continued

产品名称	Name	计量单位	Unit	2022 年	增长（±%） Increase（±%）
橡胶轮胎外胎	Rubber Tire Casing	万条	10000 tires	4637.62	-7.99
机械工业产品	**Products of Machinery Industry**				
工业锅炉	Industrial Boiler	蒸发量吨	ton（evaporation amunt）	17734.07	-22.56
交流电动机	AC Motors	万千瓦	10000 kW	194.81	-17.93
金属切削机床	Metal-cutting Machine	台	set	358	-7.49
改装汽车	Refitted Motor Vehicles	辆	set	43575	-1.55
民用钢质船舶	Civil Steel Ships	载重吨	syn-ton	2200000	-17.95
电子产品	**Electronic Products**				
彩色电视机	Color TV sets	万台	10000 sets	2545.61	28.13
电子元件	Electronic Component	亿只	10000 units	206.47	-39.80
建材工业产品	**Products of Construction Industry**				
水泥	Cement	万吨	10000 tons	456.69	-12.58
平板玻璃	Plate Glass	万重量箱	10000 wt. cases	853.05	-14.54

12-13 续表 2
Continued

产品名称	Name	计量单位	Unit	2022 年	增长（±%）Increase（±%）
纺织工业产品	**Products of Textile Industry**				
纱	Yarn	吨	ton	40841.75	-33.81
布	Cloth	万米	10000 m	24346.70	-2.02
印染布	Printed Fabric	万米	10000 m	28242.00	-21.18
化学纤维	Chemical Fibers	吨	ton	13114.16	-24.47
轻工产品	**Products of Light Industry**				
机制纸及纸板	Machine-made Paper and Paperboards	万吨	10000 tons	4.03	-79.47
家用洗衣机	Home Washing Machines	万台	10000 sets	776.06	6.20
糖果	Sugar	吨	ton	844.8	-12.55
食用植物油	Vegetable Oil	万吨	10000 tons	152.65	14.71
饮料酒	Beverage Liquor	万千升	10000 KL	205.98	2.05
#白酒	White Spirit	万千升	10000 KL	2.31	7.41
#啤酒	Beer	万千升	10000 KL	203.01	2.02
塑料制品	Plastic Products	万吨	10000 tons	49.41	-3.10
家具	Furniture	万件	10000 articles	696.60	-16.69
家用电冰箱	Home Refrigerators	万台	10000 sets	832.13	-7.05
皮革鞋靴	Leather Shoes	万双	10000 pairs	523.99	-33.81
服装	Clothing	万件	10000 articles	40106.59	-8.97

12-14 规模以上工业主要产品生产能力
PRODUCTION CAPACITY OF MAJOR PRODUCTS OF INDUSTRY ABOVE DESIGNATED SIZE

产品名称	Name	计量单位	Unit	2022 年生产能力 Production Capacity of 2022	2021 年生产能力 Production Capacity of 2021
发电设备容量总计 / 发电量	Total Capacity of Generation Equipment	万千瓦 / 万千瓦时	10000 kW/ 10000 kW · h	500	445
化学纤维	Chemical Fiber	吨	ton	32520	36350
棉纺锭 / 纺纱量	Knitting Spindle	锭 / 吨	spindle/ton	137218	141858
棉布织机 / 布	Cotton Cloth Loom	台 / 万米	set/10000 m	10050	1974
焦炭	Coke	吨	ton	1700000	1700000
农用氮、磷、钾化学肥料总计（折纯）	Chemical Fertilizer (convert to pure amount)	吨	ton	165000	80100
水泥	Cement	吨	ton	7660000	7702000
平板玻璃	Plate Glass	重量箱	weight cases	11606679	11241440
生铁	Pig Iron	吨	ton	4350000	4350000
粗钢	Crude Steel	吨	ton	4275000	4275000
钢材	Rolled-steel	吨	ton	7142416	6970540
金属切削机床	Metal-cutting Machine	台	set	1404	966
家用电冰箱	Home Refrigerators	台	set	10867416	10916400
房间空气调节器	Air Conditioner	台	set	22038717	16930000
移动通信手持机（手机）	Cell Phone	台	set	5080000	3600000
彩色电视机	Color TV Sets	台	set	28480485	28079000

主要统计指标解释

工业总产值　是以货币表现的工业企业在一定时期内生产的已出售或可供出售工业产品总量，它是反映一定时间内工业生产的总规模和总水平。

资产总计　指企业拥有或控制的能以货币计量的经济资源，包括各种财产、债权和其他权利。资产按其流动性（即资产的变现能力和支付能力）划分为：流动资产、长期投资、固定资产、无形资产、递延资产和其他资产。

负债合计　指企业所承担的能以货币计量，将以资产或劳务偿付的债务，偿还形式包括货币、资产或提供劳务。负债一般按偿还期长短分为流动负债和长期负债。

利润总额　指企业生产经营活动的最终成果，是企业在一定时期内实现的盈亏相抵后的利润总额（亏损以“–”号表示），它等于营业利润加上补贴收入加上投资收益加上营业外净收入再加上以前年度损益调整。

Explanatory Notes on Main Statistical Indicators

Gross Industrial Output Value　is the total volume of final industrial products produced and industrial services provided during a given period. It reflects the total achievements and overall scale of industrial production during a given period

Total Assets　refers to the economic resources that can be measured in currency owned or controlled by an enterprise, including various properties, claims and other rights. Assets are divided into: current assets, long–term investments, fixed assets, intangible assets, deferred assets and other assets according to their liquidity (that is, the ability to realize assets and payment capabilities) .

Total Liabilities　refers to the debts that an enterprise bears that can be measured in currency and will be repaid in assets or services. The form of repayment includes currency, assets or the provision of services. Liabilities are generally divided into current liabilities and long–term liabilities according to the length of the repayment period.

Total Profits　refer to the final achievements of production and operation of the enterprises, represented by the total profits after deducting losses (loss is expressed by the negative figure) . It is the sum of profits from operation, income from subsidies, investment earnings, net income from activities other than operation, and adjustment of profits and losses of previous years.

服务业 13

SERVICE ENTERPRISES

简要说明

一、本篇资料的主要内容

本篇资料主要反映全市规模以上服务业企业主要财务状况，规模以上服务业企业分行业财务状况，规模以上服务业企业分登记注册类型财务状况，分区市规模以上服务业企业财务状况等方面的内容。

二、本篇资料的来源

本篇中规模以上服务业企业资料来源于规模以上服务业统计年报，由市统计局服务业统计处整理提供。

Brief Introduction

Ⅰ. Main Content

This document mainly reflects the major financial indicators of service enterprises above designated size in the city, the financial indicators of service enterprises above designated size by industry, the financial indicators of service enterprises above designated size by registration type, and the financial indicators of service enterprises above designated size in regional cities content.

Ⅱ. Source of Data

The data of service enterprises above designated size in this chapter are derived from the annual statistical report of service industries above designated size, which are compiled and provided by the Service Statistics Department of the Municipal Statistics Bureau.

13-1 规模以上服务业企业主要财务状况
MAIN FINANCIAL INDICATORS OF SERVICE ENTERPRISES ABOVE THE DESIGNATED

单位：亿元（100 million yuan）

项　目	Item	2022	2021	2022 年比 2021 年增长（%）Growth Rate in 2022 Over 2021（%）
营业收入	Business Revenue	4123.35	3773.83	9.26
营业成本	Business Costs	3623.47	3283.68	10.35
税金及附加	Tax and Extra Charges on Business	18.32	16.58	10.45
销售费用	Sales Expenses	88.22	80.65	9.38
管理费用	Management Expenses	230.62	225.63	2.21
财务费用	Financial Expenses	79.09	80.35	-1.57
营业利润	Business Profits	209.48	215.50	-2.79
利润总额	Total Profits	220.64	219.32	0.61
所得税费用	Income Taxes Payable	46.48	41.48	12.08
应付职工薪酬	Employee Compensation Payable	531.72	482.00	10.32
应交增值税	Value-added Tax Payable	70.54	54.79	28.75

注：增速按可比口径计算。
Note：The growth rates are calculated on comparable coverage.

13-2 规模以上其他营利性服务业企业主要财务状况
MAIN FINANCIAL INDICATORS OF OTHER FOR-PROFIT SERVICE ENTERPRISES ABOVE THE DESIGNATED

单位：亿元（100 million yuan）

项　目	Item	2022	2021	2022年比2021年增长（%）Growth Rate in 2022 Over 2021（%）
营业收入	Business Revenue	1333.88	1154.34	15.55
营业成本	Business Costs	1041.24	879.38	18.41
税金及附加	Tax and Extra Charges on Business	7.03	6.83	2.87
销售费用	Sales Expenses	48.84	47.32	3.21
管理费用	Management Expenses	117.56	116.04	1.31
财务费用	Financial Expenses	12.96	14.24	-9.01
营业利润	Business Profits	69.37	57.43	20.80
利润总额	Total Profits	74.38	56.75	31.08
所得税费用	Income Taxes Payable	12.39	10.19	21.61
应付职工薪酬	Employee Compensation Payable	266.51	231.02	15.36
应交增值税	Value-added Tax Payable	32.94	27.47	19.91

注：增速按可比口径计算。
Note：The growth rates are calculated on comparable coverage.

13-3 规模以上服务业企业分登记注册类型财务状况（2022 年）
FINANCIAL INDICATORS OF SERVICE ENTERPRISES ABOVE DESIGNATED SIZE BY REGISTRATION TYPE（2022）

单位：亿元（100 million yuan）

类 别	Category	企业单位数（个）Number of Enterprises（unit）	营业收入 Business Revenue	营业成本 Business Costs	税金及附加 Tax and Extra Charges on Business
总 计	**Total**	**2775**	**4123.35**	**3623.47**	**18.32**
按登记注册类型分	**by Status of Registration**				
内资企业	**Domestic Funded Enterprises**	**2645**	**3613.41**	**3220.60**	**16.76**
国有企业	State-owned Enterprises	77	100.56	84.31	0.43
集体企业	Collective-owned Enterprises	9	4.49	2.87	0.10
股份合作企业	Cooperative Enterprises	1			
有限责任公司	Limited Liability Corporations	756	1647.14	1486.54	10.76
股份有限公司	Share-holding Corporations Limited	62	289.16	250.93	1.57
私营企业	Private Enterprises	1725	1567.80	1393.63	3.86
其他企业	Other Enterprises	15	4.04	2.33	0.02
港、澳、台商投资企业	**Enterprises with Funds from Hong Kong, Macao and Taiwan**	**46**	**133.11**	**103.48**	**0.55**
合资经营企业（港或澳、台资）	Joint-ventures Enterprises	25	65.41	42.08	0.21
合作经营企业（港或澳、台资）	Cooperative Enterprises	1			
港澳台商独资经营企业	Enterprises with Sole Investment	19	64.14	58.29	0.31
港澳台商投资股份有限公司	Share-holding Corporations Ltd. With Funds from Hong Kong, Macao and Taiwan	1			
其他企业	Other Enterprises				
外商投资企业	**Foreign Funded Enterprises**	**84**	**376.82**	**299.39**	**1.01**
中外合资经营企业	Joint-venture Enterprises	36	174.70	137.14	0.35
中外合作经营企业	Cooperation Enterprises	3	0.33	0.19	0.03
外资企业	Foreign Investment	41	196.77	157.52	0.59
其他企业	Other Enterprises	4	5.02	4.54	0.04

13-3 续表 1
Continued

单位：亿元（100 million yuan）

类　别	Category	销售费用 Selling Expenses	管理费用 Management Expenses	财务费用 Financial Expenses	营业利润 Business Profits
总　计	**Total**	**88.22**	**230.62**	**79.09**	**209.48**
按登记注册类型分	**by Status of Registration**				
内资企业	**Domestic Funded Enterprises**	**75.07**	**208.79**	**77.52**	**138.11**
国有企业	State-owned Enterprises	1.06	10.21	2.74	3.21
集体企业	Collective-owned Enterprises	0.01	1.16		0.34
股份合作企业	Cooperative Enterprises				
有限责任公司	Limited Liability Corporations	33.45	85.14	59.71	75.33
股份有限公司	Share-holding Corporations Limited	8.45	18.61	9.09	31.11
私营企业	Private Enterprises	32.06	91.21	5.97	28.67
其他企业	Other Enterprises	0.05	2.25		-0.57
港、澳、台商投资企业	**Enterprises with Funds from Hong Kong, Macao and Taiwan**	**3.74**	**5.48**	**1.27**	**20.30**
合资经营企业（港或澳、台资）	Joint-ventures Enterprises	2.94	2.74	1.02	16.44
合作经营企业（港或澳、台资）	Cooperative Enterprises				
港澳台商独资经营企业	Enterprises with Sole Investment	0.80	2.56	0.23	3.61
港澳台商投资股份有限公司	Share-holding Corporations Ltd. With Funds from Hong Kong, Macao and Taiwan				
其他企业	Other Enterprises				
外商投资企业	**Foreign Funded Enterprises**	**9.41**	**16.35**	**0.30**	**51.08**
中外合资经营企业	Joint-venture Enterprises	4.66	8.36	-0.32	22.50
中外合作经营企业	Cooperation Enterprises	0.13	0.13	0.03	0.33
外资企业	Foreign Investment	4.61	7.71	0.60	27.94
其他企业	Other Enterprises	0.00	0.16	-0.01	0.31

13-3 续表 2
Continued

单位：亿元（100 million yuan）

类　别	Category	利润总额 Total Profits	所得税费用 Income Taxes Payable	应付职工薪酬 Total Wages Payable	应交增值税 Value-added Tax Payable
总　计	**Total**	**220.64**	**46.48**	**531.72**	**70.54**
按登记注册类型分	**by Status of Registration**				
内资企业	**Domestic Funded Enterprises**	**148.45**	**35.06**	**476.50**	**64.63**
国有企业	State-owned Enterprises	3.16	1.91	18.45	2.73
集体企业	Collective-owned Enterprises	0.34	0.07	1.00	0.10
股份合作企业	Cooperative Enterprises				
有限责任公司	Limited Liability Corporations	78.41	21.02	254.20	31.95
股份有限公司	Share-holding Corporations Limited	31.91	5.51	44.23	5.30
私营企业	Private Enterprises	35.20	6.50	156.86	24.48
其他企业	Other Enterprises	-0.57	0.04	1.76	0.05
港、澳、台商投资企业	**Enterprises with Funds from Hong Kong, Macao and Taiwan**	**20.70**	**4.38**	**9.39**	**2.28**
合资经营企业（港或澳、台资）	Joint-ventures Enterprises	16.56	3.56	6.68	2.02
合作经营企业（港或澳、台资）	Cooperative Enterprises				
港澳台商独资经营企业	Enterprises with Sole Investment	3.88	0.76	2.58	0.27
港澳台商投资股份有限公司	Share-holding Corporations Ltd. With Funds from Hong Kong, Macao and Taiwan				
其他企业	Other Enterprises				
外商投资企业	**Foreign Funded Enterprises**	**51.49**	**7.05**	**45.83**	**3.63**
中外合资经营企业	Joint-venture Enterprises	22.53	5.60	23.79	1.21
中外合作经营企业	Cooperation Enterprises	0.33		0.13	0.01
外资企业	Foreign Investment	28.31	1.37	21.66	2.27
其他企业	Other Enterprises	0.31	0.09	0.25	0.14

13-4 规模以上服务业企业分行业财务状况（2022 年）

FINANCIAL INDICATORS OF SERVICE ENTERPRISES ABOVE DESIGNATED SIZE BY SECTOR（2022）

行　业	Category	企业单位数（个）Number of Enterprises（unit）	营业收入 Business Revenue	营业成本 Business Costs	税金及附加 Tax and Extra Charges on Business
总　计	**Total**	**2775**	**4123.35**	**3623.47**	**18.32**
按行业分	**Grouped by Sector**				
交通运输、仓储和邮政业	Transport，Storage and Post	905	2396.01	2293.45	6.89
信息传输、软件和信息技术服务业	Information Transmission, Software and Information Technology Services	265	587.37	423.29	2.08
房地产业	Real Estate	196	122.68	93.23	3.56
租赁和商务服务业	Leasing and Business Services	718	507.99	442.36	2.79
科学研究和技术服务业	Scientific Research and Technical Services	338	338.31	245.76	1.66
水利、环境和公共设施管理业	Management of Water Conservancy, Environment and Public Facilities	45	45.56	35.46	0.33
居民服务、修理和其他服务业	Resident Services, Repairs and Other Services	68	28.85	20.91	0.12
教育	Education	17	7.81	4.50	0.03
卫生和社会工作	Health and Social Work	74	39.88	28.05	0.01
文化、体育和娱乐业	Culture，Sports and Entertainment Industry	149	48.87	36.45	0.85

单位：亿元（100 million yuan）

销售费用 Selling Expenses	管理费用 Management Expenses	财务费用 Financial Expenses	营业利润 Business Profits	利润总额 Total Profits	所得税费用 Income Taxes Payable	应付职工薪酬 Total Wages Payable	应交增值税 Value-added Tax Payable
88.22	**230.62**	**79.09**	**209.48**	**220.64**	**46.48**	**531.72**	**70.54**
24.14	75.57	48.11	99.99	104.83	27.77	186.91	27.69
26.36	30.11	2.31	63.70	64.67	6.66	81.92	13.60
2.44	18.43	15.05	1.89	3.76	1.69	31.32	6.12
10.87	37.59	10.24	13.43	15.49	4.91	76.04	9.63
11.69	42.62	0.03	27.65	28.30	3.01	103.14	9.16
0.41	4.76	0.82	3.43	3.63	0.87	14.26	1.42
3.98	3.39	–0.04	0.56	1.03	0.43	8.84	0.96
0.39	3.24	0.37	–0.83	–1.24	0.03	3.86	0.20
3.64	6.96	0.76	0.10	0.20	0.37	13.14	0.07
4.31	7.96	1.43	–0.44	–0.01	0.74	12.29	1.70

13-5 规模以上服务业企业分市、区财务状况（2022年）
FINANCIAL INDICATORS OF SERVICE ENTERPRISES ABOVE DESIGNATED SIZE BY REGION（2022）

市、区名称	Region	企业单位数（个）Number of Enterprises（unit）	营业收入 Business Revenue	营业成本 Business Costs	税金及附加 Tax and Extra Charges on Business
全　市	**Whole Municipality**	**2775**	**4123.35**	**3623.47**	**18.32**
市南区	Shinan District	554	1365.13	1226.96	2.58
市北区	Shibei District	323	386.56	373.02	2.12
李沧区	Licang District	242	101.95	90.79	0.95
崂山区	Laoshan District	331	638.35	524.25	2.95
黄岛区	Huangdao District	637	924.18	754.49	3.78
城阳区	Chengyang District	301	299.82	254.17	2.10
即墨区	Jimo District	100	103.04	90.06	0.95
胶州市	Jiaozhou	197	259.05	271.25	2.72
平度市	Pingdu	50	34.91	30.55	0.14
莱西市	Laixi	40	10.36	7.93	0.02

单位：亿元（100 million yuan）

销售费用 Selling Expenses	管理费用 Management Expenses	财务费用 Financial Expenses	营业利润 Business Profits	利润总额 Total Profits	所得税费用 Income Taxes Payable	应付职工薪酬 Total Wages Payable	应交增值税 Value-added Tax Payable
88.22	**230.62**	**79.09**	**209.48**	**220.64**	**46.48**	**531.72**	**70.54**
21.73	55.74	4.54	58.85	60.05	9.30	130.67	11.13
8.98	27.32	17.91	19.87	20.40	3.46	76.53	5.06
1.51	9.99	2.86	–0.52	1.29	0.69	20.30	4.20
19.01	38.83	2.53	47.17	48.86	4.92	100.35	12.68
20.70	47.83	14.66	124.30	128.05	23.01	113.99	16.64
9.20	23.65	7.50	9.13	10.17	2.16	44.02	9.96
2.91	9.53	3.42	–0.98	–0.22	1.14	10.22	2.47
3.59	14.49	25.13	–49.99	–49.82	1.12	31.85	7.63
0.43	2.00	0.34	1.00	1.15	0.37	2.55	0.47
0.15	1.24	0.21	0.65	0.71	0.31	1.23	0.30

13-6 规模以上其他营利性服务业企业分行业财务状况（2022 年）

FINANCIAL INDICATORS OF OTHER FOR-PROFIT SERVICE ENTERPRISES ABOVE DESIGNATED SIZE BY SECTOR（2022）

行　业	Category	企业单位数（个）Number of Enterprises（unit）	营业收入 Business Revenue	营业成本 Business Costs	税金及附加 Tax and Extra Charges on Business
总　计	**Total**	**1517**	**1333.88**	**1041.24**	**7.03**
按行业分	**Grouped by Sector**				
互联网和相关服务	Internet and Related Services	33	37.24	31.51	0.06
软件和信息技术服务业	Software and Information Technology Services	211	372.62	264.24	1.55
租赁业	Leasing	37	13.57	11.54	0.04
商务服务业	Business Services	681	494.42	430.82	2.75
研究和试验发展	Research and Experimental Development	38	53.86	42.15	0.29
专业技术服务业	Professional Technical Service Industry	278	267.82	191.92	1.34
科技推广和应用服务业	Technology Promotion and Application Service Industry	22	16.63	11.69	0.03
居民服务业	Services to Households	23	7.13	4.41	0.01
机动车、电子产品和日用产品修理业	Motor Vehicle, Electronic Products and Consumer Products Repair	17	14.75	10.43	0.07
其他服务业	Other Services	28	6.98	6.07	0.03
新闻和出版业	News and Publication	10	15.34	9.41	0.16
广播、电视、电影和影视录音制作业	Production of Radio, Television, Film and Video Recording	63	14.36	10.98	0.09
文化艺术业	Culture and Arts	17	8.11	6.15	0.15
体育	Sports	21	4.15	4.04	0.27
娱乐业	Entertainment	38	6.92	5.87	0.19

单位：亿元（100 million yuan）

销售费用 Selling Expenses	管理费用 Management Expenses	财务费用 Financial Expenses	营业利润 Business Profits	利润总额 Total Profits	所得税费用 Income Taxes Payable	应付职工薪酬 Total Wages Payable	应交增值税 Value-added Tax Payable
48.84	**117.56**	**12.96**	**69.37**	**74.38**	**12.39**	**266.51**	**32.94**
1.18	1.40	-0.01	1.88	2.21	0.00	2.46	0.36
16.81	24.60	1.31	26.30	27.36	3.31	63.73	11.13
0.66	1.17	0.31	0.05	0.15	0.05	1.23	0.73
10.22	36.42	9.93	13.38	15.34	4.85	74.81	8.90
1.36	6.33	-0.46	2.98	3.17	0.37	18.59	0.62
9.62	35.04	0.12	21.88	22.30	2.54	82.81	8.32
0.71	1.26	0.37	2.80	2.83	0.11	1.75	0.22
0.36	1.74	0.13	0.47	0.81	0.25	2.29	0.07
3.56	0.85	-0.18	0.10	0.20	0.17	3.11	0.63
0.05	0.80	0.01	-0.01	0.02	0.01	3.45	0.26
1.61	1.96		2.27	2.54	0.02	3.64	0.53
0.88	1.99	0.20	0.31	0.39	0.41	1.48	0.31
0.46	1.40	0.50	-0.09	-0.12	0.28	3.17	0.19
0.52	1.05	0.13	-0.95	-1.12	0.01	2.37	0.13
0.83	1.54	0.60	-1.98	-1.71	0.02	1.63	0.53

13-7 规模以上其他营利性服务业企业分市、区财务状况（2022 年）
FINANCIAL INDICATORS OF OTHER FOR-PROFIT SERVICE ENTERPRISES ABOVE DESIGNATED SIZE BY REGION（2022）

市、区名称	Region	企业单位数（个）Number of Enterprises（unit）	营业收入 Business Revenue	营业成本 Business Costs	税金及附加 Tax and Extra Charges on Business
全　市	**Whole Municipality**	**1517**	**1333.88**	**1041.24**	**7.03**
市南区	Shinan District	241	305.03	240.23	1.52
市北区	Shibei District	183	139.82	111.74	0.66
李沧区	Licang District	147	52.42	44.46	0.35
崂山区	Laoshan District	224	308.21	217.64	1.56
黄岛区	Huangdao District	330	272.38	222.82	1.18
城阳区	Chengyang District	200	140.17	106.98	1.09
即墨区	Jimo District	46	26.72	21.54	0.27
胶州市	Jiaozhou	88	57.86	48.37	0.33
平度市	Pingdu	27	23.02	21.06	0.05
莱西市	Laixi	31	8.26	6.41	0.02

单位：亿元（100 million yuan）

销售费用 Selling Expenses	管理费用 Management Expenses	财务费用 Financial Expenses	营业利润 Business Profits	利润总额 Total Profits	所得税费用 Income Taxes Payable	应付职工薪酬 Total Wages Payable	应交增值税 Value-added Tax Payable
48.84	**117.56**	**12.96**	**69.37**	**74.38**	**12.39**	**266.51**	**32.94**
9.45	27.94	3.14	16.26	17.34	2.76	70.96	7.97
4.40	12.79	2.76	7.15	7.64	1.78	29.27	3.69
0.72	5.49	1.16	–0.23	0.18	0.12	10.38	1.39
13.36	25.43	–0.08	32.04	32.76	2.93	69.34	7.81
10.03	20.79	1.20	10.04	11.67	2.88	45.99	5.28
7.32	14.50	3.24	7.18	7.43	1.06	26.57	3.67
1.60	4.65	1.36	–6.29	–6.25	0.10	6.08	1.27
1.64	3.95	0.08	2.26	2.44	0.35	6.00	1.34
0.23	1.14	0.07	0.28	0.39	0.10	1.10	0.21
0.07	0.88	0.04	0.69	0.79	0.31	0.81	0.30

主要统计指标解释

营业收入 指企业经营主要业务和其他业务所确认的收入总额。营业收入合计包括“主营业务收入”和“其他业务收入”。根据会计“利润表”中“营业收入”项目的本年累计数填报。

营业成本 指企业经营主要业务和其他业务所发生的成本总额。包括企业（单位）在报告期内从事销售商品、提供劳务等日常活动发生的各种耗费。包括“主营业务成本”和“其他业务成本”。根据会计“利润表”中“营业成本”项目的本年累计数填报。

税金及附加 指企业因从事生产经营活动按税法规定应缴纳的消费税、城市维护建设税、资源税、教育费附加及房产税、土地使用税、车船使用税、印花税等相关税费。根据会计“利润表”中“税金及附加”项目的本年累计数填报。

销售费用 指企业在销售商品和材料、提供劳务的过程中发生的各种费用，包括保险费、包装费、展览费和广告费、商品维修费、预计产品质量保证损失、运输费、装卸费等以及为销售本企业商品而专设的销售机构（含销售网点、售后服务网点等）的职工薪酬、业务费、折旧费等经营费用。

管理费用 指企业为组织和管理企业生产经营所发生的费用，包括企业在筹建期间内发生的开办费、董事会和行政管理部门在企业经营管理中发生的，或者应当由企业统一负担的公司经费等。根据会计“利润表”中“管理费用”项目的本年累计数填报。

财务费用 指企业为筹集生产经营所需资金等而发生的筹资费用，包括企业生产经营期间发生的利息支出（减利息收入）、汇兑损失（减汇兑收益）以及相关的手续费等。根据会计“利润表”中“财务费用”项目的本年累计数填报。

利润总额 指企业在一定会计期间的经营成果，是生产经营过程中各种收入扣除各种耗费后的盈余，反映企业在报告期内实现的盈亏总额。根据会计“利润表”中“利润总额”项目的本年累计数填报。执行《企业会计准则》或《小企业会计准则》的企业，利润总额为营业利润加上营业外收入，减去营业外支出后的金额；执行其他企业会计制度的企业，利润总额为营业利润加上投资收益、营业外收入，再减去营业外支出后的金额。

应交增值税 指按照税法规定，以销售货物、服务、无形资产、不动产或提供加工、修理修配劳务的增值额和货物进口金额为计税依据而课征的一种流转税。

Explanatory Notes on Main Statistical Indicators

Business Revenue refers to the total income of the business recognized by business and other business. Total operating revenue includes the main business income and other operating income. Fill in according to the cumulative number of the current year's “Business Revenue” item in the “profit statement” of accounting.

Business Costs refers to the total amount of costs incurred by an enterprise in operating its main business and other businesses. Including the enterprise (unit) in the reporting period engaged in selling goods, providing labor services and other daily activities of all kinds of consumption. Include "main business cost" and "other business cost" . The current year' s cumulative counting is reported according to the operating cost item in the accounting "income statement" .

Taxes and surcharges refers to the excise duty, urban maintenance and construction tax, resource tax, education surcharge, property tax, land use tax, vehicle and vessel use tax, stamp tax and other related taxes and fees that the enterprise should pay in accordance with the tax law for its production and business activities. Fill in according to the cumulative number of the current year' s "Taxes and surcharges" item in the "profit statement" of accounting.

Sales expense refers to the various expenses incurred by the enterprise in the process of selling goods and materials and providing labor services, including insurance, packaging, exhibition and advertising fees, product maintenance fees, estimated product quality assurance losses, transportation fees, loading and unloading fees, etc. Operating expenses such as employee salaries, business expenses, depreciation expenses and other operating expenses of specialized sales organizations (including sales outlets, after–sales service outlets, etc.) that sell the products of the enterprise.

Management Cost refers to the costs of organizing and managing enterprise operation, including the operational cost of the board of directors and the executive body in management that shall be borne by the enterprise. Fill in according to the cumulative number of the current year' s "Management Cost " item in the "profit statement" of accounting.

Financial Cost refers to the cost from raising fund for production and operation, including expenditure of interests, loss of momentary exchange and related charges. Fill in according to the cumulative number of the current year' s "Financial Cost" item in the "profit statement" of accounting.

Total Profits refers to the operating results of an enterprise in a certain accounting period. It is the surplus after deducting various expenses from various incomes in the production and operation process, reflecting the total profit and loss realized by the enterprise during the reporting period. Fill in according to the cumulative number of the current year' s "Total Profits" item in the "profit statement" of accounting. For companies that implement the "Accounting Standards for Business Enterprises" or "Accounting Standards for Small Businesses," the total profit is the amount of operating profit plus non–operating income, minus non–operating expenses ; for companies implementing other corporate accounting systems, the total profit is the operating profit plus Investment income, nonoperating income, minus the amount of non–operating expenses.

VAT payable refers to a transfer tax levied on the basis of tax on the value added of goods, services, intangible assets, real estate or the provision of processing, repair and repair services and the amount of import of goods, as stipulated in the tax law.

建筑业 14

CONSTRUCTION

简 要 说 明

一、本篇资料的主要内容

本篇资料主要反映全市建筑业基本情况，主要包括建筑业总产值、增加值、建筑企业生产指标、财务指标、重点建筑企业名单等方面的内容。

二、本篇资料的来源

本篇资料来源于建筑业统计年报，由市统计局固定资产投资统计处整理提供。

Brief Introduction

Ⅰ. Main Content

Data in this chapter show the basic conditions of construction of the whole city, mainly including the gross output value of construction, value added, major production and financial indicators and list of key enterprises of construction, etc.

Ⅱ. Source of Data

Data in this chapter are based on the annual report of construction industry, and complied by the Division of Investment and Construction Statistics of Qingdao Municipal Bureau of Statistics.

14-1 建筑业企业生产情况（2022 年）
PRODUCTION SITUATION OF CONSTRUCTION ENTERPRISES（2022）

项　目	Item	单位	Unit	合计 Total	#中央 Central Enterprises	国有企业 State-owned Enterprises	集体企业 Collective-owned Enterprises	其他所有制企业 Other Ownership Enterprises
施工企业单位数	Number of Construction Enterprises	个	unit	961	17	23	3	935
建筑业总产值	Gross Output Value of Construction	万元	10000 yuan	35801968	7857897	726216	7861	35067891
#建筑工程	Construction	万元	10000 yuan	31212326	6194247	704191	7861	30500275
安装工程	Installation	万元	10000 yuan	3304381	1221780	17564		3286816
建筑业增加值	Value Added of Construction	万元	10000 yuan	12505600				
全年竣工产值	Output Value of Buildings Completed in the Year	万元	10000 yuan	13462213	1060763	165508	2600	13294104
施工房屋面积	Floor Space of Buildings under Construction	万平方米	10000 sq.m	25884	6394	233	8	25643
#新开工	Newly Operating	万平方米	10000 sq.m	7986	1688	80		7906
竣工房屋面积	Floor Space of Buildings Completed	万平方米	10000 sq.m	4374	221	30		4344
#住宅	Residential Buildings	万平方米	10000 sq.m	2750	169			2750
计算建筑业劳动生产率平均人数	Average Number of Persons for Calculating the Labor Productivity	人	person	689084	111657	12720	266	676098

14-2 建筑业企业财务状况（2022年）
FINANCIAL SITUATION OF CONSTRUCTION ENTERPRISES（2022）

项　目	Item	单位	Unit	合计 Total
流动资产	Circulating Funds	万元	10000 yuan	33983202
#存货	Inventory	万元	10000 yuan	4155368
年末固定资产原价	Original Value of Fixed Assets（year-end）	万元	10000 yuan	2261798
本年固定资产折旧	Depreciation of Fixed Assets in the Year	万元	10000 yuan	162801
年末资产合计	Total Assets（year-end）	万元	10000 yuan	40064310
年末负债合计	Total Liabilities（year-end）	万元	10000 yuan	32475206
所有者权益合计	Total Owners' Equity	万元	10000 yuan	7589105
#实收资本	Paid-in Capitals	万元	10000 yuan	3886891
主营业务收入	Revenue from Principal Business	万元	10000 yuan	32237340
主营业务成本	Cost of Principal Business	万元	10000 yuan	29432821
主营业务税金及附加	Taxes and Extra Charges on Principal Business	万元	10000 yuan	82095
管理费用	Management Expenses	万元	10000 yuan	844284
利润总额	Total Profits	万元	10000 yuan	795861
利税总额	Total Pre-tax Profits	万元	10000 yuan	1360189
年末应收工程款	Account Receivable（year-end）	万元	10000 yuan	10260761

#中央 Central Enterprises	国有企业 State-owned Enterprises	集体企业 Collective-owned Enterprises	其他所有制企业 Other Ownership Enterprises
8090980	1049219	3885	32930098
439161	75569	1197	4078602
791594	112847	1487	2147465
50298	13529	17	149256
10170684	1179651	6411	38878248
8795219	991577	2127	31481502
1375464	188075	4284	7396746
691165	110136	2328	3774427
9446802	1016973	5786	31214581
8835583	787941	5381	28639500
15572	1723	23	80350
129077	15068	277	828939
237020	40338	100	755423
325049	72342	263	1287585
1639206	159527	1044	10100190

14-3 建筑业企业主要经济效益指标（2022年）
MAIN INDICATORS ON ECONOMIC BENEFIT OF CONSTRUCTION ENTERPRISES（2022）

项　目	Item	单位 Unit	合计 Total	#中央 Central Enterprises	国有企业 State-owned Enterprises	集体企业 Collective-owned Enterprises	其他所有制企业 Other Ownership Enterprises
建筑业劳动生产率	**Labor Productivity of Construction**						
按总产值计算	In Terms of Gross Output Value	元/人 yuan/person	519558	703753	570924	295526	518680
竣工率	**Rate of Buildings completed**						
按产值计算	In Terms of Gross Output Value	%	37.6	13.5	22.8	33.1	37.1
产值工资率	Ratio of Wages to Gross Output Value	%	15.3	13.7	7.5	35.4	15.5
资金利润率	Ratio of Profit to Funds	%	2.3	2.8	3.5	1.9	5.1
产值利润率	Ratio of Profit to Gross Output Value	%	2.2	3.0	5.6	1.3	2.2
流动比率	Current Ratio	%	112.4	94.5	110.3	183.6	112.4
资产负债率	Assets-Liability Ratio	%	81.1	86.5	84.1	33.2	81.0

14-4 建筑业增加值（2022 年）
VALUE ADDED OF CONSTRUCTION（2022）

单位：亿元（100 million yuan）

市、区名称	Region	增加值 Value Added
全　市	**Whole Municipal**	**1250.56**
市南区	Shinan District	95.13
市北区	Shibei District	161.11
李沧区	Licang District	45.45
崂山区	Laoshan District	145.99
黄岛区	Huangdao District	325.22
城阳区	Chengyang District	122.09
即墨区	Jimo District	137.11
胶州市	Jiaozhou	124.74
平度市	Pingdu	31.95
莱西市	Laixi	89.41

14-5 重点建筑企业一览表（2022 年）
LIST OF KEY CONSTRUCTION ENTERPRISES（2022）

序 号 Precedence	企业单位名称	Name	所在地区 Location	资质等级 Qualification Criteria
1	中交一航局第二工程有限公司	Second Engineering Company Co., Ltd. of China Communications Central Airlines	市南区 Shinan District	A104
2	恒华数字科技集团有限公司	Henghua Digital Technology Group Co. Ltd.	市南区 Shinan District	B123
3	青岛青房建安集团有限公司	Qingdao Qingfang Jianan Group Co., Ltd.	市南区 Shinan District	A101
4	青岛博海建设集团有限公司	Qingdao Bohai Construction Group Co., Ltd.	市南区 Shinan District	A001
5	青岛市政空间开发集团有限责任公司	Qingdao Municipal Construction Group Co., Ltd.	市南区 Shinan District	A110
6	青岛建设集团股份有限公司	Qingdao Construction Group Co., Ltd.	市南区 Shinan District	B103
7	中建青岛投资建设有限公司	China Construction Qingdao Investment Construction Co., Ltd.	市南区 Shinan District	A110
8	青岛建设装饰集团有限公司	Qingdao Construction Decoration Group Co., Ltd.	市南区 Shinan District	B103
9	青岛中大建设集团有限公司	Qingdao Zhongda Construction Group Co., Ltd.	市南区 Shinan District	A101
10	青岛颐金建设装饰集团有限公司	Qingdao Yijin Construction Decoration Group Co., Ltd.	市南区 Shinan District	B103
11	青岛海川建设集团有限公司	Qingdao Hai Chuan Construction Group Co., Ltd.	市北区 Shibei District	A001
12	青岛东捷建设集团有限公司	Qingdao Dongjie Construction Group Co., Ltd.	市北区 Shibei District	A101
13	青岛艺高城市建设工程有限公司	Qingdao Yi Gao City Construction Engineering Co., Ltd.	市北区 Shibei District	B103
14	青岛市房屋建设集团股份有限公司	Qingdao Housing Construction Group Limited by Share Ltd.	市北区 Shibei District	A101
15	青岛嘉华鼎基建设工程有限公司	Qingdao Jiahua Dingji Construction Engineering Co., Ltd.	市北区 Shibei District	A301
16	青岛第一市政工程有限公司	Qingdao First Municipal Engineering Co., Ltd.	市北区 Shibei District	A110
17	青建国际集团有限公司	Qingjian International Group Co., Ltd.	市北区 Shibei District	A101
18	青建集团股份公司	Qingjian Group Co., Ltd.	市北区 Shibei District	A001
19	中铁四局集团第七工程有限公司	CTCE Group the 7th Engineering Co., Ltd.	市北区 Shibei District	A101
20	中铁十局集团青岛工程有限公司	China Railway Ten Bureau Group Qingdao Engineering Co., Ltd.	市北区 Shibei District	A110
21	中青建安建设集团有限公司	Zhongqing Jianan Construction Group Co., Ltd.	市北区 Shibei District	A001
22	东亚装饰股份有限公司	East Asia Decoration Limited by Share Ltd.	市北区 Shibei District	B103
23	青岛一建集团有限公司	Qingdao Yi Jian Group Co., Ltd.	市北区 Shibei District	A001
24	青岛城建集团有限公司	Qingdao Urban Construction Group Co., Ltd.	市北区 Shibei District	A110
25	中建筑港集团有限公司	Zhongjian Zhu Gang Group Co., Ltd.	市北区 Shibei District	A104
26	青岛安装建设股份有限公司	Qingdao Installation and Construction Limited by Share Ltd.	市北区 Shibei District	A112
27	山东兴华建设集团有限公司	Shandong Xinghua Construction Group Co., Ltd.	黄岛区 Huangdao District	A001
28	青岛瑞源工程集团有限公司	Qingdao Ruiyuan Engineering Group Co., Ltd.	黄岛区 Huangdao District	A105
29	中石化第十建设有限公司	Sinopec tenth Construction Company Limited	黄岛区 Huangdao District	A109
30	青岛环城建工集团有限公司	Qingdao Ring City Construction Engineering Group Co., Ltd.	黄岛区 Huangdao District	A101
31	青岛福瀛建设集团有限公司	Qingdao Fu ying Construction Group Co., Ltd.	黄岛区 Huangdao District	A101
32	青岛金沙滩建设集团有限公司	Qingdao Jinsha ConstructionGroup Co., Ltd.	黄岛区 Huangdao District	A101
33	青岛土木建工集团有限公司	Qingdao Civil Engineering Group Co., Ltd.	黄岛区 Huangdao District	A101
34	青岛滨海建设集团有限公司	Qingdao Binhai Construction Group Co., Ltd.	黄岛区 Huangdao District	A101
35	青岛昆泉建设工程有限公司	Qingdao Kunquan Construction Engineering Co., Ltd.	黄岛区 Huangdao District	A101
36	青岛德泰建设工程有限公司	Qingdao De Tai Construction Engineering Co., Ltd.	黄岛区 Huangdao District	A101

14-5 续表 1
Continued

序 号 Precedence	企业单位名称	Name	所在地区 Location	资质等级 Qualification Criteria
37	青岛前盛业建设工程有限公司	Qingdao Qianshengye Construction Engineering Co., Ltd.	黄岛区 Huangdao District	A101
38	青岛诚通建筑工程有限公司	Qingdao Chengtong Construction Engineering Co., Ltd.	黄岛区 Huangdao District	A201
39	荣泰建设集团有限公司	Rongtai Construction Engineering Group Co., Ltd.	黄岛区 Huangdao District	A001
40	青岛亿联建设集团股份有限公司	Qingdao Elink Construction Group Co., Ltd.	黄岛区 Huangdao District	A001
41	青岛西海岸城市建设集团有限公司	Qingdao West Coast City Construction Group Co., Ltd	黄岛区 Huangdao District	A110
42	中铁十七局集团第一工程有限公司	China Railway No.17 Bureau Group First Engineering Co., Ltd.	黄岛区 Huangdao District	A003
43	中建八局发展建设有限公司	China Construction Eight Engineering Division Co., Ltd.	黄岛区 Huangdao District	A101
44	青岛林海建设工程有限公司	Qingdao Linhai Construction Engineering Co., Ltd	黄岛区 Huangdao District	A210
45	中化学交通建设集团第二工程有限公司	Zhonghuaxue Transportation Construction Group the 2ndEngineering Co., Ltd	黄岛区 Huangdao District	A210
46	青岛港（集团）港务工程有限公司	Harbor Engineering Co., Ltd of Qingdao Port (Group)	黄岛区 Huangdao District	A204
47	青岛亿佰建工集团有限公司	Qingdao Yibai Construction Engineering Group Co., Ltd.	黄岛区 Huangdao District	A201
48	青岛旭华建设集团有限公司	Qingdao Xuhua Construction Group Co., Ltd	黄岛区 Huangdao District	A201
49	山东高速莱钢绿建发展有限公司	Laigang Lvjian Development Co. Ltd of Shandong Hi-speed Group	崂山区 Laoshan District	A101
50	青岛高新建筑安装工程有限公司	Qingdao High-tech Construction and Installation Engineering Co., Ltd.	崂山区 Laoshan District	A101
51	青岛海纳云智能系统有限公司	Qingdao Haina Cloud Intelligent System Co., Ltd	崂山区 Laoshan District	B223
52	合建嘉城（青岛）装饰工程有限公司	Hejian Jiacheng (Qingdao) Decoration Engineering Co., Ltd	崂山区 Laoshan District	B103
53	中建八局第四建设有限公司	Fourth Construction of China Construction Eight Bureau Co., Ltd.	崂山区 Laoshan District	A001
54	青岛新华友建工集团股份有限公司	Qingdao Xinhuayou Construction Engineering Group Limited by Share Ltd.	崂山区 Laoshan District	A101
55	德才装饰股份有限公司	Decai Decoration Limited by Share Ltd.	崂山区 Laoshan District	B103
56	中铁二十五局集团第五工程有限公司	The 5th Engineering Co., Ltd. of China Railway 25th Bureau Group	崂山区 Laoshan District	A110
57	青岛海元建设工程有限公司	Qingdao Haiyuan Construction Engineering Co., Ltd	崂山区 Laoshan District	A101
58	青岛市崂山区古建建筑工程有限公司	Qingdao Laoshan ancient building engineering Co., Ltd.	崂山区 Laoshan District	A101
59	中铁二十局集团第四工程有限公司	Fourth Engineering of China Railway twenty Bureau Group Co., Ltd.	崂山区 Laoshan District	A002
60	山东电力建设第三工程有限公司	Third Engineering Co., Ltd. of Shandong Electric Power Construction	崂山区 Laoshan District	A006
61	中国石油天然气第七建设有限公司	China Petroleum and Natural Gas Seventh Construction Co., Ltd.	崂山区 Laoshan District	A109
62	青岛中建联合集团有限公司	Qingdao Sino United Group Co., Ltd.	崂山区 Laoshan District	A101
63	青岛海德工程集团股份有限公司	Qingdao Hyde Road and Bridge Engineering Limited by Share Ltd.	崂山区 Laoshan District	B111
64	山东国建工程集团有限公司	Shandong State Construction Engineering Group Co., Ltd.	崂山区 Laoshan District	A101
65	青岛交建集团有限公司	Qingdao Construction Group Co. Ltd.	崂山区 Laoshan District	A002
66	青岛巨源建工集团有限公司	Qingdao Juyuan Construction Engineering Group Co., Ltd.	崂山区 Laoshan District	A110

14-5 续表 2
Continued

序 号 Precedence	企业单位名称	Name	所在地区 Location	资质等级 Qualification Criteria
67	青岛东建建设有限公司	Qingdao Dongjian Construction Co., Ltd.	李沧区 Licang District	A101
68	中嘉建盛建工集团有限公司	Zhongjia Jiansheng Construction Group Co., Ltd	李沧区 Licang District	A101
69	中诚祥建设集团有限公司	Zhongchengxiang Construction Engineering Co., Ltd.	李沧区 Licang District	A101
70	青岛鑫兴泰建筑工程有限公司	Qingdao Xinxingtai Construction Engineering Co., Ltd.	城阳区 Chengyang District	A201
71	山东威如建设工程有限公司	Shandong Weiru Construction Engineering Co., Ltd.	城阳区 Chengyang District	A101
72	青岛恒基伟泰建筑有限公司	Qingdao Hengji Weitai Construction Co. Ltd.	城阳区 Chengyang District	A201
73	中铁建工集团第二建设有限公司	China Railway Construction Group the 2nd Construction Co., Ltd.	城阳区 Chengyang District	A201
74	中铁十四局集团青岛工程有限公司	Qingdao Engineering Co., Ltd. of China Railway 14th Bureau Group Co., Ltd.	城阳区 Chengyang District	A110
75	青岛恒生源集团建设有限公司	Qingdao Hengshengyuan Group Construction Co., Ltd.	即墨区 Jimo District	A101
76	青岛华山广泰建设集团有限公司	Qingdao Huashan Guangtai Construction Group Co., Ltd.	即墨区 Jimo District	A201
77	青岛营上建设集团有限公司	Qingdao Yingshang Construction Group Co., Ltd.	即墨区 Jimo District	A101
78	青岛即建建设集团有限公司	Qingdao JiJian Construction Group Co., Ltd.	即墨区 Jimo District	A101
79	青岛温泉建设集团有限公司	Qingdao Hot Spring Construction Group Co., Ltd.	即墨区 Jimo District	A101
80	中即控股集团有限公司	Zhongji Holding Group Limited	即墨区 Jimo District	A101
81	中交一公局（青岛）工程有限公司	China Communications First Public Bureau (Qingdao) Engineering Co., Ltd.	即墨区 Jimo District	A305
82	中建科工集团山东有限公司	China Construction Engineering Group Shandong Co., Ltd.	即墨区 Jimo District	A310
83	青岛胶城建设集团有限公司	Qingdao Rubber City Construction Group Co., Ltd.	胶州市 Jiaozhou	A101
84	青岛亨通建设有限公司	Qingdao Hengtong Construction Co., Ltd.	胶州市 Jiaozhou	A101
85	中启胶建集团有限公司	Zhongqi Rubber Construction Group Co., Ltd.	胶州市 Jiaozhou	A001
86	青岛泰佳建筑工程有限公司	Qingdao Taijia Construction Engineering Co., Ltd.	胶州市 Jiaozhou	A201
87	青岛胶州湾建设集团有限公司	Qingdao Jiaozhou Bay Construction Group Co., Ltd.	胶州市 Jiaozhou	A101
88	青岛元昌盛房建集团有限公司	Qingdao Yuanchangsheng Housing Construction Group Co., Ltd.	胶州市 Jiaozhou	A201
89	青岛海骊住居科技股份有限公司	Qingdao Hailizhuju Technology Co., Ltd.	胶州市 Jiaozhou	B103
90	青岛建祥建设集团有限公司	Qingdao Jian Xiang Construction Group Co., Ltd.	胶州市 Jiaozhou	A101
91	青岛营海建设（集团）有限公司	Qingdao Ying hai Construction Group Co., Ltd.	胶州市 Jiaozhou	A101
92	青岛云川建筑有限公司	Qingdao Yun Chuan Architecture Co., Ltd.	胶州市 Jiaozhou	A210
93	平度市兴业建筑有限公司	Pingdu Xingye Construction Co., Ltd.	平度市 Pingdu	A201
94	青岛平建建筑安装股份有限公司	Qingdao Pingjian Construction and Installation Co., Ltd.	平度市 Pingdu	A101
95	中青建安建设集团（青岛）莱西有限公司	Zhongqing Jianan Construction Group (Qingdao) Laixi Co., Ltd.	莱西市 Laixi	A201
96	荣华建设集团有限公司	Ronghua Construction Group Co., Ltd.	莱西市 Laixi	A001
97	中建中新建设工程有限公司	China State Construction Zhongxin Construction Engineering Co., Ltd.	高新区 High tech District	A101
98	中铁二十五局集团轨道交通建设有限公司	China Railway 25th Bureau Group Rail Transit Construction Co. Ltd.	高新区 High tech District	B124
99	青岛建设集团建兴工程有限公司	Qingdao construction group LITE-ON Engineering Co., Ltd.	高新区 High tech District	A101
100	青城建工集团有限公司	Qingcheng Construction Group Co., Ltd.	高新区 High tech District	A101

主要统计指标解释

建筑业统计单位 指从事房屋、构筑物建造和设备安装活动的法人企业。建筑业法人企业应具有建筑业资质并能够独立核算，同时其应具备以下条件：①依法成立，有自己的名称、组织机构和场所，能够承担民事责任；②独立拥有和使用资产，承担负债，有权与其他单位签订合同；③独立核算盈亏，能够编制资产负债表。

建筑业总产值 是以货币形式表现的建筑业企业在一定时期内生产的建筑业产品和提供的服务的总和。建筑业总产值包括：

（1）建筑工程产值：指列入建筑工程预算内的各种工程价值。

（2）安装工程产值：指设备安装工程价值，不包括被安装设备本身的价值。

（3）其他产值：建筑业总产值中除建筑工程、安装工程以外的产值。包括房屋构筑物修理产值、非标准设备制造产值、总包企业向分包企业收取的管理费以及不能明确划分的施工活动所完成的产值。

建筑业增加值 指建筑业企业在报告期内以货币形式表现的建筑业生产经营活动的最终成果。

建筑业现价增加值 按生产法和分配法（收入法）两种方法计算，以收入法的计算结果为准，即从收入的角度出发，根据生产要素在生产过程中应得的收入份额计算。具体计算方法：经济普查年度建筑业增加值按照《经济普查年度 GDP 核算方案》计算，非经济普查年度建筑业增加值按照《非经济普查年度 GDP 核算方案》计算。

Explanatory Notes on Main Statistical Indicators

Statistical Unit in Construction refers to corporate enterprise engaged in the construction of buildings and structures and in the installation of equipment. A corporate construction enterprise should have qualification certificates with independent accounting system, and should meet the following 3 requirements：(1) being set up in line with relevant legal basis, having its full name, organization and location, and capable of taking civil liabilities；(2) independently possessing and using its assets and assuming its liabilities, and entitled to sign contracts with other institutions；(3) making independent accounts of its profits and losses, and capable of compiling its own balance sheet.

Gross Output Value of Construction refers to total of construction products and services, expressed in money terms, produced or rendered by construction and installation enterprises during a given period of time. It includes：

(1) Output value of construction projects, that is the value of projects covered by the project budgets；

(2) Output value of installation projects, that is the value of the installation of equipment, excluding the value of the equipment to be installed；

(3) Output value of others, that is the output value of construction industry excluding that of construction projects and installation projects. It includes：output value of repair of buildings and structures；output value of non-standard equipment manufacturing；overhead expenses received by contracted enterprises to the sub-contracted enterprises and the completed output value of construction activities that have no clear definition.

Added Value Of Construction Industry refers to the final results of construction industry production and operation activities expressed in currency by construction enterprises during the reporting period.

Value Added At Current Price Of Construction Industry Calculate according to the two methods of production method and distribution method (income method) . The calculation result of income method shall prevail, that is, from the perspective of income, it is calculated according to the income share of production factors in the production process. Specific calculation method : The annual added value of the construction industry in the economic census is calculated in accordance with the "Annual GDP Accounting Plan for the Economic Census", and the annual added value of the construction industry in the non-economic census is calculated in accordance with the "Non-economic Census Annual GDP Accounting Plan" .

运输、邮电 15

TRANSPORT，POSTAL AND TELECOMMUNICATION SERVICES

简 要 说 明

一、本篇资料的主要内容

本篇资料主要反映全市交通运输业和邮电业通讯业发展的基本情况，主要包括客货运输及港口吞吐量、民用汽车拥有量、独立核算运输邮电单位主要财务指标、邮电通讯基本情况、邮政行业发展情况、快递企业发展情况、电信行业基本情况、城市轨道交通发展情况等方面的内容。

二、本篇资料的来源

1. 本篇资料中交通运输邮电资料来源于全市交通运输邮电业统计年报。

2. 交通运输资料来源于青岛市交通运输局、青岛港（集团）有限公司、青岛国际机场集团有限公司、青岛地铁集团有限公司。

3. 邮政业资料来源于青岛市邮政管理局、中国邮政集团公司青岛市分公司。

4. 电信业资料来源于青岛市通信管理局、中国电信集团公司山东省青岛市电信分公司、中国电信股份有限公司青岛分公司、中国联合网络通信有限公司青岛市分公司、中国移动通信集团山东有限公司青岛分公司。

5. 民用汽车拥有量资料来源于青岛市公安局交警支队车辆管理所。

本篇资料由市统计局服务业统计处整理提供。

Brief Introduction

Ⅰ. Main Content

Data in this chapter show the basic conditions of the development of transport, post and.telecommunications in Shandong Province, mainly including the freight traffic and passenger traffic, cargo handled at port, possession of civil motor vehicles, major financial indices and basic conditions of transport postal and telecommunication services, development of the postal services, express company development development of urban rail transit.

Ⅱ. Source of Data

1. Data on transport are based on the annual report of transport.

2. Transportation data comes from Qingdao Municipal Transportation Bureau, Qingdao Port (Group) Co., Ltd. Qingdao International Airport Group Co., Ltd., and Qingdao Metro Group Co., Ltd.

3. Data on postal and telecommunication are based on Qingdao Municipal Postal Administration, Qingdao Post Bureau.

4. Data on business of telecommunication services Qingdao Communication Administration, China Telecom Group Corporation Qingdao Branch of Shandong Province, China Telecom Co., Ltd. Qingdao Branch, China United Network Communications Co., Ltd. Qingdao Branch, China Mobile Communications Group Shandong Co., Ltd. Qingdao Branch.

5. Date on possession of civil motor vehicles are provided by Qingdao Municipal Public Security Bureau Traffic Police Detachment Vehicle Management Office.

Data in this chapter are prepared and provide by the Division of Industry Statistics of Qingdao Municipal Bureau of Statistics.

15-1　主要年份客货运输及港口吞吐量

MAJOR YEAR'S PASSENGER & FREIGHT TRAFFIC AND HANDLING CAPACITY OF THE PORTS

年份 Year	客运量（万人） Passenger Traffic（10000 persons）			货运量（万吨） Freight Traffic（10000 tons）			港口货物吞吐量（万吨） Volume of Freight Handled in Ports（10000 tons）	集装箱吞吐量（万标箱） Volume of Containers Handled（10000 TEUs）	航空旅客吞吐量（万人） Air Passenger Throughput（10000 persons）	航空货邮吞吐量（万吨） Air Cargo and Mail Throughput（10000 tons）
	铁路 Railways	公路 Highways	海运 Waterways	铁路 Railways	公路 Highways	海运 Waterways				
1949	327	14	9	386	162	22	73			
1952	571	49	13	447	399	44	181			
1957	1054	149	13	747	548	118	269			
1962	3100	141	39	909	524	97	391			
1965	1424	230	19	1257	690	158	524			
1970	1329	373	20	1856	736	232	695			
1975	1803	159	30	2325	817	282	1542			
1978	1986	274	49	2917	1561	528	2081			
1980	1896	713	73	2596	1642	941	1779			
1985	2063	1 894	86	3009	2303	919	2610		2.17	0.06
1988	2083	3 300	234	3418	6486	1160	3153		17.48	0.32
1990	1488	3 639	316	3741	6433	1556	3068		28.12	0.54
1991	1453	4144	366	3774	6896	1789	3194		38.36	0.70
1992	1488	4965	437	3899	6822	1981	3240		54.17	0.57
1993	1499	6436	499	4044	7685	1910	3650		70.77	0.70
1994	1564	6787		4112	8336	1804	4331		92.64	0.88
1995	1480	9785		4205	11788	2185	5165		132.71	1.26
1996	1230	10738		4415	10749	474	6056	81.1	157.61	1.73
1997	1308	11855		4466	11232	544	6944	103.3	178.68	1.96
1998	1549	11754		4028	14311	1792	7044	121.3	184.66	2.15
1999	1674	12103		3919	14550	1926	7282	154.3	203.11	2.89
2000	1780	12145		4256	17234	2998	8661	212.0	243.15	3.44
2001	1678	13686		4778	20906	3432	10423	264.0	281.01	3.62
2002	1530	14516	777	5079	24480	2530	12252	341.0	321.99	4.63

15-1 续表
Continued

年份 Year	客运量（万人）Passenger Traffic (10000 persons)			货运量（万吨）Freight Traffic (10000 tons)			港口货物吞吐量（万吨）Volume of Freight Handled in Ports (10000 tons)	集装箱吞吐量（万标箱）Volume of Containers Handled (10000 TEUs)	航空旅客吞吐量（万人）Air Passenger Throughput (10000 persons)	航空货邮吞吐量（万吨）Air Cargo and Mail Throughput (10000 tons)
	铁路 Railways	公路 Highways	海运 Waterways	铁路 Railways	公路 Highways	海运 Waterways				
2003	1366	13132	786	4929	27241	2773	14135	424.0	349.10	5.46
2004	1496	16420	862	5119	29937	3503	16303	514.0	480.84	7.55
2005	552	17212	972	2299	31009	4471	18727	630.7	587.96	8.91
2006	810	17752	999	2790	32047	4768	22438	770.0	679.12	10.13
2007	1101	18800	1080	2781	33336	4019	26507	946.6	786.80	11.57
2008	1278	19909	1055	3225	34172	5080	30029	1037.7	820.04	13.05
2009	1425	19612	1145	3772	16297	4332	31668	1027.6	966.01	13.54
2010	1537	20460	1302	5031	17525	4407	35012	1201.0	1110.12	16.37
2011	1693	21560	791	5697	19208	4220	37971	1302.0	1171.64	16.65
2012	1881	22724	414	6126	21312	1791	41465	1450.0	1260.12	17.19
2013	2056	23588	333	6266	23270	1313	45782	1552.0	1451.67	18.62
2014	2301	5588	324	5564	19043	1434	47701	1658.0	1641.18	20.44
2015	2421	5370	288	5486	20073	1456	49749	1743.0	1820.21	20.81
2016	2701	4532	225	5569	20701	1685	51463	1805.0	2050.50	23.69
2017	3179	4534	215	6021	24716	1800	51314	1830.9	2321.06	23.21
2018	3455	4602	161	6280	27453	2502	54250	1931.5	2453.57	22.45
2019	3979	4593	186	6115	29170	2493	57736	2101.2	2555.63	25.63
2020	1240	1844	66	8416	25737	2363	60459	2200.8	1456.16	20.68
2021	1912	3113	119	8494	28407	3068	63029	2371.4	1603.20	23.76
2022	1210	1694	86	8622	26696	4393	65754	2567.2	972.01	22.00

注：1. 从 2014 年公路客、货运量统计口径进行调整，与以前年度不可比。
　　2. 根据市交通运输局提供数据，对航空部分吞吐量历史数据进行了修正。

Notes：1. In 2014, the Ministry of Transportation made an adjustment to the statistical gauge for highway passenger and freight transportation and the data are not comparable directly.
　　2. According to the data provided by the Municipal Transportation Bureau, some historical data of aviation throughput have been revised.

15-2 民用车辆拥有量(2022 年底)

POSSESSION OF CIVIL MOTOR VEHICLES（END OF 2022）

单位：辆（unit）

项目	Item	合计 Total 辆数 Number	#个人 Private Vehicles 辆数 Number
一、汽车	**Automobile**	**3551240**	**3081723**
1. 载客汽车	Passenger Vehicles	3195406	2888754
其中：轿车	Sedan	2034121	1872453
2. 载货汽车	Trucks	340964	188032
3. 其他汽车	Other Automobile	20321	10261
二、电车	**Tram**	**125**	
三、摩托车	**Motorcycle**	**139216**	**135302**
四、农用运输车	**Agricultural Camion**		
五、挂车	**Trailer Trucks**	**42177**	**820**
六、其他类型车	**Other Vehicles**		
七、校车	**School Bus**	**2674**	

补充资料：机动车驾驶员（4296145 人），其中：汽车驾驶员（4250206 人）。
Supplementary information：Motor drivers（4296145 persons），Of which：Automobile drivers（4250206 persons）.

15-3　客货运输及港口吞吐量（2022 年）
PASSENGER & FREIGHT TRAFFIC AND HANDLING CAPACITY OF THE PORTS（2022）

项目 Item	货运量（万吨）Freight Traffic（10000 tons）	货物周转量（亿吨公里）Cargo Turnover（100 million tons·km）	客运量（万人）Passenger Traffic（10000 persons）	旅客周转量（亿人公里）Passenger Turnover（100 million persons-km）	项目 Item	旅客吞吐量（万人）Passenger Throughput（10000 persons）	货物吞吐量（万吨）Cargo Throughput（10000 tons）	集装箱（万标箱）Containers（10000 TEUs）
总计 Total	**39711**	**4327.92**	**2991**	**43.81**	**总计 Total**	**972**	**65776**	**2567**
铁路 Railways	8622	81.91	1210	30.89	机场 Civil Aviation	972.01	22.00	
公路 Highways	26696	698.85	1694	12.82	港口 Ports		65754	2567
水运 Waterways	4393	3547.16	86	0.10				

15-4　规模以上运输邮电单位主要财务指标（2022 年）
MAJOR FINANCIAL INDICATORS OF TRANSPORTATION，POST AND TELECOMMUNICATION UNITS ABOVE DESIGNATED SCALE（2022）

单位：亿元（100 million yuan）

项目	Item	营业收入 Revenue from principal Business	营业成本 Cost of principal Business	营业利润 Operating Profits	营业税金及附加 Business taxes and surtax	利润总额 Total Profits
总　计	**Total**	**2573.53**	**2420.99**	**135.51**	**7.36**	**139.92**
铁路运输业	Railway Transport	35.57	29.67	-1.62	0.10	-1.62
道路运输业	Road Transport	396.14	434.24	11.19	2.11	13.55
水上运输业	Water Transport	164.63	111.71	75.83	1.46	76.16
航空运输业	Air Transport	29.56	59.15	-51.73	1.26	-51.18
管道运输业	Pipeline Transport	15.91	7.35	9.63	0.12	9.67
多式联运和运输代理业	Multimodal Transport and Transport Agent	1537.78	1472.75	37.65	0.66	38.08
装卸搬运和仓储业	Loading And Unloading And Storage	157.53	124.59	18.74	1.06	19.90
邮政业	Post	58.89	53.99	0.31	0.11	0.27
电信、广播电视和卫星传输服务	Telecommunications, Broadcast Television and Satellite Transmission Services	177.51	127.54	35.53	0.46	35.09

注：该表数据来源于规模以上服务业统计年报。
Note：The data in this table comes from the statistical annual report of the service industry above designated size.

15-5 邮政行业基本情况(2022 年)

BASIC SITUATION OF THE POSTAL INDUSTRY（2022）

指　标	Indicator	计量单位	Unit	本年实际 Actual Situation of the current year	去年实际 Actual Situation of last year
营业网点	Business Outlets	处	unit	3871	4058
其中：快递营业网点	Express Business Outlets	处	unit	1645	1860
邮路总长度	Total Length of Postal Route	公里	km	86646	85716
邮运汽车	Postal Car	辆	unit	3439	4168
邮筒信箱	Mail Box	个	unit	391	267
平均每一营业网点服务面积	Average Service Area of Each Business Outlet	平方公里	aq.km	3.0	3.0
平均每一营业网点服务人口	Average Service Population of Each Business Outlet	万人	10000 persons	0.3	0.3
平均每人每年发函件数	Average Number of Letters Sent Per Person Per Year	件	articles	0.0	1.0
平均每百人每年订有报刊数	Average Number of Newspapers Per 100 People Per Year	份	copies	8.0	8.0

注：该表数据由青岛市邮政管理局提供。
Note：The data in this table is provided by Qingdao Post Management Bureau.

15-6 邮政行业发展情况
DEVELOPMENT OF THE POSTAL SERVICES

指 标	Indicator	计量单位	Unit	2022 年	2021 年
一、邮政行业业务收入	**Postal Services Business Income**	**亿元**	**100 million yuan**	**103.85**	**110.76**
1、邮政寄递服务	Postal Delivery Service	亿元	100 million yuan	1.64	2.44
2、快递业务	Express Service	亿元	100 million yuan	86.03	94.87
二、邮政行业业务总量	**Total Business Volume Of Postal Industry**	**亿元**	**100 million yuan**	**92.10**	**88.01**
1、邮政寄递服务	Postal Delivery Service	万件	10000 articles	16993	18381
其中：函件	Number of Letters	万件	10000 articles	346	609
包裹	Package	万件	10000 articles	23	33
订销报纸累计数	Cumulative Number of Newspapers Ordered and Sold	万份	10000 copies	13519	13752
订销杂志累计数	Cumulative Number of Magazines Ordered and Sold	万份	10000 copies	589	611
汇兑	Exchange	万笔	10000 sums	3	4
2、快递业务	Express Service	万件	10000 articles	80929	77252
其中：同城	Same City	万件	10000 articles	12829	14322
异地	Different Places	万件	10000 articles	67496	62242
国际 / 港澳台	International/Hong Kong, Macao and Taiwan	万件	10000 articles	604	689

注：该表数据由青岛市邮政管理局提供。
Note：The data in this table is provided by Qingdao Post Management Bureau.

15-7 快递企业发展情况
EXPRESS COMPANY DEVELOPMENT

指　标	Indicator	计量单位	Unit	2022 年	2021 年
快递业务量	**Express Business Volume**	**万件**	**10000 articles**	**80929**	**77252**
同城	Same City	万件	10000 articles	12829	14322
异地	Different Places	万件	10000 articles	67496	62242
国际及港澳台	International/ Hong Kong, Macao and Taiwan	万件	10000 articles	604	689
快递业务收入	**Express Revenue**	**亿元**	**100 million yuan**	**86.03**	**94.87**
同城	Same City	亿元	100 million yuan	8.24	10.79
异地	Different Places	亿元	100 million yuan	43.36	50.41
国际及港澳台	International/ Hong Kong, Macao and Taiwan	亿元	100 million yuan	15.54	16.35
其他	Others	亿元	100 million yuan	18.89	17.33

注：该表数据由青岛市邮政管理局提供。
Note: The data in this table is provided by Qingdao Post Management Bureau.

15-8 电信行业基本情况
BASIC SITUATION OF TELECOM INDUSTRY

指 标	Indicator	计量单位	Unit	2022 年	2021 年
一、电信业务总量及收入	**Total Telecommunications Services and Revenue**				
电信业务总量（上年不变价）	Total Telecommunications Services（constant price of the previous year）	亿元	100 million yuan	153.41	117.03
电信业务收入	Telecommunications Revenue	亿元	100 million yuan	130.98	119.76
二、电信主要通信能力	**Primary Communication Capability of Telecommunications**				
光缆线路长度	Line Length of Optical Cable	公里	km	355125	353655
其中：长途光缆线路长度	Line Length of Long-distance Optical Cable	公里	km	3709	3590
移动电话交换机容量	Mobile Phone Switch Capacity	万户	10000 households	3434.98	3390.98
移动电话基站	Mobile Phone Base Station	万个	10000 unit	9.24	8.47
其中：4G 基站	4G Base Station	万个	10000 unit	4.80	4.85
其中：5G 基站	5G Base Station	万个	10000 unit	3.68	2.18
（固定）互联网宽带接入端口	（Fixed）Internet Broadband Access Port	万个	10000 unit	866.47	812.86
其中：FTTH/O 端口	FTTH/O Port	万个	10000 unit	832.98	766.84
三、电信服务业务	**Telecommunications services**				
固定电话主叫通话时长（含 IP）	Fixed-line Calling Duration of the calling party（IP Phone Included）	万分钟	10000 minutes	66355	76602
移动电话通话时长	Mobile Phone Calling Duration	万分钟	10000 minutes	4209338	4099047
其中：去话通话时长	Calling Duration of the Calling Party	万分钟	10000 minutes	905544	875882
移动短信业务量	Mobile SMS Service Volume	万条	10000 items	905465	975012
期末移动电话用户数	The Number of Mobile Phone Users at the End of the Period	万户	10000 households	1345.32	1295.34
其中：4G 移动电话用户	4G Mobile Phone Users	万户	10000 households	740.00	841.81
其中：5G 移动电话用户	5G Mobile Phone Users	万户	10000 households	445.91	287.93
固定电话用户	The number of Fixed Telephone Users	万户	10000 households	167.40	158.96
（固定）宽带互联网用户	The number of（Fixed）Broadb and Internet Users	万户	10000 households	498.64	498.09
其中：FTTH/O 用户	FTTH/O port users	万户	10000 households	455.38	416.98
其中：城市宽带接入用户	Urban Broadband Access Users	万户	10000 households	409.35	367.55
农村宽带接入用户	Rural Broadband Access Users	万户	10000 households	89.29	87.60
其中：家庭宽带接入用户	Home Broadband Access Users	万户	10000 households	443.72	411.37
政企宽带接入用户	Government-enterprise Broadband Access Users	万户	10000 households	54.18	43.53
移动互联网接入流量	Mobile Internet Access Traffic	万 GB	10000 GB	196052.00	169118.77
物联网终端用户	Terminal User of the Internet of things	万户	10000 households	2086.29	1436.77
IPTV 用户	IPTV Subscriber	万户	10000 households	139.66	130.10
四、电信固定资产投资	**Fixed-asset investment in Telecom industry**				
电信固定资产投资完成额	Completion of Fixed-asset Investment in Telecom Industry	万元	10000 yuan	264076	274338
其中：互联网及数据通信	Internet and Data Communication	万元	10000 yuan	194286	220254
五、电信营业网点	**Telecom Business Outlets**				
电信营业网点（自有）	Telecom Business Outlets（self-owned）	个	unit	413	397

注：1. 电信业务总量、电信业务收入、（固定）互联网宽带接入端口、FTTH/O 端口、期末移动电话用户数、固定电话年末用户、固定宽带互联网用户、其中：FTTH/O 用户等指标为青岛市通信管理局提供。
2. 其他指标由中国电信集团公司山东省青岛市电信分公司、中国电信股份有限公司青岛分公司、中国联合网络通信有限公司青岛市分公司、中国移动通信集团山东有限公司青岛分公司等企业报表数据汇总。

Notes：1. Business volume of total Telecommunication service, Telecommunication service revenue, and the number of(fixed) Internet broadband access port, FTTH/O port, mobile phone users at the end of the period, fixed telephone users at the end of the year, fixed broadband Internet users, and other indicators are provided by Qingdao Communication Administration Bureau.
2.Other indicators are summarized by the report data of China Telecom Corporation Shandong Qingdao Telecom Branch, China Telecom Corporation Qingdao Branch, China United Network Communications Co., Ltd. Qingdao Branch, China Mobile Communications Group Shandong Co., Ltd. Qingdao Branch, etc. .

15-9 城市轨道交通发展情况
DEVELOPMENT OF URBAN RAIL TRANSIT

指　标	Indicator	计量单位	Unit	2022 年	2021 年
客运量	**Passenger Traffic**	**万人次**	**10000 person-times**	**28290**	**24659**
日均客运量	**Average Daily Passenger**	**万人次**	**10000 person-times**	**78**	**68**
旅客周转量	**Passenger Turnover**	**万人公里**	**10000 passenger-km**	**289253**	**238201**
运营车数	**Number of Vehicles Operated**	**辆**	**unit**	**1486**	**1214**
其中：地铁	Subway	辆	unit	1486	1214
轻轨	Subway	辆	unit	0	
运营线路总数	**Total Number of Operating Lines**	**条**	**line**	**7**	**6**
其中：新增运营线路	New Operating Line	条	line	1	
其中：地铁	Subway	条	line	1	
轻轨	Light Rail	条	line	0	
运营线路总长度	**Total Length of Operating Line**	**公里**	**km**	**315**	**284**
其中：新增运营线路长度	New Operating Line Length	公里	km	31	38
其中：地铁	Subway	公里	km	31	38
轻轨	Light Rail	公里	km	0	
地铁站点总数	**Total Number of Subway Stations**	**个**	**unit**	**146**	**128**
其中：换乘站点个数	Number of Transfer Stations	个	unit	13	7
其中：新增站点个数	Number of New Sites	个	unit	18	22
其中：新增换乘站点个数	Increase the Number of Transfer Stations	个	unit	6	3
总开行次数	**Total Number of Trips**	**列次**	**train number**	**668419**	**666720**
总运营里程	**Total Operating Mileage**	**公里**	**km**	**24299894**	**21767244**
列车准点率	**Train on Time Rate**	**%**	**%**	**100**	**100**

注：该表数据由青岛市交通运输局提供。
Note：The data in this table are provided byQingdao Municipal Transport Bureau.

15-10 按行业分企业信息化及电子商务情况（2022 年）
INFORMATIZATION AND E-COMMERCE OF ENTERPRISES BY INDUSTRIAL SECTOR （2022）

行　业	Sector	企业数（个）Number of Enterprises (unit)	期末使用计算机数（台）Computers Used at the End of Period (unit)	每百人使用计算机数（台）Computers Used Per 100 Persons (unit)
总　计	**Total**	**14894**	**672479**	**45**
采矿业	Mining	4	174	41
制造业	Manufacturing	4438	258663	38
电力、热力、燃气及水生产和供应业	Production and Supply of Electricity, Heat, Gas and Water	125	10124	51
建筑业	Construction	953	69225	39
批发和零售业	Wholesale and Retail Trades	4560	88174	64
交通运输、仓储和邮政业	Transport, Storage and Post	891	50017	45
住宿和餐饮业	Hotels and Catering Services	948	15175	28
信息传输、软件和信息技术服务业	Information Transmission, Software and Information Technology Services	254	53612	136
房地产业	Real Estate	1346	33744	50
租赁和商务服务业	Leasing and Business Services	693	27227	33
科学研究和技术服务业	Scientific Research and Technical Services	336	47738	84
水利、环境和公共设施管理业	Management of Water Conservancy, Environment and Public Facilities	44	2959	13
居民服务、修理和其他服务业	Resident Services, Repairs and Other Services	67	1980	17
教育	Education	17	2237	65
卫生和社会工作	Health and Social Work	74	5946	57
文化、体育和娱乐业	Culture, Sports and Entertainment Industry	144	5484	64

注：有电子商务交易活动的企业是指通过计算机网络开展电子商务销售或电子商务采购的企业。
Note：Enterprises with E-Commerce Transactions refers to those enterprises which performed sales or purchases through internet.

企业拥有网站数（个）Websites of Enterprises（unit）	每百家企业拥有网站数（个）Websites Per 100 Enterprises（unit）	有电子商务交易活动 With E-Commerce Transactions		电子商务销售额（万元）Sales of E-Commerce（10000 yuan）	电子商务采购额（万元）Purchases of E-Commerce（10000 yuan）
		企业数（个）Enterprises（unit）	比重（%）Proportion（%）		
7480	**50**	**6104**	**41.0**	**71150088**	**50128456**
3	75				
3242	73	2094	47.2	31585340	19202577
49	39	56	44.8	47468	93364
433	45	366	38.4	46610	2008958
1501	33	1618	35.5	33075825	25133785
368	41	362	40.6	3498370	2608750
274	29	489	51.6	534562	9491
269	106	163	64.2	1225569	343444
562	42	251	18.6	49020	12807
299	43	308	44.4	647711	205438
279	83	205	61.0	280007	475958
18	41	23	52.3		1036
32	48	34	50.7	72252	20531
19	112	11	64.7	3125	608
56	76	53	71.6	23623	10753
76	53	71	49.3	60608	956

15-11 分市、区企业信息化及电子商务情况（2022 年）

INFORMATIZATION AND E-COMMERCE OF ENTERPRISES BY REGION（2022）

市、区名称	Region	企业数（个）Number of Enterprises（unit）	期末使用计算机数（台）Computers Used at the End of Period（unit）	每百人使用计算机数（台）Computers Used Per 100 Persons（unit）
全　市	**Whole Municipality**	**14894**	**672479**	**45**
市南区	Shinan District	1505	100751	66
市北区	Shibei District	1066	63178	56
李沧区	Licang District	972	21996	37
崂山区	Laoshan District	991	88966	62
黄岛区	Huangdao District	3495	153726	40
城阳区	Chengyang District	2150	104477	49
即墨区	Jimo District	1165	44527	37
胶州市	Jiaozhou	1903	50101	32
平度市	Pingdu	947	24779	29
莱西市	Laixi	700	19978	34

注：有电子商务交易活动的企业是指通过计算机网络开展电子商务销售或电子商务采购的企业。
Note：Enterprises with E-Commerce Transactions refers to those enterprises which performed sales or purchases through internet.

企业拥有网站数（个）Websites of Enterprises (unit)	每百家企业拥有网站数（个）Websites Per 100 Enterprises (unit)	有电子商务交易活动 With E-Commerce Transactions		电子商务销售额（万元）Sales of E-Commerce (10000 yuan)	电子商务采购额（万元）Purchases of E-Commerce (10000 yuan)
		企业数（个）Enterprises (unit)	比重（%）Proportion (%)		
7480	**50**	**6104**	**41.0**	**71150088**	**50128456**
819	55	596	39.6	13257951	5687705
461	43	477	44.7	2405571	1859363
371	38	431	44.3	3211707	3055466
593	60	558	56.3	20817869	19282051
1602	46	1435	41.1	20573921	16186224
1164	54	1047	48.7	2662514	1482863
689	59	484	41.5	2000098	797363
961	51	642	33.7	4516764	1198415
477	50	275	29.0	468539	369163
343	49	159	22.7	1235154	209843

主要统计指标解释

货（客）运量　指在一定时期内，各运输部门实际运送的货物（旅客）数量。是反映运输业为国民经济和人民生活服务的数量指标，也是制定和检查运输生产计划，研究运输发展规模和速度的重要指标。货运按吨计算，客运按人计算。货物不论运输距离长短，货物类别，均按实际重量统计；旅客不论行程远近或票价多少，均按一人一次作为客运量统计。半价票、小孩票也按一人统计。

货物（旅客）周转量　指在一定时期内，由各种运输工具运送的货物（旅客）数量与其相应运输距离的乘积之总和，是反映运输业生产总成果的重要指标，也是编制和检查运输生产计划，计算运输效益、劳动生产率以及核算运输单位成本的主要基础资料。通常以吨公里和人公里为计算单位。计算货物周转量通常按发出站与到达站之间的最短距离，也就是计费距离计算。

港口货物吞吐量　指经水运进出沿海主要港区范围，并经过装卸的货物数量，包括邮件及办理托运手续的行李、包裹以及补给运输船舶的燃、物料和淡水。货物吞吐量按货物流向分为进口、出口吞吐量，按货物交流性质分为外贸货物吞吐量和国内贸易货物吞吐量。货物吞吐量的货类构成及其流向，是衡量港口生产能力大小的重要指标。

邮政行业业务总量　指以货币形式表现的邮政企业为社会提供各类邮政通信服务或其他服务的总数量。计算方法为各类邮政通信服务业务的实物量分别乘以相应的不变单价，求出各类业务的货币量后加总求得。该指标反映了一定时期邮政通信业务发展的总成果，是观察邮政通信业务发展变化总趋势的综合性指标。

邮政行业业务收入　指邮政企业和快递企业从事各种邮政业务、快递业务取得的收入总和。

快递业务量　指企业收寄的各类快递业务总数量，由受理用户委托的企业负责统计。包括国内同城快递业务量、国内异地快递业务量、港澳台快递业务量、国际快递业务量。

快递业务收入　指企业从事快递业务取得的收入。快递业务收入 = 国内同城快递业务收入 + 国内异地快递业务收入 + 港澳台快递业务收入 + 国际快递业务收入 + 其他快递业务收入。

电信业务总量　指以货币形式表示的电信企业为社会提供的各类电信服务的总数量。包括固定话音业务总量、固定数据及互联网业务总量、固定增值及其他业务总量、移动话音业务总量、移动数据及互联网业务总量、移动增值及其他业务总量。

电信业务收入　指电信企业经营的基础电信业务和增值电信业务所取得的资费收入，以及电信企业之间网间互联电信业务的结算收入。

长途光缆线路长度　指长途光缆线路的实际长度。架空的光缆按实际杆路长度统计，埋设地下、水底的光缆按沟长统计。

本地网中继光缆线路长度　指本地网内各业务节点之间，从起点至终点所经由的光缆线路实际长度。架空光缆按实际杆路长度统计，埋设地下、水底的光缆按埋设光缆的沟长统计。

移动电话基站数　指为小区服务的无线收发信设备，处理基站与移动台之间的无线通信，在移动交换机与移动台之间起中继作用，监视无线传输质量的全套设备数。

3G 移动电话基站数　指报告期末本电信企业 3G 移动通信网络上实际使用的 NoFe-B 数量。包括 TF-SCFMA 基站、WCFMA 基站和 CFMA2000 基站。

4G 移动电话基站数 指报告期末本电信企业 4G 移动通信网络上实际使用的 Node-B 数量。包括 TD-LTE 基站和 FDD-LTE 基站。

互联网宽带接入用户 指报告期末在电信企业登记注册，通过 xDSL、FTTx+LAN、FTTH/O 以及其他宽带接入方式和普通专线接入公众互联网的用户。互联网宽带接入用户按行政区划分为城市宽带接入用户和农村宽带接入用户；按客户类别分为家庭宽带接入用户和政企宽带接入用户。

移动互联网用户 指报告期内通过移动通信网络接入公众互联网或 WAP 网站的用户。

互联网宽带接入端口 指用于接入互联网用户的各类实际安装运行的宽带接入端口的数量。

网站数 指报告期末企业拥有和维护的，在互联网上可浏览的网站数，不包括企业内网。网站是指在公共互联网上，面向公众使用的，基于 TCP/IP 协议的计算机系统，以域名本身或者“WWW. + 域名”为网址的 web 站点，由地址、软件、硬件和内容组成。

电子商务销售金额 指报告期内企业（单位）借助网络订单而销售的商品和服务总额。借助网络订单指通过网络接受订单，付款和配送可以不借助于网络。

电子商务采购金额 指报告期内企业（单位）借助网络订单而采购的商品和服务总额。借助网络订单指通过网络发送订单，付款和配送可以不借助于网络。

电子商务交易平台 指在电子商务活动中为交易双方或多方提供交易撮合及相关服务的信息网络系统的总和。

Explanatory Notes on Main Statistical Indicators

Freight (Passenger) Traffic refers to the volume of freight (passenger) transported with various means. Freight transport is calculated in tons and passenger traffic is calculated in the number of persons. Despite the type of freight and traveling distance, the freight transport is calculated in the actual weight of the goods : and despite the traveling distance and ticket price, the passenger traffic is calculated by the principle that one person can be counted only once in one travel. The passengers who travel with a half price ticket or a child ticket is also calculated as one person. The freight (passenger) traffic provides a quantitative measure to show how the transport industry serves the national economy and people, and is also an important indicator for planning the transport industry and for studying the development scale and speed of the transport industry.

Freight Ton-kilometers (Passenger-kilometers) refer to the sum of the products of the volume of transported cargo (passengers) multiplying by the transport distance. It is an important indicator to reflect the achievement of transportation industry. Normally, the shortest distance between the departure station and the destination station (i.e., the payable distance) is the basis to calculate the freight ton-kilometers. This is an important indicator to show the total results of the transport industry, to prepare and examine the transport plan and to measure the efficiency, the labour productivity and the unit cost of transport.

Volume of Freight Handled in Ports refers to the volume of cargo passing in and out the harbor area of the major coastal ports and having been loaded and unloaded. The volume includes that of the postal matters, registered luggage and fuels, materials and fresh water as supplies of the ships. The volume of freight handled may be classified by direction of flow as freight for import and freight for export, or by nature of cargo as freight for domestic trade and freight for foreign trade. As an important indicator, the volume of freight handled by type of cargo and by main flow direction reflects the production capacity of ports.

Business Volume of Post Services refers to the total amount of post services or other services provided by the post departments for society. The calculation method is that the physical quantity of each type of postal communication service business is multiplied by the corresponding constant unit price, and the monetary quantity of each type of service is obtained and summed up. This indicator reflects the total results of the development of postal communication services in a certain period of time, and is a comprehensive indicator for observing the general trend of development and change of postal communication services.

Postal Services Business Income refers to the total income obtained by postal enterprises and courier enterprises from various postal services and express delivery services.

Business Volume of Express Services refers to the total number of various types of express delivery services received and received by the enterprise, and the enterprises entrusted by the user are responsible for statistics. Including domestic city express business volume, domestic off–site express business volume, Hong Kong, Macao and Taiwan express business volume, international express business volume.

Express Revenue refers to the income obtained by enterprises engaged in express business. Express business income = Income from domestic intra–city express business + Income from domestic long–distance express business +Income from Hong Kong, Macao and Taiwan express business + Income from international express business + other express business income.

Business Volume of Telecommunication Services refers to the total number of telecommunication services provided by telecommunication enterprises in the form of money for the society. Including the total volume of fixed voice services, fixed data and total Internet services, fixed value–added and other services, total mobile voice services, total mobile data and Internet services, mobile value–added and other business.

Telecommunications Service Revenue refers to the income obtained from basic telecommunication service and value–added telecommunication service operated by telecommunication enterprises, as well as the settlement income from telecommunication service of interconnection among telecommunication enterprises.

Long–Distance Cable Line Length refers to the actual length of the long–distance cable line. The overhead optical cable is counted according to the actual length of the pole. The underground and underwater cables are counted according to the length of the trench.

Local Network Trunk Cable Length refers to the actual length of the cable line between the service nodes in the local network and from the starting point to the destination. The overhead optical cable is counted according to the actual length of the pole. The underground and underwater optical cables are counted according to the length of the buried optical cable.

Number of Mobile Phone Base Stations refers to the wireless transceiver device serving the cell, handles the wireless communication between the base station and the mobile station, and acts as a relay between the mobile switch and the mobile station to monitor the total number of devices for wireless transmission quality.

Number of 3G Mobile Phone Base Stations refers to the number of NoFe–B actually used on the 3G mobile communication network of the telecommunications enterprise at the end of the reporting period. It includes TF–SCFMA base station, WCFMA base station, and CFMA2000 base station.

Number of 4G Mobile Phone Base Stations refers to the number of Node–B actually used on the 4G mobile communication network of the telecommunications enterprise at the end of the reporting period. It includes TD–LTE base station and FDD–LTE base station.

Internet Broadband Access Users refer to those who are registered with telecom enterprises at the end of the report period and access the public Internet through xDSL, FTTx+LAN, FTTH/O, and other broadband access methods and ordinary special lines. Internet broadband access users are divided into urban broadband access users and rural broadband access users according to administrative regions. According to the customer category they are divided into home broadband access users and government and enterprise broadband access users.

Mobile Internet Users refer to those who access public Internet or WAP websites through mobile communication networks during the reporting period.

Internet Broadband Access Port refers to the number of broadband access ports that are actually installed and operated for accessing Internet users.

Websites refers to the number of websites owned and maintained by enterprises at the end of the reporting period, excluding the intranet. A website is a web site on the public Internet, accessible to the public, based on the TCP/IP protocol, with the domain name itself or the "WWW.+ domain name" as its URL, consisting of address, software, hardware and content.

E–commerce sales amount refers to the total amount of goods and services sold by an enterprise (unit) through online orders during the reporting period. With the help of a network order refers to the acceptance of orders over the network, payment and distribution can be made without the help of the network.

E–commerce purchase amount refers to the total amount of goods and services purchased by an enterprise (unit) through the help of a network order during the reporting period. With the help of a network order, an order is sent over the network, and payment and distribution can be made without the help of the network.

E–commerce trading platform refers to the sum of information network systems that provide transaction matching and related services for both parties or parties in e–commerce activities.

批发和零售业 16

WHOLESALE AND RETAIL TRADES

简要说明

一、本篇资料的主要内容

本篇资料主要反映全市批发和零售业经营情况和效益情况，主要包括批发和零售业商品流转及财务情况、亿元以上商品交易市场、社会消费品零售总额等内容。

二、本篇资料的来源

本篇资料来源于批发和零售业统计年报和定期报表统计资料，由市统计局外经贸易统计处整理提供。

Brief Introduction

Ⅰ. Main Content

Data in this chapter show the development of wholesale and retail trade of the whole city, mainly including the circulation and financial indices of commodities in the wholesale and retail trade commodity exchange markets over 100 million yuan, total retail sales of consumer goods, etc.

Ⅱ. Source of Data

Data in this chapter are based on annual report and regular reports of wholesale and retail trade. Data in this chapter are prepared and compiled by the Division of Trade and External Economic Relations Statistics of Qingdao Municipal Bureau of Statistics.

16-1 社会消费品零售总额(1985—2022年)
TOTAL RETAIL SALES OF CONSUMER GOODS（1985—2022）

单位：万元（10000 yuan）

年份 Year	消费品零售总额 Total Retail Sales of Consumer Goods	批发和零售业 Wholesale and Retail Trades	住宿和餐饮业 Hotels and Catering Services	其他行业 Others
1985	307222	231477	16996	18753
1986	364091	269418	21384	27118
1987	432569	310658	23319	32617
1988	590538	434572	32304	45449
1989	619941	450812	34083	56303
1990	658264	484770	35568	67863
1991	760562	566767	43320	56812
1992	888411	666911	53045	67392
1993	1381791	1029750	79918	96567
1994	1873212	1346723	126809	202134
1995	2362682	1627640	184925	304133
1996	2687133	1858214	218582	318787
1997	2979302	2084958	239542	357685
1998	3328902	2294750	274412	406348
1999	3710897	2678209	310962	385994
2000	4215480	3067944	381840	397499
2001	4824874	3498744	498046	426179
2002	5464940	4080963	625827	394750
2003	6315866	5169609	830717	315540
2004	7299288	6119422	993279	186587
2005	8479672	7118804	1146604	214264
2006	9885247	8226694	1403617	254936
2007	11805893	9702897	1783908	319089
2008	14456246	12590079	1505564	360603
2009	16728814	13761257	2464719	502838
2010	18923835	16550240	2373595	
2011	22172581	19408076	2764505	
2012	25331596	22147219	3184377	
2013	28650167	25076367	3573800	
2014	32182505	28179596	4002909	
2015	35481601	31012690	4468911	
2016	39141939	34175128	4966811	
2017	43214295	37751718	5462577	
2018	47427204	41340208	6086996	
2019	51265971	44158221	7107750	
2020	52034957	46836540	5198417	
2021	59754345	53434436	6319909	
2022	58917785	52807678	6110106	

注：1. 自2003年开始消费品零售总额不再包括制造业零售额和农民对非农居民的销售额分组。
2. 自2005年起，住宿业从其他行业调整到住宿餐饮业中。
3. 根据第四次经济普查结果，对1993年以来的历史数据进行了调整。

Notes：1. Since 2003, retail sales of manufacturing and retail sales of rural residents to urban residents are excluded in total retail sales of consumer goods.
2. Since 2005, hotels is adjusted to hotels and catering services from the others.
3. Historical data since1993 have been adjusted according to results of the Fourth China Economic Census.

16-2 分市、区社会消费品零售总额(2022年)
TOTAL RETAIL SALES OF CONSUMER GOODS BY REGION(2022)

单位:万元(10000 yuan)

市、区名称	Region	消费品零售总额 Total Retail Sales of Consumer Goods	按行业分 Grouped by sectors 批发和零售业 Wholesale and Retail Trades	住宿和餐饮业 Hotels and Catering Services
全　市	**Whole Municipal**	**58917785**	**52807678**	**6110106**
市南区	Shinan District	7208442	6224006	984436
市北区	Shibei District	6874501	6046857	827643
李沧区	Licang District	4411151	4105248	305903
崂山区	Laoshan District	4446398	4110308	336090
黄岛区	Huangdao District	13127945	11721865	1406080
城阳区	Chengyang District	4477057	3960520	516537
即墨区	Jimo District	5361873	4960419	401454
胶州市	Jiaozhou	6442078	5889249	552829
平度市	Pingdu	3485264	3121429	363836
莱西市	Laixi	3083077	2667778	415299

16-3 限额以上批发和零售业商品销售、库存情况(2022年)

SALES AND INVENTORIES OF WHOLESALE AND RETAIL COMMODITIES ABOVE DESIGNATED SIZE (2022)

单位：万元（10000 yuan）

项目	Item	商品销售额 Commodity Sales	#批发额 Wholesale Amount	零售额 Retail Sales	库存额 Inventory
总计	**Total**	**210516095.5**	**189697527.1**	**20262036.8**	**10369657.0**
国有企业	State-owned Enterprises	8456771.3	8381032.8	75490.4	258024.3
集体企业	Collective-owned Enterprises	105219.3	105219.3		525.5
其他企业	Other Enterprises	201954104.9	181211275.0	20186546.4	10111107.2
农、林、牧产品批发	Products Wholesale of Agriculture, Forestry and Animal Husbandry Products Wholesale	7352464.1	7329294.8	12544.8	419686.7
食品、饮料及烟草制品批发	Wholesale of Food, Beverages and Tobaccos	17205675.4	16602918.2	405624.3	847883.1
纺织、服装及家庭用品批发	Retail of Textiles, Garments and Daily Consumer Articles	18314229.5	17470828.4	834487.1	1447687.1
文化、体育用品及器材批发	Wholesale of Culture, Sports Appliances and Equipments	1526385.2	1456340.2	55924.7	127385.2
医药及医疗器材批发	Wholesale of Medicines and Medical Appliances	4521919.5	4497493.2	24426.3	365090.1
矿产品、建材及化工产品批发	Wholesale of Mineral Products, Building Materials and Chemical Products	129106919.1	127473986.2	1355044.7	4546546.7
机械设备、五金产品及电子产品批发	Wholesale of Machinery, Hardware and Electronic Equipment	10421924.8	10046922.9	338432.3	518700.0
贸易经纪与代理	Trade Broker and Agency	328015.6	328015.6		14472.2
其他批发业	Other Wholesale not Classified Elsewhere	2978166.3	2964228.4	7248.1	32575.8
综合零售	Integrated Retail Trade	2689862.0	21762.5	2668099.5	322027.5
食品、饮料及烟草制品专门零售	Retail of Food, Beverages and Tobaccos	433522.0	34616.7	398905.3	68408.2
纺织、服装及日用品专门零售	Retail of Textiles, Garments and Daily Consumer Articles	370892.3	81459.2	289433.1	85185.7
文化、体育用品及器材专门零售	Retail of Culture, Sports Appliances and Equipments	233293.2	5975.9	227317.3	63953.5
医药及医疗器材专门零售	Retail of Medicines and Medical Appliances	1117294.9	70366.1	1046928.8	139037.0
汽车、摩托车、燃料及零配件专门零售	Retail of Motor Vehicles, Motorcycles, Fuel and Parts	7573112.7	456594.6	7114886.8	791268.6
家用电器及电子产品专门零售	Retail of Household Electric Appliances and Electronic Products	498085.6	23850.8	474234.8	44976.0
五金、家具及室内装饰材料专门零售	Retail of Hardware, Furniture and Decoration Materials	117247.1	1215.4	116031.7	29800.2
货摊、无店铺及其他零售业	Non-shop and Other Retails	5727086.2	831658.0	4892467.2	504973.4

16-4 限额以上批发和零售业商品分类销售额（2022 年）

CLASSIFIED SALES OF WHOLESALE AND RETAIL AND RETAIL COMMODITIES ABOVE DESIGNATED SIZE（2022）

单位：万元（10000 yuan）

项目	Item	销售额 Total Sales Value	#批发额 Wholesale Value	零售额 Retail Value
销售总额	**Total Sales Value**	**200015102.6**	**181233940.3**	**18781162.3**
1. 粮油、食品类	Grain & Oil and Food	14248606.5	12240624.7	2007981.8
其中：粮油类	Grain and Oil	4010725.1	3793191.5	217533.6
肉禽蛋类	Meat，Poultry and Eggs	5632528.7	5360551.7	271977.0
水产品类	Aquatic Products	1098631.5	894135.4	204496.1
蔬菜类	Vegetable and Fruit	366200.0	238720.4	127479.6
干鲜果品类	Dried and Fresh Fruit	1112659.0	785566.1	327092.9
2. 饮料类	Beverages	641376.7	289085.6	352291.1
3. 烟酒类	Tobacco and Liquor	2381820.3	2104411.0	277409.3
4. 服装、鞋帽、针纺织品类	Clothing，Shoes，Hats and Textiles	4405782.0	3445162.0	960620.0
（1）服装类	Clothing	1644882.2	1005737.0	639145.2
（2）鞋帽类	Shoes and Hats	666097.4	423035.2	243062.2
（3）针纺织品类	Knitwear and Textiles	2094802.4	2016389.8	78412.6
5. 化妆品类	Cosmetics	560004.2	232643.1	327361.1
6. 金银珠宝类	Gold，Silver and Jewellery	607343.9	125951.4	481392.5
7. 日用品类	Articles for Daily Use	1260476.8	673355.5	587121.3
其中：可穿戴智能设备	Wearable Smart Devices	248944.4	155785.1	93159.3
8. 五金、电料类	Hardware and Electrical Materials	1108779.0	1094203.8	14575.2
9. 体育、娱乐用品类	Sports and Recreation Articles	214933.4	34231.5	180701.9
其中：照相器材类	Photographic Apparatus	159898.2	13241.7	146656.5
10. 书报杂志类	Newspapers and Magazines	203816.2	59757.8	144058.4
11. 电子出版物及音像制品类	E-journals and Video Products	3858.1	1099.1	2759.0
12. 家用电器和音像器材类	Household Appliances and Video Appliances	16791250.6	13462397.1	3328853.5
其中：能效等级为 1 级和 2 级的商品	Products with Energy Efficiency Grades 1 and 2	3419911.0	1232497.4	2187413.6
其中：智能家用电器和音像器材	Smart Household Appliances and Audio-visual Equipment	3639774.3	3245979.2	393795.1
13. 中西药品类	Traditional Chinese and Western Medicines	3852438.8	2850454.3	1001984.5
其中：西药类	Western Medicines	3160277.8	2408657.8	751620.0
中草药及中成药类	Traditional Chinese Medicines	190921.0	94470.7	96450.3
14. 文化办公用品类	Cultural and Offices Appliances	943825.0	572383.8	371441.2
其中：计算机及其配套产品	Computer and Related Products	695286.4	391361.3	303925.1
15. 家具类	Furniture	375109.5	252625.4	122484.1
16. 通讯器材类	Communication Appliances	1381796.9	507917.5	873879.4
其中：智能手机	Smart Phones	879294.7	551052.2	328242.5
17. 煤炭及制品类	Coal and Related Products	5580101.7	5513932.3	66169.4
18. 木材及制品类	Wood and Wooden Products	1583214.2	1583214.2	
19. 石油及制品类	Petroleum and Related Products	48114531.1	45842622.1	2271909.0
20. 化工材料及制品类	Chemical Materials and Related Products	20938851.4	20938851.4	
其中：化肥类	Fertilizers	767197.3	767197.3	
21. 金属材料类	Metal Materials	47762575.2	47762575.2	
22. 建筑及装潢材料类	Building and Decoration Materials	1798216.2	1724631.2	73585.0
23. 机电产品及设备类	Mechanical and Electrical Products	2909224.7	2864210.6	45014.1
其中：农机类	Agricultural Machineries	22879.7	22879.7	
24. 汽车类	Automobiles	8493462.5	3529166.3	4964296.2
其中：新能源汽车	New Energy Vehicles	1617022.0	599505.1	1017516.9
25. 种子饲料类	Seeds and Feedstuff	3772634.0	3772634.0	
26. 棉麻类	Cotton，Flax	1402643.0	1396567.2	6075.8
27. 其他类	Others	8678430.7	8359232.2	319198.5

注：此表为定期报表数据。

Note：The data are from regular reports.

16-5 限额以上批发业财务状况（2022 年）

FINANCIAL POSITION OF ENTERPRISES ABOVE DESIGNATED SIZE OF WHOLESALE TRADE（2022）

单位：万元（10000 yuan）

指 标	Indicator	合计 Total	国有经济 State-owned Enterprises	集体经济 Collective-owned Enterprises	外商及港澳台经济 Foreign Funded Enterprises and Enterprises with Funds from Hong Kong，Macao and Taiwan	其他 Others
单位数	**Number of Enterprises**	**3714**	**45**	**2**	**105**	**3562**
年末资产负债	**Year-end Assets-Liability**					
资产总计	Total Assets	76500353	3568775	50596	8683852	64197131
流动资产合计	Sub-total of Current Assets	68434881	2998174	48813	8072603	57315291
负债合计	Total Liabilities	64743388	2746010	45487	7570336	54381555
所有者权益合计	Total Owners' Equities	11665270	822524	5108	1113516	9724122
损益及分配	**Loss，Profits and Distribution**					
营业收入	Revenue from Principal Business	174411487	7468119	93424	20930818	145919126
营业成本	Cost of Principal Business	169326715	7057151	84064	20630964	141554537
营业税金及附加	Taxes and Extra Charges on Principal Business	310776	161809	155	12954	135859
营业利润	Profits from Principal Business	653838	145034	1233	-101269	608841
其他业务利润	Profits from other Business	118252	1266	2	3805	113179
销售费用	Operating Costs	2414679	41856	809	202182	2169832
管理费用	Management Expenses	1109297	62532	7413	115649	923703
财务费用	Financial Expenses	539678	7423	-101	10717	521639
利润总额	Total Profits	753389	147040	1281	-99296	704365
经济效益	**Economic Benefit**					
商品经营费用率 %	Ratio of Operating Costs to Revenue from Principal Business	1.38	0.56	0.87	0.97	1.49
商品销售利润率 %	Ratio of Profit to Sales Revenue	0.43	1.97	1.37	-0.47	0.48

注：限额以上批发业企业中，由于包含了部分视同法人单位，因此财务指标数据资产≠负债+所有者权益。

Note：In wholesale enterprises above designated size, as some deemed legal entities are included, the financial index data asset ≠ liability + owner's equity.

16-6 限额以上零售业财务状况（2022年）
FINANCIAL POSITION OF ENTERPRISES ABOVE DESIGNATED SIZE OF RETAIL TRADE（2022）

单位：万元（10000 yuan）

指 标	Indicator	合计 Total	国有经济 State-owned Enterprises	集体经济 Collective-owned Enterprises	外商及港澳台经济 Foreign Funded Enterprises and Enterprises with Funds from Hong Kong, Macao and Taiwan	其他 Others
单位数	**Number of Enterprises**	**938**	**7**		**56**	**875**
年末资产负债	**Year-end Assets-Liability**					
资产总计	Total Assets	10452020	80159		3660721	6711139
流动资产合计	Sub-total of Current Assets	7388133	25369		2657138	4705626
负债合计	Total Liabilities	9052017	31787		2783409	6236822
所有者权益合计	Total Owners' Equities	1865165	48372		754849	1061944
损益及分配	**Loss, Profits and Distribution**					
营业收入	Revenue from Principal Business	16515002	61161		3132425	13321415
营业成本	Cost of Principal Business	14712158	52460		2710775	11948923
营业税金及附加	Taxes and Extra Charges on Principal Business	47514	314		15469	31732
营业利润	Profits from Principal Business	39805	3055		24233	12517
其他业务利润	Profits from other Business	155543			26365	129178
销售费用	Operating Costs	1220596	3846		237457	979293
管理费用	Management Expenses	429857	4279		132150	293429
财务费用	Financial Expenses	76090	197		9517	66376
利润总额	Total Profits	55499	3632		24073	27794
经济效益	**Economic Benefit**					
商品经营费用率 %	Ratio of Operating Costs to Revenue from Principal Business	7.39	6.29		7.58	7.35
商品销售利润率 %	Ratio of Profit to Sales Revenue	0.34	5.94		0.77	0.21

注：限额以上批发业企业中，由于包含了部分视同法人单位，因此财务指标数据资产≠负债+所有者权益。

Note：In wholesale enterprises above designated size, as some deemed legal entities are included, the financial index data asset ≠ liability + owner's equity.

16-7 分市、区亿元以上商品交易市场成交情况（2022 年）
BASIC STATISTICS ON COMMODITY EXCHANGE MARKETS OF TRANSACTION VALUE OVER 100 MILLION YUAN BY REGION（2022）

市、区名称	Region	亿元商品交易市场数量（个）Number of Commodity Exchange Markets of Transaction Value over 100 Million Yuan（unit）			亿元商品交易市场成交额（万元）Turnover of Commodity Exchange Markets of Transaction Value over 100 Million yuan（10000 yuan）		
		合计 Total	#综合市场 Integrated Markets	#专业市场 Special Markets	合计 Total	#综合市场 Integrated Markets	#专业市场 Special Markets
全　市	**Whole Municipal**	**51**	**15**	**36**	**12617421**	**5107267**	**7510154**
市南区	Shinan District						
市北区	Shibei District	7	1	6	670107	421458	248649
李沧区	Licang District	3	1	2	281685	97805	183880
崂山区	Laoshan District	2		2	35807		35807
黄岛区	Huangdao District	7	2	5	822645	275551	547094
城阳区	Chengyang District	1	1		2573079	2573079	
即墨区	Jimo District	6	1	5	5991640	1150160	4841480
胶州市	Jiaozhou	16	7	9	1537576	427300	1110276
平度市	Pingdu	9	2	7	704882	161914	542968
莱西市	Laixi						

主要统计指标解释

社会消费品零售总额 指各种经济类型的批发和零售业、住宿和餐饮业以及其他行业对城乡居民和社会集团的消费品零售额总和。该指标从 2003 年开始不再包括制造业零售额和农民对非农居民的零售额。

商品购进总额 指从本企业（单位）以外的单位和个人购进（包括从国外直接进口）作为转卖或加工后转卖的商品金额（含增值税）。这个指标反映批发零售贸易业从国内、国外市场上购进商品的总价。商品购进总额包括：

（1）从工农业生产者购进的商品；

（2）从出版社、报社的出版发行部门购进的图书、杂志和报纸；

（3）从各种类型的批发零售贸易企业（单位）购进的商品；

（4）从其他单位购进的商品，如从机关、团体、企业、单位购进的剩余物资，从餐饮业、服务业购进的商品，从海关、市场管理部门购进的缉私和没收的商品，向居民收购的废旧商品等；

（5）从国（境）外直接进口的商品，但不包括企业（单位）为自身经营用和未通过买卖行为而收入的商品以及销售退回、商品损益等。

商品销售总额 指对本企业（单位）以外的单位和个人出售（包括对国（境）外直接出口）的商品金额（包括售给本单位消费用的商品，含增值税）。这个指标反映批发零售贸易业在国内市场上销售商品以及出口商品的总价。商品销售总额包括：

（1）售给城乡居民和社会集团消费用的商品；

（2）售给工业、农业、建筑业、运输邮电业、批发零售贸易业、餐饮业、服务业等作为生产、经营使用的商品；

（3）售给批发零售贸易业作为转卖或加工后转卖的商品；

（4）对国（境）外直接出口的商品。

不包括：出售本企业（单位）自用的废旧包装用品，未通过买卖行为付出的商品，经本单位介绍，由买卖双方直接结算，本单位只收取手续费的业务，购货退出的商品以及商品损耗和损失等。

Explanatory Notes on Main Statistical Indicators

Total Retail Sales of Consumer Goods refers to the sum of retail sales of consumer goods sold by all sectors of the national economy to urban and rural residents and social groups. Sectors of the national economy include wholesale and retail trade, accommodation and catering trade and others. Since 2003, retail sales of manufacture and retail sales of rural residents to urban residents are excluded in total retail sales.

Total Purchases of Commodities refers to the total value (VAT included) of purchases of commodities by the enterprises (establishments) from other establishments or individuals (including direct import from abroad) for the purpose of re-selling, either with or without further processing of the commodities purchased. This indicator is used to show the total value of purchases of commodities by wholesale and retail establishments from domestic and overseas markets. The total purchases include:

(1) agricultural and industrial products purchased from producers;

(2) books, magazines and newspapers purchased from distribution departments of the publishers;

(3) commodities purchased from wholesale and retail establishments of different status of registration;

(4) commodities purchased from other units, such as surplus materials purchased from government agencies, enterprises or institutions, commodities purchased from catering and service establishments, confiscated goods purchased from customs authorities or

market management agencies, second–hand goods and wastes purchased from residents ;

(5) commodities directly imported from abroad. Excluded are commodities purchased by enterprises (establishments) for use in their own business operation, commodities obtained without buying or selling procedures, rejected commodities, etc.

Total Sales of Commodities refers to value of commodities sold by the establishments to other establishments and individuals (including commodities sold to the establishments for consumption, VAT included), including those directly exported to foreign countries. This indicator is used to show the total value of sales of merchandise by wholesale and retail establishments at domestic markets and overseas markets. The total sales include :

(1) commodities sold to urban and rural residents and social groups for their consumption ;

(2) commodities sold to establishments in industry, agriculture, construction, transportation, post and telecommunications, wholesale and retail trades, hotels and catering services, and public utility for their production and operation ;

(3) commodities sold to wholesale and retail establishments for re–selling, with or without further processing ;

(4) commodities for direct export to other countries.

Excluded are selling of waste packaging materials used by the establishments (units) themselves, commodities transferred without buying or selling procedures, commission income from brokerage in transactions for which settlement is directly handled by buyers and sellers, rejected commodities in the purchase, loss in commodities, etc.

17 住宿、餐饮业和旅游

HOTELS, CATERING SERVICES AND TOURISM

简要说明

一、本篇资料的主要内容

本篇资料主要反映全市住宿和餐饮业的经营情况和效益情况以及旅游的基本情况，主要包括住宿和餐饮业经营情况和财务情况、涉外以及国内旅游基本情况等方面的内容。

二、本篇资料的来源

本篇资料中住宿和餐饮业经营情况和财务情况资料来源于住宿和餐饮业统计年报和定期报表统计资料；旅游资料来源于市文化和旅游局。由市统计局外经贸易统计处整理提供。

Brief Introduction

Ⅰ. Main Content

The information in this chapter mainly reflects the operating conditions and benefits of the accommodation and catering industry in the city, as well as the basic conditions of tourism, mainly including the operating conditions and financial conditions of the accommodation and catering industry, foreign-related and domestic tourism, and other aspects.

Ⅱ. Source of Data

The information on the operating and financial status of the accommodation and catering industry in this article comes from the accommodation and catering industry statistical annual reports and periodic statement statistics; the tourism information comes from the Qingdao Municipal Bureau of Culture and Tourism. Provided by the Foreign Economic and Trade Statistics Department of Qingdao Municipal Bureau of Statistics.

17-1　限额以上住宿和餐饮业经营情况（2022 年）

OPERATION OF ACCOMMODATION AND CATERING SERVICES ABOVE DESIGNATED SIZE（2022）

单位：万元（10000 yuan）

项目	Item	营业额 Turnover	客房收入 Income from Guest Rooms	餐费收入 Catering Income	商品销售收入 Income from Commodity Sales	其他收入 Other Income
总　计	**Total**	**1564687.6**	**376682.1**	**1050887.1**	**43164.2**	**93954.2**
一、住宿业	**Hotels**	**607905.1**	**354064.0**	**169787.1**	**7526.6**	**76527.4**
国有企业	State-owned Enterprises	64815.1	22962.8	26637.1	1505.3	13709.9
集体企业	Collective-owned Enterprises	817.4	693.0	124.4		
其他企业	Other Enterprises	542272.6	330408.2	143025.6	6021.3	62817.5
独立门店	Freestanding Stores	531751.4	293967.3	157189.3	6789.0	73805.8
连锁总店	General Chain Stores	3310.9	1757.4	1415.4		138.1
连锁直营店	Chain Store	6949.6	5241.2	756.3	24.9	927.2
连锁加盟店	Franchise Store	41877.1	37920.2	2638.1	285.5	1033.3
其他	Others	24016.1	15177.9	7788.0	427.2	623.0
五星	Five Star Class	100297.8	41121.1	43643.0	2157.5	13376.2
四星	Four Star class	65551.3	30576.9	23723.5	885.0	10365.9
三星	Three Star class	48696.8	28658.4	14917.5	754.5	4366.4
二星	Two Star class	2633.5	1471.6	1113.3	25.1	23.5
一星	One Star class	607.2	607.2			
其他	Others	390118.5	251628.8	86389.8	3704.5	48395.4
二、餐饮业	**Catering Services**	**956782.5**	**22618.1**	**881100.0**	**35637.6**	**17426.8**
国有企业	State-owned Enterprises	15116.3	6980.2	7394.4	659.4	82.3
集体企业	Collective-owned Enterprises					
其他企业	Other Enterprises	941666.2	15637.9	873705.6	34978.2	17344.5
独立门店	Freestanding Stores	480706.0	18264.9	419044.8	27633.5	15762.8
连锁总店	General Chain Stores	289917.2	40.6	286180.6	2990.4	705.6
连锁直营店	Chain Store	27682.2	1219.7	26218.9	123.9	119.7
连锁加盟店	Franchise Store	59298.5		59298.5		
其他	Others	99178.6	3092.9	90357.2	4889.8	838.7

注：2022 年统计口径不含海员数。
Note：The statistical caliber of 2022 does not include the number of seafarers.

17-2 限额以上住宿业财务状况（2022 年）
FINANCIAL SITUATION OF HOTELS ABOVE DESIGNATED SIZE（2022）

单位：万元（10000 yuan）

指 标	Indicator	合计 Total	国有经济 State-owned Enterprises	集体经济 Collective-owned Enterprises	外商及港澳台经济 Foreign Funded Enterprises and Enterprises with Funds from Hong Kong, Macao and Taiwan	其他 Others
单位数	**Number of Enterprises**	**416**	**24**		**11**	**380**
年末资产负债	**Year-end Assets-Liability**					
资产总计	Total Assets	1648269	138691		233957	1274214
流动资产合计	Sub-total of Current Assets	851563	73878		102468	674726
负债合计	Total Liabilities	1475328	90031		183250	1201595
所有者权益合计	Total Owners' Equities	178151	48660		58601	69937
损益及分配	**Loss, Profits and Distribution**					
营业收入	Revenue from Principal Business	580872	62069		53674	464314
营业成本	Cost of Principal Business	255661	21255		17437	216628
营业税金及附加	Taxes and Extra Charges on Principal Business	7663	1019		2344	4300
营业利润	Profits from Principal Business	-51563	-8949		-3151	-39597
其他业务利润	Profits from other Business	6683	480		3129	3074
销售费用	Operating Costs	157901	31915		10564	115419
管理费用	Management Expenses	202896	17205		28558	156795
财务费用	Financial Expenses	18928	-31		403	18556
利润总额	Total Profits	-41398	-2666		-3327	-35540
其他	**Others**					
应付职工薪酬	Employee Compensation Payable	179984	33137		16209	130504
营业利润率	Operating Profit Margin	-7.13	-4.30		-6.20	-7.65

17-3 限额以上餐饮业财务状况（2022 年）
FINANCIAL SITUATION OF CATERING SERVICES ABOVE DESIGNATED SIZE（2022）

单位：万元（10000 yuan）

指　标	Indicator	合计 Total	国有经济 State-owned Enterprises	集体经济 Collective-owned Enterprises	外商及港澳台经济 Foreign Funded Enterprises and Enterprises with Funds from Hong Kong, Macao and Taiwan	其他 Others
单位数	**Number of Enterprises**	**550**	**7**		**14**	**529**
年末资产负债	**Year-end Assets-Liability**					
资产总计	Total Assets	685679	22637		195705	467337
流动资产合计	Sub-total of Current Assets	388856	15384		66077	307395
负债合计	Total Liabilities	586818	19097		177673	390049
所有者权益合计	Total Owners' Equities	98258	3540		18032	76685
损益及分配	**Loss，Profits and Distribution**					
营业收入	Revenue from Principal Business	909108	13714		257342	638052
营业成本	Cost of Principal Business	560355	11478		137118	411760
营业税金及附加	Taxes and Extra Charges on Principal Business	1216	101		309	805
营业利润	Profits from Principal Business	–4050	–5479		20797	–19368
其他业务利润	Profits from other Business	1740	3		495	1242
销售费用	Operating Costs	222640	1445		70394	150801
管理费用	Management Expenses	122849	6340		26305	90204
财务费用	Financial Expenses	10666	–41		4844	5863
利润总额	Total Profits	–1454	–5434		20730	-16751
其他	**Others**					
应付职工薪酬	Employee Compensation Payable	209599	4894		60575	144130
营业利润率	Operating Profit Margin	–0.16	–39.62		8.06	–2.63

17-4 入境旅游人数(2000—2022年)

NUMBER OF OVERSEA VISITOR ARRIVALS（2000—2022）

项　目	Item	2000年	2005年	2010年	2012年
总　计	**Total**	**237465**	**684407**	**1080511**	**1270113**
一、外国人	**Foreigner**	**177098**	**596177**	**826628**	**877593**
#韩国	Korea	69878	295111	382225	338383
日本	Japan	67215	177121	242082	185613
美国	USA	10384	23284	35539	48431
俄罗斯	Russia	4820	12062	15793	26432
德国	Germany	3820	10646	21626	26311
新加坡	Singapore	6321	6060	13444	16316
英国	UK	2798	5744	17639	28385
加拿大	Canada	1865	4397	9279	11678
法国	France	2491	5166	11766	15595
意大利	Italy	1555	3963	3867	5622
澳大利亚	Australia	1817	4257	8223	16644
菲律宾	Philippines	7947	3459	14140	7546
泰国	Thailand	780	3261	2572	2369
印尼	Indonesia	1241	2349	7863	4571
新西兰	New Zealand	442	710	1597	6448
二、港澳和台湾同胞	**Chinese Compatriots from Hong Kong，Macao and Taiwan**	**60367**	**88230**	**253883**	**392520**

注：2022年统计口径不含海员数。
Note：The statistical caliber of 2022 does not include the number of seafarers.

17-5 入境旅游收入(2000—2019年)

EARNINGS FROM INTERNATIONAL TOURISM（2000—2019）

项　目	Item	2000年	2005年	2010年	2011年
总　计	**Total**	**118164**	**340899**	**399688**	**441171**
旅游购物	Shopping	20742	67047	74104	80823
住宿费	Accommodation	17443	37277	43933	59823
餐饮费	Dining	11223	33557	38747	40191
交通费	Transportation	35252	128112	145551	134425
邮电费	Postal and Telecommunication	5502	18394	19081	16720
文化娱乐费	Culture and Entertainment	6894	20240	24032	36132
游览	Sightseeing			22978	51705
其他	Others		36272	31262	21353

注：因新冠肺炎疫情影响，2020年、2021年、2022年未开展此项统计。
Note：Due to the impact of the COVID-19 epidemic, this statistic was not conducted in 2020, 2021, and 2022.

单位：人次（person-time）

2013 年	2014 年	2015 年	2016 年	2017 年	2018 年	2019 年	2020 年	2021 年	2022 年
1282814	**1280526**	**1338702**	**1410494**	**1443715**	**1535733**	**1702568**	**188361**	**222857**	**24546**
905415	**951732**	**996191**	**1042213**	**1056800**	**1118860**	**1258240**	**155124**	**201691**	**20472**
338191	366584	389832	68010	432430	451046	507854	73266	87137	6480
146080	135179	140762	151832	164095	174147	192257	41274	70244	4860
54178	57907	62771	68010	73905	79392	87014	9079	6567	1224
26519	25356	28529	30534	32540	37053	44720	4896	2646	171
19014	21723	23425	25456	26636	28646	33256	5874	3536	1387
16305	19975	21310	23713	25257	26060	29001	3942	5043	626
19496	22817	23812	26133	28006	28942	31577	3582	3816	703
9727	9483	10659	11592	12544	15473	16849	2245	2278	868
21422	17828	19388	21836	23507	25035	27218	2708	2335	353
5679	7705	8747	9234	10627	11559	12904	1563	1182	294
11149	15339	16798	18839	20304	21491	23344	1679	1008	529
18630	6668	7300	7891	8489	9837	11300	1327	274	78
3692	4803	5331	5784	6628	7367	8331	2075	1262	181
10011	6568	5692	6220	7388	9816	11161	515	403	104
1452	2549	2872	3352	4230	7367	7965	429	430	139
377399	**328794**	**342511**	**368281**	**386915**	**416873**	**444328**	**33237**	**21166**	**4074**

单位：万元（10000 yuan）

2012 年	2013 年	2014 年	2015 年	2016 年	2017 年	2018 年	2019 年
519495	**511158**	**503900**	**566742**	**656966**	**694103**	**798374**	**1084000**
93872	94055	109246	122473	141970	129381	102192	264604
59378	58577	62232	69879	81004	77184	150893	134308
51378	51065	44041	49589	57483	68091	122950	95717
170238	180945	160492	180791	209573	249113	273842	351975
23014	22950	19400	21593	25031	33248	16766	42059
32832	32103	33409	36271	42045	42201	62273	70243
32832	32152	44192	49930	57879	40674	33532	90839
55951	39311	30888	36216	41982	54211	35927	34254

17-6 国内旅游人数及收入(2022年)
NUMBER OF DOMESTIC TOURISTS AND INCOME（2022）

指　　标	Indicator	单位	Unit	2022年
国内旅游人数	Number of Domestic Tourists	万人次	10000 person-times	6581.3
1. 过夜旅游者人数	Number of Overnight Tourists	万人次	10000 person-times	2975.9
2. 不过夜旅游者（一日游人数）	Number of Non-overnight（One-day Sightseeing）Tourists	万人次	10000 person-times	3605.4
国内旅游人均花费	Per Capita Expenditure of Domestic Tourist	元	yuan	1529.2
国内旅游收入	Earings from Domestic Tourism	亿元	100 million yuan	1006.4
1. 接待过夜旅游者收入	Earings from Overnight Tourists	亿元	100 million yuan	691.3
2. 接待不过夜旅游者（一日游）收入	Earnings form Non-overnight（One-day Sightseeing）Tourists	亿元	100 million yuan	315.1

主要统计指标解释

住宿餐饮业营业额 指住宿和餐饮业法人企业、产业活动单位在经营活动中因提供服务或销售商品等取得的收入，包括客房收入、餐费收入、商品销售收入和其他收入。客房收入指住宿和餐饮业法人企业、产业活动单位在经营活动中因提供住宿服务取得的客房收入。餐费收入指住宿和餐饮业法人企业、产业活动单位因为顾客提供就餐服务取得的收入，包括经烹饪、调制加工后出售的各种食品，如主食、炒菜、凉拌菜等的收入。商品销售收入指住宿和餐饮业法人企业、产业活动单位伴随服务而出售商品所取得的收入。其他收入指营业收入中除客房收入、餐费收入、商品销售收入以外的其他收入，包括娱乐、健身和商务服务等。

国内旅游者 是指不以谋求职业、获取报酬为目的，离开惯常居住环境，到国内其他地方从事参观、游览、度假等旅游活动（包括外出探亲、疗养、考察、参加会议和从事商务、科技、文化、教育、宗教活动过程中的旅游活动），出行距离超过 10 公里，出游时间超过 6 小时，但不超过 12 个月的我国大陆居民。

入境旅游者 指来我国参观、访问、旅行、探亲、访友、休养、考察、参加会议和从事经济、科技、文化、教育、体育、宗教等活动的外国人、华侨、港澳和台湾同胞的人数。不包括外国在我国的常驻机构，如领事馆、通讯社、企业办事处的工作人员；来我国常住一年以上的外国专家、留学生人员。

Explanatory Notes on Main Statistical Indicators

Business Revenue of Hotels and Catering Services refer to revenue received from providing services or selling commodities by corporate enterprises and establishments engaged in hotel and catering services, including income from hotel rooms, from catering services, from selling of commodities and from other services. Income from hotel rooms refers to income of corporate enterprises and establishments by providing lodging services. Income from catering services refers to income of corporate enterprises and establishments by providing catering services, including selling of cooked or prepared foods such as stable food, cooked dishes or cold dishes. Income from selling of commodities refers to income of corporate enterprises and establishments by selling commodities that accompany the services they provide. Income from other activities refers to income received other than income from hotel rooms, catering services or selling of commodities, such as income from providing recreation, fitness or business services.

Domestic Tourists refers to residents Chinese mainland who are not for the purpose of seeking employment, remuneration, and leaving the usual living environment, elsewhere to engage in domestic visitors, sightseeing, vacation travel (including to go out to visit relatives, infirmary, observing, participate in the meeting and engage in business, science and technology, culture, education, religious activities in the course of tourism activities), trip distance of more than 10 km, trips longer than six hours, but not more than 12 months.

Entrance Tourists refer to the foreigners, overseas Chinese, Hong Kong, Macao and Taiwan compatriots who come to China to tour, visit, travel, visit relatives and friends, recuperate, investigate, attend conferences and engage in economic, technological, cultural, educational, sports, religious and other activities. It does not include staff of foreign permanent institutions in China, such as consulates, news agencies, and corporate offices; foreign experts and overseas students who have come to China for more than one year.

主要统计指标解释

Explanatory Notes on Main Statistical Indicators

教育、科技和文化 18

EDUCATION, SCIENCE & TECHNOLOGY AND CULTURE

简 要 说 明

一、本篇资料的主要内容

本篇资料主要反映全市教育、科技和文化事业基本情况。教育部分主要包括高等教育、中等教育、初等教育、成人教育、职业教育、幼儿园等方面的基本情况。科技部分主要包括科研机构、科学技术奖励。文化部分主要包括文化、文物、广播、电视、报纸杂志出版、图书出版等方面的发展状况。

二、本篇资料的来源

1. 教育部分，技工学校的资料来源于市人力资源和社会保障局，其他资料来源于市教育局。

2. 科技部分，科研机构及科技奖励资料来源于市科技局。

3. 文化部分，图书、杂志、报纸出版有关资料来源于青岛出版集团、海大出版社，其他资料来源于市文化和旅游局。

本篇资料由市统计局人口就业和社会科技文化统计处整理提供。

Brief Introduction

Ⅰ. Main Content

Data in this chapter show the basic conditions of education, science & technology and culture. Data on education show the development of higher education secondary education, primary education, adult education, vocational education and kindergartens. Data on science & technology show the basic conditions of science research institutions, scientific and technological achievements and prizes, scientific& technological activities of large and medium- size industrial enterprises. Data on culture show the basic conditions of arts, cultural relics,broadcasting, television and publication of newspapers magazines and books.

Ⅱ. Source of Data

1.In education component, data on the basic conditions of technical schools are provided by Qingdao Municipal Bureau of Human Resources and Social Security, and the other data on education are provided by Qingdao Municipal Bureau of Education.

2.In science & technology component, data on science research institutions and scientific & technological achievements and prizes are provided by Qingdao Municipal Bureau of Science and Technology Data on scientific and technological activities are from the annual report of scientific and technological activities, which is provided by Qingdao Municipal Bureau of Statistics.

3.In the cultural part, the related materials for books, magazines, and newspapers are from Qingdao Publishing Group and Haida Publishing House, Other materials are from the Municipal Bureau of Culture and Tourism.

The information in this article was compiled and provided by the Population, Employment and Social Science, Technology and Culture Statistics Department of Qingdao Bureau of Statistics.

18-1　各级各类学校基本情况（2022 年）
BASIC STATISTICS ON SCHOOLS BY LEVEL AND TYPE OF SCHOOL（2022）

项　目	Item	学校数（所）Schools（unit）	毕业生数（人）Graduates（person）	招生数（人）New Students Enrollment（person）	在校学生数（人）Students Enrollment（person）	教职工数（人）Teachers and Staff（person）	#专任教师 Full-time Teachers
研究生	Postgraduates	8	15495	21970	67281	23654	15663
普通高等学校	Regular Institutions of Higher Education	27	125058	146859	472280	37080	25885
普通中等职业学校	Regular Secondary Vocational School	53	29746	27782	92381	8472	7064
技工学校	Technical Schools	17	8796	15316	39973	3330	2196
普通中学	Regular Secondary Schools	363	139383	151609	450106	46850	39715
#初中	Junior Secondary Schools	274	95004	93682	292537	28795	25943
#高中	Senior Secondary Schools	89	44379	57927	157569	18055	13772
小学	Primary Schools	672	93153	125367	664452	37542	40505
特殊教育学校	Special Education Schools	15	322	303	2486	863	707
幼儿园	Kindergartens	2274	112301	89698	352406	50145	29341
成人高等学校	Adult Institutions of Higher Education	1	86264	88127	196713		

注：1. 普通中等职业学校包含普通中专学校、成人中专学校、职业高中学校。
2. 普通中等职业学校自 2021 年起按照学校类别统计学生数，2020 年以前是按学生身份统计学生数。
3. 因九年一贯制学校的教职工数计入初中，完全中学、十二年一贯制学校的教职工数计入高中，而专任教师是按照教育层次进行归类，存在小学教职工数据小于专任教师数据的情况。

Notes：1.Regular Secondary Vocational Schools include: Secondary Specialized Schools, Adult Secondary Specialized Schools, Vocational High schools.
2.The number of students in regular secondary vocational schools has been counted by school category from 2021, and by student identity before 2020.
3.Because the number of teaching and administrative staff in nine-year schools is included in junior high schools, and the number of full-central schools and 12-year schools is included in senior high schools, while full-time teachers are classified according to education levels, therefore, the data of primary school teaching and administrative staff is less than that of full-time teachers.

18-2 主要年份各级各类学校在校学生数
MAJOR YEAR' S STUDENTS ENROLLMENT OF SCHOOLS BY LEVEL AND TYPE OF SCHOOL

单位：人（person）

年份 Year	普通高等学校 Regular Institutions of Higher Education	中等学校 Secondary Schools	普通中学 Regular Secondary Schools	普通中等职业学校 Regular Secondary Vocational School	技工学校 Technical Schools	中等专业学校 Specialized Secondary Schools	职业中学 Vocational Schools	小学 Primary Schools
1949	1007	13804	12204			1600		213470
1952	2761	27951	24181			3770		413286
1957	3133	56689	51604			4985	100	482397
1962	4381	62646	58639		973	2791	243	522921
1965	2987	99605	88187		523	9405	1490	788485
1970	320	222521	220262			105	2154	728433
1975	1151	350309	346403		762	3144		928153
1978	3465	464584	457460		865	4269	2000	634905
1980	6783	325935	318193		1203	5195	1344	816970
1985	10631	327446	279915		2111	11475	33945	691341
1988	14408	352576	306943		4881	11819	28933	629212
1990	15433	351365	296163		5516	15118	34568	632314
1991	15491	353410	298568		5803	14618	34421	612772
1992	16470	367480	307903		6572	14763	38242	585381
1993	23858	383043	318179		7244	16877	40743	583585
1994	25018	420077	347667		8094	20582	43734	593419
1995	24908	450212	372335		8089	23744	46044	595891
1996	26076	468561	382760		8719	26951	50131	607284
1997	27434	463619	362305		11131	28543	61640	626749
1998	29507	442525	336918		10861	28757	65989	625308
1999	33681	459520	352238		10091	26955	70236	583594

注：自 2021 年起中等学校校生学生数包含普通中学、普通中等职业学校和技工学校在校生数。

Note：The number of students enrolled in secondary schools from 2021 includes the number of students enrolled in regular secondary schools, regular secondary vocational schools, and technical schools.

18-2 续表
Continued

单位：人（person）

年份 Year	普通高等学校 Regular Institutions of Higher Education	中等学校 Secondary Schools	普通中学 Regular Secondary Schools	普通中等职业学校 Regular Secondary Vocational School	技工学校 Technical Schools	中等专业学校 Specialized Secondary Schools	职业中学 Vocational Schools	小学 Primary Schools
2000	46131	497391	398458		9847	25192	63894	534922
2001	60728	542400	443693		11346	25358	62003	499147
2002	82539	575599	467628		13465	27421	67085	478634
2003	168439	586704	461435		21100	28948	75221	467560
2004	201739	598804	436117		30253	30881	101553	476897
2005	239761	569230	391148		38160	33522	106400	479781
2006	260339	554308	365192		40578	32051	116487	483892
2007	264917	558527	360410		39950	28011	130156	484775
2008	269314	582932	373884		40592	25330	143126	477230
2009	275157	564476	377427		36518	22739	127792	465031
2010	284788	535079	380025		32480	24014	98560	462722
2011	291453	505051	373226		31028	25905	74892	479513
2012	296645	489103	369580		27099	27005	65419	484985
2013	300246	484025	365110		28932	28389	61594	496343
2014	313486	479260	362599		29740	28751	58170	516529
2015	322260	467231	355401		30202	33038	48590	536492
2016	340875	470333	356107		30589	32710	50927	547231
2017	346328	490796	372196		33179	32882	52539	550540
2018	397982	500872	385443		32110	31879	51440	569923
2019	415824	521758	408953		32733	30555	49517	583784
2020	430671	546747	430426		33432	33122	49767	603763
2021	457201	571597	445941	90220	35436			630538
2022	472280	582460	450106	92381	39973			664452

18-3 主要年份普通高等学校基本情况
MAJOR YEAR'S BASIC STATISTICS ON REGULAR INSTITUTIONS OF HIGHER EDUCATION

单位：人（person）

年份 Year	学校数（所）Schools（unit）	毕业生数 Graduates	招生数 New Students Enrollment	在校学生数 Students Enrollment	教职工数 Teachers and Staff	#专任教师 Full-time Teachers
1949	1		250	1007	779	226
1952	2	262	565	2761	12530	308
1957	2	356	755	3133	1308	622
1962	5	647	653	4381	1866	749
1965	3	741	529	2987	1539	623
1970	2	684		320	1178	486
1975	2	460	473	1151	1353	582
1978	4	739	1782	3465	2829	1176
1980	6	431	1717	6783	4182	1606
1985	7	1828	3823	10631	5561	2181
1988	7	3496	4687	14408	6875	2499
1990	7	4495	4745	15433	7305	2624
1991	7	4880	4954	15491	7282	2489
1992	7	4458	5428	16470	7344	2523
1993	7	3140	9449	23858	7366	2520
1994	4	7059	8042	25018	7466	2650
1995	4	7828	7978	24908	7545	2682
1996	4	6691	7956	26076	7606	2745
1997	4	7091	8503	27434	7790	2813
1998	4	6912	8849	29507	7662	2907
1999	4	7202	11584	33681	7662	2928
2000	6	7128	18427	46131	8030	3278

18-3 续表
Continued

单位：人（person）

年份 Year	学校数（所） Schools （unit）	毕业生数 Graduates	招生数 New Students Enrollment	在校学生数 Students Enrollment	教职工数 Teachers and Staff	#专任教师 Full-time Teachers
2001	6	8991	22787	60728	8706	4058
2002	7	13053	29731	82539	9517	4723
2003	25	25747	61975	168439	18911	10293
2004	25	34860	70022	201739	21437	12347
2005	25	46114	79725	239761	23078	13894
2006	25	55931	79094	260339	24881	15195
2007	25	68354	78728	264917	25956	16005
2008	25	75198	86878	269314	26654	16805
2009	25	69475	81025	275157	26983	16870
2010	25	70450	82220	284788	28145	16996
2011	22	79466	84434	291453	28151	17120
2012	22	79791	87981	296645	29445	18183
2013	22	78974	85707	300246	28958	18396
2014	22	77503	90127	313486	28944	18587
2015	24	79784	92251	322260	29620	19213
2016	26	86270	100525	340875	30390	20151
2017	25	95006	98983	346238	32013	21231
2018	25	105580	118247	397982	32628	21576
2019	24	103684	126423	415824	34259	22849
2020	27	107147	133158	430671	35540	24321
2021	27	114731	146306	457201	36263	25059
2022	27	125058	146859	472280	37080	25885

18-4 分市、区普通中学情况(2022 年)
BASIC STATISTICS ON REGULAR SECONDARY SCHOOLS BY REGION（2022）

单位：人(person)

市、区名称	Region	普通高中 Regular Senior Secondary Schools				普通初中 Regular Junior Secondary Schools			
		学校数(所) Schools (unit)	毕业生数 Graduates	招生数 New Students Enrollment	在校生数 Students Enrollment	学校数(所) Schools (unit)	毕业生数 Graduates	招生数 New Students Enrollment	在校生数 Students Enrollment
全 市	**Whole Municipality**	**89**	**44379**	**57927**	**157569**	**274**	**95004**	**93682**	**292537**
市直属	Municipal Level	27	11499	14389	39630	6	3404	3614	11019
市南区	Shinan District					11	3627	3527	10370
市北区	Shibei District					24	7707	8864	26107
李沧区	Licang District	2	6	21	40	15	4587	5717	15823
崂山区	Laoshan District	3			5	14	2881	3430	10041
黄岛区	Huangdao District	17	6883	11084	26630	44	16500	17053	51160
城阳区	Chengyang District	8	3165	5556	14192	22	9241	11074	31493
即墨区	Jimo District	12	6461	8549	22959	35	15566	13574	43739
胶州市	Jiaozhou	7	5437	6003	16837	25	11495	10299	32033
平度市	Pingdu	9	6745	7591	23681	48	12392	10569	34312
莱西市	Laixi	4	4183	4734	13595	30	7604	5961	26440

18-5　分市、区职业中学、小学情况（2022 年）

BASIC STATISTICS ON VOCATIONAL SECONDARY SCHOOLS AND PRIMARY SCHOOLS BY REGION（2022）

单位：人（person）

市、区名称	Region	普通中等职业学校 Regular Secondary Vocational School				小学 Primary School			
		学校数（所）Schools（unit）	毕业生数 Graduates	招生数 New Students Enrollment	在校生数 Students Enrollment	学校数（所）Schools（unit）	毕业生数 Graduates	招生数 New Students Enrollment	在校生数 Students Enrollment
全　市	**Whole Municipality**	**53**	**29746**	**27782**	**92381**	**672**	**93153**	**125367**	**664452**
市直属	Municipal Level	30	10306	10815	32122	1	767	1092	7079
市南区	Shinan District					29	4980	6245	36072
市北区	Shibei District					64	9910	12165	67226
李沧区	Licang District					41	6290	9526	48745
崂山区	Laoshan District					24	3964	5506	28354
黄岛区	Huangdao District	10	7225	5331	22877	99	16640	25412	127843
城阳区	Chengyang District	3	2228	1304	5293	56	10839	16736	84768
即墨区	Jimo District	3	1646	2068	7234	144	13431	16108	89689
胶州市	Jiaozhou	1	3064	2723	8610	64	9925	13990	72083
平度市	Pingdu	2	2176	2752	8130	102	10559	11679	69029
莱西市	Laixi	4	3101	2789	8115	48	5848	6908	33564

注：1. 市直属中有一所十二年一贯制学校，校数在高中中统计。
2. 自 2021 年起按照学校类别统计学生数，2020 年以前是按学生身份统计学生数。

Notes：1. There is a twelve-year consistent school in the municipality, and the number of schools is counted in high schools.
2. The number of students has been counted by school category from 2021 and by student identity before 2020.

18-6　分市、区中小学教职工情况(2022年)

BASIC STATISTICS ON TEACHERS AND STAFF IN SECONDARY AND PRIMARY SCHOOLS BY REGION（2022）

单位：人（person）

市、区名称	Region	普通中学 Regular Secondary Schools		普通中等职业学校 Regular Secondary Vocational School		小学 Primary Schools	
		教职工数 Teachers and Staff	#专任教师 Full-time Teachers	教职工数 Teachers and Staff	#专任教师 Full-time Teachers	教职工数 Teachers and Staff	#专任教师 Full-time Teachers
全　市	**Whole Municipality**	**46850**	**39715**	**8472**	**7064**	**37542**	**40505**
市直属	Municipal Level	5439	4162	3194	2501	126	587
市南区	Shinan District	1210	1003			2193	2201
市北区	Shibei District	2639	1991			3491	3800
李沧区	Licang District	1806	1317			2417	2667
崂山区	Laoshan District	1627	1095			1660	2074
黄岛区	Huangdao District	7407	6612	1713	1463	6619	6953
城阳区	Chengyang District	4491	3693	645	567	4072	4544
即墨区	Jimo District	7004	5918	894	811	5521	6005
胶州市	Jiaozhou	4487	4169	628	503	4634	4617
平度市	Pingdu	6495	5825	661	597	4410	4613
莱西市	Laixi	4245	3930	737	622	2399	2444

注：因九年一贯制学校的教职工数计入初中，完全中学、十二年一贯制学校的教职工数计入高中，而专任教师是按照教育层次进行归类，存在小学教职工数据小于专任教师数据的情况。

Note：Because the number of teaching and administrative staff in nine-year schools is included in junior high schools, and the number of full-central schools and 12-year schools is included in senior high schools, while full-time teachers are classified according to education levels, therefore, the data of primary school teaching and administrative staff is less than that of full-time teachers.

18-7 分市、区幼儿园基本情况(2022年)
BASIC STATISTICS ON KINDERGARTENS BY REGION（2022）

单位：人（person）

市、区名称	Region	幼儿园（所）Kindergartens（unit）	幼儿数 Children	教职工数 Teachers and Staff	#专任教师 Full-time teachers
全　市	**Whole Municipality**	**2274**	**352406**	**50145**	**29341**
市直属	Municipal Level				
市南区	Shinan District	70	13602	2516	1281
市北区	Shibei District	191	35937	5436	2585
李沧区	Licang District	115	32460	4579	2209
崂山区	Laoshan District	105	16097	3150	1668
黄岛区	Huangdao District	519	75325	10165	6098
城阳区	Chengyang District	211	42023	6738	3773
即墨区	Jimo District	373	49155	6185	4023
胶州市	Jiaozhou	260	38961	6060	3509
平度市	Pingdu	292	32268	3333	2649
莱西市	Laixi	138	16578	1983	1546

18-8　科研机构基本情况（1978—2022 年）

BASIC STATISTICS ON SCIENTIFIC RESEARCH INSTITUTIONS（1978—2022）

年　份 Year	独立自然科研结构（个） Independent Institutions of Natural Scientific Research（unit）	独立自然科研结构中科技人员（人） Personnel of Independent Institutions of Natural Scientific Research（person）	完成科研项目（项） Number of Scientific Research Projects Completed（item）	取得科技成果（项） Number of Achievements in S&T（item）
1978	31	2701	306	306
1980			481	297
1982	41	2345	451	451
1983	48	3182	530	530
1984	53	3312	507	507
1985	52	3673	552	552
1986	63	3998	577	577
1988	101	5199	544	510
1990	141	6046	414	931
1991	72	5665	753	753
1992	71	5726	659	659
1993	69	5545	546	546
1994	69	5540	467	467
1995	59	5286	441	441
1996	58	4738	613	613
1997	54	4577	418	418
1998	52	4142	517	517
1999	58	3771	606	606
2000	54	3637	621	621
2001	50	3191	457	457
2002	52	3248	406	406
2003	53	3246	589	589
2004	50	3226	506	506
2005	50	3234	438	438
2006	50	3291	548	548
2007	50	3432	506	506
2008	42	3709	416	416
2009	43	3727	572	572
2010	44	4088	472	472
2011	47	4548	345	345
2012	48	4967	304	304
2013	48	6057	433	433
2014	50	5438	415	415
2015	54	6037	639	639
2016	57	5722	606	606
2017	57	6017	588	588
2018	58	6017	406	406
2019	58	6417	400	400
2020	49	7379	1309	984
2021	31	5492	1349	1356
2022	32	5516	1250	1600

注：1991 年以后不包括民办科研机构。
Note：Since 1991，private institutions of scientific research are not included.

18-9　独立科学研究机构情况（2022 年）

BASIC STATISTICS ON INDEPENDENT INSTITUTIONS OF SCIENTIFIC RESEARCH（2022）

项　目	Item	单位	Unit	总　计 Total	中央属 Central	地方属 Local
机构数	Number of Institutions	个	unit	55	16	39
职工人数	Staff and Workers	人	person	7855	4647	3208
科技人员	Personnel Engaged in S&T	人	person	6843	4169	2674
经费收入	Funding for S&T	万元	10000 yuan	582457	321105	261352
经费支出	Expenditures for S&T	万元	10000 yuan	572422	322221	250201

18-10　科学技术奖励情况（2022 年）

AWARD STATISTICS ON SCIENCE AND TECHNOLOGY（2022）

项　目	Item	单位	unit	自然科学奖 Natural Science Prizes Awarded	技术发明奖 Invention Prizes Awarded	科技进步奖 Scientific and Technological Progress Prizes Awarded	国际科技合作奖 International S&T Cooperation Prizes Award	最高奖 Highest Prizes Award	青年奖 Youth Award
国家级	National Level	项	item						
特等	Special Grade	项	item						
#一等	First Prize	项	item						
二等	Second Prize	项	item						
省级	Provincial Level	项	item	13	10	55		1	1
#一等	First Prize	项	item	1	3	13			
二等	Second Prize	项	item	12	7	42			
市级	Municipal Level	项	item	10	3	105	1	1	
#一等	First Prize	项	item	3	1	22			
二等	Second Prize	项	item	7	2	83			

注：1. 国际科技合作奖、最高奖不分等级。
　　2. 国家级科学技术奖励最终结果暂未公布。

Notes：1. There is no grade in international scientific and technological cooperation prizes award and highest prizes award.
　　2. The final result of the national science and technology award has not been announced yet.

18-11 文化、文物事业机构、人员数

NUMBER OF CULTURAL AND CULTURAL RELIC INSTITUTIONS AND PERSONNEL

项　目	Item	文化机构数（个） Number of Cultural Institutions（unit）		文化人员数（人） Number of Cultural Personnel（person）	
		2022 年	2021 年	2022 年	2021 年
一、艺术事业	**Art**				
1 . 艺术表演团体	Art Performance Troupes	5	5	276	318
2 . 艺术表演场所	Art Centers	7	7	133	134
3 . 艺术研究机构	Art Research Institutions	1	1	0	38
4 . 艺术展览机构	Art Exhibition Institutions	2	2	40	38
5 . 其他	Others				
二、图书馆事业	**Libraries**				
公共图书馆	Public Libraries	11	11	316	272
#县（区）级图书馆	County Libraries	10	10	217	263
三、群众文化事业	**Nass Culture**				
1 . 群众艺术馆	Nass Art Centers				
2 . 文化馆	Cultural Palaces	11	11	214	225
3 . 文化站	Cultural Centers	137	137	680	607
4 . 其他	Others				

18-12　文化部门艺术剧团情况（2022年）
STATISTICS ON ART TROUPES OF CULTURAL DEPARTMENT（2022）

项　目	Item	剧团（院）数（个） Number of Troupes (theatres) (unit)	职工人数（人） Staff and Workers (person)	演出场次（场） Number of Performances (show)	观众人数（万人次） Number of Spectators (10000 person-times)	演出收入（万元） Income from Ticket Sales (10000 yuan)	#财政补贴（万元） Appropriation Funds (10000 yuan)
总　计	**Total**						
一、按单位性质分	**Divided by Unit Nature**						
事业	Career	5	276	600	25.13	708.3	5434.5
企业	Enterprise	3	524	500	24.7	1043.6	5303.4
二、按艺术门类分	**By Category of Art**						
1. 话剧院	Theatre Drama Troupes	1	111	200	11	489.5	64.7
2. 交响乐团	Symphony Orchestra	1	123	59	4	127.5	3534.4
3. 地方戏曲剧团	Local Opera Troupe	4	153	501	21.1	580.8	2198.1
4. 京剧院	Peking Opera Theatre	1	96	100	3.7	837	1465.9
5. 综合性艺术表演团体	Comprehensive Art Performance Group	1	317	165	10	470.4	2340.6

18-13　图书馆、文化馆情况
STATISTICS ON LIBRARIES AND CULTURAL CENTERS

项　目	Item	单位	Unit	2022年 全市合计 Total	2022年 #市区 Urban Area	2021年 全市合计 Total	2021年 #市区 Urban Area
公共图书馆	**Public Libraries**	个	**unit**	**11**	**10**	**11**	**8**
工作人员	Staff and Workers	人	person	316	217	272	226
藏书册数	Collcetion Books	千册	1000 copies	9743.5	6608.3	8896.6	7774
阅览席位	Seating Capacity of Reading Rooms	张	piece	6255	4635	5984	4663
读者人数	Readers	万人次	10000 person/times	445.5	293.4	378.27	291.9
文化馆	**Cultural Centers**	个	**unit**	**11**	**10**	**11**	**8**

主要统计指标解释

普通高等学校　指通过国家普通高等教育招生考试,招收高中毕业生为主要培养对象,实施高等学历教育的全日制大学、独立设置的学院、独立学院和高等专科学校、高等职业学校及其他普通高教机构。

大学、独立设置的学院主要实施本科及本科层次以上的教育。独立学院主要实施本科层次的教育。高等专科学校、高等职业学校实施专科层次的教育。其他普通高教机构是指承担国家普通招生计划任务不计校数的机构，包括普通高等学校分校、大专班等。

科技活动人员　指直接从事科技活动、专门从事科技活动管理和为科技活动提供直接服务，累计的实际工作时间占全年制度工作时间 10% 及以上的人员。

独立自然科研机构　按照《科学研究和技术服务业非企业单位调查表》表 1 "机构概况" 填报。其中,机构类别为 "1. 县以上政府部门属自然科学与技术领域研究与开发机构（理、工、农、医类）" 全部包含，机构类别为 "4. 县属研究与开发机构" "5. 其他事业单位" 的从事的国民经济行业代码分类中的 731、732、733、734。

取得科技成果　按照《科技研究和技术服务业非企业单位调查表》表 9 "科技产出"，未包含科技论文。

文化事业机构　指从事专业文化工作和为专业文化工作服务的独立建制的单独核算的单位。不包括这些单位另外举办独立核算的其他机构和各部门的业余文化组织。

Explanatory Notes on Main Statistical Indicators

Regular Institutions of Higher Education　refers to full–time universities, independently established colleges, independent colleges and technical colleges, higher vocational schools and other general higher education institutions that have passed the national general higher education enrollment examination and recruited high school graduates as the main training objects.

Universities and independent colleges mainly implement education at the undergraduate level and above. Independent colleges mainly implement education at the undergraduate level. Higher technical colleges and higher vocational schools implement college–level education. Other general higher education institutions refer to institutions that undertake the tasks of the national general enrollment plan without counting the number of schools, including general higher education branch schools, college classes, etc.

Personnel Engaged in S&T Activities　refer to personnel directly engaged in S&T activities, in the management of S&T activities, and in providing direct service to S&T activities, who spend over 10% of the total working hours in a year in S&T activities.

The independent research institutions　The independent research institutions fill in tables in accordance with the "Institutional profile" (Table 1) from the document Survey of non–enterprise units in scientific research and technology services. If the category of institutions is "1. Government departments at or above the county level belonging to natural science and technology research and development institutions (science, industry, agriculture and medicine)" , it covers all. And if the categories of institutions are respectively "4. research and development institutions at county level" , or "5. Other institutional organization" , the codes are 731 732 733 734 respectively according to the National economy industry code classification.

Scientific and technological achievements　are filled according to Table 9 (scientific and technological output) of *Survey of non–enterprise units in scientific research and technology services*, with scientific and technical papers excluded.

Cultural Institutions　refer to entities with independent structure and independent accounting that engage in or serve professional cultural work, and do not include other institutions and amateur cultural organizations of various departments that conduct independent accounting.

体育、卫生和民政、司法 19

SPORTS，PUBLIC HEALTH AND CIVIL AFFAIRS，JUDICIAL AFFAIRS

简要说明

一、本篇资料的主要内容

本篇资料反映全市体育、卫生、民政、司法等社会事业的基本情况。体育部分主要包括主要年份运动员、教练员、裁判员发展人数、体育运动破纪录、获奖情况。卫生部分主要包括各类卫生机构及其人员、床位数。民政部分主要包括婚姻登记、社会救济、社会福利事业基本情况、殡葬服务情况。司法部分主要包括律师、公证、调解、社会治安基本情况。

二、本篇资料的来源

1. 体育部分来源于市体育局。

2. 卫生部分来源于市卫健委。

3. 民政部分来源于市民政局。

4. 司法部分，社会治安资料来源于市公安局，其他资料来源于市司法局。

本篇资料由市统计局人口就业和社会科技文化统计处整理提供。

Brief Introduction

Ⅰ. Main Content

Data in this chapter show the basic conditions of sports, public health, civil affairs and judicial affairs Data on sports are mainly including the number of athletes, coaches and referees, conditions of record and awards. Data on public health are mainly including the number of health institutions, personnel and beds. Data on civil affairs are mainly including the conditions of marriage registration, social relief, social welfare and funeral services. Data on judicial affairs are mainly including the conditions of lawyers, notarization, mediation and social order.

Ⅱ. Source of Data

1. Data on sports are provided by Qingdao Municipal Bureau of Physical.

2. The health part comes from the Qingdao Municipal Health Commission.

3. Data on civil affairs are provided by Qingdao Municipal Bureau of Civil Affairs.

4. In judicial affairs component, data on social order are provided by Qingdao Municipal Bureau of Public Security and the other data are provided by Qingdao Municipal Bureau of Justice.

The information in this article was compiled and provided by the Population, Employment and Social Science, Technology and Culture Statistics Department of Qingdao Bureau of Statistics.

19-1 体育事业情况(2000—2022 年)

STATISTICS ON SPORTS（2000—2022）

单位：人（person）

项 目	Item	2000 年	2005 年	2010 年	2015 年	2016 年	2017 年	2018 年	2019 年	2020 年	2021 年	2022 年
体育部门职工人数	**Staff and Workers in Sports Commissions**	**849**	**834**	**1015**	**795**	**857**	**654**	**682**	**784**	**780**	**832**	**899**
# 运动员	Athletes	90	87	287	259		284	1123	2259	2787	2100	3865
教练员	Coaches	174	235	170		120	133	134	131	133	271	182
重点体校	Key Sports School	126	117	115			1061	1370	881	980	1248	1462
业余体校	Spare Time Sports Schools	142	223				1537	1846	1702	1807	1810	1067
体育专业队	Professional Sports Teams	135	132	192	17	17	5	5				
优秀运动员	Excellent Athletes	90	87	146								1
优秀运动队专职教练员	Full-time Coaches of Excellent Sports Teams	18	23	97	89	120						200
等级裁判员发展人数	**Certified Referees**	**1114**	**275**	**212**	**490**	**167**		**511**	**347**	**519**	**530**	**1559**
# 二级	Second Grades	451	275	169	490	116		319	122	236	437	1027
三级	Third Grades	616							90	283		
等级运动员发展人数	**Certified Athletes**	**343**	**260**	**229**	**259**		**176**	**327**	**829**	**328**	**625**	**511**
# 二级	Second Grades	209	260	229	259		176	290	730	328	568	511
三级	Third Grades	46										
少年级	Junior Grades	88										

19-1 续表
Continued

项 目	Item	单位	Unit	2000 年	2005 年	2010 年	2015 年	2016 年	2017 年	2018 年	2019 年	2020 年	2021 年	2022 年
全年获得奖牌数	**Number of Medals Won in the Year**	枚	**piece**	**347.5**	**669**	**754**	**596**	**729.5**	**3032**	**849**	**1507.5**	**666.5**	**1242**	**1138**
#国家级金牌	Golden Medals at National Level	枚	piece	45	62	14	51	101	104	76	142	40	81	95
国家级银牌	Silver Medals at National Level	枚	piece	28	48	7	44	56	91	81	127	32	81	75
省级金牌	Golden Medals at Provincial Level	枚	piece	116.5	187	459	149	219.5	214.5	264	428.5	372.5	321	313
省级银牌	Silver Medals at Provincial Level	枚	piece	62	174	116	126	135	140	161	289	222	385	273
体育运动破全国记录	**Records Broken the National Records**													
项目	Number of Events	项	item		2	1				1				
人数	Number of Persons	人	person		2	1				1				
次数	Number of Times	人次	person-times		4	1				1				
体育运动破全省记录	**Records Broken the Provincial Records**													
项目	Number of Events	项	item	7	3	1								
人数	Number of Persons	人	person	7	1	1								
次数	Number of Times	人次	person-times	7	3	1				15				

19-2　主要年份卫生事业基本情况
MAJOR YEAR'S BASIC STATISTICS ON PUBLIC HEALTH

年份 Year	卫生机构数（个）Health Institutions（unit）	#医院 Hospitals	医疗床位数（张）Beds in Health Institutions（bed）	#医院 Hospitals	卫生技术人员（人）Medical and Technical Personnel（person）	#医生 Doctors	每千人口拥有医生数（人）Number of Doctors per 1000 Population（person）	每千人口拥有床位数（张）Number of Hospital Beds per 1000 Population（bed）
1949	80	26	1079	970	2637	1292	0.32	0.27
1952	260	34	2943	1691	3748	1559	0.37	0.70
1957	624	45	5163	2656	6941	2578	0.53	1.07
1962	849	149	7167	4526	8279	2972	0.64	1.55
1965	912	162	8428	5003	9051	3586	0.73	1.72
1970	712	170	8613	6603	9591	3761	0.70	1.60
1975	959	181	10902	9078	13558	4566	0.80	1.90
1978	1192	212	13084	10709	16921	5893	1.01	2.24
1980	1253	212	14170	11345	19265	6781	1.14	2.38
1985	1517	219	18469	13214	23413	9694	1.55	2.95
1990	1563	235	23541	16586	27932	13761	2.08	3.56
1991	1579	235	23727	16796	27772	13227	1.98	3.54
1992	1562	236	24765	17269	28305	13157	1.95	3.67
1993	1540	237	24885	17469	28705	13312	1.97	3.68
1994	1335	242	24732	17882	28938	13535	1.99	3.64
1995	1347	228	25282	18126	29816	13840	2.02	3.69
1996	2216	228	24334	18344	30048	13790	2.00	3.53
1997	2193	239	25201	19046	31121	14400	2.07	3.62
1998	2190	237	24887	19083	31623	14327	2.05	3.56
1999	2185	235	25481	19798	31965	14453	2.06	3.62
2000	2911	231	24392	20057	32160	14860	2.10	3.45
2001	3199	217	24755	20313	32765	15772	2.22	3.48
2002	3050	213	21370	20662	31469	13371	1.87	2.99
2003	3111	213	23980	21605	32337	13452	1.87	3.33
2004	2923	219	25432	23465	32937	13953	1.91	3.48
2005	2609	235	30627	28564	33942	15008	2.03	4.13
2006	2834	232	28724	26653	34360	15451	2.06	3.83
2007	2006	251	30062	28107	33807	15018	1.98	3.97
2008	1985	249	32350	29874	36574	16260	2.14	4.25
2009	2017	252	32803	30527	40217	16734	2.19	4.30
2010	2147	254	36066	33383	43285	17696	2.32	4.72
2011	2549	280	39980	35600	47347	18310	2.39	5.22
2012	2607	288	47254	41186	54488	21593	2.81	6.14
2013	2936	285	44876	39725	59961	24113	3.12	5.80
2014	3126	297	47081	42961	62738	24946	3.20	6.03
2015	3146	308	48601	45066	65264	26270	3.35	6.20
2016	7564	322	50649	47309	87733	27675	3.49	6.39
2017	7927	410	55798	46282	76146	30867	3.84	6.94
2018	8027	421	53154	50842	83975	34578	4.23	6.82
2019	8317	427	60519	58492	90361	37813	4.55	7.28
2020	8531	460	64423	62450	94854	39708	4.74	7.70
2021	8574	449	67748	65041	97048	39969	3.90	6.61
2022	8763	456	67984	65360	99121	41279	3.99	6.57

注：自 2016 年起，卫生机构及人员包含村卫生室。
Note：Health agency and personnel includes village clinic as of 2016.

19-3 各类卫生机构、床位、人员数(2022年底)

NUMBER OF HEALTH INSTITUTIONS, BEDS AND EMPLOYED PERSONS (END OF 2022)

项　目	Item	机构数（个）Health Institutions (unit)	床位数（张）Beds in Health Institutions (bed)	人员数（人）Personnel (person)
总　计	**Total**	**8763**	**67984**	**118110**
一、医院合计	**Sub-total of Hospitals**	**456**	**65360**	**82354**
1. 医院	Hospitals	353	58455	73292
#综合医院	General Hospitals	176	32431	45417
中医医院	Hospitals Specialized in Traditional Chinese Medicine	41	7404	9432
中西医结合医院	Hospitals of Combination of Chinese and Western Medicine	2	486	567
专科医院	Specialized Hospitals	127	17700	17739
#口腔医院	Stomatological Hospitals	12	165	1160
眼科医院	Ophthalmology Hospitals	14	822	1197
肿瘤医院	Tumor Hospitals	2	60	78
心血管病医院	Cardiovascular Diseases Hospitals	3	1105	1221
精神病医院	Mental Hospitals	37	8338	4418
传染病医院	Infectious Disease Hospitals	2	636	709
皮肤病医院	The Skin Disease Hospitals	2	100	120
骨科医院	Orthopaedics Hospitals	3	280	272
2. 卫生院	Sanitation Stations	103	6905	9062
二、社区卫生服务中心	**Neighborhood Service Centers**	**99**	**798**	**4685**
三、门诊部	**Outpatient Service Stations**	**407**	**108**	**6327**
四、诊所	**Clinics**	**3222**	**8**	**9767**
五、卫生所、医务室、护理站	**Medical Houses Nursing Station**	**338**	**33**	**900**
六、社区卫生服务站	**Neigborhood Service Stations**	**215**	**204**	**2941**
七、急救中心	**First Aid Centers**	**7**		**241**
八、采供血机构	**Institutions of Blood Collection and Supply**	**2**		**285**
九、妇幼保健院（所、站）	**Maternity and Child Care Centers**	**12**	**363**	**1571**
十、专科疾病防治院（所、站）	**Specialized Disease Prevention & Treatment Institutions**	**6**	**224**	**260**
十一、疾病预防控制中心（防疫站）	**Centers for Disease Control and Prevention (Epidemic Prevention Stations)**	**41**		**1517**
十二、卫生监督所	**Sanitation Control Stations**	**12**		**468**
十三、卫生监督检验所（站）	**Sanitation Control and Test Stations**			
十四、计划生育技术服务机构	**Family Planning Service Institutions**			
十五、健康教育所（站、中心）	**Health Education Stations**			
十六、其他卫生机构	**Other Health Institutions**	**40**	**886**	**1684**
十七、村卫生室	**Village Clinic**	**3906**		**5110**

注：床位数指实有床位数。

Note: The number of beds refers to the number of beds actually available.

#卫生技术人员 Medical and Technical Personnel	#医生 Doctors	注册护士 Registered Nurses	药剂人员 Pharmacists	技师人员 Technician staff
99121	**41279**	**44440**	**4750**	**5551**
70557	**25242**	**35191**	**3675**	**4405**
62903	22228	32274	3079	3820
39573	14370	20011	1847	2360
8083	3084	3735	525	504
486	178	219	61	22
14641	4561	8232	643	929
873	422	361	12	33
814	281	451	31	31
59	25	30	3	1
1027	353	529	45	84
3900	717	2879	158	98
621	173	360	35	44
98	34	48	10	6
208	87	89	12	17
7654	3014	2917	596	585
3941	**1705**	**1548**	**357**	**214**
5309	**2605**	**2258**	**182**	**202**
9518	**6406**	**2893**	**147**	**36**
871	**554**	**298**	**13**	**1**
2530	**1238**	**918**	**253**	**80**
162	**60**	**95**	**1**	**4**
205	**53**	**79**	**1**	**70**
1285	**502**	**547**	**66**	**116**
196	**76**	**73**	**13**	**19**
1091	**560**	**68**	**15**	**157**
361				
918	**218**	**359**	**23**	**247**
2177	**2060**	**113**	**4**	

19-4 分市、区各类卫生机构数(2022年底)

NUMBER OF HEALTH INSTITUTIONS IN VARIOUS TYPES BY REGION (END OF 2022)

市、区名称	Region	机构数(个) Number of Institutions (unit)	医院小计 Sub-total of Hospitals	#医院 Hospitals	#卫生院 Sanitation Stations
全　市	**Whole Municipality**	**8763**	**456**	**353**	**103**
市南区	Shinan District	449	30	30	
市北区	Shibei District	808	63	63	
李沧区	Licang District	536	30	30	
崂山区	Laoshan District	507	27	25	2
黄岛区	Huangdao District	1458	64	48	16
城阳区	Chengyang District	885	40	35	5
即墨区	Jimo District	1136	58	37	21
胶州市	Jiaozhou	1015	38	24	14
平度市	Pingdu	1162	61	32	29
莱西市	Laixi	807	45	29	16

19-4 续表

Continued

市、区名称	Region	采供血机构 Institutions of Blood Collection and Supply	妇幼保健院(所、站) Maternity and Child Care Centers	专科疾病防治院(所、站) Specialized Disease Prevention & Treatment Institutions
全　市	**Whole Municipality**	**1**	**12**	**6**
市南区	Shinan District	1	1	1
市北区	Shibei District		2	
李沧区	Licang District		1	
崂山区	Laoshan District		1	
黄岛区	Huangdao District		2	2
城阳区	Chengyang District		1	
即墨区	Jimo District		1	1
胶州市	Jiaozhou		1	
平度市	Pingdu		1	2
莱西市	Laixi		1	

社区卫生服务中心 Neighborhood Service Centers	社区卫生服务站 Neighborhood Service Stations	门诊部 Outpatient Service Stations	诊所、卫生所、医务室、护理站 Clinics Medical Houses	急救中心 First Aid Centers
98	**216**	**407**	**3560**	**7**
12	25	46	325	
26	63	64	583	1
15	46	39	399	
3	36	29	277	
18	14	76	604	1
12	6	71	346	1
4	20	26	387	1
4		22	269	1
2		25	262	1
2	6	9	108	1

疾病预防控制中心（防疫站） Centers for Disease Control and Prevention（Epidemic Prevention Stations）	卫生监督所 Sanitation Control Stations	村卫生室 Village health room	计划生育技术服务机构 Family Planning Service Institutions	其他卫生机构 Other Health Institutions
41	**12**	**3906**		**41**
1	1			6
2	2			2
1	1			4
1	1	128		4
1	1	668		7
9	1	388		10
23	1	611		3
1	1	677		1
1	1	804		2
1	2	630		2

19-5 分市、区各类卫生床位数(2022 年底)
NUMBER OF SANITARY BEDS IN VARIOUS TYPES BY REGION （END OF 2022）

市、区名称	Region	床位数(张) Beds in Health Institutions (bed)	#医院小计 Sub-total of Hospitals
全　市	**Whole Municipality**	**67984**	**65360**
市南区	Shinan District	8947	8013
市北区	Shibei District	15815	15716
李沧区	Licang District	4070	4014
崂山区	Laoshan District	1468	1319
黄岛区	Huangdao District	10023	9229
城阳区	Chengyang District	4471	4461
即墨区	Jimo District	5803	5726
胶州市	Jiaozhou	5419	5201
平度市	Pingdu	7260	7073
莱西市	Laixi	4708	4608

19-6 分市、区各类卫生人员数(2022 年底)
NUMBER OF HEALTH PERSONNEL BY REGION （END OF 2022）

市、区名称	Region	人员数（人） Personnel (person)	#卫生技术人员 #Medical and Technical Personnel
全　市	**Whole Municipality**	**118110**	**99121**
市南区	Shinan District	15564	13290
市北区	Shibei District	26263	23005
李沧区	Licang District	8452	7370
崂山区	Laoshan District	5324	4219
黄岛区	Huangdao District	18111	14534
城阳区	Chengyang District	9823	8109
即墨区	Jimo District	9554	8003
胶州市	Jiaozhou	8443	6957
平度市	Pingdu	9839	8102
莱西市	Laixi	6737	5532

医院 Hospitals	卫生院 Sanitation Stations	门诊部 Outpatient Service Stations	妇幼保健院（所、站） Maternity and Child Care Centers	专科疾病防治院（所、站） Specialized Disease Centers
58455	**6905**	**108**	**363**	**224**
8013		34		
15716		17		
4014		15		
1292	27			
7780	1449	19	100	114
4213	248			
4784	942	16	40	
4108	1093	2	98	
4883	2190	5	65	110
3652	956		60	

# 医生 #Doctors	注册护士 Registered Nurses	药剂人员 Pharmacists	技师人员 Technician staff	其他人员 Other Personnel
41279	**44440**	**4750**	**5551**	**18989**
5125	6476	557	722	2274
9892	10150	1093	1370	3258
3127	3471	378	338	1082
2054	1619	230	226	1105
5949	6558	722	841	3577
3241	3551	410	490	1714
3473	3411	418	393	1551
2896	3201	293	320	1486
3248	3685	339	503	1737
2274	2318	310	348	1205

19-7 提供住宿的社会服务机构单位情况(2022年)
SITUATION OF SOCIAL SERVICE INSTITUTIONS PROVIDING ACCOMMODATION (2022)

市、区名称	Region	单位数(个) Number of Institutions (unit)	年末职工人数(人) Number of Staff and Workers at Year-end (person)	年末床位数(张) Number of Beds at Year-end (bed)
全　市	**Whole Municipality**	**307**	**7661**	**44408**
市本级	Municipal Level	4	183	1257
市南区	Shinan District	24	1282	3355
市北区	Shibei District	71	1581	9839
李沧区	Licang District	39	1029	5142
崂山区	Laoshan District	15	409	2689
黄岛区	Huangdao District	35	854	5198
城阳区	Chengyang District	24	736	4933
即墨区	Jimo District	19	277	2588
胶州市	Jiaozhou	23	397	3026
平度市	Pingdu	33	491	3038
莱西市	Laixi	20	422	3343

19-8 社会救济情况(2022年)
BASIC STATISTICS ON SOCIAL RELIEF (2022)

市、区名称	Region	城镇居民最低生活保障人数(人) Number of Persons Receiving Minimun Living Allowance in Urban Area (person)	城镇居民最低生活保障家庭数(户) Number of Households Receiving Minimum Living Allowance in Urban Area (household)	城镇低保资金支出(万元) Urban low-security capital expenditure (10000 yuan)
全　市	**Whole Municipality**	**16668**	**11889**	**20586.8**
市南区	Shinan District	2769	2047	3499
市北区	Shibei District	10014	7054	12553.7
李沧区	Licang District	1653	1150	1970.2
崂山区	Laoshan District	114	63	116.8
黄岛区	Huangdao District	593	446	646.3
城阳区	Chengyang District	179	131	232.3
即墨区	Jimo District	463	338	544.6
胶州市	Jiaozhou	454	339	527.3
平度市	Pingdu	287	207	321.4
莱西市	Laixi	142	114	175.2

年末在院人数（人） Residences at Year-end （person）	老年人 Senior Citizens	青壮年 Young and middle-aged	少年儿童 Youth
16446	**16260**		**159**
190	4		159
1411	1411		
3889	3889		
2160	2160		
720	720		
1583	1583		
1756	1756		
747	747		
1237	1237		
1517	1517		
1236	1236		

农村居民最低生活保障人数（人） Number of Persons Receiving Minimum living Allowance in Rural Area（person）	农村居民最低生活保障家庭数（户） Number of Households Receiving Minimum Living Allowance in Rural Area（household）	农村低保资金支出（万元） Rural low-security capital expenditure（10000 yuan）
60828	**41406**	**55451.3**
1585	836	1507.4
11006	7665	9898
3108	2022	3363.9
15392	11009	17292.4
8919	6091	7167.6
16005	10482	12539
4813	3301	3683

19-9 分市、区婚姻登记情况(2022年)

BASIC STATISTICS ON MARRIAGE REGISTRATION BY REGION (2022)

市、区名称	Region	准予登记结婚 Registered Marriages		
		合计(对) Total (couple)	初婚(人) First Marriages (person)	恢复结婚(对) Resumed Marriages (couple)
全　市	**Whole Municipality**	**50006**	**74212**	**4514**
市本级	Municipal Level			
市南区	Shinan District	3693	5395	436
市北区	Shibei District	5378	7369	588
李沧区	Licang District	3500	5152	336
崂山区	Laoshan District	3047	5045	164
黄岛区	Huangdao District	9854	14375	903
城阳区	Chengyang District	5401	8155	565
即墨区	Jimo District	5661	9204	276
胶州市	Jiaozhou	4694	6806	518
平度市	Pingdu	5911	8555	513
莱西市	Laixi	2867	4156	215

再婚（人）Remarriages（person）		准予登记离婚（对）Registered Divorces（couple）	涉外婚姻登记 Registered Marriages with Foreigner	
男 Male	女 Female		结婚登记（对）Marriage registration（couple）	离婚登记（对）Divorce registration（couple）
12573	**13227**	**16060**	**88**	**12**
1038	953	1290	16	1
1723	1664	2232	24	6
936	912	1331	5	1
557	492	637	10	1
2560	2773	3299	9	
1296	1351	1531	11	2
1021	1097	1463	3	
1221	1361	1543	5	
1490	1777	1817	2	1
731	847	917	3	

19-10 律师、公证、调解、社会治安基本情况(2000—2022 年)
BASIC STATISTICS ON LAWYERS，NOTARIZATION，MEDIATION AND SOCIAL ORDER（2000—2022）

项　目	Item	单位	Unit	2000 年	2005 年	2009 年	2010 年	2012 年
一、律师工作	**Lawyers**							
律师事务所	Law Offices	个	Unit	76	116	203	222	266
律师工作者	Lawyers	人	person	1439	1941	3144	2487	3130
专职	Full-time Lawyers	人	person	971	1542	1934	2377	2944
兼职(含特邀)	Part-time Lawyers	人	person	150	73	86	94	107
请常年法律顾问单位	Units with Permanent Legal Advisors	个	Unit	2508	3564	4457	4779	5228
全年办理民事代理	Agent of Civil Gases	件	case	5571	11104	29025	26935	30586
刑事辩护	Defender of Criminal Cases	件	case	1755	3003	3758	3964	4935
非诉讼事件	Agent of Non-litigious Legal Affairs	件	case	5251	6501	5897	4274	4251
解答法律询问	Agent of Legal Advisory Services	件	case	58385	27880	30123	21102	45388
代写法律事务文书	Agent of Legal Documents Written on Behalf of Clients	件	case	9335	8595	6015	6210	6388
二、公证工作	**Notarization**							
公证处	Notary Offices	个	Unit	15	15	13	13	13
公证人员	Notarial Personnel	人	person	152	196	214	214	225
公证员	Notaries	人	person	106	112	118	117	118
办理公证文书	Notarized Documents	件	case	120849	105787	97019	94077	87703
三、人民调解	**People's Mediation**							
人民调解委员会	People's Mediation Committees	个	Unit	9750	11480	9643	8014	8426
调解人员	Mediators	人	person	34714	46735	32675	27820	27421
调解民间纠纷	Civil Disputes Mediated	件	case	18501	13658	14660	20550	23999
四、社会治安	**Social Order**							
交通事故发生次数	Traffic Accidents	次	time	15601	7051	2570	2313	1951
#死亡人数	Deaths	人	person	1371	776	402	393	343
#受伤人数	Injuries	人	person	8620	6639	2943	2504	1913
#经济损失	Losses	万元	10000 yuan	4815.70	2208.20	854.80	811.27	652.10
火灾发生次数	Fire Accidents	次	time	3088	1948	773	683	366
#死亡人数	Deaths	人	person	10	3	5	9	6
#受伤人数	Injuries	人	person	43	3		4	2
#经济损失	Losses	万元	10000 yuan	1531.06	550.40	865.50	5566.11	601.90

注：1. 自 2020 年起，火灾发生次数改为全口径统计，含轻微火灾发生次数。

2. 2021 年火灾发生死亡人数含刑事死亡人数；火灾发生受伤人数含刑事受伤人数。

Notes：1. Since 2020, the number of fire occurrences has been changed to full-caliber statistics, including the number of minor fires occurrences.

2. The death toll in 2021 includes criminal deaths; the number of fire injuries includes the number of criminal injuries.

2013 年	2014 年	2015 年	2016 年	2017 年	2018 年	2019 年	2020 年	2021 年	2022 年
285	322	337	355	371	394	427	458	501	519
3143	3637	3896	4260	4839	5451	5960	6470	7187	8021
2980	3443	3728	4134	4578	5179		5911	6581	7183
93	110	112	123	127	129		146	147	207
5374	5647	6101	6294	6952			7702	11133	10861
31147	36317	39640	42216	47679	63277	75116	78940	96377	104548
4858	5370	5107	4560	4936	7490	8372	6205	8952	7809
4133	4833	4900	4624	5386	8486	9795	14569	12068	12726
53775	33717	34003	40884	55320					
7376	5961	6272	7326	7112					
13	13	12	12	12	12	12	14	13	13
244	249	242	250	264	265	256	294	318	326
113	119	129	125	127	125	121	129	124	130
99852	100553	96085	104423	105200	88619	88370	71102	84466	91776
8448	8027	7708	7861	7413	7366	7098	6416	2518	2543
27035	25646	25222	26318	23918	24761	24366	23396	17407	17796
19525	23737	23552	30084		29989	26880	31960	34095	34057
1896	1857	1814	1759	1847	1825	1787	1751	1734	1717
333	321	313	308	324	319	315	311	307	304
1840	1796	1785	1770	1828	1814	1782	1750	1721	1634
609.80	561.80	509.1	506.6	528.7	573.8	545.7	533.6	520.4	544.7
742	1170	1001	1654	1458	1269	704	6925	7276	7211
7	12	10	8	13	2	8	11	20	10
11	9	3	10	9	6	7	34	17	19
2348.10	1725.50	1491.0	1433.2	2739.7	3023.2	1208.2	2563.3	5704.8	5192.3

19-11 分市、区殡葬服务情况（2022 年）
BASIC STATISTICS ON FUNERAL SERVICES BY REGION（2022）

市、区名称	Region	单位数（个）Number of Institutions（unit）	年末职工人数（人）Number of Staff and Workers at Year-end（person）	火化炉数（台）Number of Crematiors（unit）	处理遗体数（具）Number of Remains Cremated（body）
全　市	**Whole Municipality**	**10**	**207**	**51**	
市本级	Municipal Level	1	40	10	
市南区	Shinan District				
市北区	Shibei District				
李沧区	Licang District				
崂山区	Laoshan District				
黄岛区	Huangdao District	2	60	11	
城阳区	Chengyang District	1	15	5	
即墨区	Jimo District	1	8	7	
胶州市	Jiaozhou	1	8	5	
平度市	Pingdu	2	35	7	
莱西市	Laixi	2	41	6	

19-11 续表
Continued

市、区名称	Region	穴位数（个） Number of Graves (unit)	本年销售穴位数 Number of Graves Sold in the Year	安葬数（具） Number of Remains Buried (body)	本年安葬数 Number of Remains Buried in the Year
全　市	**Whole Municipality**	**55480**	**833**	**56386**	**6229**
市本级	Municipal Level	22289	120	20283	470
市南区	Shinan District				
市北区	Shibei District				
李沧区	Licang District				
崂山区	Laoshan District				
黄岛区	Huangdao District	25001	428	32127	5560
城阳区	Chengyang District				
即墨区	Jimo District				
胶州市	Jiaozhou				
平度市	Pingdu	2331	166	2133	80
莱西市	Laixi	5859	119	1843	119

主要统计指标解释

卫生机构　按类别分为医院、社区卫生服务中心（站）、卫生院、门诊部（诊所、医务室、村卫生室）、急救中心（站）、采供血机构、妇幼保健院（所、站）、专科疾病防治院（所、站）、疾病预防控制中心（防疫站）、卫生监督所、卫生监督检验（监测、检测）所（站）、医学科学研究机构、医学教育机构、健康教育所（站）、其他卫生机构和社会团体16大类。

医疗卫生机构　包括医院、基层医疗卫生机构、专业公共卫生机构、其他医疗卫生机构。

（1）医院包括综合医院、中医医院、中西医结合医院、民族医院、各类专科医院和护理院，不包括专科疾病防治院、妇幼保健院和疗养院，包括医学院校附属医院。

（2）基层医疗卫生机构包括社区卫生服务中心（站）、乡镇（街道）卫生院、村卫生室、门诊部、诊所（医务室）。

（3）专业公共卫生机构包括疾病预防控制中心、专科疾病防治机构、妇幼保健机构（含妇幼保健计划生育服务中心）、健康教育机构、急救中心（站）、采供血机构、卫生监督机构、取得《医疗机构执业许可证》或《计划生育技术服务许可证》的计划生育技术服务机构。

（4）其他医疗卫生机构包括疗养院、临床检验中心、医学科研机构、医学在职教育机构、卫生监督（监测、检测）机构、医学考试中心、农村改水中心、人才交流中心、统计信息中心等卫生事业单位。

医院　包括综合医院、中医医院、中西医结合医院、民族医院、各类专科医院和护理院，不包括专科疾病防治院、妇幼保健院和疗养院，包括医学院校附属医院。

执业（助理）医师　指在医疗卫生机构中取得医师执业证书且实际从事医疗、妇幼保健、疾病防治等工作的执业医师和执业助理医师。

卫生技术人员　包括医疗卫生机构中执业医师、执业助理医师、注册护士、药师（士）、检验及影像技师（士）、卫生监督员和见习医（药、护、技）等卫生专业人员。

社会福利事业单位　指集中收养社会孤老、残、幼的机构，包括由民政部门管理的社会福利院、儿童福利院、精神病人福利院和城镇集体举办的福利院及农村集体举办的敬老院和具有收养能力的社区服务中心等。

Explanatory Notes on Main Statistical Indicators

Health Agency　according to categories, it is divided into hospitals, community health service centers (stations), health centers, outpatient departments (clinics, infirmaries, village clinics), emergency centers (stations), blood collection and supply institutions, maternal and child health care centers (stations, stations), and specialties Disease prevention and control institutes (stations, stations), disease prevention and control centers (epidemic prevention stations), sanitary supervision institutes, sanitary supervision and inspection (monitoring, testing) institutes (stations), medical scientific research institutes, medical education institutes, health education institutes (stations), 16 categories of other health institutions and social organizations.

Medical and Health Institutions　including hospitals, primary medical and health institutions, professional public health institutions, and other medical and health institutions.

(1) Hospitals include general hospitals, hospitals of traditional Chinese medicine, hospitals of integrated traditional Chinese and

western medicine, ethnic hospitals, various specialized hospitals and nursing homes, excluding specialized disease prevention and treatment hospitals, maternal and child health care hospitals, and nursing homes, including hospitals affiliated to medical schools.

(2) Primary medical and health institutions include community health service centers (stations), township (street) health centers, village clinics, outpatient departments, and clinics (medical offices).

(3) Professional public health institutions include disease prevention and control centers, specialized disease prevention institutions, maternal and child health institutions (including maternal and child health and family planning service centers), health education institutions, emergency centers (stations), blood collection and supply institutions, health supervision institutions, and Family planning technical service organizations with "Medical Institution Practicing License" or "Family Planning Technical Service License".

(4) Other medical and health institutions include nursing homes, clinical testing centers, medical research institutions, medical on-the-job education institutions, health supervision (monitoring, testing) institutions, medical examination centers, rural water reform centers, talent exchange centers, statistical information centers, etc. Institutions.

Hospitals including general hospitals, traditional Chinese medicine hospitals, integrated traditional Chinese and western medicine hospitals, ethnic hospitals, various specialized hospitals and nursing homes, excluding specialized disease prevention and treatment hospitals, maternal and child health care hospitals, and nursing homes, including hospitals affiliated to medical schools.

Practicing (Assistant) Physician refers to the practicing doctors and assistant practicing doctors who have obtained the doctor's practice certificate in medical and health institutions and are actually engaged in medical treatment, maternal and child health care, disease prevention and treatment, etc.

Health Technician including health professionals such as practicing physicians, practicing assistant physicians, registered nurses, pharmacists (persons), laboratory and imaging technologists (persons), health supervisors, and trainee doctors (medicine, nursing, technology) in medical and health institutions.

Social Welfare Institutions refers to institutions that collectively adopt social orphans, the disabled, and children, including social welfare homes, children's welfare homes, mentally ill welfare homes managed by the civil affairs department, welfare homes organized by urban collectives, nursing homes organized by rural collectives, and community services capable of adopting Central, etc.

附　录

APPENDIX

2022年省内各市主要经济指标情况

MAJOR ECONOMIC INDICATORS ON CITIES OF THE PROVINCE（2022）

指　标 Indicator	单位 Unit	全省 Whole province	青岛 Qingdao	济南 Jinan	淄博 Zibo	枣庄 Zaozhuang	东营 Dongying
生产总值（GDP）	累计（亿元） Total（100 million Yuan）	87435.0	14920.8	12027.5	4402.6	2039.0	3620.7
	增长（%） Growth（%）	3.9	3.9	3.1	4.7	4.5	4.3
规模上以工业增加值 Industrial Added Value above Designated Size	增长（%） Growth（%）	5.1	3.8	1.6	6.5	7.0	10.5
固定资产投资 Investment in Fixed Assets	增长（%） Growth（%）	6.1	4.5	3.8	18.1	10.1	12.4
货物进出口总额 Imports and Exports	累计（亿元） Total（100 million yuan）	33324.9	9117.2	2208.9	1234.1	431.0	2626.5
	增长（%） Growth（%）	13.8	7.4	13.9	3.0	42.8	27.9
#货物出口 Exports	累计（亿元） Total（100 million yuan）	20355.8	5361.1	1431.8	731.6	397.5	674.8
	增长（%） Growth（%）	16.2	9.0	22.0	1.0	42.9	21.6
货物进口 Imports	累计（亿元） Total（100 million yuan）	12969.1	3756.1	777.1	502.5	33.5	1951.7
	增长（%） Growth（%）	10.3	5.1	1.5	6.2	42.3	30.3
社会消费品零售总额 Total Retail Sales of Consumer Goods	增长（%） Growth（%）	-1.4	-1.4	-4.8	-1.1	-2.6	1.9
一般公共预算收入 General Public Budget Revenue	累计（亿元） Total（100 million yuan）	7104.0	1273.2	1001.1	375.9	168.9	265.5
	增长（%） Growth（%）	5.3	5.5	6.8	6.1	11.4	9.7
全体居民人均可支配收入 Disposable Income Per Capita of All Residents	累计（元） Total（yuan）	37560	53735	48827	44885	31477	48101
	增长（%） Growth（%）	5.2	4.9	4.5	6.2	5.7	5.0
全体居民人均消费支出 Per Capita Consumption Expenditure of All Residents	累计（元） Total（yuan）	22640	32497	29547	27204	17795	27939
	增长（%） Growth（%）	-0.8	-1.2	-1.6	-0.7	-0.6	-0.9

注：本表为快报数据。

Note：This table is for bulletin.

烟台 Yantai	潍坊 Weifang	济宁 Jining	泰安 Taian	威海 Weihai	日照 Rizhao	临沂 Linyi	德州 Dezhou	聊城 Liaocheng	滨州 Binzhou	菏泽 Heze
9515.9	7306.5	5316.9	3198.1	3408.2	2306.8	5778.5	3633.1	2779.9	2975.2	4205.3
5.1	3.7	4.4	4.3	1.5	3.8	4.2	4.4	4.3	3.9	4.2
10.8	7.4	8.6	9.0	-0.5	5.8	7.0	7.8	8.5	1.7	8.1
8.5	12.7	-16.1	17.4	-18.9	3.1	12.3	18.5	16.3	14.1	18.3
4547.4	3419.9	848.2	405.9	2095.6	1397.7	1875.1	622.1	614.0	1227.1	654.3
10.5	30.6	25.0	39.5	3.1	20.4	6.7	21.4	15.7	19.3	15.1
2750.9	2477.2	637.8	352.4	1567.5	545.3	1711.3	489.1	408.3	506.3	313.0
12.4	36.4	31.4	82.4	4.9	35.4	8.3	46.6	11.4	9.5	11.0
1796.5	942.7	210.3	53.5	528.2	852.4	163.8	133.0	205.7	720.9	341.3
7.8	17.5	8.9	-45.3	-1.9	12.5	-7.1	-25.7	25.2	27.3	19.2
0.5	-1.3	0.1	0.0	-4.4	0.3	-0.4	-0.3	0.0	-0.3	-1.4
635.4	608.0	447.7	222.7	225.2	185.5	420.2	235.0	230.6	275.7	300.6
7.3	-1.7	8.6	5.7	-8.9	6.6	9.6	9.6	7.4	5.3	10.8
45143	39365	33628	35260	46638	32490	33231	27321	25863	34099	25190
5.9	6.1	5.6	5.2	4.5	4.6	5.4	5.8	5.5	5.3	5.6
28001	22916	19051	20193	27293	18004	16325	17130	15566	20828	16574
-0.1	-0.5	0.1	-0.4	-1.1	0.3	-0.2	0.2	-0.4	-1.0	-0.8

2022年十五个副省级城市主要经济指标情况

MAJOR ECONOMIC INDICATORS ON CITIES UNDER PROVINCIAL LEVELS (2022)

指　标 Indicator	单位 Unit	青岛 Qingdao	沈阳 Shenyang	大连 Dalian	长春 Changchun	哈尔滨 Haerbin
全市生产总值(GDP)	累计(亿元) Total(100 million yuan)	14920.8	7695.8	8430.9	6744.6	5490.1
	增长(%) Growth(%)	3.9	3.5	4.0	-4.5	2.5
第一产业 Primary Industry	累计(亿元) Total(100 million yuan)	478.1	335.2	563.0	551.3	672.1
	增长(%) Growth(%)	2.2	2.1	3.2	2.1	2.6
第二产业 Secondary Industry	累计(亿元) Total(100 million yuan)	5197.3	2885.5	3712.5	2695.0	1285.0
	增长(%) Growth(%)	2.8	3.7	4.5	-9.3	0.6
第三产业 Tertiary Industry	累计(亿元) Total(100 million yuan)	9245.4	4475.1	4155.4	3498.3	3533.0
	增长(%) Growth(%)	4.5	3.5	3.7	-1.8	3.2
三产占比 Three-yield Ratio	占比(%) Ratio(%)	62.0	58.2	49.3	51.9	64.4
规模以上工业增加值 Industrial Added Value above Designated Size	增长(%) Growth(%)	3.8	3.1	5.1	-10.1	1.0
固定资产投资 Investment in Fixed Assets	增长(%) Growth(%)	4.5	6.1	6.5	-11.8	-7.6
社会消费品零售总额 Total Retail Sales of Consumer Goods	累计(亿元) Total(100 million yuan)	5891.8	3864.5	1846.9	1907.8	2195.9
	增长(%) Growth(%)	-1.4	-3.0	-3.3	-14.0	-7.7
货物进出口总额 Imports and Exports	累计(亿元) Total(100 million yuan)	9117.2	1406.6	4792.1	1107.6	387.0
	增长(%) Growth(%)	7.4	-0.7	12.8	-6.2	12.5
#货物出口 Exports	累计(亿元) Total(100 million Yuan)	5361.1	522.3	2086.7	208.5	136.3
	增长(%) Growth(%)	9.0	7.7	8.0	25.6	-20.4
货物进口 Imports	累计(亿元) Total(100 million yuan)	3756.1	884.3	2705.4	899.1	250.6
	增长(%) Growth(%)	5.1	-5.0	16.7	-11.4	45.2
一般公共预算收入 General Public Budget Revenue	累计(亿元) Total(100 million yuan)	1273.2	713.7	669.7	459.7	262.2
	增长(%) Growth(%)	5.5	1.3	0.6	-21.0	-20.8
城镇居民人均可支配收入 Annual Per Capita Disposable Income of Urban Households	累计(元) Total(yuan)	62584	51702	51904	43240	43981
	增长(%) Growth(%)	3.9	2.2	2.7	-0.1	3
农村居民人均可支配收入 Annual Per Capita Net Income of Rural Households	累计(元) Total(yuan)	27701	22352	24759	18919	22260
	增长(%) Growth(%)	6.0	3.2	4.2	2.4	4
居民消费价格指数 Consumer Price Indices	上年同期=100 Preceding Year=100	102.0	101.7	102.2	101.9	101.9

注：本表为快报数据。

Note: This table is for bulletin.

南京 Nanjing	杭州 Hangzhou	宁波 Ningbo	厦门 Xiamen	济南 Jinan	武汉 Wuhan	广州 Guangzhou	深圳 Shenzhen	成都 Chengdu	西安 Xian
16907.9	18753.0	15704.3	7802.7	12027.5	18866.4	28839.0	32387.7	20817.5	11486.5
2.1	1.5	3.5	4.4	3.1	4.0	1.0	3.3	2.8	4.4
315.6	346.0	382.0	29.3	420.5	475.8	318.3	25.6	588.4	323.6
3.4	1.8	4.1	1.4	3.1	3.2	3.2	0.8	3.8	3.7
6069.6	5620.0	7413.5	3233.6	4180.2	6716.7	7909.3	12405.9	6404.1	4071.6
1.7	0.4	3.2	3.8	3.2	7.3	1.1	4.8	5.5	10.7
10522.7	12787.0	7908.8	4539.8	7426.7	11674.0	20611.4	19956.2	13825.0	7091.4
2.2	2.0	3.8	4.7	3.0	2.3	1.0	2.4	1.5	1.3
62.2	68.2	50.4	58.2	61.7	61.9	71.5	61.6	66.4	61.7
2.4	0.3	3.8	4.3	1.6	5.0	0.8	4.8	5.6	13.9
3.5	6.0	10.4	9.9	3.8	10.8	−2.1	8.4	5.0	10.5
7832.4	7294.0	4896.7	2665.4	4878.1	6936.2	10298.2	9708.3	9096.5	4642.1
−0.8	5.8	5.3	3.1	−4.8	2.1	1.7	2.2	−1.7	−5.2
6292.1	7565.0	12671.3	9225.6	2208.9	3532.2	10948.4	36737.5	8346.4	4474.1
0.3	2.7	6.3	4.0	13.9	5.3	1.1	3.7	1.6	0.8
3827.9	5141.0	8230.6	4657.4	1431.8	2153.0	6194.8	21944.8	5005.1	2801.5
−1.8	10.6	8.0	8.2	22.0	11.6	−1.8	13.9	3.7	17.3
2464.2	2424.0	4440.7	4568.2	777.1	1379.2	4753.6	14792.7	3341.3	1672.6
3.6	−10.8	3.4	0.1	1.5	−3.3	5.3	−8.5	−1.4	−18.4
1558.2	2450.6	1680.2	883.8	1001.1	1504.7	1854.7	4012.3	1722.3	834.1
0.1	8.4	5.1	6.6	6.8	3.7	5.5	−0.6	5.8	9.7
76643	77043	76690	70467	59459	58449	76849	72718	54897	48418
4.1	3.1	3.8	4.9	3.5	5.7	3.3	3	4.3	3.2
34664	45183	45487	32323	23844	29304	36292		30931	18285
6.0	5.8	5.9	8.1	5.6	7.7	5.1		6.2	5.2
102.2	102.4	102.3	101.8	101.4	102.3	102.4	102.3	102.4	102.2

2022 年部分城市主要经济指标情况

MAJOR ECONOMIC INDICATORS OF SOME CITIES（2022）

指　标 Indicator	单位 Unit	北京 Beijing	天津 Tianjin	上海 Shanghai	重庆 Chongqing	苏州 Suzhou	无锡 Wuxi
全市生产总值（GDP）	累计（亿元） Total（100 million yuan）	41610.9	16311.3	44652.8	29129.0	23958.3	14850.8
	增长（%） Growth（%）	0.7	1.0	−0.2	2.6	2.0	3.0
第一产业 Primary Industry	累计（亿元） Total（100 million yuan）	111.5	273.2	97.0	2012.1	193.0	133.7
	增长（%） Growth（%）	−1.6	2.9	−3.5	4.0	3.0	1.1
第二产业 Secondary Industry	累计（亿元） Total（100 million yuan）	6605.1	6038.9	11458.4	11693.9	11521.4	7177.4
	增长（%） Growth（%）	−11.4	−0.5	−1.6	3.3	1.8	3.6
第三产业 Tertiary Industry	累计（亿元） Total（100 million yuan）	34894.3	9999.3	33097.4	15423.1	12244.0	7539.8
	增长（%） Growth（%）	3.4	1.7	0.3	1.9	2.1	2.4
三产占比 Three-yield Ratio	占比（%） Ratio（%）	83.8	61.3	74.1	53.0	51.1	50.8
规模以上工业增加值 Industrial Added Value above Designated Size	增长（%） Growth（%）	−16.7	−1.0	−0.6	3.2	2.4	5.4
固定资产投资 Investment in Fixed Assets	增长（%） Growth（%）	3.6	−9.9	−1.0	0.7	1.5	2.2
社会消费品零售总额 Total Retail Sales of Consumer Goods	累计（亿元） Total（100 million yuan）	13794.2		16442.1	13926.1	9010.7	3337.6
	增长（%） Growth（%）	−7.2	−5.2	−9.1	−0.3	−0.2	1.0
货物进出口总额 Imports and Exports	累计（亿元） Total（100 million Yuan）	36445.5	8448.5	41902.8	8158.4	25721.1	7373.1
	增长（%） Growth（%）	19.7	−1.4	3.2	2.0	1.6	8.0
#货物出口 Exports	累计（亿元） Total（100 million yuan）	5890.0	3803.6	17134.2	5245.3	15475.0	4852.6
	增长（%） Growth（%）	−3.8	−1.9	9.0	1.5	4.0	15.0
货物进口 Imports	累计（亿元） Total（100 million yuan）	30555.5	4644.9	24768.5	2913.0	10246.1	2520.4
	增长（%） Growth（%）	25.7	−1.0	−0.5	2.9	−1.9	−3.3
一般公共预算收入 General Public Budget Revenue	累计（亿元） Total（100 million yuan）	5714.4	1846.6	7608.2	2103.4	2329.2	1133.4
	增长（%） Growth（%）	2.6	−13.8	−2.1	−2.5	0.1	1.6
城镇居民人均可支配收入 Annual Per Capita Net Income of urban Households	累计（元） Total（yuan）	84023	53003	84034	45509	79537	73332
	增长（%） Growth（%）	3.1	2.9	1.9	4.6	3.4	4.0
农村居民人均可支配收入 Annual Per Capita Net Income of Rural Households	累计（元） Total（yuan）	34754	29018	39729	19313	43785	41934
	增长（%） Growth（%）	4.4	3.8	3.1	6.7	5.5	5.8
居民消费价格指数 Consumer Price Indices	上年同期 =100 Preceding Year =100	101.8	101.9	102.5	102.1	102.1	102.1

注：本表为快报数据。

Note：This table is for bulletin.